HMAS SYDNEY

TOM FRAME

Dedicated to the memory of my father
Robert Frame
1921–1986
Royal Navy Volunteer Reserve, 1941–46

This edition published in Australia and New Zealand in 2018
by Hachette Australia
(an imprint of Hachette Australia Pty Limited)
Level 17, 207 Kent Street, Sydney NSW 2000
www.hachette.com.au

Originally published in 1993
by Hodder Headline Australia Pty Limited

 A catalogue record for this
book is available from the
National Library of Australia

978 0 7336 4017 9 (paperback)

Cover design by Luke Causby/Blue Cork
Cover image of HMAS *Sydney* courtesy of Australian War Memorial 002290
Cover image of sailors courtesy of Newspix
Text design by Post Pre-Press Group
Typeset in 12/15pt Sabon Roman by Post Pre-press Group, Brisbane
Printed and bound in Australia by McPherson's Printing Group

 The paper this book is printed on is certified against the Forest Stewardship Council® Standards. McPherson's Printing Group holds FSC® chain of custody certification SA-COC-005379. FSC® promotes environmentally responsible, socially beneficial and economically viable management of the world's forests.

Contents

Introduction

Human beings have difficulty in living with the unknown, and they are even more uncomfortable with the unknowable. The seas are probably the world's largest store of both the unknown and the unknowable. Under the oceans are countless ill-fated ships that had carried many unfortunate people. If the stricken ships could be refloated and if their dead could speak, they would disclose many secrets and truths which the seas hide.

Of the sea's many mysteries, few seemed as impenetrable as the fate of the Australian light cruiser HMAS *Sydney* and the 645 men who were lost with her on 19 November 1941 after a short engagement with the German auxiliary cruiser HSK *Kormoran* off the coast of Western Australia. Other than a small carley float measuring three metres in length and one and a half metres in width, and two charred lifebelts, the sea swallowed up the entire ship and every man who sailed in her. Apart from the little that the German survivors could recall or were willing to disclose, the reasons behind her final and inexplicable movements and the total disappearance of the ship and her men were destined to remain a mystery for more than six decades.

Despite detailed and wide-ranging historical research carried out in Australia, Britain, the United States and Germany, the absence of even a single survivor from *Sydney* to describe the action through Australian eyes meant that the prospects of solving the mystery would always be limited. Something could be learned from analysing the Australian cruiser's movements as they were observed and interpreted by the German survivors. It would be a complicated exercise in historical analysis, and it would need to recognise that some matters would remain unknowable.

The first half-century after the engagement produced rigorous attempts by historians to explain the loss of *Sydney*. In addition to the Navy's efforts following the action, the official historian of the RAN in World War II and two private researchers had undertaken detailed studies into the *Sydney–Kormoran* engagement. The least comprehensive account was that of the official historian, George Hermon Gill, who was commissioned to produce a comprehensive wartime history of all Australian naval operations. He was naturally constrained by the inherent editorial limits of his task in what he could say about *Sydney*.

The books produced by writers Michael Montgomery and Barbara Winter took vastly different approaches to the subject. Montgomery in *Who Sank the Sydney?*[1] tended to focus on the actions of the Australian cruiser while Winter, in *HMAS Sydney: Fact, Fantasy and Fraud*,[2] concentrated on the German ship. Montgomery's work was deliberately polemical and revisionist. Winter's book was more conservative and restrained. Nonetheless, the two books had much in common because Winter, who published three years after Montgomery, was constrained to examine the issues and evidence on which Montgomery had based his provocative statements.

Since 1985, the controversy over *Sydney* continued unabated. Fuelled by the work of Montgomery and Winter, the matters in dispute multiplied. Unfortunately, historians working in this area were suspected of ulterior motives and personal affiliations and the debate surrounding the loss of *Sydney* became acrimonious. The exchange of personal abuse and insults created rival parties and divisions within the naval history community. It perhaps does not need to be said that none of this served to clarify or resolve the many contentious matters that required light rather than heat.

It is never helpful for history to be researched, written and then presented in the midst of a controversy, particularly when the history has contemporary consequences. The existence of motives that transcend academic interest, such as a determination to blame an individual, can make it very difficult for the historian to write objective history. When the historian is subject to these influences, the history is likely to be polemical, or even propagandist.

There will, of course, always be people unconnected with history who will seek to use historians for purposes for which their craft was not intended. However, once history has been used for an illegitimate purpose, it becomes the responsibility of other historians to reassert the essentials of the historian's noble charter and calling.

There are very few *really* controversial events within Australian naval history and just as few controversial interpretations of that history. The loss of *Sydney* and the loss of HMAS *Voyager* after a collision during night exercises off Jervis Bay in 1964 are the two best-known examples of both controversial events and interpretations. But the sinking of *Sydney* surpasses the *Voyager* tragedy in that the controversy over the actual event has been compounded by the controversy generated by historians.

Consequently, the historical interest prompted by speculation over the loss of *Sydney* has been productive in some respects, and unproductive in others. The positive outcomes are principally archival and historiographical. Historians and researchers have had to examine areas of Australian naval history that had not been touched before, such as signal intelligence, convoy routing and gunnery fire control. The drawback is the preponderance of research and writing into one isolated area of history. The *Sydney–Kormoran* action has limited scope to enhance our understanding of other areas of naval history or to season our judgments about the history of the RAN as a whole. Some of the effort that has been expended in this area of research would have been more productively directed in areas where practically nothing is known of the RAN's history. However, the *Sydney–Kormoran* action is probably the only event in Australian naval history which illustrates some important historiographical principles that need to be observed in assessing what has been written about the subject to date.

There is a view that history is characterised by a well-known taxonomy, passing through at least three well-defined stages. The *Sydney–Kormoran* action has been described in all three.

In the *first* stage, history is written by the victors or survivors, largely from published sources, within a framework of 'conventional wisdom' shared by the participant writers. In the *second* stage, the conventional paradigm handed down from the participant writers is challenged, often *a priori*, by a later generation of non-participant writers. In the *third*, non-participant writers challenge the received paradigm and perceive and question the evidence in entirely different ways.

The first stage is more likely to be flawed by self-justification. This needs to be remembered when the various accounts of the *Sydney–Kormoran* action are considered. At either the second or third stage, the historian is able to draw upon a wider range of primary archival source material, if not from every document that records the event or the period under review. Of course, progression through the stages is also determined by the range and depth of source material. It is difficult to write history when little evidence exists of what occurred. There is, however, no shortage of material relating to the loss of *Sydney*.

Australian naval history as a whole is fast emerging as a distinct entity as a consequence of its passage from the first stage into the second stage of the taxonomy I have described. This is only a recent development, having been in the second stage for two decades. Although progress has been made, the future for naval history will be substantially affected by the availability of sources both in Australia and in Britain where a great body of information about the RAN is stored. Thus, it needs to be remembered that the debate over the loss of *Sydney* has been in the third stage of the taxonomy for some considerable time, and that it has gone beyond scholarship in related areas of historical inquiry which might, in the future, offer some new insight. Widespread public interest in the loss of *Sydney* has been the catalyst for its accelerated progress through the stages of the taxonomy.

Virtually every known official document with either a direct or indirect connection to the *Sydney–Kormoran* action has been identified and made available to historians. Those documents which have been withheld from public access are known to historians.

If all the official sources are available to the public, and three major studies have already been published, what else could possibly be said about the *Sydney–Kormoran* action?

In my view, as someone with an academic background in the discipline of history, neither the account of Gill, nor the more populist works of Montgomery or Winter deserved to stand as the sum total of writing or the final word on this subject. In different ways, each is demonstrably flawed. Considered collectively, they create a false impression of the issues involved in solving questions about the loss of *Sydney* and the likelihood that an accurate account can ever be produced.

It is for these reasons that I decided in 1990 to write a book on the loss of *Sydney*. In writing this book it has been difficult to decide what to include and what to leave out. The *Sydney* mystery has unearthed so much primary material and the controversy has prompted so many secondary accounts that the story seems almost infinite. Deciding the sources to include and which to omit is a delicate process and the supreme test of the historian. To avoid writing a book of nearly one thousand pages, I have restricted myself to those parts of the story which bear directly on both the mystery and the controversy associated with the loss of *Sydney*.

I have not attempted, as Winter painstakingly did, to identify and discredit all the 'fantasies and frauds', which have been advanced over the last six decades to explain the loss of *Sydney*. Many of the questionable allegations and theories have been ignored for either one of two reasons. First, to consider them in detail would be to ascribe to them a credibility they do not deserve. Secondly, many are plainly irrelevant to the main points in dispute and fail to add anything to our understanding of how *Sydney* was sunk. It would be unfair, therefore, for someone to allege that I did not consider this theory or that allegation because I did not have an answer to it. Although I do not claim to have all the answers, the need for careful selection has brought with it a value judgment of various theories and allegations which I hope I have exercised judiciously. This selection is naturally a product of my personal bias and overall view of Australian naval history.

Admiral Alfred Thayer Mahan, that great American navalist and historian, recognised while he was writing about Britain's naval campaigns with Napoleon that pure objectivity in historical writing was impossible. Mahan conceded that the admiration he developed for Prime Minister Pitt 'aroused in me an enthusiasm which I did not seek to check'. In other words, Mahan had come to that inevitable conclusion that all historians are indeed biased. As historians possess different personalities, and assess events and ideas on the basis of varied formative experiences and dissimilar world views, bias is unavoidable. Barbara Tuchman remarks that 'historical bias means a *leaning* which *is* the exercise of judgement as well as a source of insight'.[5] Bias only becomes a problem when it is concealed from the reader.

I readily confess that when I write the history of the RAN, and this includes the loss of *Sydney*, I am biased. At the age of 16 I joined the Navy as a junior entry cadet midshipman at the RAN College at Jervis Bay. I was taught to have pride in the Service which I had joined and to protect its reputation and public standing. When I started writing Australian naval history for publication in 1984, I never tried to conceal my affiliation with the Navy. Being in the Service seemed to be a decided advantage. I was familiar with its customs and acquainted with its culture. Perhaps not unexpectedly, I was criticised by civilians for being too generous in my appraisal of the Navy's past just as often as I was chastised by serving and retired officers for being too harsh.

If public and private reactions to my 1992 book *Where Fate Calls: The HMAS* Voyager *Tragedy* are a guide, I have perhaps been too severe in my criticisms of the Navy and too demanding in my expectations of its people. However, I have defended the Navy when it has been unfairly attacked by those who fail to acquaint themselves with the vagaries of the sea, who show an unwillingness to grasp the sheer complexity of naval operations, or who neglect to understand the corporate Service ethos. Although I am no longer a serving naval officer, my empathy for the Navy remains.

The bias that I bring consciously to this book is found in my insistence that the circumstances surrounding the loss of *Sydney* should be considered through the eyes of the professional naval officers who were involved. Some were quite junior, others very senior. Their actions reflected their training, their experience and the expectations that were associated with their positions. There were also limits to what each officer could do. Their responsibilities varied with their authority. Some, such as those on board *Sydney*, were totally involved in their ship's role in the war. Throughout 1941 they had more to think about than the threat posed by a lone German raider. Others, such as the Australian Commonwealth Naval Board (ACNB) in Melbourne, were responsible for the operation and administration of a wartime Navy. The Naval Board was aware of the raider threat at the same time that it planned for imminent combat at sea with Japan. If it appears that after the loss of *Sydney* some senior officers seemed distracted or even uninterested in her sinking, it was because they were totally preoccupied in trying to prevent the consolidation of Japanese naval power in Australia s northern waters.

The loss of *Sydney* was a major blow to the Navy and to the nation. The same can be said for the loss of the sloop HMAS *Parramatta* and the cruiser HMAS *Perth* in the three months that followed. In 1942, a large part of Australia's fighting fleet was lost in combat. The loss of *Sydney* needs to be placed in a comparative perspective when one assesses the Navy's reaction to her sinking at the hands of a German raider which was, of course, no longer a threat.

The Navy survived the tragic loss of *Sydney* and the 645 men who perished with her. The loss of *Sydney* did not result in the disestablishment of the RAN nor did it change the training of Australian naval officers for command at sea. Australian warships under Australian captains have continued to defend Australia from aggression. Since its foundation in 1911, the RAN has quickly learned from its mistakes. That no other ship was lost in the same circumstances as *Sydney* during the war suggests that the Navy learned all there was to learn from her loss. That no other men lost their lives in this way was a tribute to those who had been killed learning the hard lessons of naval warfare.

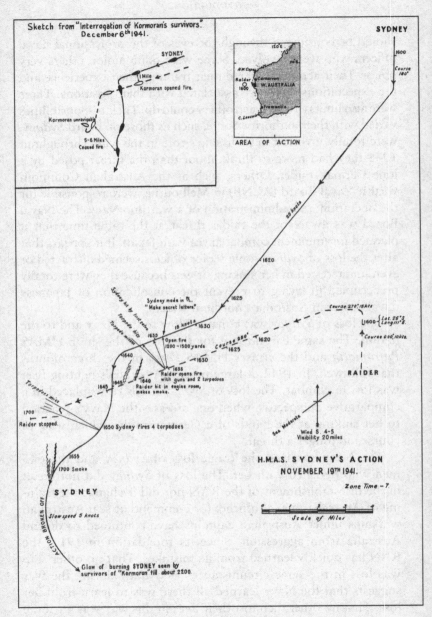

Diagram of the engagement (Australian War Memorial)

I

The Aftermath

As darkness fell on 19 November 1941, hundreds of men struggled to hold on to life in West Australian coastal waters off Carnarvon. The seas began to settle. There were stars but no shoreline. At first light on 20 November, five boats and two rafts containing more than 300 German sailors were all that remained after the short and savage naval gun battle which had broken the calm of the previous afternoon. They remained in a confined area more than 100 miles from the coast, keeping together during the night by means of green and white flares fired from one of the boats. There was nothing and no-one else to be seen. One of the lifeboats was a cutter equipped with sails carrying 46 men under the command of Chief Petty Officer Telegraphist Paul Kohn.

Two of the craft were steel lifeboats which had been slightly damaged when launched. Although they had filled with water, air tanks kept them afloat. One of these steel lifeboats, in which 57 men were embarked, was commanded by Lieutenant Commander Henry Meyer. It also contained Lieutenant (Baron) Reinhold von Malapert who kept a diary of the boat's easterly progress as it proceeded under oars and sail towards the coast of Western Australia. When the wind freshened from the south-west several days later, the sail was lowered and a sea-anchor was deployed to give the boat stability. When the winds eased, they were assisted by south-easterly and then south-westerly winds as they proceeded towards the north-east. The other steel lifeboat contained 62 men under Commander Theodor Detmers. Behind it, several floats had been secured. During the night, several men had fallen from them and were not seen again.

The fourth boat was a workboat that had formerly been carried in the German supply ship *Kulmerland*. Although built with a pedal-gearing propulsion system, this had recently been removed for maintenance. The three-inch circular hole in the boat's hull where the propeller shaft had been fitted was sealed with a bung which now leaked. The original commander of the boat, Sub-Lieutenant Wilhelm Bunjes, was later relieved by Lieutenant Joachim von Gosseln. There were 70 Germans and two Chinese on board.

The fifth boat came from the Greek ship *Nicolaos D.L.* Commanded by Petty Officer Hans Kuhl, it contained 31 men. During the first night at sea it overturned and the provisions, sail and rudder were lost overboard. It was later righted and a few provisions were provided by another boat.

While the Germans were making their way towards the coast, the District Naval Officer in Fremantle, Captain Charles Farquhar-Smith RAN, despatched a routine signal at 0940 (Time Zone H)[1] to Navy Office in Melbourne on 21 November regarding the light cruiser HMAS *Sydney*. 'HMAS *Sydney* has not yet arrived.' She was expected to return to Fremantle on 20 November after escorting the troopship *Zealandia* to a rendezvous with the cruiser HMS *Durban* in the Sunda Strait (7 degrees 56 minutes S, 104 degrees 40 minutes E). The Naval Board in Melbourne was not immediately concerned. As *Sydney* was directed to maintain normal wireless telegraphy (W/T) silence during her passage and any number of contingencies could have delayed her return, she was expected to arrive in the next twenty-four hours. The Naval Board learned the next morning that *Zealandia* had arrived in Singapore one day later than expected. This led the Board to assume *Sydney* would not return until 21 November. It was still not concerned at this stage for her safety.

At 0600(H) on the morning of Sunday 23 November, a raft was sighted from the converted military transport, *Aquitania*,[2] approximately 100 nautical miles off the coast of Carnarvon

(24 degrees 35 minutes S, 110 degrees 57 minutes E).[3] The majestic Cunard liner stopped and 26 sailors, who were thought to be victims of a possible German raider attack, were taken on board. As the captain of *Aquitania* feared that a German raider might still be operating in the area, he maintained radio silence and the ship's passage to Port Jackson on the east coast of the continent resumed. By this stage, *Sydney* had not returned to Fremantle and nothing had been heard from her. *Aquitania* was also sighted by the boat commanded by Commander Detmers. However, he did not allow his men to fire a flare as he was hoping to be picked up by a neutral steamer and conveyed to a friendly or neutral port.

At sunset the same day, a signal was sent from Navy Office ordering *Sydney* to report her present position, course and speed. There was no response to this signal so it was sent a second time. The absence of a reply was ominous. Naval communications stations in Fremantle and Darwin were directed to call the cruiser continuously. The Commander-in-Chief of the China Station reported that the rendezvous between *Sydney* and *Durban* occurred as planned on 17 November. The delay in *Zealandia*'s arrival occurred between the Sunda Strait and Singapore. This meant that *Sydney* was already more than three days overdue. However, the signal sent from Fremantle on 21 November reporting that *Sydney* was overdue gave the Naval Board in Melbourne the impression that she was due earlier that day rather than on the morning of the previous day (20 November).

Signals were sent to Admiral Sir Geoffrey Layton, Commander-in-Chief of the British Eastern Fleet, and to Vice Admiral C.E.L. Helfrich, commanding the Dutch naval forces in Batavia.[4] The Dutch light cruiser *Tromp* was in the western Java Sea and was ordered to search the area where *Sydney* had rendezvoused with the *Durban*. Four days after *Sydney* was due back in Fremantle, six Royal Australian Air Force (RAAF) bombers from No. 14 Squadron based at Pearce, Western Australia, commenced a search off the coast. After searching for five hours, the Squadron reported at 1300 on Monday 24 November that nothing had been found. In his private diary, the Rear Admiral

Commanding the Australian Squadron (RACAS), John Crace, commented on 26 November that Navy Office 'are very worried about *Sydney* . . . She has been called by wireless without result. Naval Board think there is a possibility that a Vichy submarine escorting a Vichy ship has torpedoed her'. Fearing the worst, the Chief of Naval Staff, Admiral Sir Guy Royle, informed the Minister for the Navy, Norman Makin, that afternoon that radio contact with *Sydney* had been lost. 'It is most unlikely that she has received instructions from other Naval Authorities to proceed outside Australia Station . . . I will keep you informed of developments.'[5]

By this time, 1500 on 24 November, the Shell tanker *Trocas*,[6] on passage from Palembang in Sumatra to Fremantle, picked up 25 German sailors about 120 nautical miles north-west of Carnarvon at position 24 degrees 6 minutes S, 111 degrees 40 minutes E. The ship's master sent a radio message to Carnarvon reporting what had occurred. The message from *Trocas* was also received in Singapore and relayed to Navy Office at 1616. RAAF Catalina flying boats based in Townsville and Port Moresby were ordered to Carnarvon. Efforts to contact *Sydney* by signal were terminated. Nearly three hours later, the tanker was asked for further information on the men she had rescued. In reply, *Trocas* reported that the German sailors claimed they were from a ship named *Kormoran* and they had been sunk by a 'raider'.

The Naval Board held grave fears for the safety of *Sydney*. According to Admiral Crace, this led the Naval Board to believe that 'there was an action between *Sydney* and [Armed Merchant Cruiser] *Cormoran* [sic] and both ships were sunk'. At first light the next morning (25 November), seven Lockheed Hudson reconnaissance aircraft[7] from RAAF 14 Squadron and five Wirraway fighters from RAAF 25 Squadron went looking for the cruiser in a fan-shaped search area that extended 300 miles off Rottnest Island. There was immediate success. One of the Hudsons located a lifeboat, 50 miles south of the raft sighted by *Trocas*, but was unable to identify its occupants. Another Hudson sighted four lifeboats. The lifeboat commanded by Kohn containing 46 men had reached the shore near 17-Mile Well adjacent to a stock route on Quobba Station to the north of Carnarvon. Another lifeboat, that commanded by Meyer, was approaching Red Bluff. Two boats were seen making their way slowly towards the coast. Later in the day, the occupants of the lifeboats that had landed were rounded up by the manager and staff at Quobba Station, the civil police and available military personnel. The German sailors had survived an ordeal and they offered no resistance to capture. One of them later recalled:

> We existed on scraps of bacon and biscuit . . . We were terrified at the thought of being cast ashore on a desert and dying miserably of starvation. Some of the men were half crazy with the pain of swollen and blistered limbs. We had to watch them all the time to prevent them jumping out of the crowded boat. There were 57 men in our boat. It was impossible to lie down, we had to take our turns at standing and sitting.

Lieutenant von Malapert's diary revealed that in his lifeboat the shortage of food and water, the unrelenting sun and the struggle to bail out water was becoming too much for some of the men. The sighting of land on 24 November produced 'great jubilation in the boat'.

> At 0830 [on Tuesday 25 November] we landed in front of a cave which lay quite sheltered in the south corner of the bay. We pulled the boat up the beach, unpacked everything, everyone got something to drink and had to lie down on the white sand in the shade of the cave and rocks. After being such a long time in the boat one is so weak on the feet that when one steps on land for the first time one feels as if drunk. Towards noon we had something to eat and everything was got ready to pass the night in the open.

Later that day, the men in both lifeboats ashore were reunited. There was still no sign of any Australian wreckage or survivors.

In a minute from Royle early on 25 November, Makin was

advised that *Trocas* had recovered some German sailors from a ship called '*Cormoran*' which had been sunk by a cruiser. At the same time, Prime Minister John Curtin received a minute from his secretary regarding a conversation he just had with Royle. Curtin was told that:

> A raft has been picked up carrying some German sailors from a raider, which they said was sunk by a cruiser. The Admiral is coming by air tomorrow with the Chief of the Air Staff to discuss the matter and wishes to attend War Cabinet in the afternoon, leaving as soon as possible for Singapore [where he would attend a high level naval planning conference]. I said you would do your best to meet him by such an arrangement.[8]

The next morning (26 November), *Aquitania* had entered the relatively safe waters within the Great Australian Bight and attempted to send a radio message to Adelaide and Melbourne reporting the recovery of a raft and the German sailors. The transmissions were unsuccessful. At sunset, the coastal passenger ship *Koolinda*[9] noticed a lifeboat on the open sea and recovered another 31 German sailors before proceeding to Carnarvon. Later that night (2230), guided by a red signal flare, the *Centaur*,[10] a former passenger ship, took the lifeboat commanded by Detmers in tow and headed for Carnarvon. Ten of the German sailors in this lifeboat were ill or wounded and were taken on board *Centaur*. When the lifeboat was in danger of sinking during the night, Captain Walter Dark transferred the German sailors into two of *Centaur*'s lifeboats in which they completed the passage in tow to Carnarvon.

At the Advisory War Council[10a] meeting in Canberra on 26 November, there was a joint report from Makin and Royle. They advised that no trace of *Sydney* had been found. The Council agreed that there was little chance of the ship still being afloat and decided that

> the next-of-kin of the crew of the *Sydney* be informed, the notification being to the effect that their relatives are missing, due to enemy action. No public statement is to be made at present, and steps are to be taken

to ensure complete censorship of all references to the *Sydney* in press and broadcasts.

If and when it is established that the *Sydney* has been sunk, the initial announcement regarding its loss is to be in a form which does not convey any useful information to the enemy.

The Naval Staff prepared a brief statement on the action for release at short notice.[11] The Secretary to the Naval Board, George Macandie, sent Royle a draft prime ministerial statement. After mentioning that *Sydney* had probably been in an action with an enemy warship the statement concluded:

No subsequent information has been received from HMAS *Sydney*. It is known that this vessel suffered some damage in the action, but since there has as yet been no direct communication from this vessel, the Naval Board are not aware of the extent of such damage. All possible action is being taken to secure further information.[12]

A condensed history of *Sydney*'s service in the RAN and 'casualty lists' were to be made available in each district naval office.[13] Telegrams to next-of-kin stated 'With deep regret I have to inform you that your [relationship and name] is missing as a result of enemy action. Minister for Navy and Naval Board desire to express to you their sincere sympathy.' Eulogies for her senior officers were also written. The Public Censorship Liaison Officer, George Gill, advised Royle to maintain public silence even after the next-of-kin of those in *Sydney* were contacted.

Trocas and *Koolinda* reached the coast on 26 November and disembarked the German sailors. Some of those in *Trocas*, interviewed by Naval Intelligence staff from Fremantle, told of a naval battle. The Naval Intelligence officers 'generally considered that, with few exceptions, the survivors spoke the truth'.[14] The naval auxiliary ship, HMAS *Yandra*,[15] recovered a further 70 German sailors from the lifeboat commanded by von Gosseln just before midday and sailed for Carnarvon.[16] Several hours later, *Centaur* arrived in Carnarvon and the British freighter *Evagoras*, also in the area, picked up an RAN lifebelt. Another lifebelt was found by the naval auxiliary ship HMAS *Wyrallah* at 1815. By this time, *Aquitania* was again closer to the coast. As she rounded Wilson's Promontory, the southern-most point on the Australian mainland, *Aquitania* was finally able to signal visually that she had recovered a number of German sailors from the sea off Carnarvon. This information was passed to the Navy.

Wyrallah picked up a German lifebelt at 0800 the next morning (Friday 28 November) and an hour later she sighted two small German four-man carley floats lashed together. One of the floats contained a body. The clothes were removed from the corpse and the German sailor was buried at sea. Meanwhile, the Naval Intelligence staff in Fremantle sent the Naval Board a summary of information that had been obtained from the German sailors.[17] Later in the morning, the War Cabinet met to discuss what action it would take to account for *Sydney* being overdue in Fremantle. By this stage, Parliament was in recess. The recovery of an empty RAN carley float by HMAS *Heros* 160 miles off Carnarvon (24 degrees 07 minutes S, 110 degrees 58 minutes E) suggested the worst. The float had been damaged, possibly by gunfire.

A sailor who served in *Heros* also observed a

'huge patch of linseed oil . . . This large mass was circular in pattern and generally of unbroken formation. My immediate reaction was that a ship lay below us and this oil was welling up from it'.[18]

[He also] 'spotted a pipe and slipper float past some thirty feet apart'.

Rumours were circulating publicly about the ship's possible fate, and families and friends of those on board were demanding information from the Navy.[19] An American radio station had broadcast the news that *Sydney* had been sunk in the Timor Sea and 'all 616 men' on board had been lost. The place of the action and the number of men killed were incorrect but the information would still be used by Germany for a propaganda broadcast.[20] The Australian government had to ensure that it was the first to announce the news. The next day *Koolinda* arrived in Fremantle and *Aquitania* sailed into Port Jackson. The Naval Board instructed Admiral Crace to arrange for these prisoners to be 'interviewed'. At sunset on 29 November, the final air patrols reported that nothing had been seen after a thorough search of the sea near Carnarvon and Geraldton.

On 30 November, the Naval Board sent a message 'for transmission to His Excellency the Governor General and the Prime Minister' after the final searches of the previous day had proved unsuccessful:

> The Naval Board regret that after intensive air and surface search of the area no (no) evidence of HMAS *Sydney* has been . . . sighted except two RAN . . . lifebelts and one carley float badly damaged by gunfire. It is concluded that *Sydney* sank after the action and further search has been abandoned.[21]

This was the first formal indication that the ship had been lost with no survivors. Every man, including her commanding officer, Captain Joseph Burnett, was gone. There seemed no useful purpose in further delaying a public announcement. Prime Minister Curtin made a brief statement on Sunday, 30 November at 1800:

> HMAS *Sydney* has been in action with a heavily armed enemy merchant raider, which she sank by gunfire. The intimation was received from survivors from the enemy vessel who were picked up some time after the action. No subsequent communication has been received from HMAS *Sydney*, and the Government regrets that she must be presumed lost.[22]

The nation was stunned. Of all the RAN ships which might be lost in the war, no-one thought that *Sydney* would possibly be among them. She seemed to have an aura of invincibility about her as former Navy Minister Billy Hughes remarked:

> This magnificent ship had seemed to have a charmed life. She had run the gauntlet of the toughest fighting in the Mediterranean and escaped

with not much more than a scratch on her paint. Everyone of her countrymen had thrilled to her exploits.

The war had come to Australia's door-step. As a mark of respect, flags on all public buildings in Sydney were flown at half-mast on the morning of 1 December. The city had enjoyed a close association with the ship that had carried its name. The Lord Mayor, Alderman Stanley Crick, said that 'the city has suffered the greatest heartache in its history'. An 'HMAS *Sydney* Replacement Fund' was launched in every capital city.[23]

The *West Australian* summed up the national sentiment:

> The *Sydney* had a fighting record of which we are justifiably proud. Her fame has echoed round the world. It was not her fate to rust away. The grievous shock of her loss is tempered by the knowledge that she found a glorious end on the high seas in the service of a just cause; victorious in her defeat and defiant of the enemy to the last. It is for us to salute her heroes in final homage and to avenge them.[24]

The *West Australian* spoke for many who were critical of the government's decision to withhold information:

> There are doubtless some impatient murmurings at the delay in the official statement which gave rise to much rumour and heart-burning among the public as news of a serious action at sea was bruited about. But it will now be conceded by the fair-minded that Mr Curtin's explanation [that there was a 'remote yet not impossible eventuality of the *Sydney* still being afloat'] gives ample justification for withholding temporarily news the premature publication of which might have been of much value to the enemy.[25]

But the public continued to demand more information. The Navy was against disclosing anything further on operational grounds, and because interrogation of the *Kormoran* survivors had just started. However, in the absence of detailed information, rumours continued to circulate. Several of the newspapers contacted the Navy on 1 December wanting to know whether it was true that the wreck of *Sydney* had been found on the West Australian coast.[26] The Prime Minister's office was asked whether two raiders might have been involved in the loss of *Sydney* and could some survivors from the cruiser have been picked up by the second ship? Another editor asked: 'From the viewpoint of bringing the war close to Australia and awakening national interest in perils likely for Australia, can place and date of action be revealed?'[27] Because an enemy ship might have scheduled a rendezvous with *Kormoran*, Curtin decided against announcing any further details of the action.

On 4 December, the Acting Chief of Naval Staff, Commodore Durnford, attended a meeting of the War Cabinet and gave a reconstructed account of the action.[28] As the account presented to the War Cabinet seemed so certain and very 'matter of fact', it formed the basis of a statement issued by Prime Minister Curtin later that day. The detailed information provided by Curtin was appreciated.

Curtin was obliged to relay further bad news to the Australian people before the day ended.[29] On 27 November, the sloop HMAS *Parramatta* had been sunk in the Mediterranean after a torpedo attack from the German submarine U-559, with heavy loss of life. Only 24 of her ship's company of 160 had survived. The *Bulletin* said that '1 December will be remembered in the ports of the Commonwealth as the beginning of the worst week of mourning the RAN has known in its splendid history'.[30]

Despite the grief and sadness, the Navy was still faced with the responsibility of finding out what had happened in the Indian Ocean off Carnarvon on 19 November 1941.

2

HMAS Sydney

'Sydney' was an appropriate name for an Australian warship to carry. It honoured Australia's largest and best-known city and reflected the nation's naval heritage. Sydney Cove within Port Jackson was the location of the first European settlement in Australia with the name chosen in 1788 by Captain Arthur Phillip RN, the first viceroy of New South Wales, who named the site after Lord Sydney, Secretary of State for the Home Department.

It was traditional in the Royal Navy for warships to be named in honour of British counties, cities and towns. The bigger the county, city or town, the bigger the ship. So that 120 years later it was not surprising that one of the ships commissioning into the newly created Royal Australian Navy (RAN) was named Sydney.

The first Australian ship[1] to bear the name was a Town Class Light Cruiser which was laid down in February 1911 and completed in June 1913. Sister-ship to *Melbourne* and *Brisbane* and similar to the British *Chatham* Class, *Sydney* displaced 5400 tons and carried eight 6-inch guns, one 3-inch gun, four 3-pounders, ten machine-guns and two 21-inch torpedo tubes. Having been built in Britain for the Commonwealth government, *Sydney*, commanded by Captain John Glossop RN, was part of the Australian Fleet that made its first ceremonial entry into Port Jackson on 4 October 1913. In the middle of the following year, the RAN was preparing for war with Germany. Six days after hostilities commenced on 4 August 1914, *Sydney* was dispatched north from Thursday Island and deployed in waters around New Guinea in search of the German East Asiatic Squadron under Vice Admiral Graf von Spee. After a fruitless search for the enemy fleet, the light cruiser supported the Australian Naval and Military Expeditionary Force (ANMEF) which sought to destroy enemy wireless stations in and around German New Guinea in September–October 1914.

After a successful campaign which led to the capture of all German possessions in the South-west Pacific, the cruisers *Sydney* and *Melbourne* escorted a convoy of 38 transports carrying the Australian Imperial Force (AIF) from Albany in Western Australia to the Middle East. The Australian ships were joined by the British cruiser *Minotaur* and the Japanese cruiser *Ibuki* in making up the escort screen. The escort was necessary because the German raider *Emden* was known to be lurking in the eastern Indian Ocean.

Mention of the name *Emden* created consternation in the first few months of World War I in the Pacific and Indian Oceans. SMS *Emden* was launched on 26 May 1908 and was described by the Imperial German Navy as a 'small cruiser'. She was armed with ten 4.1-inch guns and two 17.7-inch torpedo tubes. Under the command of Captain Karl von Muller, *Emden* was in the Yellow Sea proceeding towards the Russian port of Vladivostok when news was received that Germany and Russia were at war. Von Muller decided to raid merchant shipping and within the first 24 hours of hostilities commencing, von Muller had captured the Russian mail-passenger ship *Rjasan*. After meeting with Admiral von Spee at a rendezvous in the Mariana Islands on 12 August, von Muller was given permission to detach from the main German squadron and commence operations as a lone merchant raider. In company with the supply ship *Markomannia*, von Muller called at the German colony of Angaur before heading for Koepang in Dutch Timor. By this time, Japan had entered the war on the Allied side and von Muller was denied a secure base for his operations. Mounting a false funnel, *Emden* disguised herself as the four-funnelled British Town Class cruiser, HMS *Yarmouth*.

On 9 September, von Muller claimed his first victim: the Greek steamer *Pontoporos*. The ship, with her cargo of coal, was captured and became part of von Muller's supply line. For the next eight weeks, *Emden* operated in the Bay of Bengal and the Indian Ocean sinking another 18 ships, totalling more than 74 000 tons; capturing another five; and intercepting a further four of which three were used to transport the crews of sunk or captured ships to friendly or neutral ports. The fact that not one merchant mariner was killed throughout this period is testimony enough of von Muller's enormous skill as a raider captain. *Emden* also shelled British oil installations at Madras.

By late October 1914, von Muller decided on a change of tactics to boost the morale of his men who had been at sea for a long period in trying conditions without respite. With 16 ships from five navies in pursuit, *Emden* would raid the Cocos Islands.

Apart from the material damage the enemy would have suffered by the destruction of the cable and wireless station and the temporary interruption of telegraphic communications between Australia on the one hand and England and other countries on the other, I hoped also to effect (1) a general unrest among shipping to and from Australia by creating the impression that the *Emden* would proceed to harry steamer traffic south and west of Australia, (2) a withdrawal from the Indian Ocean of at least some of the English cruisers which were taking part in the hunting down of the *Emden*. My intention was, after carrying out the raid on the Cocos Group, to make for Socotra and cruise in the Gulf of Aden and then on the steamer route between Aden and Bombay.[2]

After *Emden* took on coal from the prize ship *Exford* before dawn on 8 November 30 miles north of North Keeling Island, the raid was postponed until the next day when wireless operators in the German ship noted unusual coded radio transmissions between the Cocos Islands and ships at sea. When *Emden* signalled to the collier *Buresk* on the morning of 9 November in a code unknown to the wireless operators on the Cocos Islands, a brief signal, 'Strange warship approaching', was transmitted and received in Perth. A second signal from *Emden* was intercepted by *Sydney*.[3]

Melbourne was ordered to proceed at once to investigate, but as she was the senior ship in the absence of the *Minotaur* which had been detached from the convoy, *Melbourne* passed the order to *Sydney* which left the convoy to intercept the 'strange warship'. Meanwhile, Lieutenant Commander von Mucke, second-in-command in *Emden*, had proceeded ashore on Cocos Island with a party of 50 armed men to destroy the cable and wireless stations. The task was not completed when a smoke plume was sighted from *Emden*'s bridge and von Mucke was ordered to 'speed up the work at hand'. Before the shore party's return to the ship, *Emden* weighed anchor and put to sea.

Glossop, in *Sydney*, sighted the German cruiser at 0930. He believed that the maximum range of *Emden*'s 4.1-inch guns was 9000 yards. It was actually 13 347 yards and at more than 10 000 yards the third salvo from *Emden* struck *Sydney*'s gunnery fire control room. Another round hit the foremost rangefinder but did not explode. Four men were killed and the Australian cruiser's main armament then had to be operated in local control. At 9500 yards, Glossop opened fire with *Sydney*'s 6-inch guns and inflicted major damage on the German raider before closing to 5500 yards for a torpedo attack. Although the torpedo attack was unsuccessful, *Emden*'s steering gear was not functioning and von Muller had few options available. He later wrote:

> I decided to put my ship . . . on the reef in the surf of the weather side of North Keeling Island and to wreck it thoroughly in order not to sacrifice needlessly the lives of the survivors.[4]

With *Emden* beached, the Australian cruiser ceased fire at 1120 and started to chase the collier *Buresk*. When the ship was scuttled by the German crew, Glossop returned to the raider on North Keeling Island. As *Sydney* closed *Emden* at 1600, Glossop observed that *Emden*'s battle ensign was still flying. This signified, to Glossop at least, that Captain von Muller had not surrendered. A signal, sent by light and flag-hoist, from *Sydney* asked 'Do you surrender?' This was effectively a request that the German ensign be struck from its staff. Glossop was answered with 'What signal? No signal books.' The signal 'Do you surrender?' was sent to *Emden* a second time. When this was apparently ignored by the stricken raider, Glossop signalled 'Have you received my signal?' But was Glossop justified in thinking that the battered and burning *Emden*, wrecked on a coral reef, had the capacity to fire on *Sydney*? When there was no reply to his signals and the German ensign continued to flutter in the breeze, two salvoes fired from *Sydney* crashed onto the upper deck of *Emden* and 20 men were killed. Von Muller was indignant.

> I had not expected her to resume the attack and was very astonished when she suddenly opened up again. As I afterwards learned from the *Sydney*'s captain, they twice made the signal 'Do you surrender?' but this was not understood on board *Emden*. As there was no reply, the *Sydney* assumed that the *Emden* wished to continue the fight, the more so as an ensign was still flying from the top-mast. In order to avoid the useless sacrifice of my men's lives, and as the *Emden* was no longer a warship but a wreck, I showed a white flag as a sign of surrender and ordered the ensign from the top mast to be taken down and burned. I am not quite certain what judgment will be passed on my decision to wreck the *Emden* and on the final surrender of the remaining crew.[5]

Meanwhile, von Mucke had seized the old yacht *Ayesha* from Cocos Island and sailed towards Asia. After a long and dangerous escape, von Mucke and the *Emden* shore party reported to the German admiral at Constantinople in Turkey in June 1915.

Emden's brief but highly successful raiding career was over. Glossop in *Sydney* sent a signal conveying the exciting news: '*Emden* beached and done for.' In the German ship, 134 men died, 65 were wounded and 110 taken prisoner.

This was the RAN's first and only major engagement of the 1914–18 war. Despite German complaints about Glossop's questionable decision to fire on *Emden* in the later afternoon, the victory over *Emden* brought instant international attention and fame to the fledgling Dominion navy. The Australian

Prime Minister, Andrew Fisher, told Parliament: 'I do not think that there is a soul in Australia that is not pleased that such an opportunity arose and such success was achieved by our own ship.' The Admiralty sent a message to Glossop: 'Warmest congratulations on the brilliant entry of the Australian navy into the war. Signal service has been rendered to the Allied cause, and peaceful commerce by the destruction of *Emden*.' '*Emden* 1914' was added to the ship's battle honours and Captain Glossop was made a Companion of the Order of the Bath (CB). Von Muller was awarded the Iron Cross (First Class) while the Kaiser announced that 'a new and stronger *Emden* shall arise, on whose bow the Iron Cross shall be fixed'.

With von Spee's squadron fleeing to German home waters and the Pacific and Indian Ocean basins rid of any German presence, there was little left for the RAN to do in defence of Australian sovereign interests. Both *Sydney* and *Melbourne* were despatched initially to Malta before being transferred to the West Indies Station. For the remainder of the war, *Sydney*'s service was largely uneventful. After service off the east coast of North America in 1915 and most of the following year, *Sydney* joined the Grand Fleet in late 1916 and was deployed in North Sea patrols until the end of the war. The only notable event came on 4 May 1917 when *Sydney* engaged the Zeppelin *L 43*. Neither the cruiser nor the zeppelin, which dropped its entire payload of bombs on *Sydney*, suffered any major damage. *Sydney*'s feat in sinking the first *Emden* was honoured in late 1918 when she was nominated to escort the second *Emden*, another cruiser, at the surrender of the German High Seas Fleet.

Following the cessation of hostilities, *Sydney* returned to Australia and a regular routine of peacetime refits, work-ups and exercises. She was finally paid off in May 1928 and scrapped at Cockatoo Island in January the following year. Her distinctive tripod mast was removed and placed upright on Bradley's Head in Port Jackson as a memorial to her achievements. The name *Sydney* had already achieved an aura and a sizeable reputation.

After the RAN was reduced to a mere four ships and 3200 men during the Great Depression, the growing belligerence of Japan and rising fears of the re-emerging fascist Germany prompted the Commonwealth government to strengthen Australia's defences. In April 1934, the government approved a three-year development program which would include the purchase of the light cruiser of the Modified *Leander* Class, HMS *Phaeton*, which was still under construction at Swan, Hunter and Wigham Richardson's shipyard at Wallsend-on-Tyne. The Modified *Leander* Class cruisers were built to a basic late 1920s design which the Admiralty constantly altered and developed in the years before the war. The first five ships of the unmodified class, *Leander*, *Neptune*, *Orion*, *Achilles* and *Ajax*, were launched between 1931 and 1934. The modified class consisted of three ships, *Amphion*, which was ordered first, *Apollo* and *Phaeton*.

The first ship of the class, *Leander*, was 1000 tons heavier than the original draft displacement of 6500 tons. This was corrected in the later ships, all of which were within 7000 tons. By the time the first five ships had been completed, the Admiralty decided to alter the main machinery layout in the remaining vessels. This change, which resulted in two separate machinery units, was a feature of other cruiser classes being built at that time. Instead of having a single machinery system, the creation of two self-contained machinery units would reduce the possibility of battle damage or a technical fault resulting in a complete power failure. Whereas in the *Leander* Class the funnel uptakes were raked into a distinctive single funnel, the funnel uptakes in the modified ships would be vertical with a single funnel for each of the two machinery units. As the machinery spaces were changed, the modified ships had their side armour extended from 84 feet to 141 feet. Thus, the weight saved in the machinery spaces was lost with the extra armour. The machinery unit system also affected the accommodation arrangements in the modified ships which were cramped and would be overcrowded if a wartime complement were embarked.

The British were also under pressure, not only from the Australian government, to consider the use of triple and quadruple 6-inch gun turrets, that is, three or four gun barrels in each turret, to increase firepower. In 1932, the Admiralty decided that one of the modified class two turrets, one forward and one aft, would be fitted with a triple turret as a trial. However, after further consideration the Admiralty decided that the alteration of the original design would decrease the maximum speed of the class and cause problems with the existing fire control and spotting systems.[6]

The Admiralty was pleased with the completed ship despite the many changes which had been made to the design. 'The end result was the most handsome cruisers ever built by the Royal Navy, with a symmetry that was as attractive as it was functional.'[7]

The announcement that Australia would buy *Phaeton* caused local political controversy. Although the government announced at the same time that a second sloop would be built at Cockatoo Island Dockyard, the first having been ordered in 1933, the Leader of the Opposition, James Scullin, argued that

> whatever is needed for the defence of Australia should not be purchased overseas if it can be made in Australia . . . with thousands of Australians unemployed and eking out a miserable existence on sustenance, the placing of a contract overseas is monstrous.[8]

However, the last cruiser to be built in Australia was HMAS *Adelaide*, which was commenced in 1915 but not completed until 1922. In addition to the time and cost involved, Australian naval shipbuilding lacked the experience necessary to build a vessel as complex as the latest British light cruisers. With war looming, there was not the time for them to gain that experience. In any case, construction of the ship offered by Britain was well advanced.

Phaeton had been laid down on 8 July 1933. She was 562 feet long, with a beam of 56 feet eight inches and a mean draught of 15 feet eight inches, displacing 7198 tons. The ship was powered by four Parsons geared turbines producing 72 000 shaft horsepower. Her armament consisted of eight 6-inch guns, four 4-inch anti-aircraft guns, four 3-pounder saluting guns, three

4-barrel 0.5-inch machine guns and eight 21-inch torpedo tubes. The ship carried one Walrus amphibian. The peacetime complement was 550 which was increased to 645 in wartime. She underwent sea trials in July 1935.

On a displacement of 8,138 tons with 71,972 [shaft horsepower], a speed of 32.137 knots was achieved. The trials took place off St Abbs Head in a Force 2 wind, with a calm sea. Further trials on a displacement of 7,105 tons with 72,340 [shaft horsepower] produced a speed of 33.05 knots. All trials were run in shallow water and it was estimated that in deep water an extra half knot would have been obtained. As with the *Leanders*, the class responded beautifully to the helm, and vibration was negligible. After acceptance trials, the ship was examined for welding defects, but none were found and the work appeared to be of a very high standard.[9]

HMS *Phaeton* was taken over by the RAN and launched on 22 September 1934 as HMAS *Sydney* by Mrs Ethel Bruce, the wife of the Australian High Commissioner in London and former Prime Minister, Stanley Melbourne Bruce.[10] Although the old sailor's superstition promised ill-fortune for a ship whose name was changed, the ship had to have an Australian name. One year later, the new *Sydney* completed her trials and sailed to Portsmouth under the command of Captain John Fitzgerald, an officer on loan from the Royal Navy.[11]

Commander John Collins RAN, a gunnery specialist, was the Executive Officer (second-in-command) and the senior Australian officer on board. The remainder of *Sydney*'s ship's company arrived in Portsmouth on board HMAS *Brisbane* which was to pay off for scrap. The new ship's company marvelled at what they saw when *Brisbane* came alongside the new cruiser.

All around *Sydney*, above and below decks, parties of sight-seers were engaged in the job of giving the ship the once over, inspecting the mess decks, workshops, galleys and the electric bakery with a very critical eye, and by the wide grins on their faces it was obvious that they were extremely pleased with what they saw. Everything was of new design and some of the fittings so unconventional that we had not encountered them before. The spaciousness and comfort of the decks and flats, and the modern design of the furniture and equipment was the more emphasised by the fact that we had just left a ship some twenty years old.[12]

On 29 October 1935, the second *Sydney* sailed for Australia. However, with the Italian invasion of Abyssinia (Ethiopia) she was diverted to Gibraltar for service with the 2nd Cruiser Squadron, enforcing League of Nations sanctions against Italy, where she remained based until January 1936.[13] *Sydney* docked at Malta on 26 February and then in Alexandria where she joined the 1st Cruiser Squadron under Admiral Sir Max Horton. After exercises and an independent cruise to Cyprus designed to rid the ship of mumps which had affected the ship's company since late 1935, *Sydney* docked again at Malta before arriving at Alexandria in July. She finally sailed for Australia on 14 July 1936.

After being delayed many months, the arrival of *Sydney* in her home port was a major occasion for the city and the RAN. After a short maintenance period, *Sydney* joined the normal peacetime exercise program which included longer cruises, such as to New Zealand for exercises with the New Zealand Squadron, and short visits to Australian ports. In July 1937, Fitzgerald handed over command to Captain J.W.A. Waller RN;[14] Collins was also relieved as Executive Officer. Prime Minister Lyons announced in March 1938 that a new three-year defence program would also include the purchase of the other two Modified *Leander* Class light cruisers: *Apollo* and *Amphion*, completed in 1936, and renamed *Hobart* and *Perth*.

With war looming, attention was focused on *Sydney*'s weapons. The turret and the fire control system of the main armament of 6-inch guns was modern in every respect. *Sydney* was well armed and fast but speed was achieved at the expense of armour-plating. The only area protected with armour was the ship's side between the funnels.

The guns could be fired from a number of positions around the ship. The Gunnery Officer could give the order to fire the guns using information obtained from the main director situated above the bridge. His assistant could give the order to open fire using a director located near the after mast. Each turret could also be fired under what was called 'local control' with the order given by the officer responsible for each of the four turrets.

In a fleet action, the guns were usually fired under Director Control using information obtained from both the main and after directors. Information from the directors was processed by a series of dials in the transmitting room. As variables such as the target's course and speed, and prevailing winds were entered, other variables would be affected. The aim was to achieve a bearing and elevation on which the guns could fire to hit the target. The ship's movement was negated by each gun being gyro-stabilised so as to allow fire only when the turret was level.

When the guns fired, the fall of shot would be observed and buttons marked 'Over', 'Short' and 'Straddle' were pressed in either director tower or by the officer in charge of a turret to indicate the correction required. The fire control solution would then be altered accordingly. The dials in the transmitter room effectively averaged fall-of-shot observations although the Gunnery Officer could intervene as he chose. The cruiser's secondary armament of 4-inch and anti-aircraft mountings were operated in local control and aimed using visual observation.

Although it was up to date, doubts were raised about the ability of Sydney's gunnery system to survive battle damage. In October 1938, Waller told the Naval Board that:

> The primary gun control systems in HMAS Sydney are extremely vulnerable to gunfire and bombs, even of small calibre, between the Director Control Tower or High Angle Control Tower and the Platform Deck.[15]

What Sydney's captain may not have known is that the Admiralty asked its ship designers to work on a protected fire control system in the early 1930s. But as this would have adversely affected the placement and operation of other weapon systems, the Admiralty had accepted the limitations of the Modified *Leander* design.

Waller's chief concern about *Sydney* was the lack of protection for the non-duplicated cables running to and from the gun directing tower. Were Power Room No. 1 to suffer damage, the primary system for controlling the main armament would be inoperative. The alternative system was, Waller stated, either inefficient or impractical.

> The position of the commanding officer is therefore the uncomfortable one of desiring to close to an effective fighting range while knowing that at any moment he may find his rate of hitting seriously reduced or even vanished due to very minor damage.[16]

The Fleet Commander, Rear Admiral Wilfred Custance RN, considered Waller's representation as 'a matter of anxiety to me, and that the primary control might be put out of action by a lucky hit is a matter of grave concern'.[17] Captain John Collins, who was a gunnery specialist and possessed first-hand knowledge of the ship from his time as her Executive Officer, suggested that Waller's concerns be relayed to the Admiralty as it had built the Modified *Leander* Class and operated a large number of the ships. Given that Collins did not propose immediate remedial action, it is possible that Collins did not agree with Waller's sentiments.

Sydney's fire control system was not altered or improved and the peace-time exercise program continued into 1938 and throughout most of 1939 until *Sydney* was ordered to her war station at Fremantle on 22 August where she remained until war was declared on 3 September 1939.

The Modified *Leander* Class light cruisers were integral to both Australia's contribution to the war in Europe and to local naval defence. In September 1939, the Dominions Office in London outlined its views on how Australian naval assets could be most effectively employed. The minute, relayed by the Secretary of the Department of Defence, Frederick Shedden, to the Naval Board, asked Australia to contribute a light cruiser and five destroyers to join HMAS *Perth* which was already under the operational control of the Admiralty.

> . . . So long as Japan remains neutral it is considered that Australian waters may be regarded as unlikely to suffer submarine attack. The most likely danger to be guarded against on [the] Australian station under present conditions is that of attack on shipping by enemy raiders. It is considered that two cruisers and HMAS *Australia* (when ready) should prove adequate for this purpose.[18]

The Naval Board was prepared to approve placing five destroyers, the Flotilla Leader HMAS *Stuart* and the four V & W Class destroyers, *Vampire*, *Vendetta*, *Voyager* and *Waterhen*, under Admiralty control. As these ships were technically on loan from the Royal Navy, there could be no reasonable objection to the request. Regarding a second cruiser, the Board

> recommended that a second 6-inch cruiser (HMAS *Hobart* or *Sydney*) should be made available forthwith for service when required. With two cruisers playing their part in the defence of sea communications to and from Australia in distant waters, and the remaining cruisers employed in Australian waters, the best distribution of our available force is achieved.[19]

On 6 October, the War Cabinet agreed to release a second 6-inch cruiser to serve in the Mediterranean. *Sydney* was chosen.

Captain Waller was relieved in command of *Sydney* by Captain John Collins on 16 November 1939. The first two months of the war had involved the ship in patrol and escort duties, and in the continual activity of working-up the command team and weapons crews. When the tanker *Africa Shell* was sunk by the German pocket battleship *Graf Spee* in the Indian Ocean on 19 November, *Sydney*, in company with the Australian 8-inch heavy cruisers *Australia* and *Canberra*, patrolled the Indian Ocean shipping routes in search of the German ship. After a four-day search commencing on 28 November which failed to find *Graf Spee*, the ships returned to Fremantle. *Sydney* was relieved on station by the aged light cruiser HMAS *Adelaide* on 13 December, and went to Cockatoo Island for docking.

Sydney rejoined the fleet in late January 1940 and formed the first Anzac convoy, US 1, with *Canberra* and HM Ships *Ramillies* and *Leander*. The light cruiser returned to Fremantle on 8 February and resumed her duties patrolling the shipping routes and escorting merchant ships off the West Australian coast. Collins described this period, 'which included intensive exercising, operating aircraft, high angle and surface firings and torpedo running' as the 'most valuable in the strenuous days ahead'.[20] In April and May, *Sydney* escorted convoy US 2 and planned to escort US 3 before receiving a signal which directed her to make best speed to Colombo where she arrived on 8 May. It was from here that *Sydney* was ordered to the Mediterranean where the Admiralty was building a fleet to counter the possible Italian entry into the war. The Australian light cruiser arrived in Alexandria on 26 May and came under the command of Vice Admiral Sir John Tovey in the 7th Cruiser Squadron.[21]

By this time, *Sydney* had a competent and experienced command team led by Collins and the Executive Officer, Commander Thomas Hilken. Commander Lionel Dalton was the Chief Engineer, Lieutenant Commander Clive Montgomery the Navigating Officer and Lieutenant Commander Michael Singer the Gunnery Officer. The latter two were British officers seconded to the RAN.

When hostilities with Italy started after midnight on 10 June 1940, *Sydney* was in Alexandria Harbour with the ships of the Australian 'Scrap Iron Flotilla'. The ships of the 10th Destroyer Squadron, consisting of *Stuart*, *Vendetta*, *Vampire*, *Voyager* and *Waterhen*, were so named after Dr Goebbels referred to the aged ships scathingly as the 'scrap iron' from Australia. The First Division of the 7th Cruiser Squadron put to sea and patrolled between Benghazi and the Ionian Islands and then refuelled in Alexandria. Bardia was bombarded on 20 June by the British cruisers *Orion* and *Neptune*, the French battleship *Lorraine* and *Sydney*.[22] With the French surrender looming, the Fleet returned and remained in Alexandria to prevent the French ships from falling into enemy hands. *Sydney* sailed from Alexandria again on 27 June when the 7th Cruiser Squadron covered the passage of a Malta-bound convoy. The following day, three Italian destroyers were spotted by an Allied flying boat and engaged at long range in the deteriorating daylight.

The *Espero* suffered minor damage, lost speed and was to be sunk by *Sydney*. But as the Australian cruiser closed the range, the Italian destroyer returned fire and despatched torpedoes. As Collins had prudently kept *Sydney* 'bows on' to the enemy ship to reduce the size of the target area, he was able to avoid the torpedoes before sinking *Espero*. In the darkness, Collins could hear the cries of the Italian sailors and began a rescue operation. Being directed to rejoin the Squadron and mindful of submarine attack, Collins left behind one of *Sydney*'s cutters for the Italians still in the water. Collins later said, 'It was felt that the company of a ship that had put up such a gallant defence deserved every chance of survival, even at the expense of losing one cutter.'[23]

The next morning *Sydney* rejoined the Squadron as it was attacked by Italian bombers south of Crete.[24] No damage was sustained during the attack and the ships returned to Alexandria on 1 July. *Sydney* returned to sea on 7 July and, as part of the Mediterranean Fleet, prepared to engage the Italian fleet in a major action. The Allied force, led by the carrier *Eagle*, the battleships *Warspite*, *Malaya* and *Royal Sovereign* and the cruisers *Orion*, *Neptune*, *Gloucester*, *Liverpool* and *Sydney*, was subjected to intense Italian air attack on 9 July. Later in the day, three enemy battleships, six cruisers and a number of destroyers were reported to be north of Benghazi. The Allied fleet then manoeuvred to cut the route between the Italian fleet and its base. At 1500, *Sydney* observed smoke and eight minutes later the enemy force was in sight.[25] The Italians opened fire at maximum range. The 6-inch cruisers of the 7th Cruiser Squadron did not return fire until the range had closed to 23 000 yards. While fire was directed at the Australian cruiser, no damage was sustained. The Italian fleet made for Calabria at full speed behind a smoke screen. The only enemy ship to be sunk was the destroyer *Zeffiro*. The Italians responded with air attacks the next day without success. The Allied fleet returned to Alexandria on 13 July.[26]

After a quick hull cleaning, *Sydney* put to sea on 18 July in support of an anti-submarine sweep north of Crete. Although *Sydney* was able to operate independently after escorting the anti-submarine destroyers through the Kaso Strait, Collins remained approximately 20 miles to the north of the destroyers rather than proceeding towards Piraeus, the port of Athens, in search of enemy shipping. The Kaso Strait, 15–20 miles wide between Crete and then in Greek possession, and Kaso Island to the east, were the site of an Italian fast attack craft and air base. Shortly after dawn on 19 July, *Sydney* received an enemy sighting report from HMS *Hyperion*. The destroyers turned towards *Sydney* and were followed by the Italian cruisers *Bartolomeo Colleoni* and *Giovanni delle Bande Nere*. Both ships, which displaced over 5000 tons and were armed with eight 6-inch guns, were capable of speeds of over 40 knots for eight hours. *Sydney* turned towards the destroyers at full speed but kept radio silence to avoid detection.[27]

Collins took a risk in engaging the Italian ships as he had a reduced capability to determine fall of shot. The cruiser's Walrus aircraft had not been replaced after suffering damage on 4 July. But just as *Sydney* sighted the Italian cruisers, Collins sent an enemy report and, making best use of the available light and the prevailing misty conditions, engaged the *Bande Nere* at 20 000 yards apparently undetected. In his report Collins stated, 'It was not possible to distinguish what type of cruisers they were and I was concerned in case they were heavy 8-inch cruisers. However, I decided to go for them and opened fire.'[28]

The Italians were caught completely by surprise and took some time to determine the origins of the firing. By this time the destroyers were in a suitable position to launch their torpedoes. In the mistaken belief that the destroyer HMS *Havoc* was a cruiser, the two Italian ships made smoke and turned away. The Allied ships chased the enemy cruisers with *Sydney* concentrating her fire from her forward gun turrets on the *Colleoni*. Nearly one hour after the initial sighting, *Sydney* altered course to bring a broadside to bear on the Italian cruiser. The *Colleoni* lost speed. She was on fire and appeared down by the bows.

For a moment it appeared that the *Bande Nere* would remain with the stricken *Colleoni*. But after firing a salvo, one shell of which struck the fore funnel of *Sydney*, she fled at full speed. While the *Colleoni* was sunk by the destroyers, *Sydney* proceeded to chase the *Bande Nere* with very little prospect of success. Although the *Bande Nere* was indeed struck by a shell from *Sydney*, the Italian ship was too fast and escaped.[29] With her outfit of 6-inch ammunition practically expended, Collins had reason to be alarmed when he heard that another enemy force was expected and that *Havoc* was operating at reduced speed after a near miss disabled her boiler room. *Sydney* rejoined *Havoc* and headed back towards Alexandria. Other than intermittent air attacks, the Italian fleet did not return.

An engineering officer who survived the engagement, Lieutenant Gallupini, later reported that a 6-inch shell from *Sydney* had exploded in the *Colleoni* to be followed by repeated hits to the base of the bridge which disabled the gunnery control and started a fire which spread throughout the ship. Some 550 Italian officers and sailors were recovered.

Sydney returned to Alexandria after what became known as the Battle of Cape Spada[30] on 20 July to a hero's welcome. In the official history, Gill recorded that as the cruiser entered the harbour:

Her own destroyers started it off by hauling out of line in the channel near the boom and cheering her as she passed them. Her berth lay at the far end of the harbour, a distance of about two miles from the boom. Every ship in harbour cleared lower deck, and as she passed down harbour they cheered her in turn. To one of *Sydney*'s company it was 'a continuous roar for about fifteen minutes . . . something I will never forget'. The Australian destroyers—each flying seven Australian flags for the occasion, gave her a tremendous welcome, and [Commander Hec] Waller, leading the cheering in *Stuart*, gave an Australian flavour to his greeting with the signal, 'Whacko, *Sydney*!' It was a great Australian day in Alexandria.

The Commander-in-Chief (CINC) of the Mediterranean Fleet, Admiral Sir Andrew Cunningham, was overjoyed with *Sydney*'s important morale-boosting success.[31] Mussolini's son-in-law, Count Ciano, noted in his diary entry for 22 July that the Duce 'was depressed on account of the loss of the *Colleoni*, not so much because of the sinking itself as because he feels the Italians did not fight very brilliantly'. The captain of the *Colleoni*, Captain Umberto Navaro, died in an Allied hospital ship from wounds he received during the action and was buried in Alexandria on 24 July.

Sydney had finally achieved a surface action with the Italian fleet and demonstrated the Allied superiority in that mode of warfare. However, the Axis Command was not going to let this incident affect morale. The German account of the action was broadcast by 'Lord Haw Haw':

Two British heavy armoured cruisers and a large force of destroyers attacked two Italian light cruisers off the coast of Crete and in the ensuing battle the two British cruisers were heavily damaged. Slight damage was inflicted on one of the Italian cruisers. Italian super bombers attacked the British force on its way back to harbour; one ship was set on fire and sunk.[32]

In his subsequent report to the Admiralty, Cunningham praised Collins for 'his quick appreciation of the situation, offensive spirit and resolute handling of the ship'. In sum:

HMAS *Sydney* achieved a victory over a superior force which has had important strategical effects . . . *Sydney*'s gunnery narrative is of great interest both technically and from the more general point of view. It shows the results obtainable by an efficient control team backed by good material, and it should be given the weight due to the experience of a ship which has had the unique opportunity of firing 2,200 main armament rounds in action in six weeks.

Sydney's achievements were reflected in decorations and awards: Collins was made a Companion of the Bath (CB);

Commanders Hilken and Dalton received the Distinguished Service Order (DSO), Lieutenant Commanders Singer and Thruston the Distinguished Service Cross (DSC) while Lieutenant Commander Montgomery was Mentioned in Despatches (MID). Senior sailors were awarded the Distinguished Service Medal (DSM) or were Mentioned in Despatches. Like the first ship to bear the name, the second *Sydney* had earned a world-wide reputation.[33]

After repairs and with new Walrus aircraft, *Sydney* was refuelled, rearmed and ready for sea on 27 July. That afternoon, escorting a convoy, *Sydney* again came under attack from enemy bombers but evaded being struck. The following morning in company with *Neptune*, the Australian cruiser was detached from the main force to intercept and sink the tanker *Ermioni* which was thought to be in the Aegean Sea delivering fuel to the Dodecanese. After another unsuccessful bomber attack, *Sydney* identified the *Ermioni* at 2130 and, after recovering the crew, sank the tanker. *Neptune* and *Sydney* returned to Alexandria on 30 July in time for final preparations for another patrol operation in company with *Orion* which lasted until 2 August. *Sydney*'s ship's company were granted a well-earned rest and the opportunity to express their artistic talent by repainting the ship.

When the cruiser sailed with *Neptune* and five destroyers on 12 August to locate enemy shipping off the North African coast and in the Aegean Sea, *Sydney* was impressively camouflaged for the first time. This operation lasted two days and failed to locate the enemy. A week later, *Sydney* sailed from Alexandria to support a squadron of destroyers which were shelling Bomba and Bardia. Another Malta convoy escort operation, MB 5, commenced on 30 August.

The ship was later detached in company with HMS *Ilex* to bombard the Makri Yalo airstrip on the island of Scarpanto. This was the site of a vital Italian air base located north-east of Crete. It supported air operations against Crete, Greece and the sea approaches from Egypt. *Sydney* approached the shore at dawn successfully disguised as an Italian cruiser. Five Italian E-boats were sent against *Sydney* and *Ilex*; two were sunk by

Ilex, and the other three returned to their base. This was another operation that earned *Sydney* and Collins the praise of the Mediterranean Fleet. With the airstrip destroyed, Cunningham relayed his pleasure in a signal to the ship: 'Well done. You are a stormy petrel.'

Sydney had earned a rest and a refit which commenced in the Alexandria dry dock on 8 September. After returning to the Fleet, *Sydney* was on convoy escort and patrol missions before returning to Alexandria on 3 October and preparing for the next Malta convoy—MB 6. After reaching Malta on 11 October, the Fleet turned eastward again and, rejoining the main force after a rendezvous with *Ramillies*, *Sydney* pursued the remaining elements of a fleeing Italian force. Following a short stay in Alexandria, *Sydney* was at sea again escorting other convoy and patrolling into the North Aegean.

At the end of October 1940, the Australian cruiser sailed with the main battle-fleet into the central Mediterranean in an effort to prevent attacks on Greece from Italy. Another short stay in Alexandria on 3–4 November preceded *Sydney*'s departure for Port Said in company with *Ajax* for the embarkation of military stores, guns and ammunition destined for Crete. After supporting the establishment of a new advanced base at Suda Bay, *Sydney* returned to the main battle-fleet which was preparing for Malta convoy MB 8 and the Fleet Air Arm attack on the Italian naval base at Taranto. On her return to Alexandria, *Sydney* was despatched to Piraeus with stores and military personnel. She then rejoined the 7th Cruiser Squadron which was escorting a convoy in the Aegean. The remainder of the month of November saw *Sydney* support Malta convoy MB 9 which also involved operations around Malta and Greece. After spending the first half of December in and around the Aegean escorting convoys and bombarding the port of Valona, *Sydney* needed a refit in Malta.

Shortly after *Sydney* rejoined the fleet on 8 January, Admiral Cunningham ordered her to detach from the main force, to conduct a final sweep along the coast of North Africa and to close any convoys which might require escorting during the ship's return to Australia. The CINC sent a final signal as *Sydney* departed the station.

> Much regret that there will be no opportunity for me to come on board and personally say goodbye to you all. *Sydney* has been with us from the beginning of the Italian war and has borne with us the rough when things were difficult and better times which we have had lately. We have all admired her efficiency and the fiery spirit which animated all on board. She was the first to show the enemy that, whatever the odds, he ran great risk of destruction if he encountered our ships. We part with you with great regret and the best wishes of the Mediterranean Fleet go with you. I hope you will have a happy home coming and that your countrymen will give you the reception you deserve.

After briefly diverting to patrol off Mogadishu in Somalia, and refuelling at Seychelles, *Sydney* arrived in Fremantle on 5 February 1941. The reception the ship deserved had to wait until the cruiser arrived in Port Jackson late on the night of 9 February.[34] The following morning, the Rear Admiral Commanding the Australian Station (RACAS), John Crace, was embarked at Watsons Bay before *Sydney* made the short passage to Sydney Cove to be welcomed formally by the Governor General, Lord Gowrie, the Minister for the Navy, Billy Hughes, and the Chief of Naval Staff, Vice Admiral Sir Ragnar Colvin. The Lord Mayor of Sydney, Alderman Stanley Crick, presented Collins with a plaque the next day to commemorate the ship's success in the Mediterranean. This was followed by a triumphant march of *Sydney*'s officers and ship's company through the streets of the city after which their ship had been named. One officer recalled:

> Through Macquarie Street, Martin Place and George Street we were given a really overwhelming reception. Each square inch of path and roadway—except for a narrow laneway left for us to march through— was packed and the continuous applause was deafening. It has been estimated that a quarter of a million onlookers were packed between [Circular Quay] and the Town Hall.[35]

When the euphoria of the ship's return eventually abated, *Sydney* received a short refit before sailing for Fremantle on 28 February. For the next month, *Sydney* resumed the convoy work which had occupied her service off the West Australian coast nine months before. *Sydney* escorted the giant transport *Queen Mary* to Jervis Bay in early April before sailing to Port Phillip Bay to embark Admiral Colvin for a secret passage to Singapore where she arrived on 19 April.[36] By the end of the month, *Sydney* was back in Fremantle and the time had come for Collins to relinquish command.

During his time in command Collins did not pursue the matters relating to *Sydney*'s fire control system that were raised by Waller before the war. Neither is there any record of the Admiralty proposing any modification to this class of ship to overcome deficiencies in the fire control system. Battle experience demonstrated that the ships were more robust and versatile than the Admiralty may have expected. The 'unmodified' *Leander* Class cruiser, HMS *Achilles*, had suffered a direct hit on her director tower during the Battle of the River Plate on 13 December 1939 and continued to fight.[37] HMS *Orion* was bombed in May 1941 during the Battle of Crete. Waller in 1938 may have overstated an unavoidable weakness in the design of the ship's gunnery system; eighteen months of combat seems to have proved that the fire control system was not as 'flimsy' as Waller imagined.

If there were a problem with the gunnery system, it would also have come to the attention of Collins's relief, Captain Joseph Burnett RAN, who assumed command of *Sydney* on 15 May 1941.

Burnett was fortunate that the first four weeks of his command were taken up with the straightforward demands of convoy escort work in the Indian Ocean. On 24 June, *Sydney* sailed for Port Jackson where she arrived on 2 July. With little delay, the cruiser sailed as escort for a Pacific Ocean convoy before docking and minor maintenance. On 8 August, *Sydney* resumed her escort duties, on this occasion sailing with *Awatea* to Auckland and Suva. The cruiser was back in her home port by the end of the month before escorting convoy US 12A, consisting of the

transports *Queen Mary* and *Queen Elizabeth*, from Jervis Bay
to a rendezvous with *Canberra* in the Great Australian Bight.
Sydney was back in Fremantle at the end of September after a
maintenance period in Williamstown and a series of fleet exercises with main armament firings. The cruiser then rendezvoused
in the Bight with convoy US 12B, comprising *Aquitania*, *Johan
Van Oldenbarnevelt*, *Marnix Van St Aldebonde* and *Sibajak*,
which she escorted into the Indian Ocean.

Meanwhile, the 6700-ton troopship *Zealandia*, with nearly
1000 men of the Australian 8th Division reinforcements and
RAAF embarked, sailed from Port Jackson in company with
the cruiser *Adelaide* bound for Singapore. *Sydney* sailed into the
Bight to escort *Zealandia* during her passage to the Sunda Strait,
where the cruisers *Danae* and *Durban* would escort *Zealandia*
to her destination of Singapore. On 8 November, *Canberra* left
Fremantle with *Queen Mary* and *Queen Elizabeth* bound for
a rendezvous with the cruiser HMS *Cornwall* near the Cocos
Islands. Three days later, *Sydney* departed Fremantle with
Zealandia. It appeared that the passage from Fremantle to the
Sunda Strait had been executed without incident when *Sydney*
detached *Zealandia* on 17 November. By this time, *Canberra*
had returned to Fremantle and was on her way back to Port
Jackson. In the absence of any signal amending her arrival time,
Sydney was expected back in her home port of Fremantle on the
afternoon of Thursday 20 November.

If she did fail to arrive on time, the Naval Board would not
be overly concerned at first. It was expected that during such
a long passage, *Sydney* would encounter any number of merchant ships. In the previous two months, she had challenged a
number of vessels including *Bramora*, *Islander* and *Salland*. The
latter sighting provoked more than passing interest at the District Naval Office in Fremantle. *Sydney* sighted *Salland* shortly
after noon on 4 October about 900 miles to the north-west of
Rottnest Island bound for Fremantle.[38]

The identification procedure promulgated by the Admiralty
on 25 December 1940 was straightforward. A merchant ship
would be asked by a warship using signal light for her four

international signal letters. When these were given, usually with signal flags, they were converted to a secret callsign in the Admiralty code book. The warship would then signal the two inner letters of the secret callsign (by light or flag-hoist) with the merchant ship replying with the outer two letters. The warship was not to demand the secret callsign in a separate signal because the merchant ship was meant to know the significance of the two-letter hoist. If a ship was unable to give the outer two letters of her secret callsign, the warship would order her to stop (if she had not done so earlier) and a boarding party would check the merchant ship's identity. If the merchant ship failed to heave to when ordered, the warship could fire warning shots before firing for effect. This procedure was followed precisely by Burnett in the identification of *Salland*, and during previous encounters with merchant ships. Some other naval units were not as efficient.

During a rain-squalling night on 5 October, HMAS *Yandra* was deployed off Rottnest Island as the guard ship for the port of Fremantle. At 2220, she challenged an inward-bound ship which apparently identified herself as *Salland* which had sailed from Calcutta. This was reported to Port War Signal Station (PWSS) on Rottnest Island who duly informed the naval staff in Fremantle. However, the District Naval Office was not expecting *Salland* for another two days. The Naval Duty Plotting Officer suggested that the signal letters for *Saidja* (PHHE), a ship which was due in Fremantle, could have been misread for those of *Salland* (PHHV). When both the PWSS and *Yandra* lost contact with the ship alleged to be *Salland* during the night, the only recourse was to wait until the morning when her identity could be positively confirmed.[39]

When *Salland* had not proceeded into the harbour by dawn but *Saidja* came alongside shortly afterwards, the mystery appeared to be solved and the naval staff would be proved correct about *Yandra*'s mistake. However, when the master of *Saidja* stated that he had not been challenged during the night, suspicion was raised about the vessel claiming to be *Salland*. That afternoon, the watchkeeping officer from *Yandra* was interviewed and all ships expected in the area were identified by routine RAAF air surveillance. When *Sydney* reported the position of her sighting of *Salland* in response to a signal from Fremantle, it became obvious that the ship challenged by *Yandra* was not *Salland*. With the troopship *Queen Mary* bound for Fremantle and the suspicious ship thought to be a minelayer, *Sydney* was directed to intercept *Queen Mary* before she reached a possible mine-field. Minesweepers were also sent to sweep a channel for the troopship. *Queen Mary* arrived in Fremantle without incident and no mines were observed.

An official inquiry was subsequently held on board *Sydney*. The watchkeeping officer and the signalman in *Yandra* who had allegedly sighted *Salland* had earlier had their ability to read signal-light tested. Neither could read morse at the required rate. When the officers from *Yandra* were told at the inquiry that, in any event, they should have demanded the ship's secret callsign and checked its silhouette in addition to ascertaining its signal letters, they pointed out that *Yandra* had not been supplied with either the secret codebook or the manual containing silhouettes. In his report on the inquiry, Burnett concluded that *Yandra* had probably sighted *Armadale*, which had been challenged well over an hour earlier, twice. The confusion possibly resulted from *Yandra* having changed course after the first challenge. Burnett was also critical of the identification procedures in use.

> It seems entirely wrong that the identification of ships at night should be left merely at accepting the plain language name and port of departure of a ship on the list of expected arrivals as sufficient evidence. Patrol ships here are not supplied with secret callsigns of merchant ships, and their orders do not appear to include any instruction that they should make close investigation unless there are specially suspicious features.[40]

Burnett was also generally critical of the local examination procedures around Fremantle and believed that a more rigorous approach was needed. He was certainly aware of what ought to be done and had ensured that his ship followed the correct identification procedures.

On the afternoon of 19 November, *Sydney* was in the Indian Ocean south-west of Carnarvon proceeding on a south-easterly course when she sighted an unidentified merchant ship on the horizon.

3

The Men in Command

The navy that Joseph Burnett joined in 1913 as a 14-year-old boy was imbued with centuries of naval tradition despite having been in existence for less than two years. The Royal Australian Navy, created by royal decree in 1911, was drawn from the Royal Navy and would remain under the influence of the parent service for more than fifty years. The training of the Australian junior officers was the means by which the RAN would be placed and maintained on a sound professional footing. The Committee of Imperial Defence stated that 'the navies of each component part of the Empire must be trained to the same standards—the systems of tactics, gunnery, fire control, torpedo work, and signalling must be identical'.[1] It would also ensure that Australian ships could be interchanged with those of the Royal Navy in operations around the globe.

The Navy and the nation held high hopes for what the young Australian officers would achieve. The *Sydney Morning Herald* remarked in 1914 that

> the son of an Australian boundary rider today may be the Commander-in-Chief of the British fleet in the Pacific tomorrow—for all one knows he might be a second Nelson who will some day preserve the British Empire.[2]

But the boys who made up the first entry to the Naval College in 1913 endured hardships unknown to their successors.[3] After beginning their naval training at Osborne House on Corio Bay in Geelong, Victoria, the temporary site of the Naval College, the 1913 term was relocated to Jervis Bay on the New South Wales south coast in 1915.[4,5]

At the end of 1916, members of the first term had completed their four-year course studying engineering, seamanship, gunnery, navigation, mathematics, physics, chemistry, English, French, history, geography, physical training and Bible study, and were prepared to graduate from the College. When they joined the Navy in February 1913, the average age was thirteen years and seven months. Most were now seventeen and a half years old and more than eight inches taller and forty-three pounds heavier. Cadet Midshipman Burnett, born on St Stephen's Day (26 December) 1899, was the second son of Richard and Emily Burnett of Singleton, New South Wales. As his father died when he was seven, the prospect of a free education and going to sea attracted young Joseph to the Navy. He was a promising young officer. He was made a cadet captain in 1914 and soon gained sporting colours for cricket, tennis, athletics and, his first love, rugby. In September 1916, the Naval College rugby team defeated the Royal Military College, Duntroon by 20–9. Burnett played at half-back and was commended for his 'swift attack from the scrum base'.[6]

The graduation parade for the 1913 entry was a proud and important occasion for the Australian government.[7] The reviewing officer was the Governor General, Sir Ronald Munro Ferguson, who addressed the graduating class.

This is a notable occasion. The first draft of His Majesty's Sea Service is putting out from Jervis Bay—an institution bearing the name of one of the greatest of all seamen. You, who are of the same blood, have been trained here in the traditions of a race which for 300 years and more has never lost its hold on the sea . . . Your bearing, good manners and conduct testify to the high tone maintained in the College, and we may confidently expect that you are qualified to exhibit that character and personality which, from Nelson downwards, has ever distinguished the British sea officer. All at home are anxious to see what Australia has made of her Cadets. Your progress will be keenly watched by comrades of the Old Country who will judge by you whether an Australian shapes into a good seaman and naval officer ... I'm sure I hope all concerned will come out well of the ordeal. But after the first few months you will soon cease to discriminate between Australian and English born, and you will remember only that you belong to the greatest of all British Services that of the sea.

Promoted to midshipman on 1 January 1917, Burnett sailed to Britain to join the battlecruiser and RAN flagship, HMAS *Australia*, which was operating in the North Sea. After joining the ship in April, Burnett was detached to the destroyer HMS *Tower* to broaden his experience. In September 1918, Burnett was promoted to probationary acting sub-lieutenant and completed his professional courses for that substantive rank gaining First Class Certificates in all subjects. Confirmed in the rank of sub-lieutenant at the end of 1918, Burnett remained in Britain for the next five years, completing courses for the rank of lieutenant and gaining watchkeeping experience in *Australia* and the battleship HMS *Royal Oak*.

It remained important that Australian officers like Burnett were trained in a manner identical with their British contemporaries as the Minister for the Navy, Sir Joseph Cook, explained on 20 December 1918.

It is fundamental to the idea of Empire naval defence that there should be a complete standardisation of personnel and ships and equipment and that this should be to the level of the best. Only the best is good enough for any Navy in the British Empire.[8]

This was endorsed by Lord Jellicoe, latterly First Sea Lord at the Admiralty in London, who toured Australia in 1919 to advise the Commonwealth government on the Dominion's naval defence requirements. He suggested that the Admiralty 'endeavour to give Dominion officers experience in large fleets and in the British Navy by frequent interchange with officers of the Royal Navy'.[9] This was the guiding principle of Burnett's professional development.

As a junior lieutenant, Burnett decided he would specialise in gunnery. He completed the long gunnery course at the Royal Navy's Gunnery School, HMS *Excellent*, in 1922 before service in the light cruiser HMAS *Adelaide* which was then on a goodwill cruise around the United Kingdom. Burnett was also a champion rugby footballer, representing the British United Services, Hampshire and the Royal Navy. As the RAN's tennis champion, he was invited to play in the Royal Navy tournament at Wimbledon. Burnett returned to the Gunnery School in early 1927 and then joined the newly commissioning heavy cruiser HMAS *Canberra* in which he served as gunnery officer for two years. He was promoted lieutenant commander on 1 January 1928.

Opportunities for varied service were limited during the Depression with the RAN reduced to four operational vessels. Lieutenant Commander Burnett returned to Britain in the summer of 1930 and served for the next twelve months in the destroyer flotilla leaders *Wallace* and *Montrose* as squadron gunnery officer. This was followed by the War Staff Course at HMS *President* in Shrewsbury during 1932 and promotion to the rank of commander at the end of that year.

There was some resistance to Burnett's promotion. It was administrative rather than personal in nature. In a memorandum entitled 'Officering the RAN', produced in 1931 by the Chief of Naval Staff, Admiral Hyde expressed his concern that promoting the Australian officers prematurely might prevent them from consolidating their experience at each rank level and might lead the Royal Navy to refusing their services on exchange.[10] This was not a valid concern in the case of Burnett whose expertise continued to be welcomed in British ships.

Commander Burnett returned to Australia on completion of his staff course and spent the next two years as a staff officer at Navy Office in Melbourne. In 1936, Burnett returned to *Canberra* and he was appointed an Honorary Aide-de-Camp to the Governor General. After eighteen months service as Executive Officer in HMS *Royal Oak*, including service in the Spanish Civil War, Burnett was promoted captain at the end of 1938 and completed the Imperial Defence College course. He was then appointed to Navy Office as the Assistant (later Deputy) Chief of Naval Staff (ACNS). The CNS, Admiral Colvin, later wrote that 'his thoroughness, his appetite for hard work and his powers of organisation were invaluable and he had a special faculty for getting at the heart of a problem and of stripping it of unessentials which is given to few'.

Burnett was certainly aware of the way in which the war was being fought. In October 1940 he was the RAN's representative in the Allied working-level conference which was considering the requirements of defending Asia against a possible Japanese invasion. In a minute to Admiral Colvin on his return, Burnett was critical of the parochial attitude of the British staff in Singapore who were 'interested in any suggestions for making good their own local deficiencies but rather uninterested in Australia's and New Zealand's naval activities'.[11] Burnett remained in Navy Office until May 1941 when he became the fourth officer to command HMAS Sydney. Colvin later wrote: 'When the time came for him to go to sea—a time to which he eagerly looked forward—I had no doubt that as captain of the Sydney he would acquit himself successfully as he had at the Navy Office.'

Burnett was an active and industrious thinker. In the final letter to his two sons he wrote:

Don't forget what I said when at home about thinking things and problems out for yourselves and not to do or believe things just because everyone else does. Be independent and stand on your own views—but not in a too argumentative way.[12]

Burnett was also well regarded by his RAN College term mates.

Joe Burnett was one of our finest officers. An outstanding sport with a good brain—an unusual combination. With these qualifications and . . . a happy and cheerful disposition, it is not surprising that he was one of the most popular of our year.[13]

John Ross, who served in *Sydney* from the time of her commissioning until she departed on her last cruise, remembered Burnett as

a very pleasant and congenial man, quiet of manner and not at all abrasive or over-bearing. I do not recall ever seeing or hearing of any occasion when he had over-ridden or ignored any advice of his subordinates . . . From my limited experience with him I would have said that Burnett was prudent and meticulous with his duties and most certainly not a man who would not have fitted in well with any group of officers or senior ratings . . . knowing that he had a group of experienced officers and senior ratings under him must have given him a great deal of confidence.

Burnett was not a physically imposing man despite his prowess in rugby. He was of medium height and build with soft facial features. He possessed an attractive personality, an engaging demeanour, and was a man people easily liked. Burnett could be generous and compassionate without being seen as weak. This was probably a reflection of his deep Christian faith which played a large part in his professional and personal life; one of his favourite books was *Running a Big Ship by the Ten Commandments*, by Captain Rory O'Connor RN.

Joe Burnett was a most accomplished sportsman and athlete. He enjoyed his leisure time and valued his family life away from the Navy. These attributes probably obscured Burnett's inner strength and determination. Burnett was a capable officer who wanted to do well in the Navy. Although he would have been justified in hoping for promotion to flag rank in due course, he was neither boastful nor arrogant. However, his ambition was not as obvious as that displayed by his two better-known 1913 Naval College term mates, Harold Farncomb and John Collins. The careers and attainments of both Farncomb and Collins provide a useful comparison with the professional progress and achievements of Joseph Burnett.

Farncomb was born at Sydney in 1899.[14] At his graduation in 1916, Farncomb was awarded the Grand Aggregate Prize and set his sights on reaching the top of his Service and being the first in his term to be promoted to the ranks of commander and captain.[15] He completed his sea service as a midshipman in HMS *Royal Sovereign* and was promoted to lieutenant in October 1919 after achieving First Class Certificates in all subjects.

Unlike Burnett and Collins, Farncomb did not choose to specialise. Instead, he spent much of his early career in operations and intelligence work. He was promoted lieutenant commander in 1927 and served for the next two years in the battlecruiser HMS *Repulse*. Farncomb completed the Imperial Defence College course in 1930 and was promoted commander in June 1932. He then returned to sea as Executive Officer of the heavy cruiser HMAS *Australia* which escorted the Duke of Gloucester back to England in 1935, for which he was made a Member of the Royal Victorian Order (MVO). Farncomb remained in Britain to take up a posting to the Americas desk of the Admiralty Naval Intelligence Division. He was promoted captain on 30 June 1937, six months before Collins and eighteen months before Burnett.

To compensate for his perceived lack of command experience, Farncomb commanded the newly commissioning sloop HMAS *Yarra* in 1937–38. He returned to Britain to complete the Senior Officers' Course and the Tactical Course in the first half of 1939 after which he was appointed commissioning captain of HMAS *Perth*. Farncomb was to serve the entire war at sea in command positions. In June 1940 he took command of the heavy cruiser HMAS *Canberra* and then of her sister-ship *Australia* in December 1941.

Farncomb was a highly gifted sailor. He was technically proficient and possessed the ideal temperament for wartime operations. He was an aggressive and resolute man who trusted his judgment occasionally against the advice of others. Farncomb was not an easy man to know and was respected rather than liked by those serving under him. Unlike Burnett, Farncomb was often harsh, abrasive and intolerant of lapses. He was a strict disciplinarian and he made no secret of his ambition. Farncomb's only weakness, and it became known during the war, was his liking for alcohol. While he never drank at sea,

Farncomb's drinking ashore made some senior officers feel that his reliability in all circumstances was suspect.

There were no such reservations about John Collins, the most famous and successful of the 1913 Naval College term. Collins was born in Deloraine in Tasmania in 1899.'[16] After graduation, Collins continued his training at sea in the battleship HMS *Canada* and the destroyer HMS *Spencer*. After completing courses for sub-lieutenant and lieutenant, Collins returned to Australia in 1921 and served in HMAS *Melbourne* as a watchkeeping officer. Also specialising in gunnery, Collins completed the long gunnery course and achieved first place one year before Burnett. This course was intended to produce experts in all facets of naval gunnery. After brief service in the survey ship HMAS *Moresby*, Collins returned to *Melbourne* as gunnery officer when she joined the Mediterranean Fleet in 1926.

It came as little surprise when Lieutenant Commander Collins was appointed Squadron Gunnery Officer in the newly completed HMAS *Australia* in 1928, after which he was appointed in command of the destroyer HMAS *Anzac*. Following promotion to commander in 1932, Collins completed the War Staff Course in the same year as Burnett but remained in Britain on the staff of the Admiralty War Plans Division. After the War Staff Course which he undertook in the latter part of 1934, Collins was appointed Executive Officer of the soon-to-be commissioned *Sydney*. After promotion to captain in December 1937, Collins was posted from the ship to Navy Office as ACNS and Director of Naval Intelligence (DNI). He was in command of HMAS *Sydney* from 16 November 1939 until being relieved by Burnett.

Collins was described by the Chief of Naval Staff, Admiral Colvin, as 'decisive and quick-thinking'. He was also professional, very competent and politically astute. Like Burnett, Collins was not physically imposing. He could almost be described as 'weedy'. But this is where the similarities between Collins and Burnett ended. Collins could be petty and pedantic. He was more forthright, more aggressive and more egocentric than Burnett. Collins's natural ability brought him to the notice of senior officers and he worked hard on being well regarded by those above him. His self-view and ambition were subdued with personal charm and polished social skills. Collins was the best all-round naval officer of his Naval College term. He did well in the RAN and would have done just as well in the Royal Navy; this could also be said of Burnett and Farncomb.

It is difficult to rate the three captains in terms of their ability and their performance of command at sea. Whereas Farncomb and Collins had completed long periods in command at sea by the time Burnett was appointed to *Sydney*, nevertheless it is reasonable to suggest that Collins would be ranked first; Farncomb would be second; and Burnett would be placed third. But this is not to suggest that Burnett was not worthy or suitable for appointment in command of *Sydney*. It is rather a reflection of how fortunate the RAN was to have within its first graduating class so many highly talented officers.

Joseph Burnett and Theodor Anton Detmers—*Kormoran*'s captain—were men of vastly different backgrounds with largely dissimilar professional experiences. Burnett was a naval lieutenant with wartime experience when the nineteen-year-old Detmers joined the German Navy in April 1921. After a short training period ashore in Wilhelmshaven, Detmers went to sea for training in the battleship *Hannover* in September 1921. The following year he spent some time in the sail training ship *Niobe*, before being appointed to the cruiser *Berlin*. In April 1923, Detmers returned ashore to the naval training school at Flensburg where he remained until January 1925 when he joined the battleship *Elsass*. Ten months later on promotion to sub-lieutenant, Detmers was posted to the newly commissioned cruiser *Emden* to gain further watchkeeping experience. Having served in *Emden* and being schooled in the exploits of the first German ship to bear that name, Detmers was well aware of the role of German raiders and he seemed attracted by the fine challenge of wits entailed.

After a year spent in *Emden*, Detmers returned to Wilhelmshaven where he was later promoted lieutenant in July 1927. From October 1928, Detmers served as a seagoing staff officer for two years with the 4th Torpedo Boat Flotilla in the destroyer

Albatross. After a staff posting in Berlin, Detmers was back at sea in October 1932 in the cruiser *Koln* in which he served as a watchkeeping officer. It was during his service in *Koln* that Detmers visited Australia for the first time. The cruiser made a number of port visits around Australia, including Port Jackson where Detmers was one of a number of German officers who were entertained in HMAS *Canberra*.

Detmers was promoted to lieutenant commander at the end of 1933. By this time he was a broadly experienced officer who was devoted to the Navy. He had not married and had little interest in pursuing activities beyond his career.

In October 1934, Detmers was appointed captain of the pre-World War I torpedo boat *G 11*. Completed in 1912 and weighing 760 tons, *G 11* was armed with two 4.1-inch guns and three deck torpedo tubes. She was capable of 25 knots and was crewed by 100 men. It was in this appointment that Detmers learned the importance of taking care of ships' engines. *G 11* was rebuilt and lengthened during the Great Depression and was now the fastest vessel in her flotilla. However, it was thought by the flotilla staff that her operational life was limited to the next three months. Detmers set about proving that he could do more with less.

My chief [engineer] and deck officers were given detailed instructions, and the longer manoeuvre times [created by sparing the engines] were respected even when risks had to be taken. Every time we put alongside or cast off, the necessary manoeuvres were carefully discussed and thoroughly checked, and my officers were so precisely drilled that they managed to get by with the least possible strain on our machinery.

At first this must have seemed rather strange for a torpedo boat, but before long we had all learned what was necessary, and got used to it, with the result that we managed with only a fraction of the power a torpedo boat really possesses. When we took part in torpedo practice manoeuvres at the beginning of December [1934], the three other vessels of the Half Flotilla had to put into dock on account of machinery defects, but the *G 11* carried on for fourteen days and nights executing repeated torpedo practice attacks without suffering the slightest breakdown.

Despite the gloomy predictions that were made when Detmers took command of *G 11*, it remained in service until July 1936 when he was posted to the 1st Destroyer Division with responsibility for training. In January 1937, Detmers was appointed First Officer (the equivalent of Executive Officer) of the destroyer *Leberecht Maass*. Ten months later, he was promoted to Korvettenkapita (equivalent to a junior commander) and posted to Berlin in the personnel office.

In October 1938, Detmers was given his second command. For nearly two years he was captain of the aged destroyer *Hermann Schoemann*.[17] It was in this ship that Detmers established a reputation for command at sea. Detmers' careful use of main engines prolonged her operational availability. By the time the war began in September 1939, Detmers had found that the destroyer was hampered by constantly bursting engine steam pipes. In the early stages of the war, Detmers feared that his ship would be rendered non-operational by the increasingly unserviceable steam pipes.

> I sailed her for about nine months; and sometimes we were lucky and sometimes we weren't. Sometimes we could get by without any bursts; sometimes we would have several in quick succession. In consequence some of our undertakings had to be abandoned, whilst others, on the other hand, were carried out successfully.

By the time of the invasion of Norway in May–June 1940, the German Navy was desperately short of destroyers to escort and support its larger ships. Detmers' ship had become a disproportionately valuable asset. During the two battles of Narvik, ten German destroyers were lost. When Operation Juno was launched on 4 June 1940, only four destroyers, including *Hermann Schoemann*, were available to escort the battleships *Gneisenau* and *Scharnhorst*, and the heavy cruiser *Admiral Hipper*. After refuelling in heavy seas, *Schoemann* patrolled the sea lanes between Narvik and Scotland in the hope of sinking or capturing any British shipping which may have been slow in evacuating Norwegian ports after the Allied withdrawal. The

German fleet's first victims were the tanker *Oil Pioneer*, which was disabled by gunfire from *Scharnhorst*, and her escort, *Juniper*. The British tanker was finally sunk with a torpedo from *Hermann Schoemann*. These ships were followed by the troopship *Orama*, which was sunk, and later the battleships *Gneisenau* and *Scharnhorst* after *Admiral Hipper* and the four destroyers had to return to Trondheim for refuelling.

Detmers was able to keep his ship at sea for the duration of the operation:

> We put into Trondheim the next morning, and the destroyer flotilla commander, Commodore Bey, came onboard the *Hermann Schoemann* and presented me with the Iron Cross, First Class, saying that throughout the action he had been on tenterhooks, expecting a signal from the *Hermann Schoemann* to say that she would have to fall out, and that he had been very glad not to receive it, although others had in fact fallen out.[18]

When Detmers brought *Hermann Schoemann* alongside the repair dock at Wilhelmshaven on 17 June 1940 in company with *Scharnhorst*, he learned that he was to assume command immediately of the enigmatically named Ship No. 41. After his initial efforts to learn more about his new command proved fruitless, Detmers was directed to contact the Admiral of the Hamburg Station who would inform him of all that he needed to know about Ship No. 41.

The following day he received the pleasing news that he was to command an HSK, *Handelstorkreuzer*, a merchant navy protection cruiser, later known as *Kormoran*. Detmers was delighted to be given such a command because he believed that auxiliary cruiser operations suited his personal temperament and professional style, and presented him with a perfect opportunity to use his initiative and display his well-developed tactical skills. His selection for the appointment originated with Admiral Otto Schniewind, the Chief of Staff to the Chief of Naval War Staff (Seekriegsleitung (SKL)), the German equivalent of the British Admiralty, and Chief of the Naval Command Office, who had earlier been Detmers' commanding officer in the cruiser *Koln*. The young destroyer captain had evidently demonstrated that he was a suitable choice. Detmers later reflected:

> How many times had I read descriptions of the exploits of such vessels in the First World War and become enthusiastic at the way they did the job, cut off from the Fleet and all its sources, completely on their own on the High Seas.[19]

As Barbara Winter well explains:

> Such a captain had to combine rather contradictory characteristics: daring but not foolhardy; cautious but not timid; able to work harmoniously with the same group of men for a long period under trying conditions, yet individualistic enough to bear alone the responsibilities of command, for once he put to sea there would be no-one to consult; not afraid to use his initiative, yet willing for the most part to do exactly as he was told, and able to do it well; above all, able to obtain loyalty by his character, not just by his rank.[20]

Detmers was justifiably proud of the professional achievement this appointment represented. The commanding officers of auxiliary cruisers were men who had previous experience in command of a cruiser and were of captain or commander rank. Comparatively inexperienced, Detmers would be the youngest of all the German raider captains to serve in World War II. But he had shown throughout his career that he was a reliable officer whose approach to naval operations made him ideally suited to raider warfare despite his more limited experience. Detmers relished the challenge:

> I was not dismayed at my new job and its special responsibilities. I didn't think I was too young, and I felt that my service with the cruiser *Koln* on her world cruise—not to speak of my varied experience with torpedo boats and destroyers—had given me all I needed in the way of suitable background and training: so I entered on my new command with confidence and a light heart.[21]

Detmers' reputation and actions at the time he commanded *Kormoran* reveal a man of enormous determination who never had any doubt about himself or his ability as a naval officer. Detmers, eminently practical, preferred doing to thinking. He was invariably thorough in completing a task. He may have appeared dour and conservative to those who did not know him well, but he had earned wide respect as a capable and reliable officer. Not surprisingly, he loathed administration and paperwork. Happily for Detmers, he liked being at sea and longed for the challenge of command.

He was never over-confident, his professional outlook working against any such weakness. Detmers was conceited but not vainglorious. He was a romantic who saw himself as an inheritor of Germany's naval traditions and a direct descendant of those German naval captains in World War I, like von Muller in SMS *Emden*, who had succeeded by superior skill and tactics against the Allies rather than merely by greater firepower. As captain of *Kormoran*, Detmers felt a strong sense of history and his own destiny. Command of this ship was his chance to prove his greatness and to achieve a place in history.

Detmers believed in his country and its cause in resorting to war to achieve national aims, which he never questioned. In addition to the opportunity it presented for demonstrating his prowess in naval operations, Detmers' professional ruthlessness and dedication in prosecuting the war at sea were primed by enthusiasm for the conflict and what it would achieve for Germany and its navy. However, it appears that his general indifference towards politics was largely the reason for his lukewarm attitude towards National Socialism. Detmers saw himself as a patriotic German who would contribute to his nation's struggle to achieve its rightful place in the world.

There are no obvious similarities between Burnett and Detmers and the differences in their professional experiences make it impossible to compare their competence in command. When the two men were pitted against each other at sea off Carnarvon on 19 November 1941, the vast gunnery and engineering superiority enjoyed by *Sydney* over *Kormoran* should have made the result irrelevant to the comparative abilities of their captains. With even the most mediocre officer in command, *Sydney* should have sunk *Kormoran* without suffering any damage in doing so. Trying to establish why *Sydney* was lost without placing the blame squarely on Burnett's shoulders would be a difficult task for the Naval Board.

4

HSK Kormoran

Before 1939, the German naval staff knew that the auxiliary cruisers would play a major role in Germany's conduct of the war at sea. The surrender and scuttling of the High Seas Fleet at Scapa Flow in 1919 ended Germany's brief reign as the most powerful naval nation after Britain. All that the 1919 Treaty of Versailles allowed Germany to retain were eight elderly pre-dreadnought battleships for use in coastal defence. Provision was made for these ships to be replaced but strictly on a ship-for-ship basis. The size of the replacements was limited to 10 000 tons displacement and 11-inch guns. The *Reichsmarine* was also limited to a personnel strength of 15 000. On this basis, a revitalised German Navy would never be able to challenge the major Allied navies, even with the limitations imposed on naval construction by the Washington Naval Treaty of 1922. There was no immediate effort in Germany to rebuild the navy. In 1926, the oldest of the pre-dreadnought survivors, *Zahringren*, was converted to a radio-controlled target ship. Replacements for *Preussen* and *Elsass* were ordered in 1930 and the ships were scrapped in 1931.

The completion of the so-called 'pocket battleship', *Deutschland*, in 1933 marked the re-emergence of the *Reichsmarine*. Despite the claims of her admirers and detractors, *Deutschland* was a high-performance, long-range, well-armoured heavy cruiser, and not a battleship. Although the displacement was stated to be 10 000 tons, as defined by the Washington Treaty, her standard displacement was actually 11 700 tons. Another two ships were built with very similar designs—*Admiral Scheer* in November 1934 and *Admiral Graf Spee* fifteen months later. The three ships were politically significant. The pocket battleships were suitable for commerce-raiding but were over-armed for the task. They were slightly too slow for major fleet actions or major convoy interdiction. However, when the major powers had met in 1930 to endorse the London Naval Agreement to extend the prohibition on any new battleship construction until 1936, the French cited the building of *Deutschland* as the reason for their refusal to ratify the Agreement. The French believed that *Deutschland* would be used to disrupt trade between France and North Africa. France claimed that it needed new battleships of 25 000 tons armed with 13-inch guns to counter the threat posed by the German ship. They built the battlecruisers *Dunkerque*, launched in December 1932, and her sister-ship, *Strasbourg*, launched in December 1936.

When Hitler came to power in 1933, he claimed that Germany had a 'right' to build a ship which met the threat posed by *Dunkerque*. As France had refused to ratify the 1930 London Naval Agreement, and Hitler rose to power on the promise of reversing the humiliation of Versailles, a new naval arms race was imminent. In June 1935, the Anglo-German Naval Agreement, proposed by Germany, was signed by the British government on the advice of the Admiralty. Under this Agreement, Germany would be able to build a new fleet with a tonnage that would not exceed 35 per cent of the aggregated tonnage of the British Fleet in all classes of vessel, except submarines of which Germany was permitted 45 per cent. This figure could be raised to 100 per cent at the expense of the approved ratio in other classes of vessel.

Having been freed from restrictions, Germany announced that it would build a 26 000-ton battlecruiser armed with 11-inch guns. The new ship, *Scharnhorst*, was actually found to displace 32 000 tons when she was completed in 1938. However, no increase in calibre was achieved for her gunnery. Although the British, French and Americans would operate ships with heavier armament, German naval dockyards made provisions for the 11-inch mountings to be replaced with 15-inch turrets at a later stage. The following year, another battlecruiser, *Gneisenau*, was ordered although this was kept secret by the renamed *Kriegsmarine*. When Hitler denounced the Treaty of Versailles in early 1935, it was not long before an order was placed for a new battleship, armed with eight 15-inch guns, to be named *Bismarck*. Germany would also build an aircraft carrier, *Graf Zeppelin*, a heavy cruiser, *Prinz Eugen*, an additional six destroyers and 12 torpedo boats. Another battleship, *Tirpitz*, was ordered the following year.

The Spanish Civil War between 1936 and 1938 also gave the *Kriegsmarine* an opportunity to gain operational experience. Although most of the German ships then in commission spent some time off the Spanish coast, only two saw any action. On 29 May 1937, Republican aircraft scored two hits on *Deutschland* off Ibiza. In response, *Admiral Scheer* shelled the Republican port of Almeria two days later. For most of the time, the *Kriegsmarine* trained in German waters for the forthcoming war.

With a massive naval construction program underway, the German Navy prepared plans for a naval war against Britain and France. Requirements were set out in Z-Plan, prepared in 1937–38. To be successful in a trade war with Britain, Germany would need six battleships to be ready by 1944, eight battlecruisers by 1948, four aircraft carriers (the first two to be operational by 1941) and 223 U-boats by 1947. The key planning date for the German naval staff was 1944; Hitler was adamant that 'For my political aims I shall not need the fleet before 1944'.[1] Without knowing the details of the German plan, British naval construction was already a long way ahead in every class of vessel except submarines. When Z-Plan became known to the British, it added further impetus to new construction and the refurbishment of older ships. When Germany was building two battleships, *Bismarck* and *Gneisenau*, Britain had started construction of *King George V*, *Prince of Wales*, *Duke of York*, *Anson* and *Howe*.

By the second half of 1939, Germany was a long way behind the surface strength of the Royal Navy, while the Italians and the French were fairly evenly matched. In contrast to the fleet envisaged under Z-Plan, which Hitler approved on 29 January 1939, the German Navy consisted of two old battleships, three

pocket battleships, two battlecruisers, eight cruisers, 22 destroyers, 57 U-boats and a number of support ships. The battleships
were obsolete and were unable to leave the shelter of the Baltic
while only 26 of the U-boats were capable of operations in the
Atlantic. German shipbuilding yards did not have the capacity
of the British yards to expand the fleet during the war and Hitler
was opposed to a direct confrontation with Britain for control
of the seas. The Fuehrer was prone to seasickness and did not
like ships. He did not have a well-developed understanding of
seapower and believed that German resources had been wasted
on the inactive High Seas Fleet in World War I. The German
strategy was to disrupt the 68 million tons of imports which
were conveyed to Britain in 21 million tons of shipping each
year. On any given day, 2500 British-registered ships were at
sea. If enough of this shipping could be sunk or prevented from
reaching its destination, Britain would be prevented from continuing the war.

Of the three German armed forces, the Navy was given the
least opportunity to prepare. The Commander-in-Chief of the
Navy, Grand Admiral Erich Raeder, was pessimistic about the
Kriegsmarine's prospects in a naval war against Britain.

As far as the Navy is concerned, obviously it is in no way very adequately equipped for the great struggle with Britain by autumn 1939.
It is true that in the short period since 1935, the date of the [Anglo–
German Naval] Treaty, it has built up a well-trained, suitably organised
submarine arm, of which at the moment about twenty-six boats are
capable of operations in the Atlantic; the submarine arm is still much
too weak, however, to have any *decisive* effect on the war. The surface
forces, moreover, are so inferior in number and strength to those of the
British Fleet that, even at full strength, they can do no more than show
that they know how to die gallantly and thus are willing to create the
foundations for later construction.[2]

In the absence of conventional warships, Germany would once
again turn to raider operations as a quick and cheap method of
waging trade war against the Allies. This was a form of warfare

on which Germany could make the most of past experience. The World War I experience, which was fully documented by retired Vice Admiral von Manthey in *Die deutschen Hilfskreuzer,* which was published in 1937 as part of the official German history *Der Krieg zur See 1914–18,* gave the German naval staff a wealth of insight. Instead of regarding every German merchant ship as a potential raider, a policy which caused many problems during World War I, a list of suitable ships was prepared before World War II. Their conversion for raider operations would begin with the declaration of war. In addition to the six conventional warships—*Scharnhorst, Gneisenau, Deutschland, Graf Spee, Admiral Hipper* and *Admiral Tirpitz*—which would be used against Allied shipping, the nine auxiliary cruisers would sail where conventional warships could not go and would disrupt the global flow of sea trade. The flaw in the German strategy was the lack of overseas bases which prevented surface attacks on concentrations of shipping. Not even the pocket battleships could risk attacking a convoy of merchant ships for fear of being damaged so far from German repair bases.

The size of the British surface force consisting of battleships, cruisers and destroyers, and the need to observe international law, all curtailed attacks on merchant shipping. When the war began on 3 September 1939, Britain declared a blockade against Germany in large areas off the French and British coasts and the Royal Air Force launched a bombing raid on *Scharnhorst* and *Gneisenau,* at Brunsbuttel, and on *Admiral Scheer,* at Wilhelmshaven. While the heavier German ships remained in the German North Sea ports, the remaining ships of the surface force were deployed in laying a minefield in the Heligoland Bight. This was followed the next month by the laying of magnetic mines along the English coast.

Diplomatic reactions in neutral countries to the declaration of war in Europe had a serious effect on the war at sea. Six weeks after the war started, the Pan-American Conference declared a neutrality zone 300 miles wide off the coasts of neutral North and South American countries. On 21 November, the British blockade was extended to German ports. Hitler's initial response was to overstate the value of the German Navy as a force-in-being by restricting it to its ports. He also severely circumscribed the scope of naval operations. The *Kriegsmarine* was prohibited from attacking passenger ships or French ships. The latter could, however, be fired upon in self-defence. However, Hitler was persuaded that the navy, particularly the auxiliary cruiser force, was of greater service being at sea attacking shipping with fewer restrictions. In War Directive No. Four issued on 25 September, Hitler ordered that: 'At sea, trade war according to International Prize Law is to be waged against France and England, free from previous restrictions.' The rules of engagement were outlined in War Directive No. Five.

> Merchant ships and troopships definitely established as being hostile may be attacked without warning. This also applies to ships sailing without lights in waters around England. Merchantmen which use their radio transmitters on being stopped will be fired upon.

These rules would apply to conventional surface combatants, submarines and raiders. There were further requirements placed on raider warfare. They must 'show the external signs of warships—ensign and pennant—before engaging in acts of warfare'. Raiders were permitted to disguise themselves with foreign flags but the German Ensign had to be raised when 'engaging in acts of war'. Those auxiliary cruisers that had a foreign emblem painted on the hull were required to show the German Ensign when 'engaging in acts of war', and were to cover the painted foreign emblem if possible.

In March 1940, the first German raiders were ready for operations. It had taken longer than expected to convert the ships. They would be the first German warships at large in the Atlantic since *Graf Spee* the previous December. *Atlantis* sailed for the Indian Ocean on 11 March and *Orion* for the Pacific on 6 April. After a short break, *Widder* left for the Atlantic on 6 May; *Thor* headed for the South Atlantic on 6 June; and on 15 June, *Pinguin* sailed for the Indian Ocean. The last of the 'first wave', *Komet*, sailed on 9 July from Bergen bound for the Pacific.

All the raider captains were officers on the active list of the German navy, except Captain Hellmuth von Ruckteschell in *Widder*. He had been a U-boat commander in World War I and was on the reserve list at the commencement of World War II. Three of the captains, Kahler, Rogge and Weyher, had commanded sail training ships during the 1930s. Of the 26 men who would command raiders during the war, six would be killed during operations.

On 6 September 1940, Raeder reported to Hitler that 'The successes of all the auxiliary cruisers have exceeded expectations'.[3] On 14 November, he advised the Fuehrer that 'Ship 41 will put out to sea in December for operations in the Atlantic and Indian Ocean'.[4]

The 'second wave' would not be unleashed until the end of 1940. Detmers realised he had previously known nothing of Ship 41 when he learned that her name was *Steiermark*. A cargo ship of 9800 tons, the *Steiermark* was built, together with her sister-ship *Ostmark*, for the Hamburg–Amerika Line at the shipbuilding yards in Kiel. Listed in *Lloyd's Register of Shipping* with an incorrect gross tonnage and the callsign—DUBL—of a 440-ton trawler with the same name, *Steiermark* was destined for service on the East Asia run when the war intervened. Although she had completed her trials before the war began, *Steiermark* had not entered merchant service.

As was common in ships of her type, *Steiermark* was driven by four diesel-electric engines which also provided power for the main shipboard services, such as pumps, hoists, lights and heaters. Additional power required for wartime operations was provided by two small diesel engines fitted into cargo hold No. 3. Two small boilers were used to provide drinking water. With modification, *Steiermark* was able to carry 5000 tons of fuel oil. This capacity, if used judiciously at an economical cruising speed of 11 knots, would allow the ship to remain at sea for twelve months.

Her main armament consisted of six 15-centimetre (5.9-inch) guns which were arranged so that two guns trained on the port side and two guns on the starboard side, both located within the forecastle and the quarterdeck, while another two guns were located within hatches No. 3 and No. 4 on the ship's centre-line. This gave *Steiermark* a combined firing arc of 160 degrees although the centre-line guns were restricted to a firing arc of 50 degrees both sides of the beam. The 20-degree blind arc, located right ahead and right astern, was dictated by the ship's superstructure. The only drawback in this arrangement was that *Steiermark* was limited to a full broadside of four guns rather than six. The guns themselves were antiquated. Detmers noted that No. 3 gun had been removed from the battlecruiser *Seydlitz* after the Battle of Jutland in 1916 and, after some mistreatment, was refurbished and fitted to *Steiermark*. The fire control system was also rudimentary. All the 15-centimetre guns were located behind counter-weighted iron hatch covers which were opened and closed manually.

The auxiliary cruiser's secondary armament consisted of five 2-centimetre anti-aircraft guns. Located on platforms which could be raised hydraulically, two guns were sited on the forecastle. Another two were hidden in the after funnel deck. The fifth was fitted in a recess in the quarterdeck. This armament was complemented by two (not four, as planned) army 3.7-centimetre anti-aircraft guns behind sheet metal screens outboard and slightly abaft, and below the bridge. There were six torpedo tubes; four fitted to the upper deck and two submerged. The four upper-deck tubes were sited outboard of No. 3 hatch, two on each side. The submerged tubes were placed slightly aft of the upper-deck fittings. They were fitted when raider captains from the 'first wave' stated that torpedoes fired from upper-deck tubes made a splash as they hit the surface of the water and this invited evasive action. The tubes originated from torpedo boats that had also been Jutland veterans. Firing the upper-deck tubes presented difficulties, but the submerged tubes were even more cumbersome as they could be fired only when *Steiermark* was moving at less than three knots.

The torpedoes deployed in the raiders were a variation of the G 7 type used during World War I. They could be set to run at a fast speed over a short distance or at a slower rate over a longer distance.

Against Detmers' wishes, a single 6-centimetre signalling cannon was installed into the ship's stern. This cannon was to be used for firing warning shots at unco-operative merchant ships. Detmers would have preferred a completely smooth stern but as the recess had already been cut, the cannon was fitted.

A 3-metre rangefinder was fitted into the mainmast and could be retracted at will. When tactical circumstances precluded its use, small 125-centimetre anti-aircraft rangefinders were available. In addition to a searchlight fitted to the mainmast, a smoke-making machine was fitted near the stern. Hatch No. 5 contained one Arado 196 reconnaissance plane and hatch No. 6 an LS-3 fast boat for use in mine-laying.

The ship was constructed of thin plate steel and did not have any armour protection. Bunks were built for each man on board and an internal continuous passageway was added for the crew to move undetected to their action stations. Prisoner accommodation was constructed. This consisted of a large hammock space with separate facilities for the masters of captured ships and any women prisoners.

Detmers was involved in preparing *Steiermark* for her work as an auxiliary cruiser; his ship was given priority over all other dockyard activity with the exception of the U-boat fleet. As conversion work on *Steiermark* had been proceeding since early 1940, there was limited scope for Detmers to make any changes and the only aspect of the fitting out with which he disagreed was the provision and arrangement of camouflage:

I regarded the camouflage measures as far too detailed. In my opinion, which practical experience has since done nothing to change, all you need to disguise the outline of a ship is an alteration here and there amidships, with steel sheeting and liberal use of paint. Other simple but effective measures include changing the height of the masts, putting up a new mast, or adding a mock funnel. All the rest of it, such as bridge alterations, sheeting with foreign flags painted on it, superstructure alterations amidships, funnel markings, and so on, aren't worth all the trouble they involve. It is much more important to know all about ships of a similar tonnage and structure, and to know their approximate routes; after that you can choose yourself a likely disguise which has a good chance of proving impenetrable. However, the planners had their own ideas about camouflage so I let them get on with it.[5]

Detmers involved himself in the provision of important items of equipment, such as the ship's compass. He talked with the authorities providing fittings and equipment for his ship and satisfied himself that he had obtained the best that was available. It was during one such visit to Berlin that Detmers was asked by Commander Gunther Gumprich, the head of the equipment section, what name the ship would bear as a raider as its selection was his prerogative as her captain. As he had not given any serious consideration to her new name, Gumprich suggested the name *Kormoran*. Detmers liked the suggestion because it appealed to his sense of history.

A gunboat called *Cormoran* had operated with the East Asiatic Squadron in the Central Pacific shortly before World War I, taking part in the German suppression of an uprising in the colony of the Caroline Islands. When war commenced in 1914, the gunboat was obsolete. When *Emden* captured the Russian ship *Rjasan* on 4 August, the ship's company of the old gunboat took over the prize vessel which was renamed *Cormoran*. However, she was too slow to keep pace with the East Asiatic Squadron which was fleeing the Pacific Ocean. Vice Admiral Graf von Spee ordered *Cormoran* and the *Prinz Eitel Friedrich* to the Indian Ocean where they would harass Allied merchant shipping and, probably, be lost to a superior Allied naval force. After seeking refuge at the German colony on the island of Yap and in Alexishafen in northern, formerly German, New Guinea, *Cormoran* reached Lamotrek Atoll in the Western Caroline Islands. Earlier, the Allies believed *Cormoran* was hiding up the Sepik River in New Guinea and the destroyers *Warrego*, *Parramatta* and *Yarra* were sent to search for her.

When *Cormoran* moved to the American possession of Guam and was unable to obtain sufficient supplies or fuel to sustain a return passage to Germany, it was only a matter of time before the United States entered the war and in 1917 *Cormoran* was seized. But before the Americans could take possession, she was destroyed by her ship's company.

Although the name *Kormoran* possessed none of the feeling aroused by the name *Emden*, Detmers was attracted to its ornithological meaning.

The cormorant is a practical bird; it isn't much as far as looks go, but it knows its job. The Malays and the Chinese both use it for fishing. They put a ring around its neck, which does not interfere with its breathing but prevents it following its normal instincts and swallowing bigger fish. They take a cormorant equipped with such a ring out to sea fishing. The cormorant has eyes like an eagle for what goes on under water, and when it spots a likely fish it goes over the side and down, returning with a large fish in its bill; which—thanks to the ring—it is unable to swallow. The fish is therefore added to the day's catch. At the end of the day, when the work of the busy bird is done, the ring is removed and it is given its share of the spoils. I now hoped to catch a fish or two on the high seas so the name *Kormoran* seemed suitable.

But the name *Kormoran* was not widely known. For the sake of security and the tactical advantage of anonymity, *Steiermark* would continue to be administered as Ship 41—a *Sperrbrecher* or pathfinder. Consistent with her formal designation as a pathfinder, *Kormoran* had to look as though she was fitted out for steaming ahead of a convoy in search of mines. To that end, two dummy guns were placed in positions fore and aft while the signal masts and halyards were rigged as if *Kormoran* were a naval vessel. The superstructure was camouflaged with diagonal bands of different coloured paint although the ship's side from the waterline to six feet above was painted grey-brown. Detmers intended to paint the entire hull of *Kormoran* this colour once he had broken through the British blockade of German ports and had entered the open sea, thinking that this preparation would make the job much easier.

The auxiliary raider's crew were accommodated on board

Monte Pascoal which was berthed alongside in Wilhelmshaven where Detmers moved to bring the crew up to standard.

> I myself appointed Lieutenant von Gosseln to be in charge of training. It was his job to see that this mass of individual men was forged into a homogeneous crew and to make any necessary replacements. I had very little time to occupy myself with the training of the crew, but with my discussions with von Gosseln I was satisfied that he was taking the job very seriously, doing it very well, and getting all the support and assistance he needed from the departments.[7]

Although they would spend a great deal of time together and had to work as a very close-knit team, Detmers had little say over the officers appointed to *Kormoran*. In fact, he later stated that he had not previously known any of the officers who came under his command. However, he had heard of his First Officer (the Executive Officer) who was also his second-in-command. The 33-year-old Lieutenant Commander Kurt Foerster had been commissioned in 1927 from the lower deck. He had commanded the former Hapag ship and converted minelayer, *Konigin Luise*, during successful operations in the Baltic for which he had been awarded the Iron Cross (First Class). Detmers was delighted to have him on board.

> I left the men entirely to him and in that respect he took everything completely off my shoulders. Only very occasionally did he consult me on a point, and then it was usually to check his own decisions with me. We had both grown up in the navy, and we had the same general views, the same outlook, and, in particular, the same attitude towards the lower deck. All I ever had to do was to drop an occasional hint and I could be perfectly certain it would be put into operation; and, above all, I could be quite certain that my crew were being both well and justly treated.

Also posted to *Kormoran* from the *Konigin Luise* was Foerster's secretary, Lieutenant Heinz Messerschmidt, whom Detmers made his adjutant. This duty was in addition to his prime responsibility for *Kormoran*'s outfit of mines, which would be laid offensively during any passage through Allied waters. Messerschmidt was an experienced officer who had seen active service in the battleship *Schlesien* during the Spanish Civil War. The navigator was Lieutenant Commander Henry Meyer. Detmers also received navigational and ship-handling advice from one of the merchant navy officers on board, Lieutenant Commander Gustav Oetzel, who would have been the master of *Steiermark* had she remained in merchant service. Detmers obviously decided that he posed no threat to his authority as he described Oetzel as 'a grand officer, a fine man and a good comrade'.[8] The subordinate specialist officers in the seaman department were:

Lieutenant Heinfried Ahl—Air Observer
Lieutenant Wilhelm Brinkman—Anti-aircraft weapons
Lieutenant Joachim von Gosseln—Battle Watch Officer
Lieutenant Joachim Greter—Torpedoes
Lieutenant Reinhold von Malapert—Radio and Ciphers
Lieutenant Edmund Schafer—Speedboat and Searchlights
Lieutenant Fritz Skeries—Gunnery

In addition to the seaman officers with executive responsibility for *Kormoran*'s operations, a number of former merchant navy officers were posted to the ship. These men, Sub-Lieutenants Wilhelm Bunjes, Johannes Diebitsch and von Bloh, would be selected by the navigator, Meyer, to act as the captains of any prize ships captured by the auxiliary cruiser. Diebitsch was to be the boarding officer.

The Chief Engineer was a naval reserve officer, Lieutenant Commander Hermann Stehr, with another reservist, Engineer Officer Egbert von Gaza, serving as the Electrical Officer. The Administration Officer, who bore responsibility for stores and supplies, was Lieutenant Commander Herbert Bretschneider. The two medical officers appointed to the ship were Friedrich Lienhoop and Siebelt Habben. The latter arrived in the ship shortly before she sailed after undertaking a short course in dentistry. The meteorologist, Dr Hermann Wagner, was not a serving military officer but was specifically requested by

Detmers. Detmers also involved himself in the selection *of Kormoran*'s Chief Cook:

> From my former commands I was well aware how important good food was. Other things being equal, a well-fed crew is a better crew than an ill-fed one and I wanted a good man for mine; preferably a young man, but nevertheless one with plenty of experience and a high degree of skill; and, above all, not a stick-in-the-mud who wouldn't have gumption enough to ring the changes. In this respect too I found the appropriate official [in Berlin] very understanding and helpful, and from a long list of possibles we chose a man named Schuster.[9]

With his officers gathering and the conversion work on *Kormoran* proceeding satisfactorily, Detmers was disappointed when he was ordered, with the other captains of auxiliary cruisers, to bring his ship immediately to a state of readiness for the possible invasion of Britain. Although this may have been an encouraging development in the German war plan, it threatened to deny Detmers his 'dreams of scouring the high seas as an auxiliary cruiser'.[10] There was the added frustration of finding that the conversion work on *Kormoran* had now been given a low priority and little progress seemed to be made. When the cross-channel invasion, Operation Sea Lion, was cancelled, the conversion of *Kormoran* was again accorded virtually top priority.

By the end of August 1940 and after six months in dry dock, *Kormoran* was nearly ready for sea. Von Gosseln brought the crew together in Hamburg in preparation for the sea trials which would be conducted in the Baltic in September. When these were successful, Detmers brought forward to the first week in October the cruise in which the ship would be formally handed over to him by the dockyard. This cruise, which Detmers combined with a general calibration of the ship's equipment and instruments, was likewise successful. *Kormoran* appeared to be operating without any major problem. It was decided that *Kormoran* would be commissioned on 9 October. Following a short celebration, the auxiliary cruiser took on fuel and sailed the next day for Kiel. *Kormoran*'s arrival coincided with an Allied air raid which led Detmers to conclude that an alternative to Kiel was required for his ship's training and final preparations.

The next morning, Detmers was woken by reports of a small disaster on board. A fire caused by faulty electrical cable arrangements in Power Room No. 11 would take four weeks in dry dock to repair. By this time, Detmers' impatience was showing. He wanted to get to sea and achieve results. He decided that *Kormoran* could operate without Power Room No. 11 for the moment and persuaded the technical authorities in Kiel that he should be permitted to proceed as previously planned with dockyard workers to sail with the ship and effect repairs while she was underway. Later that day, *Kormoran* was moved to a buoy opposite Kitzeberg—the site of an oil storage facility and the focus of Allied bombing efforts. Allied aircraft returned that evening and dropped a bomb near the stern of *Kormoran* but caused no damage. The next day marked the start of the long and laborious task of embarking stores and supplies to last twelve months. Detmers later remarked:

> Lighter after lighter was brought alongside and one after the other they were emptied—and still there was room. It was astonishing how much the ship's maw could swallow. The transfer of the provisions went like clockwork, and both officers and men found they could manage the electric winches, the derricks and the cranes as smoothly as though they had been on cargo boats all their lives . . .
>
> And when we had finished taking our provisions on board it was the turn of the munitions, the torpedoes and the rest of the explosives—with the exception of mines. The loading of all this material went just as smoothly, and within a few days it was completed.[11]

With the stores and munitions stowed on board, *Kormoran* sailed from Kiel to Gotenhafen (now known as Gdynia), a Polish naval port on the west side of the Danzig Peninsula. This was to be her last base before attempting to penetrate the Allied blockade. It was from Gotenhafen that *Kormoran* sailed for short passages into open waters where the guns and torpedoes could be tested and seagoing routines refined. It was in these final days of preparation that Detmers realised the difficulties of deploying his motor torpedo boat and his Arado aircraft. He was also forced to concede that the radar fitted to *Kormoran* was unserviceable and that 'we had to give it up'.[12]

With Power Room No. 11 repaired, *Kormoran* was ready for full power trials, which she conducted at the same time as the battleship *Bismarck* conducted hers. Although the auxiliary cruiser managed to achieve 18 knots, half a knot above her theoretical maximum speed, her engines started to overheat. However, she could comfortably produce the speed that was necessary for the operations in which she would be engaged. After a live-firing exercise, Detmers was satisfied that his ship was ready for action. But he recognised her limitations:

> Of course, our training for action, that is to say the joint exercise of all our weapons in battle conditions, with assumed hindrances, damage, improvisations, and so on, was possible only within the relatively narrow margins determined by the nature of our ship: a passenger vessel fitted out as an auxiliary cruiser, and she was no more than that despite all the weapons which had been crowded aboard her.[13]

With *Kormoran* finally ready in every respect, Admiral Raeder travelled to Gotenhafen to inspect the ship and address the crew. Although Raeder told Detmers he understood the haste with which his ship had been converted and would accept a delay in the ship's departure, Detmers was adamant that he and the crew were ready and that any further delay was pointless.

Shortly after Raeder's visit, Detmers was instructed by the Chief Adjutant (Personnel) to accept another two officers he

> didn't really want . . . The two officers in question were both from the Propaganda Department; one of them was a war reporter and the other a film man. Let me say at once that neither of them gave me any cause for complaint, but I couldn't get rid of the feeling that when people like that were on board to report and film everything, you weren't as free as you would like to be.[14]

The reporter was Dr Fritz List and the cameraman was Walter Hrich.

After briefings in Berlin, Detmers flew to Jever near Wilhelmshaven to finalise *Kormoran*'s breaking through the Allied blockade. This included determining the date, the courses to be steered and the tactics to be pursued. There were two possible routes through the blockade to the Atlantic. The first was the most direct route through the English Channel. The second, north or south around the Faroe Islands or around Iceland and through the Denmark Strait, was much longer. The first route had a number of drawbacks although France had surrendered by this time. If *Kormoran* kept close to the French coast and proceeded at full speed for fourteen hours she could be protected under the cover of darkness by the French coastal batteries which were now operated by the German Army. This protection would be supplemented by the Luftwaffe as required. But Detmers doubted that the Luftwaffe, which did not enjoy absolute command of the air space, could give *Kormoran* the fighter aircraft cover she might need. The protection of a single pathfinder by the Luftwaffe might make the British suspect that *Kormoran* was a raider. Detmers argued against this route.

He also decided against sailing around the Faroe Islands. As he could not count on mist and fog at that time of year to conceal his presence, and he realised that the British would also know that this was the next best route to penetrate the blockade, Detmers decided on a passage around Iceland and through the Denmark Strait. This route was the furthest from British naval bases and was his best chance of not being observed. The Commander of the North Sea Station accepted Detmers' decision to attempt a break-out by this route but tried to persuade him to undertake the passage under a new moon, rather than a full moon as Detmers intended. His reasoning was that he wanted to cling to the edge of the ice line in the Denmark Strait and could do this only with the aid of moonlight. He believed he would see any British guardships before they saw him and he would flee to the south. For that, he would need moonlight for target finding and gunnery spotting if he were forced to fight a British warship at night. As Detmers was responsible for his command and the success of her operations, the final decision was left to him. It was agreed that *Kormoran* would start her attempt to reach the Atlantic on 3 December 1940.

Detmers returned to Gotenhafen as the mines were being loaded into *Kormoran*. The only concern for Detmers was the absence of Lieutenant Ahl, who was ashore in Holtenau trying to obtain a second Arado aircraft for *Kormoran*. A signal was received on the day before *Kormoran*'s departure advising that Ahl had obtained an aircraft and would be returning to the ship shortly. For *Kormoran* and her crew of 400 officers and men, their time had come.

The newest, biggest and fastest raider to set out from Germany carried with her the hopes of the German Naval War Staff that she would make a major contribution to the disruption of British sea communications. The German surface navy had not fared well in the first year of the war at sea. The pocket battleships *Deutschland* and *Graf Spee* had sailed for the Atlantic before the war began to conduct a war against British trade. *Deutschland*, later renamed *Lutzow*, sank three ships before returning to Germany in November 1939 while *Graf Spee* had much greater success, sinking nine ships in the South Atlantic and Indian Ocean by 13 December 1939. *Graf Spee* was then pursued by the cruisers *Ajax*, *Achilles* and *Exeter*; *Exeter* was badly damaged during a brief action with the more heavily armed *Graf Spee* on the morning of 13 December but the German ship was then shadowed by the British ships during daylight until she headed for the safety of the neutral port of Montevideo on the River Plate at nightfall. After four days of diplomatic activity over the status of the ship, and with the British force assembled at the estuary to the River Plate, *Graf Spee* sailed from Montevideo on 17 December and was destroyed by her crew.

During a brief sortie into the North Atlantic, the battlecruisers *Scharnhorst* and *Gneisenau* sank the British armed merchant cruiser HMS *Rawalpindi* to the south-east of Iceland on 23 November. Operations against shipping were curtailed in the early part of 1940 as the surface force was required to support military operations, particularly in the Baltic. In mid-1940, *Scharnhorst* and *Gneisenau* were both damaged by torpedoes in separate actions during the Norwegian Campaign.

German success against trade in the first year of the war could have been significantly greater if the naval dimension in German war planning had been accorded a higher priority. At the end of 1939, Hitler ordered the suspension of further surface ship construction while only two major warships would operate on the high seas at one time. Despite the advice of the German Naval War Staff who believed that the war at sea depended on submarines, Hitler also refused to authorise an increase in U-boat construction. It was not until July 1940 that a slight increase was permitted despite the loss of 28 U-boats in the first year of the war. The total number of boats capable of Atlantic operations had increased from 26 in September 1939 to just 33 one year later. Hitler's refusal to extend the U-boat program in 1940 gave the Allies an opportunity to reorganise and enhance their protection of merchant shipping.

By October 1940, the pocket battleship *Admiral Scheer* was ready for raider operations after a year of rebuilding. She was followed by the cruiser *Admiral Hipper*, which had earlier suffered main machinery defects, and the battlecruisers *Scharnhorst* and *Gneisenau*. Operation Berlin had led to attacks on several convoys and unescorted merchant ships. On their most successful day, 15 February 1940, *Scharnhorst* sank six ships and *Gneisenau* seven; in all, 115 600 tons of shipping. With access to French ports and the heavy ships having proved to be so successful in the raider role, the German Naval War Staff decided that the new battleship *Bismarck* and the new cruiser *Prinz Eugen* would also be deployed to the North Atlantic when their work-up was completed in May 1941. The other leading units of the surface fleet were suffering from repeated successful RAF bombing attacks which kept them alongside undergoing lengthening repairs. With the demand on the surface force to achieve greater success against trade, the pressure on Detmers and the crew of *Kormoran* to achieve results was enormous. They had to sink ships, and sink them as quickly as possible.

5

Under Pressure to Perform

The newest German auxiliary cruiser sailed from Gotenhafen at 1405 on 3 December. Passing through the Baltic, and several defensively laid minefields, Detmers was forced to make an unplanned stop at the Norwegian port of Stavanger on the morning of 9 December after four torpedoes broke from their fittings. Later that day, *Kormoran* was underway again. At sunset the following day, 10 December, Detmers altered course to the north-west into the North Sea.

The next morning the crew started work changing *Kormoran*'s disguise from a pathfinder to a merchant ship. The hull was now completely painted a grey-brown colour with the superstructure brown and the funnel black with a red band. The dummy guns were removed and the masts re-rigged. *Kormoran* had become a Soviet freighter, *Vyacheslav Molotov*, registered in Leningrad. A Soviet ship of this type would not be unexpected in these waters and could expect to attract little attention.

When bad weather closed in to assist his running the blockade, Detmers increased speed and set a south-westerly course through the Denmark Strait shortly before midnight on 12 December. By midday on 13 December, *Kormoran* was to the south-west of Iceland and well into the Atlantic Ocean. In penetrating the blockade, *Kormoran* had not encountered any Allied ships.

With the bad weather persisting, Detmers headed towards Greenland where some refuge from the storm was possible. When the weather did improve, *Kormoran* went south to her operational zone. Detmers' prior orders had prohibited any attack on merchant shipping before he reached a latitude 40 degrees north. During the night of 19–20 December, *Kormoran* was south of the line drawn roughly between New York and Madrid at 40 degrees latitude north of the equator and thus in her operational zone. It reported this to SKL by short-wave signal. When sending a report, *Kormoran* used what was called a *Kurzsignal* (short signal) which consisted of a special code designed to convey information with a minimum number of letters and digits. As the signal could be transmitted quickly, it reduced the likelihood of accurate detection.[1]

Detmers was now free to sink merchant shipping and lay mines in designated areas, including the sea off Calcutta:

> Our job, apart from sinking as much enemy tonnage as possible, was to appear as often as possible where we were least expected; and in this way to sow alarm and confusion in the enemy's shipping lanes, thus compelling him to abandon the shortest and most convenient routes and to use the longer and more circuitous routes instead, thereby wasting shipping space and fuel . . . We were, of course, strictly forbidden to seek any action with enemy naval units, because we were only passenger or merchant ships fitted out as warships, and not real warships. We were therefore not in a position to look for trouble with real warships, and were instructed to avoid convoys of enemy shipping, because they were always escorted.[2]

If a merchant ship were sighted, the raider would need to approach the potential victim cautiously so as to avoid raising suspicion. By altering to a slowly converging course, the raider would shadow a merchant ship during the night and mount an attack at dawn. If the raider's converging course produced no reaction in the merchant ship during daylight, the attack would begin when the victim was within range of the raider's guns. In both instances, the merchant ship would be ordered to stop engines and send no messages. If the merchant ship did not stop a warning shot could be fired across her bows. If the hapless merchant ship tried to send a distress signal, the raider would fire for effect and try to stop the transmission which would announce the presence of the raider and her location to any nearby warship. Once the merchant ship was stopped or disabled, the raider's captain would then decide whether she should be captured as a prize vessel and taken back to Germany, or used to support raider operations, or scuttled. If the merchant ship was sunk after sending a signal reporting an action with a raider, the raider would flee the scene of the action to avoid any encounter with an Allied warship.

Attacking merchant shipping would rely on chance encounters. To conserve fuel, Detmers reduced speed to nine knots once *Kormoran* had entered her operational zone. Detmers posted additional lookouts and watchkeepers. However, for the first two weeks at sea he observed that all of the ships he encountered were flying the American flag and could not be attacked. This was a great frustration because every time a ship was sighted the crew were sent to action stations only to be stood down some time later when its American flag was sighted. Despite his doubts that some of these ships really were American, Detmers could do nothing. He decided that if he did not encounter a ship he could attack the following day—7 January 1941—he would leave the western part of the mid-Atlantic and lie in wait for ships coming out of the Mediterranean.

In the early afternoon that day, Detmers' luck changed when smoke was sighted from a ship already on a converging course with *Kormoran*. When the ship held her course and speed and took no avoiding action and the range had closed to 3000 yards, Detmers signalled the ship by light to show her flag and identify herself. The Greek flag was hoisted and the name *Antonis* was the reply sent by light. As *Kormoran*'s camouflage was removed and the German battle ensign was hoisted, Detmers signalled to the Greek ship, 'Heave to. No wireless.' The signal was sent three times. The *Antonis* stopped without hesitation and waited for *Kormoran* to come alongside her. A motor boat was swung outboard with Sub-Lieutenant Diebitsch and the boarding party embarked. The raider's radio room staff monitored the 600-metre short-wave band, the frequency normally used by merchant ships at sea, to ensure that *Antonis* sent no distress signal which might have alerted any other shipping to her fate and *Kormoran*'s position. Greece was at war with Italy but not Germany. However, if her cargo had originated from an Allied country or if she were armed with Allied weapons, Detmers would be entitled to sink her.

Detmers records:

> The motor boat reached the Greek and the boarding party climbed over the rails and hurried to their respective posts and about their respective business as they had been taught to do on so many exercises at home. The leader of the boarding party went to the bridge with a signaller who immediately established contact with us. The wireless man went to the wireless cabin; the engine-room personnel clambered down into the engine room; and the ordinary seamen searched the holds to establish the nature of the ship's cargo.[3]

Diebitsch questioned the master of the *Antonis* about his ports of departure and destination, the routes used by similar ships in crossing the Atlantic and whether he had sighted any Allied warships.

The *Antonis* was carrying high-grade coal from Cardiff in Wales to Rosario in Uruguay. She was also carrying three British-made machine-guns and 1000 rounds of ammunition, which were transferred with the ship's papers and other useful items to *Kormoran*. As the coal was of little use to the German Navy, the boarding party evacuated the Greek crew and sank the ship with scuttling charges. The master of the *Antonis* had contributed to the loss of his ship when he deviated from the course he was advised to steer by the British Consul in Uruguay. As *Antonis* was not due in Rosario until 25 January and had deviated from her course, the Admiralty concluded in April after one of her lifeboats was found on 3 April some 400 miles to the south-west, that the action probably occurred on 13 January. The summary of raider activity for this period issued by the Admiralty in 1942 listed the probable position of the attack as 3 degrees S, 30 degrees W, rather than the correct position of 18 degrees 17 minutes N, 28 degrees 32 minutes W. The Admiralty assumed that the raider responsible was probably the ship they designated Raider E, known to the Germans as *Thor*.

Although *Antonis* had sent no signal, Detmers moved out of the area towards Gibraltar where he again observed several American ships. His treatment of prisoners appeared to be humane and considerate:

> [We] brought our prisoners on the forecastle deck for a breath of fresh air, and this took place for an hour three times a day: morning, afternoons and evenings. They lazed in the sun, stood at the ship's rail and looked at the flying fish or at dolphins swimming along with us . . . or they walked around in twos and threes. These precious hours in daylight meant a lot to them, and they would ask to be let out even in bad or stormy weather, of which there was not a great deal.[4]

Although the accommodation areas were hot and stifling, adequate provision had been made for personal hygiene and the crew of the *Antonis* did not complain.

After sailing across the shipping lanes leading towards Gibraltar, Detmers headed south until *Kormoran* was a considerable distance to the west of the normal convoy routes. If this proved unsuccessful, Detmers would return to the routes on which ships from or bound for America would be possible victims. He did not have to wait long. Near sunset on 18 January, smoke was sighted on the horizon on *Kormoran*'s starboard quarter. The ship from which it came appeared to be heading to the west. Detmers altered to a converging course, increased to full speed of 17 knots and hoped to avoid being seen as the sun set ahead of the merchant ship which was identified as a tanker.

As the tanker flew no flag, was not illuminated as a neutral, and started an anti-submarine zig-zag course, Detmers decided that she must be an Allied ship. The anti-submarine gun on the quarterdeck strengthened this assessment. In the rapidly failing light, Detmers ordered the camouflage dropped and the German battle ensign hoisted. It was reasonable for Detmers to expect that this ship would try to use her radio when attacked. *Kormoran* had to make a rapid and devastating strike that would

disable her wireless equipment. When the range was about 7000
yards, the masthead searchlight was turned on and the raider's
guns opened fire. However, it was extremely difficult to keep
the searchlight trained on the tanker in a rolling and pitching
sea. Detmers altered course to open the firing arc of No. 3 gun
which fired star shells to illuminate the target. The third salvo
from *Kormoran* hit the tanker which signalled 'RRR BRITISH
UNION SHELLED 2624N 3058W'. The action took place at 26
degrees 24 minutes N, 30 degrees 58 minutes W. In the early part
of the war, merchant ships were directed to use the three-letter
group QQQ if they sighted a suspicious ship and RRR if they
were attacked. These signal groups were clarified in 1940 with
revised four-letter groups; QQQQ for disguised raiders, RRRR
for conventional warships and SSSS for submarine attack. The
changes were slowly implemented and depended upon the merchant ship being able to distinguish her foe and using the correct
signal group. It is apparent that the tanker had not seen, and
could not see, the raider at the time of her first salvo.

Five minutes after being hit, *British Union* signalled *Kormoran*
by light. Detmers assumed that this indicated that she surrendered. As *Kormoran* turned towards the tanker, the raider was
fired upon with four unsuccessful rounds. *Kormoran* responded
with her main armament and the secondary weapons and set the
after part of the ship ablaze at a range of around 4000 yards.

As fire engulfed *British Union*, her crew abandoned ship and
Detmers decided to sink the empty tanker, which had departed
Gibraltar bound for Trinidad to take delivery of oil. Mindful of
the safety of his boarding party and the impossibility of placing
scuttling charges, Detmers manoeuvred *Kormoran* into a position
where he could sink the tanker with torpedoes. The first torpedo
fired detonated at the end of its safety distance and short of *British Union*, but a second torpedo hit. A morse SOS signal sent by
torch was observed on *Kormoran*'s bridge as the lifeboats from
the British ship, holed during the action, began to sink as they
struggled to reach the raider. Detmers opened fire on the tanker
with main armament but still *British Union* remained afloat. A
third torpedo which struck the tanker amidships appeared to

achieve the objective as shortly afterwards *British Union* rolled over to starboard and sank.

When the crew of the tanker were mustered on board *Kormoran*, 28 men including the ship's master had been recovered but 17 men were reported missing including the First and Second Officers. Although Detmers wanted to avoid the possibility that the missing men would be recovered by the British and his presence reported, he was unable to remain in the area for fear of an encounter with a warship. Although it was another success for *Kormoran*, Detmers noted in the ship's war diary that the

> capture of the *British Union* does not alter my opinion that there is hardly any enemy shipping in the open Atlantic. The consumption of ammunition was unfortunately very high; 3 torpedoes, 61 15-cm shells, 36 15-cm star shells. However it was a baptism of fire for the crew. The opponent's shots lay short, one of them wide.[5]

Detmers ordered full speed as *Kormoran* headed away to the west. This was a prudent action on her part as a lookout in the armed merchant cruiser HMS *Arawa*, armed with seven 6-inch guns and two 3-inch guns, noticed the glow of gunfire from ten miles away to the north-west. When *British Union*'s RRR signal was intercepted, the captain of *Arawa* believed that the pocket battleship *Admiral Scheer* must have been engaging the tanker as Allied intelligence reported that this was the only conventional German warship thought to be in the area.

As *Arawa* prepared for what would be a one-sided engagement if it really were *Admiral Scheer* in the area, they were relieved to find that no enemy warship remained around the scene of the action, which they reached shortly before midnight. Debris and the presence of a lifeboat containing survivors from *British Union* were of passing concern as the armed merchant cruiser continued to the west in pursuit of the pocket battleship. The next morning they returned to recover the men in the lifeboat and then resumed their search for *Admiral Scheer*. When these survivors from *British Union* were questioned in *Arawa* about the action, they stated that one of the other lifeboats had been fired upon by the raider before the men were recovered. But as most of these survivors were subsequently lost in a ship sailing in a convoy from Freetown that was attacked by *Admiral Hipper*, it was not possible for the allegations to be investigated fully.

When the Admiralty confirmed that the attack on *British Union* was not the work of *Admiral Scheer*, it struggled to identify the culprit. However, Detmers was disappointed when a signal arrived on 23 January reporting that *Admiral Scheer* had sunk 132 000 tons of Allied shipping. He remarked in his war diary, 'Our 10 700 tons are quite miserable compared with that'. However, *Kormoran*'s movements and chances of success were restricted by the area she had been given and the need to keep away from waters that were the province of *Thor*, another raider operating in the Atlantic, or U-boats, Italian submarines or conventional German warships, such as *Admiral Hipper* and *Admiral Scheer*. Detmers was also instructed to prepare for a rendezvous with the tanker *Nordmark* on 7 February. On 28 January, Detmers decided to cross the shipping route between Trinidad and Freetown in search of victims.

At 1316 the following day, *Kormoran* sighted a large ship which seemed to emerge suddenly from the heat haze at about 16 000 yards. On sighting *Kormoran*, the merchant vessel, which appeared to be a large refrigerator ship, altered course away from the raider at a speed of 15 knots. Detmers maintained course and speed, which evidently allayed the fears of the merchant ship, which resumed her base course. As the two ships drew nearer, Detmers altered course, increased speed to 15 knots, ordered *Kormoran* decamouflaged while he signalled the merchant ship by morse to stop and had a warning shot fired across her bows. As this was ignored, Detmers ordered his guns to fire at the merchant ship at a range of 11 000 yards. The third salvo was on target but the merchant ship attempted to send a QQQ signal giving her position. The signal was jammed by *Kormoran* as the merchant ship altered course to the southwest before stopping dead in the water. Her transmissions also ceased.

Detmers ordered the crew of the stricken vessel to 'LEAVE THE SHIP'. But when a man appeared to be manning the gun on the ship's quarterdeck, *Kormoran* opened fire again. The ship was abandoned as the raider's boarding and scuttling parties embarked in their boats. *Kormoran*'s third victim was a refrigerator ship, *Afric Star*, with a cargo of fresh meat and butter bound from Buenos Aires to England. Given that the ship was badly damaged and her complicated configuration would present a prize crew with enormous difficulties in sailing her back to Germany, Detmers decided to sink the ship. Scuttling charges were detonated but the highly compartmentalised ship refused to sink even after *Kormoran*'s guns were fired at short range. It took one of Detmers' precious torpedoes to finish the ship, which sank slowly by the stern. Seventy-two crew members and four passengers, including two women, were taken on board *Kormoran,* which quickly left the area. Although the wireless station in Freetown had not understood *Afric Star*'s signal, it was intercepted and repeated by a nearby merchant vessel.

As darkness fell, lookouts in *Kormoran* observed a vessel, which was darkened. The raider closed the merchant ship and decamouflaged in preparation for yet another action. As *Kormoran* had not been seen, the merchant ship was suddenly illuminated with star shells and Detmers gave the order to open fire. Although the opening range was over-estimated, the merchant ship was hit repeatedly but transmitted a QQQ signal. Several minutes later, with the superstructure badly damaged and on fire, the luckless merchant ship stopped and ceased transmitting. Detmers ordered his guns to cease firing as the crew started to abandon ship. But when transmission of a series of numbers was attempted again, Detmers ordered his main armament and anti-aircraft guns to resume fire. He later stated that he thought the transmission was not from this ship but another merchant ship nearby trying to attract a warship. With the aid of the *Merchant Navy Code Book* which had earlier been captured in *Afric Star*, Detmers was able to learn that the attack had been on *Eurylochus*, a British 5273-ton freighter carrying 16 engineless heavy bombers to Takoradi on the Gold Coast of

Africa, and his presence had been reported to the Air Ministry in London. As wireless activity had 'become so lively', Detmers decided to sink *Eurylochus* with a torpedo after recovering four Britons and 39 Chinese. More than half of those not taken on board *Kormoran* were later picked up by the Spanish freighter *Monte Teide*. Three and a half hours after *Afric Star* was sunk, *Eurylochus* joined her on the bottom.

Kormoran raced away from the scene pursued by the British cruisers *Norfolk* and *Devonshire*. She was now bound for waters adjacent to the shipping routes near the Cape Verde Islands. The time taken to sink the two ships on 29 January meant that *Kormoran* had to remain at full speed for several days in order to clear the area and achieve her rendezvous with *Nordmark*. In his assessment of the two actions in the ship's war diary, Detmers mentions that his disguise, which was still that of the *Vyacheslav Molotov*, remained effective while *Kormoran* possessed 'no super-structure behind which one could suspect a gun'.

As *Kormoran* sailed to the south-west, a signal was received from SKL in Germany that *Kormoran* was to hand over her prisoners to *Nordmark* who would later transfer them to the prize ship *Portland*. On 5 February, Detmers was also advised that *Nordmark* would be at the rendezvous position, code-named Andalusien, to the west of Ascension Island from early the following morning. He was also offered a whale-chaser captured by *Pinguin* for use as a mine-laying craft. If he did not want the vessel, he was ordered to proceed towards the Cape of Good Hope where he could mine the shipping lane between the Cape and Freetown and the waters around South Africa. Later that day Detmers received another signal informing him that he was to proceed to the north-east quadrant of the Indian Ocean. The following day the captain of the raider *Atlantis* requested a rendezvous with *Kormoran* to relay his experiences of operating in the Indian Ocean.

Early on 7 February, *Kormoran* sighted *Nordmark*, painted grey and disguised as the American ship *Dixie*, and the prize vessel, *Duquesa*, captured by *Admiral Scheer*. Refuelling lasted 15 hours and 1338 tons of fuel were transferred. The following morning, *Kormoran* transferred half of the U-boat equipment she carried to *Nordmark,* which also supported submarine operations. Detmers advised *Nordmark*'s captain that the most rewarding area for operations in the North Atlantic was south of the Cape Verde Islands. He was shown the war diaries of *Nordmark* and *Admiral Scheer.* Detmers also indicated that he did not want the whale-chaser and pointed to contradictory orders from SKL. On the third day of the rendezvous, *Kormoran* took on provisions, mainly eggs and meat, from *Duquesa* and 170 prisoners were transferred to *Nordmark.* Four of the Chinese from *Eurylochus* were retained on board *Kormoran* as laundrymen. At 1600, the ships parted and *Kormoran* headed towards the Cape. Detmers doubted if he would have much success there, and he was also concerned about using the magnetic mines on board in waters around South Africa because he was disinclined to have *Kormoran* venture into the shallower waters to lay them. As *Kormoran* continued to steam into waters adjacent to South-West Africa, a signal was received advising that the raider had been awarded two Iron Crosses (First Class) and fifty Iron Crosses (Second Class) to be distributed as Detmers saw fit.

The Iron Cross (Second Class) was awarded with a red, white and black ribbon, and usually presented in a small blue or cream-coloured envelope inscribed '*Eisernes Kreuz 2. Klasse 1939*'. The cross consisted of a black centre, with the date '1813' on the otherwise blank reverse. The date marked the original institution of this old Prussian award. The front of the medal had a swastika in the centre and the date '1939' on the lower leg of the cross. The Iron Cross was normally only worn at the time when the award was made; thereafter, only the ribbon was worn through the buttonhole of the tunic. There were 2.5 million Iron Crosses (Second Class) and Clasps awarded during the war. The Iron Crosses (Second Class) awarded to *Kormoran* were meant for non-commissioned personnel. The Iron Cross (First Class) was issued in a lined box and the front of the cross was identical with the second class award. Around 300 000 Iron Crosses (First Class) and Clasps were issued during the war.

As he already had the Iron Cross (First Class) Detmer hoped to be awarded the Knight's Cross of the Iron Cross. This was a much more prestigious award, the Cross being presented in an elaborate case with the citation contained in a large red and brown leather folder with a gilt metal eagle and swastika in the front. Only 318 Knight's Crosses would be awarded to the *Kriegsmarine* during the war, nearly half going to U-boat officers. Forty-four would be awarded to officers serving in battleships or cruisers.

Despite these awards, Detmers was not satisfied with his achievements to date. In the ship's war diary he recorded, almost begrudgingly, that other ships had sunk many more tons of shipping than he had. The enormous success of *Admiral Scheer* and *Admiral Hipper* made his achievements look paltry. He was clearly frustrated that he had not sunk more ships but seemed to regard his opponents with less respect than one might have expected. It annoyed him that the prisoners from *Afric Star* and *Eurylochus* firmly believed

> in the invincibility of Great Britain and the British Navy. We would get it again and again when we talked to them, and they expressed their opinions freely. They were all quite certain that we must have been out since the declaration of war, or had put out from some neutral port since. The idea that we had sailed out of a German harbour in war time and through the British blockade just wouldn't go into their heads. For them the North Sea was British. And when we tried to tell them the truth they just wouldn't believe us. Such firm faith was not to be shaken.[6]

When the Chief Engineer informed Detmers that bearings in two of *Kormoran*'s main engines were of white metal that was too soft (WM 10) and needed replacing with harder metal (WM 80), his frustration was magnified. He would not return to port and miss out on further spoils of war. Instead, he signalled SKL in Germany and requested the supply of harder metal to replace the worn bearings.

On 25 February, *Kormoran* met *Pinguin* and took on stores, including 210 kilograms of WM 80, and exchanged advice on

Indian Ocean operations. Detmers was impressed with Captain Ernst-Felix Kruder's achievement in sinking or capturing 135 000 tons of shipping. Kruder informed Detmers that after the first few months when there were plenty of ships to attack and success was frequent, the Allies had re-routed and reorganised their merchant shipping movements and success was more difficult. It appeared to Detmers as though he may have been too late and missed the best opportunities:

> I was very pleased with the success of our auxiliary cruisers, of course, but I could see that it was going to make things more difficult for me: and I regretted that I had not been sent out earlier when pickings were there for the asking. Of course, there was still valuable work to be done—my mere presence would compel the enemy to adopt new and more circuitous routes. Although that didn't altogether compensate for the missing tonnage, it was a real success.

One wonders if Detmers was really convinced but he was not without hope. Kruder suggested that the Arabian Sea and the Bay of Bengal remained a possibility, in addition to the shipping route between Cape Town and Fremantle. But before he would enter the Indian Ocean, Detmers decided to wait until he had obtained the necessary hard metal for the engine bearings.

As he waited, Detmers met U-boat *U 124* under the command of Lieutenant Commander Willi Schulz, to the north-east of Sao Paulo. *Kormoran* was able to supply seven torpedoes and some provisions to Schulz who had already sunk 92 000 tons of shipping. Detmers

> congratulated her commander and expressed the hope that with the seven torpedoes we had given him he would be able to bring the score to over 100,000 tons—which was the minimum total for an investiture with the Knight's Cross.[7]

Once again, Detmers had revealed his near obsession with tonnage sunk and the honour they brought. The following day, 16 March, Detmers went on board *Admiral Scheer* for a conference with Captain Theodor Krancke and the captain of a submarine who had also been directed to rendezvous with the pocket battle-ship. Krancke, who had already sunk 156 000 tons of shipping, confirmed Kruder's assessment that in the Indian Ocean only the Bay of Bengal and the Arabian Sea offered good chances of sink-ing Allied merchant ships. As *Kormoran* would be going into the Indian Ocean in four weeks time, 'it was all the more important that as far as possible we should add to our successes here in the Atlantic'. When *Kormoran* returned to the Freetown–South America shipping lane on the morning of 22 March, she noticed a vessel emerging from the haze.

As the two ships converged, *Kormoran* asked the merchant ship for her name. When Detmers learned that she was the British tanker *Agnita*, in transit from Freetown to Carapito in Venezuela, *Kormoran* dropped her camouflage, hoisted the Ger-man battle ensign and signalled by flag, 'Stop immediately' and by light, 'No wireless or be shelled'. *Agnita*, which was armed with one 4-inch gun and two anti-aircraft guns, altered course away from *Kormoran*, increased speed and began transmitting a raider signal. Detmers ordered his guns to fire while the radio room jammed the tanker's wireless transmission. After two sal-voes struck *Agnita*, her master surrendered with his crew of 12 Britons and 25 Chinese.

The scuttling party from *Kormoran* placed charges in the engine room which, when detonated, failed to sink the ship. After several attempts to finish her with gunfire, Detmers was forced to use yet another torpedo. Even after a torpedo crashed into *Agnita* amidships, she sank very slowly in a position 3 degrees 20 minutes S, 23 degrees 48 minutes W. The real success in attacking *Agnita* was that the boarding party found a chart of Freetown harbour showing details of the minefields. The chart was subsequently made available to the U-boat captains who were replenished from *Kormoran*. As Detmers believed the signals sent by *Agnita* were jammed successfully, he decided to head south before returning to the location of this action in three days. In doing so Detmers was well aware, of course, that what I was doing was against my usual principles. Theoretically I ought to be making my way from the spot where I had sunk the *Agnita* in case they sent a cruiser looking for me. Fundamentally my attitude was wrong, for the British naval authorities might well send one of the two cruisers which were permanently stationed in the Freetown-Bahia narrows on my trail. But it seemed to me that it might be a good idea to do the wrong thing occasionally— precisely because this might deceive the enemy. The only thing was not to make a habit of it.[8]

Detmers was fortunate in sighting the stern of a tanker through the morning haze when he returned to the site of the action with *Agnita* three days later on 25 March. *Kormoran*'s speed was increased to 15 knots and her camouflage dropped before Detmers managed to bring the raider near to the tanker without being observed. When he was in the desired position, a warning shot fired across the bows ordered the tanker to stop. In the same manner as *Agnita*, the tanker turned away from *Kormoran*, increased speed and attempted to send a raider signal. As she was a big ship, Detmers instructed Skeries, the gunnery officer, to minimise the damage caused by her gunfire. When the mist lifted, the master of the tanker realised that resistance might result in serious injury to his crew, so he stopped, ceased wireless transmission and the crew took to the boats.

The boarding party from *Kormoran* went into action. The victim on this occasion was the 11 309-ton Canadian tanker *Canadolite*. Detmers ordered her crew to remain on board until he decided whether or not she should go back to Germany as a prize vessel. As the ship was originally built in Germany and was undamaged, Detmers decided to send Lieutenant von Bloh to Bordeaux in command of *Canadolite* with 16 men and some members of the existing crew. As the fuel stocks in *Canadolite* seemed insufficient for the passage to Bordeaux, Detmers instructed von Bloh to rendezvous with *Nordmark* if additional fuel was required.

On 27 March when *Kormoran* rendezvoused with *Nordmark*, Detmers learned that *Canadolite* had had sufficient fuel

to make Bordeaux. This must have been confirmed by von Bloh
after he took command of the ship. Detmers was also pleased
to learn that *U 105*, which was also meeting *Nordmark*, had
the metal requested by *Kormoran* for bearings. Although the
quantity was less than expected by Detmers, it was sufficient for
Kormoran to continue raider operations. On 4 April, *Kormoran*
rendezvoused with the tanker *Rudolf Albrecht* and transferred
her prisoners. While remaining in the vicinity of the rendezvous
area for several days, Detmers also received a signal recognising
his ship's achievements. *Kormoran* had been awarded a further
three Iron Crosses (First Class) and another fifty Iron Crosses
(Second Class). Detmers recorded in his diary that 'these will be
saved up for the Fuehrer's birthday', and then distributed.

Kormoran returned to waters near Freetown on 9 April and
immediately sighted a merchant vessel at dawn. The ship was
astern of the raider, heading in the same direction and belching
a great deal of smoke. Detmers ordered the speed of *Kormoran*
to be decreased gradually until the funnel of the merchant ship
was visible on the horizon. When he reduced speed to five knots,
Detmers feared that *Kormoran*'s slow progress would create
suspicion in the vessel astern. The raider's speed was increased
to eight knots and Detmers estimated the merchant ship would
pass 5000 yards on *Kormoran*'s port side if she maintained her
course and speed. After nearly one hour of slow steaming, Detmers saw that the ship was a British freighter and not American.
When she was abeam of *Kormoran* at 5000 yards on a parallel
course, Detmers increased to 14 knots, ordered decamouflaging,
signalled by light, 'Stop immediately. No wireless or be shelled',
and fired a warning shot.

The freighter turned away from *Kormoran* and started
sending a raider signal. Some of her crew started to man the
anti-submarine gun on her quarterdeck. Detmers ordered his
guns to fire and the engines brought to maximum revolutions.
The British ship appeared to stop and then wireless transmissions ceased. When *Kormoran* stopped firing, the freighter
started making way while trying to send another raider report.
The British ship stopped again after she was hit by *Kormoran*'s

guns and fires raged amidships. Just as Detmers was about to cease firing, radio transmissions commenced and further gunfire inflicted major damage on the British ship. The crew finally took to the boats as Detmers despatched his boarding and scuttling parties.

Kormoran's seventh victim was the 8022-ton freighter *Craftsman*, which was on her way from Rosyth with an anti-submarine net for use at Cape Town harbour. Five men had been killed in the action and 46 were recovered by the raider. After the scuttling charges were unsuccessful, Detmers sank her with another torpedo at a position 0 degrees 32 minutes N, 23 degrees 37 minutes W. For the next two days, the raider's lookouts sighted nothing of interest to the south of where *Craftsman* was sunk until, at 0740 on 12 April, a plume of smoke was seen on the horizon.

After altering course towards the ship which had produced the smoke, Detmers was initially unable to determine her nationality and thought she was probably American. For nearly three hours, *Kormoran* manoeuvred to reduce the distance between the two ships while improving her firing position. The freighter appeared to grow less concerned about *Kormoran*'s presence. At approximately 12 000 yards with the sun behind the raider, Detmers gave the order to decamouflage while *Kormoran* altered course towards the freighter. The ship was signalled to stop and a warning shot was fired. When this produced no reaction, a second warning shot was fired. The freighter turned away from *Kormoran* and continued underway. At 11 000 yards, *Kormoran* opened fire as the freighter transmitted an SOS signal and her position. When the bridge suffered a direct hit, the ship stopped and the transmitting ceased. The crew took to the boats as *Kormoran* came alongside her opponent, the 5486-ton Greek freighter *Nicholaos D.L.*, bound for Durban with Oregon timber from Vancouver. Thirty-eight men from a number of countries were recovered by the raider as the scuttling charges were set and detonated. Just after noon, more than six hours after she was sighted, *Nicholaos D.L.* was left to sink in a position 1 degree 54 minutes S, 22 degrees 12 minutes W. Detmers was unable to finish off the ship with his smaller weapons but was unwilling to expend any further main armament ammunition or torpedoes, the ship being beyond salvage.

An inability to sink *Nicholaos D.L.* was not the least of Detmers' concerns. His radio-room staff reported that they had been unable to jam the freighter's distress signal, which had been intercepted by several merchant ships and shore wireless stations. But fortunately for Detmers, the wireless operator in *Nicholaos D.L.* sent his ship's position incorrectly as 20 degrees S, rather than 02 degrees S. And as the signal was an SOS rather than an RRR or QQQ signal, Detmers was not unduly concerned.

On 19 April, *Kormoran* returned to rendezvous position Andalusien and joined the raider *Atlantis* commanded by Captain Berhard Rogge, the 'ace of auxiliary cruiser commanders' as Detmers referred to him. Detmers was fully aware that Rogge had sunk or captured more than 100 000 tons of shipping and had been at sea for more than 12 months. While at the rendezvous, the blockade-runner *Dresden* arrived and Detmers hoped she might have brought the desperately needed bearing metal. Detmers was disappointed to learn that the metal his ship needed was carried by another blockade-runner, *Babitonga*, whose departure from South America had been delayed.

Raeder was nonetheless pleased by *Kormoran*'s cruise. He reported to Hitler the following day that

> Ship 41, operating in the Atlantic, has reported sinking 56,000 tons since the middle of December 1940 . . . The numerous supply ships engaged in replenishing the supplies of auxiliary cruisers and submarines in the Indian Ocean and South Atlantic Ocean have hitherto been remarkably successful.[9]

But Detmers was becoming angry. He had repeatedly asked for bearing metal and it seemed that in Germany SKL either refused to appreciate the full extent of his predicament or they were not overly concerned. In his view, several ships or submarines could have carried the metal he so urgently required but numerous opportunities had been missed. He had not asked for much and believed his success to date should have seen his request given priority. There were only two options. Either put up with the worn bearings in the hope of getting the necessary metal in the next few weeks, or put into a port on the French coast for repairs that could take months to complete.

> If I did this I knew perfectly well that the Naval Warfare Department [SKL] would not be prepared to let me go out again in anything like my present state. After our repeated successes that would be hard. After all, we had demonstrated that we do valuable work at sea despite our difficulties.[10]

Detmers decided to remain at sea. The next day he conferred in *Atlantis* with Captain Rogge who gave him more information and advice about operations in the Indian Ocean. Over the next few days *Kormoran* completed taking on provisions from *Duquesa*, ammunition from the supply ship *Alsterufer*, and fuel from *Nordmark*. Her prisoners were transferred to *Alsterufer*. Detmers and Rogge agreed that *Kormoran* would head northeast on 22 April where her hull would be painted before she sailed two days later for the Indian Ocean.

On entering the Indian Ocean, the hull of *Kormoran* would be painted black, the superstructure would become brown and the red band on the funnel was to be painted yellow. Perhaps a change of identity would bring with it a change of fortune.

6

The Eclipse of Raider Warfare

K*ormoran* began her passage to the Indian Ocean through heavy seas as she rounded the Cape on 24 April 1941. Detmers decided he would try his luck initially on the shipping route between Fremantle and Cape Town, disguised as the Japanese ship *Sakito Maru* with the Japanese flag painted on both sides of the hull below the bridge. The change of identity was prompted by information that the line which operated the *Kinka Maru*, the initial choice of disguise, used only older ships in that part of the Indian Ocean.

On 11 May, in a long discourse in the ship's war diary, Detmers expressed his doubts about German raider strategy in the Indian Ocean. Detmers did not agree that a raider ought to proceed into the north-west Indian Ocean; he believed that shipping there was heavily protected and that an auxiliary cruiser faced a greater risk of encountering Allied warships. He thought raiders should remain in the open seas to attack individual ships that were not plying the standard routes. Detmers believed that *Kormoran* should keep away from the major routes and so force the Allies to use convoys and regulated shipping movements. Only major combatants like *Admiral Scheer* were capable of attacking the principal shipping routes. Notably, he believed that

the continual employment of an auxiliary cruiser on the western coast of Australia is at present not worthwhile . . . In my opinion, a thrust towards the route Chagos Archipelago–Maldives or south of Madagascar would be more correct.

But his plans were upset by other events. Once in the Indian Ocean, Detmers was instructed to transfer fuel to the supply ship *Alstertor* on 12 May, which was sent home to Germany after the loss of *Pinguin* on 8 May. Two new prize officers were also transferred to *Kormoran*. They were Sub-Lieutenants Rudolf Jansen and Bruno Kube. When *Alstertor* was sent on her way, Detmers sent a signal to SKL reporting her departure from the rendezvous. Although the Allied wireless station at Mauritius intercepted the coded signal, which it could not read, direction-finding equipment on the island revealed that another German raider had entered the Indian Ocean. Detmers had to leave the Chagos Archipelago area. He was also annoyed that he had been given a number of time-consuming tasks including refuelling supply ships, something he regarded as ridiculous, and provisioning prize ships, when he should have been searching for ships to sink:

> At the present stage of the war, where traffic in the open ocean outside the central Atlantic has practically ceased and the auxiliary cruiser must operate against the heavily protected routes, it needs a lot of time for these operations. Therefore, we should be given as few special tasks as possible . . . In any case, I am glad that I now have an unlimited operational period ahead of me for the first time.

Detmers thought he might try the Colombo–Penang route, which had been free of a raider attack for six months. He also hoped to find a ship in the Bay of Bengal. He decided not to lay mines there as the minefields would be easily swept by the Allied mine-sweeping flotilla based at Rangoon. The pressure on Detmers to sink ships increased. On 22 May, Raeder was pleased to tell Hitler that Captain Kruder in *Pinguin* had overtaken the success of the famed World War I raiders *Emden* and *Wolf*. Despite the variable performance of the conventional warships, Raeder could point to the *Kriegsmarine*'s consistent success with auxiliary cruisers.

Had Raeder known how little the British Admiralty knew about *Kormoran*, he would have been especially pleased with her prospects for further success. The 'Raider Supplement' to the British *Weekly Intelligence Report* (No. 64) dated 30 May 1941,[1] listed *Kormoran* as Raider G. However, other than the suspicion that she was 'possibly' in the South Atlantic, the most the Admiralty could say was that she was distinguished by a squat funnel in the centre of a high superstructure. Her stern was half-counter and half-cruiser. Raider G was best described as 'a modified *Kulmerland*'. *Kulmerland* was known to the Admiralty as an unarmed supply ship. In effect, the Admiralty had no idea of *Kormoran*'s whereabouts or appearance. Had Detmers understood how little was known about his ship, he might have been a little more adventurous.

On 1 June, Detmers received a signal which advised him that the whole Indian Ocean was to be considered his operational zone. For days, *Kormoran* searched the open seas in the triangle formed by Chagos, Colombo and Sabang as news was received that arrangements for supplying bearing metal had been changed again. Detmers suggested in the ship's war diary that whoever was responsible for the design and construction of two of the engines in his ship 'should be called to account'.

On 5 June, *Kormoran*'s disguise was altered again. She became the *Kinka Maru* after the funnel was repainted and the ship's name was changed. Detmers was not altogether happy with the disguise *Sakito Maru* as the company which operated her, Nippon Yusen Kaisha, rarely operated in the western Indian Ocean. The operators of the *Kinka Maru*, Kokusai Kisen Kaisha, did operate in these waters with ships of similar appearance to *Kormoran*. With his new disguise, Detmers headed for the waters between Chagos and Maldives the following day. On 8 June, Detmers received more bad news about his bearing metal. The supply ship *Egerland*, which was carrying bearing metal and other items, including condenser coils, for *Kormoran*, was reported sunk. A replacement ship with the bearing metal would reach the Indian Ocean in September.

With no success near Maldives, Detmers headed towards the south of Ceylon. *Kormoran* sighted a passenger-cargo vessel in the early morning of 15 June; it appeared to be of the

British-India Company, and was not an auxiliary cruiser, so *Kormoran* manoeuvred for an attack. When the British ship altered course at 12 000 yards to cross the raider's stern, a valve in *Kormoran*'s bow smoke generator failed and thick smoke began to envelop the raider. The British ship turned away. There was little that Detmers could do but give up the chase for the moment. As the British vessel did not wireless, Detmers decided to make contact with her again at twilight.

When nothing was seen later that day, *Kormoran* began a long period of nine days of fruitless searching during her passage into the Bay of Bengal. On 24 June in the afternoon lookouts sighted a ship that appeared to be an auxiliary cruiser. When *Kormoran* altered away she was followed by the suspected British auxiliary cruiser which appeared to be slightly slower than the German raider. When the distance between the two ships had increased, the other ship returned to *Kormoran*'s previous course and appeared to Detmers to head towards Madras where he assumed the British ship would wait for the 'Japanese' ship to arrive. When the Japanese ship failed to enter port, the local naval authorities would no doubt be alerted and become suspicious. Detmers decided to postpone the mining of either Madras or Calcutta harbours. He was concerned the following day when he heard two wireless messages to all British ships; he could not read the ciphered messages.

Detmers had been in two minds as to whether he should have turned and engaged the British ship:

Ought I to have engaged that ship, although I knew perfectly well that she was an auxiliary cruiser? And what about the morale of my crew? Would my men understand my behaviour? Particularly as we had been without the slightest success for weeks. I went into the whole problem as thoroughly as possible, asking myself a good many questions and answering them as well as I could. Finally I came to the conclusion that I had done the right thing, and I decided that even if we had to waste many further weeks without a capture, and if we then found ourselves in a similar situation, I should act in exactly the same way.[2]

The news received by Detmers later the same day that *Atlantis* had sunk more than 140 000 tons of shipping could hardly have made him feel enthusiastic about raider operations in the Indian Ocean.

But his luck changed in the early morning hours of 26 June when the silhouette of a darkened merchant ship was spotted by Lieutenant Ahl, from *Kormoran*'s bridge. When the ship failed to stop after a warning shot was fired, *Kormoran*'s main armament opened fire at approximately 4000 yards. The 5.9-inch guns inflicted serious damage on the ship, which burned fiercely as the crew abandoned her. Nine crew members were recovered from the 4153-ton Yugoslavian cargo ship *Velebit*, which was on a passage from Bombay to Moulmein. It appeared that 25 were killed in the attack. However, eight of the crew remained on board *Velebit* and managed to keep the ship afloat until she grounded on the coral reefs surrounding the Andaman Islands in the northern Bay of Bengal.

In the mid-afternoon on the same day, smoke was sighted off *Kormoran*'s starboard quarter. The raider slowed down to allow the ship to come over the horizon and be identified. However, Detmers found he was steering a course to the east while the merchant ship was heading to the south-west. To avoid suspicion, *Kormoran* sailed into a rain squall and altered to a converging course. By a steady alteration of course and speed, Detmers was able to bring *Kormoran* within 14 000 yards, apparently without arousing suspicion. When the range had been reduced to approximately 6000 yards, *Kormoran* was decamouflaged as she hauled round to port to begin the attack. The merchant ship was signalled by flag to stop immediately. When this was ignored and a QQQ signal was transmitted but successfully jammed, Detmers gave the order for the raider's guns to open fire. The first salvo struck the vessel's wireless room. The second and third hit the forecastle. As *Kormoran* ceased fire, the merchant ship had stopped in the water as the boarding and scuttling parties were despatched from the raider.

Forty-eight men were recovered from the 3472-ton cargo ship, *Mareeba*, of Melbourne. *Mareeba* was on her way from

Batavia to Colombo with a cargo of 5000 tons of raw sugar. When the scuttling charges were detonated, *Mareeba* quickly sank. From the captured crew Detmers learned that the disguise of *Kinka Maru* was effective, and that the last German raider in the Indian Ocean had been reported six weeks earlier. While this was pleasing news, he was less than delighted to learn from his radio officer, Lieutenant von Malapert, that he could not be completely sure that all of *Mareeba*'s transmission had been jammed. The instruction issued by the Admiralty the next day to merchant ships to transmit emergency messages on short wave if they were not immediately acknowledged on standard frequencies led Detmers to believe that the signal from *Mareeba* had alerted the Allies to his presence in the Indian Ocean.

A notebook log which was seized by the boarding officer, Lieutenant Diebitsch, was of particular interest to Detmers. Just seven hours before the attack . . .

> the *Mareeba* had sighted the Australian cruiser *Sydney* in the Ten Degree Channel [between the Andaman and Nicobar Islands]. In other words, the *Sydney* had crossed our bows only half a day ahead! Now it was quite certain that my decision not to engage the British auxiliary cruiser earlier on was correct. Had I done so she would have called up the *Sydney*, and we should have had to fight them both. It was unfortunate for the enemy that the *Velebit* had not used her wireless. If *Sydney* had picked up a call for help from her she would have raced to the spot, and the odds against us would have been overwhelming.[3]

The notebook had not named the cruiser as *Sydney*. It made reference to a cruiser which was actually HMS *Durban*. The suggestion that it was *Sydney* later originated in an inaccurate article published in the *United States Naval Institute Proceedings* in December 1950.[4]

Four days after the sinking of *Mareeba*, British merchant ships were advised of the presence of an unknown German auxiliary cruiser in the eastern Indian Ocean although the *Weekly Intelligence Report* of 11 July concluded that *Velebit* and *Mareeba* were probably lost in bad weather.

The time had come for *Kormoran* to overhaul her engines. The work commenced in open waters on 2 July and lasted until 17 July. It was a busy time when the entire ship was cleaned and refurbished. The tedium was relieved by a signal which was received advising that *Kormoran* had been awarded another five Iron Crosses (First Class) and 100 more Iron Crosses (Second Class) in recognition of her success as a raider.

The time had also come to change the ship's disguise. The Japanese markings were removed, the superstructure was painted brown and the funnel black: *Kormoran* had become the Dutch freighter *Straat Malakka* of Batavia.[5] She was slightly different in appearance from *Kormoran*. She displaced 2000 tons less than the raider, had a counter stern and was fitted with four samson posts fore and aft, whereas *Kormoran* had a cruiser stern and two samson posts fore and aft. Detmers was glad to change from the light colours used as part of the Japanese disguise:

> I have . . . come to the conclusion that the best camouflage is in any case the greatest possible inconspicuousness, i.e., a ship on which one can see no armament or suspicious superstructure, and which is so painted that it could well be friendly. Representing any particular ship is not at all necessary. The times of a *Wolf* and a *Seeadler* are over. The opponent is on the watch and stops everything. However, if one is stopped at all, there is only one way out: battle.

There was also the news that *Kormoran* would be ordered to the Manila–Los Angeles trade route when a replacement was available for her in the Indian Ocean. Detmers had doubts that he would ever be relieved given the extreme difficulty being encountered by German ships attempting to elude the radar-fitted British ships making up the Allied blockade. He seemed resigned to remaining at sea until his ship was lost or totally unserviceable. On the day before the repairs were completed, another signal was received regarding the bearing metal and new condenser coils. A ship would be leaving Japan on 29 August and Detmers assumed that she would be carrying the items he requested in addition to a range of stores and new equipment which he assumed SKL would realise he needed after being at sea continuously for nearly 12 months by the time it finally arrived.

With the repairs completed on 17 July, Detmers decided to return to the Bay of Bengal. He believed that the Allies would not expect him to return so soon to the area and he wanted to lay some mines. Because 'the increasing tension in the Far East will probably make operations in the Bay [of Bengal] completely impossible later', Detmers risked having one last sweep through the area. But the prospects were still not good as Detmers lamented in his ship's war diary:

> For the auxiliary cruiser in the Indian Ocean, times are getting worse and worse. We put to sea at least six months too late. In the area where we have been cruising fruitlessly for six months, our predecessors got their best ships.

At least Detmers could be comforted by the news he received on 18 July that the Admiralty in London believed that *Kormoran* was Ship 46, also called *Dora*, which was supposed to have sailed in January. After three days in the Bay of Bengal and the news that the British aircraft carrier *Hermes* was in Colombo, Detmers moved to the south of Sumatra and Java where she arrived on 30 July. By 8 August, Detmers was again becoming irritated by his lack of success: 'we travel thousands of miles, see nothing but water and often feel that we are superfluous.'

Five days later as the light faded, *Kormoran* sighted her first ship in weeks at approximately 24 000 yards. As the raider was on the horizon with the setting sun behind her, *Kormoran* would have been observed first. When the range had closed by some 8000 yards, the unidentified ship altered towards *Kormoran* and Detmers suspected that she may have been a British auxiliary cruiser. When the raider turned to follow the ship, she sent a QQQ signal but without a position given in latitude and longitude. *Kormoran* decamouflaged when the range was 12 000 yards but in the darkness the gunnery staff could see nothing. When the wireless station at Singapore asked for a repetition of the QQQ signal, the vessel simply replied with its signal letters,

GKKI. Such strange behaviour prompted Detmers to believe that this ship had either just seen a warship or was attempting to lure *Kormoran* into an escorted convoy where a warship would be able to engage her. Detmers decided to flee the area although he was sorely tempted to sink the ship which appeared to be of around 6000 tons.

There were few alternative areas that really appealed to Detmers:

> [As] I have been cruising here fruitlessly for fourteen days, I will now cross the routes between Lombok and Sunda Straits in broad sweeps and then return to the west coast of Sumatra. Then I shall be in the Chagos Archipelago just in time to have the whole of the new moon period in September at my disposal for the north-western area. I have considered the question of mining Carnarvon and Geraldton. It would be quite possible at both places. On account of the sparse traffic in them even in peacetime, however, my mines are still too valuable for that.

Although *Kormoran* had achieved success, Raeder was growing increasingly concerned about the ability of the *Kriegsmarine* to continue the fight against Britain. The navy was hampered by having too few ships and insufficient resolve to risk their loss in combat. Raeder also argued that the *Kriegsmarine* needed a naval air arm to give the surface fleet adequate aerial protection. 'It is possible,' Raeder told Hitler, 'that the surface forces will gradually be destroyed. The possibility, however, must not be allowed to keep surface ships from continuing to operate in the war against merchant ships.'[6]

For the next couple of weeks, *Kormoran* sailed the Indian Ocean without success. On 22 August, his 39th birthday, Detmers handed over command to Foerster and got very drunk. In a relaxed address to his crew, he told them that they would beat all the other auxiliary raiders in tonnage of ships sunk. The next day, the crew returned to the all-too-familiar drudgery of searching for non-existent ships. The only variation came late on 25 August when a report of 'Direction 45, strange formation, not a cloud, not a smoke plume' was received from the mast lookout. It was actually the peak of the Boea Boea mountain on the island of Enggano which was forty miles away at the entrance to the Sunda Strait between Sumatra and Java. This was the first time the *Kormoran* crew had sighted land in 258 days. An hour later, the island was out of sight. As Detmers recorded in the ship's war diary:

> For us the festive hour is over, which can only be understood by somebody who has seen nothing but water for 258 days. It meant a lot to us; that is why it is mentioned here.

As the month ended, Detmers was advised by signal that the supply ship *Kulmerland* would rendezvous with *Kormoran* at the end of August. He was also advised that the captain of Ship 36, *Orion*, had received a Knight's Cross for his achievements. As if to gauge what he would have to do to receive the same honour, Detmers remarked in *Kormoran*'s war diary that 'unfortunately the final tonnage of 36 was not reported'.

As September began, Detmers was hoping for more opportunities than had come his way in the previous two months. He was not to be disappointed. Just before noon on 1 September, a modern motor ship of more than 10 000 tons appeared out of the haze at a range of 24 000 yards. As the ship had a flag hoisted, Detmers immediately feared that she might be an auxiliary cruiser. The closest point of approach between the two ships if they maintained present courses would be about 17 000 yards—beyond the range of *Kormoran*'s guns. If the vessel were an auxiliary cruiser Detmers assumed it would radio for air support from Ceylon, which was only 150 miles distant. But as she had not asked for the raider's name, Detmers assumed she was a military transport vessel. 'It would be a dereliction of duty for an auxiliary cruiser not even to ask our name, even with our innocent appearance and the nearness of Colombo.' Detmers decided that he would wait and possibly attack the ship during the night. However, the ship slipped from view in the late afternoon and, despite *Kormoran*'s search efforts, vanished.

On the second anniversary of the start of war, Detmers was

advised that he would be relieved by Ship 10, *Thor*, at the end of December. *Kulmerland*, which would depart Kobe in Japan and rendezvous with *Kormoran* some time after 12 October, would provide whatever he needed to continue until that time. Detmers continued to be disappointed by his 'meagre success' but conceded that the 'task of the auxiliary cruiser in the Indian Ocean at present is police work, in that by his presence he prevents the use of shorter [shipping] routes'. If nothing else, Detmers had forced the Allies to send most trans-Indian Ocean shipping through the northern part of the ocean basin making most use of its ports. However, with Iran and the Persian Gulf secured on the Allied side, British naval power in the northern Indian Ocean amounted to one battleship, one aircraft carrier and 16 cruisers. With so many warships patrolling at sea, raider operations were considerably more risky.

The political situation in East Asia did nothing to improve *Kormoran*'s raiding prospects. The Japanese had stopped relaying messages from raiders to Germany and were no longer a source of stores and equipment for supply ships. *Kormoran* was also instructed not to send any prisoners to Japan. But Raeder was nonetheless pleased with the work of the auxiliary cruisers. As he told Hitler, 'despite enemy countermeasures and strategy, the auxiliary cruisers have been able to achieve further success'.[7]

The lack of success continued for *Kormoran*. Even with the assistance of the Arado aircraft, which flew short-range reconnaissance sorties when the weather permitted, there was nothing to be seen in the Arabian Sea or the north-west Indian Ocean. Detmers believed that the aircraft could have been in constant use if *Kormoran* had been fitted with a catapult. SKL finally agreed with Detmers that the prospects for raider operations in the South Atlantic were better than in the Indian Ocean.

On the early evening of 23 September, however, the raider's luck changed when the watch officer saw a small light off *Kormoran*'s port bow. *Kormoran* increased speed and altered course, and the light appeared to be a green starboard sidelight from a ship heading to the east. At 5000 yards, *Kormoran* decamouflaged and asked the ship by light for her name. When the reply received was 'Greek ship. *Stamatios G. Embiricos*', she was ordered to stop and was illuminated by *Kormoran*'s search-light. Only after the order was sent three times did the vessel heave to. No attempt was made to send a signal.

The boarding party in *Kormoran* was despatched to the 3941-ton Greek freighter, which was on its way from Mombasa to Colombo to receive a cargo. As *Embiricos* was coal-burning and could not be refuelled and used as a prize or prison ship, Detmers ordered her to be sunk shortly after midnight. However, one lifeboat with 23 men attempted to avoid being taken prisoner by *Kormoran*. As Detmers wanted to remain in the area, the lifeboat had to be found. Twelve hours later, it was spotted by the Arado aircraft and the men were recovered.

After being unable to find any more victims near where *Embiricos* was sunk, *Kormoran* headed south for her rendezvous with *Kulmerland*, disguised as the American ship *Matthew Luckenbach*, on 16 October 600 miles to the west of Cape Leeuwin. Captain Pschunder from *Kulmerland* conferred with Detmers in *Kormoran*. Thanks to the German Naval Attache in Japan, Rear Admiral Paul Wenneker, all of *Kormoran*'s requests and anticipated needs could be met, including the bearing metal and condenser coils. Wenneker had also made available a list of Allied merchant shipping in which there was some detail about the movements of the *Straat Malakka*. Detmers gave a copy of *Kormoran*'s war diary to *Kulmerland* for delivery to Germany in *Spreewald*. Admiral Wenneker also held a copy, which became very important as the version carried by *Spreewald* was lost with that ship. In addition to ship's documents, the prisoners from *Kormoran* were transferred to *Kulmerland* in addition to five ill members of the crew.

The transfer of provisions, stores and equipment was completed by 24 October. In the last entry in the ship's war diary before it was transferred to *Kulmerland*, Detmers wrote:

We have received everything we need. Things were thought of for which we had not dared to hope. The cooperation with *Kulmerland* was very good. Captain Pschunder devoted himself entirely to his task, so that there was no friction at all. I respectfully suggest that a suitable recognition will be awarded to him and his crew. My sea endurance until 1 June 1942 seems to be ensured by this provisioning. I intend to proceed immediately with carrying out alterations to adapt Engine I as reserve ship's network engine. Thanks to the speedy completion of the provisioning, I hope to be back in my operational area by the next new moon period.

The next new moon was due around 19 November. In the meantime, *Kormoran* required further repair and maintenance work, particularly in the electrical department. Once the work was completed, Detmers

proposed to sail up the western coast of Australia, laying mines in Shark's [sic] Bay if opportunity afforded; and then moving northward again, leaving Java and Sumatra to starboard and penetrating into the Bay of Bengal once more, perhaps laying mines off Calcutta and other harbours. For the moment therefore I set an easterly course. With the new moon I wanted to be off Cape Leeuwin.[8]

When a signal was received advising that a heavy cruiser was making way around the south-west coast of Australia, Detmers altered course to the north-west until the warship was clear of the area he intended to mine. As he was in waters adjacent to a shipping route, Detmers decided he would proceed with his earlier intention of laying mines near Shark Bay in the hope of disrupting domestic and international shipping movements on the West Australian coast.

There was great pressure on Detmers, both external and self-imposed, to achieve success over the next few months. He had already sunk 68 274 tons of shipping. However, he was well behind the amount of tonnage sunk by the first raiders—some had exceeded 100 000 tons. The prospects of repeating their achievement seemed remote. The German surface navy had been successful but was increasingly confined to its bases as Raeder advised Hitler:

In view of the far-reaching effect of operations by auxiliary cruisers, the naval staff believes in using the vessels for warfare outside home waters despite the fact that operations are being made more difficult by enemy countermeasures and able direct control of shipping. As long as auxiliary cruisers are successful in sinking and capturing ships, it is justifiable and necessary to use them.[9]

The problem for Raeder was that raider success had slowly declined throughout the second half of 1941 and Germany was suffering from an increasingly serious shortage of oil. Raeder also advised Hitler that *Kormoran* would be returning to Germany in the spring of 1942 when replaced by *Thor*.

Whereas Britain and the Dominions were continuing with a vast naval construction program, the full capacity of German shipyards was devoted to U-boat construction and the surface fleet languished. *Bismarck* had been sunk and the only new capital ship to be completed, the battleship *Tirpitz*, could not be deployed in open waters without substantial surface and air protection.

With the increasing likelihood of Japan entering the war, Detmers realised that many more warships would be active in the Indian Ocean and that his relocation to the Manila–Los Angeles route would certainly be cancelled. There were not many opportunities remaining for Detmers to make his mark. He had to sink many more ships if he were to stand any chance of receiving the Knight's Cross of the Iron Cross. If he were to lose his ship at this point, Detmers would be relegated to the ranks of the lesser-known raider captains, bereft of a place in history alongside von Muller and Count von Luckner. Realistically, Detmers concluded that he had to do something that no other raider captain had managed to achieve.

On 19 November, *Kormoran* approached the West Australian coast on a north-easterly course. The weather was fine and the seas were moderate. At 1500, Detmers decided that *Kormoran* would continue on her present course until 2000 when he would alter course to the east and lay mines in Shark Bay. With the end of *Kormoran*'s cruise in sight, some of the 360 mines had to be expended. At 1555 that afternoon, Detmers was advised that a lookout had sighted a ship on the horizon.

7

What Happened?

The circumstances of the engagement between *Sydney* and *Kormoran* and its outcome were such that the Naval Board could only slowly learn what had occurred off the West Australian coast on 19 November 1941. The Staff Officer (Intelligence) in Fremantle, an ex-merchant navy RAN Reserve officer named Lieutenant Commander James Rycroft, was sent to Carnarvon with an interpreter, J.L. Lobstein, a modern languages teacher at Scotch College; they were to interview the 103 German survivors who had sailed their lifeboats ashore and who were being held in the small gaol at Carnarvon. The Volunteer Defence Corps guard had been relieved at this stage by the 11th Garrison Battalion.[1] As practically no preparation had been made for such a contingency, the whole interrogation was handled poorly from the beginning. It was disorganised, very amateur, lacked a sense of urgency and was indicative of the widely held feeling that the war was still a long way from the Australian continent.

The 46 sailors who had landed at 17-Mile Well were immediately reunited with the crew of the lifeboat, including thirteen officers, who had come ashore at Red Bluff. This did not assist Rycroft, who arrived after both groups had been delivered to Carnarvon gaol. He later stated that all of the survivors had 'obviously been carefully instructed by their officers to give incorrect answers to all questions regardless of their nature'. This did not necessarily mean that they would all uniformly offer a well-rehearsed account but that they would not assist the Australian authorities to determine what had occurred.

On the morning of 28 November, Rycroft went on board *Yandra* where Detmers and Foerster were being held, and took them into his custody. After a short and marginally successful interview that yielded very little useful information, Rycroft sent a signal to the Naval Board. It conveyed the information obtained from Detmers and from Radio Operator Hans Linke. Because he spoke good English, Linke was chosen from the group of survivors who came ashore at 17-Mile Well to accompany Wing Commander McLean, the local RAAF senior officer, in a vehicle to Carnarvon on 25 November. McLean reported what he had been told by Linke to the Central War Room (CWR) in Perth. This information would allow the Naval Board to brief the government, which was anxious for news.

On the same day, Admiral Crace decided that Captain Farncomb, the commanding officer of *Canberra*, would conduct the interrogation in Sydney of the *Kormoran* survivors recovered by *Aquitania*.[2] According to Crace, the Assistant Chief of Naval Staff in Navy Office, Captain Frank Getting RAN, suggested that he should have overall responsibility for the interrogation as *Sydney* had come under Crace's command, and because Navy Office 'didn't want Army butting in'. It appears that Getting was able to persuade the Chief of Naval Staff, Admiral Royle, to place Crace in charge rather than the District Naval Officer in Fremantle, Captain Charles Farquhar-Smith. This was, according to Crace's operations officer, Lieutenant Commander George Oldham, part of a continuing feud between Getting and Farquhar-Smith who was allegedly 'not doing very well' in Fremantle. Although the Second Naval Member, Commodore Durnford, tried to persuade Crace to remain in Sydney because the 'Far Eastern situation is critical and war is expected any moment', Crace decided that he had little to do in Sydney and would travel to Fremantle two days later.

On the evening of 28 November, the 103 *Kormoran* survivors held at Carnarvon gaol were embarked in *Centaur* for passage to Fremantle. Detmers and Foerster were sent to Perth in a truck because, Rycroft told the Naval Board, 'these officers [were] considered too risky to leave [in the] ship with other prisoners'.[3] The next morning (Saturday 29 November), Crace learned that Durnford had probably tried to persuade Admiral Royle that there was little point in him going to Fremantle. In reply, Royle stated that 'as present evidence is so unsatisfactory I consider RACAS [Crace] should proceed to Fremantle to reinvestigate'. Whereas it appeared earlier that Crace had actually wanted to be in Fremantle, he remarked in his diary: 'This is a confounded nuisance and I cannot understand what is meant as from all accounts the interrogation has been very good.' Crace was probably unaware that the circumstances for conducting interrogations in Sydney were very different from those prevailing in Western Australia where the prisoners had been reunited and discussion between them was taking place. The reasons for the presence of RACAS in the West were explained later in the day to Crace by both Getting and Durnford. It is reasonable to suggest that Crace was also advised that he might also need to investigate the performance of Farquhar-Smith and recommend if the Naval Board needed to take any remedial action in his command.

When he arrived in Fremantle late on Sunday 30 November, Crace was met by Farquhar-Smith's naval secretary, and the officers who had been involved in the interrogations to date. Commander Emile Dechaineux, an officer seconded from the Directorate of Naval Intelligence to assist with the interrogation, showed Crace a 'note from Royle which I think explains the reason for my being sent over. He was dissatisfied with the evidence of a man called Linke, the W/T [wireless telegraphy] operator who talked about the cruiser being with a convoy. All obvious lies and it was not felt necessary to give consideration to his evidence by Dechaineux'.

By this time, the group of *Kormoran* survivors who had sailed from Carnarvon in *Centaur* had arrived in Fremantle. The officers were reunited with their colleagues at Swanbourne Army Barracks, and the sailors were taken to an internment camp at Harvey, 80 miles south of Perth, after a brief period in the local gaol. The group recovered by *Trocas* were kept isolated and interviewed by Commander Victor Ramage, the Senior Naval

Intelligence officer in Fremantle, until 19 December when they too were sent to Harvey. Those who were recovered by *Aquitania* were sent to Murchison in northern Victoria after their interrogations were completed in Sydney.

The following day (1 December), the formal interrogation of the officers commenced at Swanbourne Barracks. Interviews with the sailors at Harvey began the next day. Crace interviewed most of *Kormoran*'s officers. Crace described Lieutenant von Malapert as 'a violent Nazi'; Lieutenant Greter, who had spent five years in the Hitler Youth Movement, as 'a surly toad' and Skeries as 'unpleasant'. Crace was not overjoyed by the results of his initial efforts:

> We could get little of real value out of them, no-one definitely knew the fate of *Sydney* but we got a pretty good description of the action . . . I don't feel I can be of any real use here and think that the interrogations can go on with [a naval officer] and two interpreters one of whom has a legal mind. If I can get this going I'm going home on Wednesday morning. Farquhar-Smith is quite hopeless and doesn't know what is going on at all.

One suspects that Crace had little faith in any of the staff from Naval Headquarters in Fremantle because he commented in his diary that 'I think nothing of Rycroft'. But it is doubtful whether a flag officer, who did not speak German and who possessed no specialist interrogation skills, was needed to conduct the interrogations personally. This is probably what Crace realised after two days.

Crace issued a memorandum, 'Instructions for Interrogating Prisoners of War ex [Raider] No. 41' for the benefit of those at Harvey on 2 December. The sailors from *Kormoran* would be interrogated by two teams, each consisting of a naval officer and two interpreters. Crace felt it necessary to advise the interrogators that they needed to use 'devious ways' in extracting answers. The Admiral thought that 'direct questioning is useless'.

The task of the interrogators was to obtain information about *Kormoran*'s 'movements in the Indian Ocean between June and

November [1941]' in addition to details of raider supply organisation and neutral ports used; German strategic policy; tactics used when attacking merchant ships; whether a *ruse de guerre* was employed in sinking *Sydney*; and the activities of other raiders, and when and where any mines may have been laid. The teams were informed that:

(a) Force is not to be used.
(b) A prisoner-of-war cannot be forced to give information, but on the other hand it is to be impressed on the prisoner that he is not allowed to lie.

Crace ended with a little encouragement:

It is appreciated that this is a dull and laborious task. It is nevertheless most important to get all we can from the prisoners. Your efforts may lead to the destruction of more than one enemy supply ship or raider. Officers are earnestly requested to keep plugging away at the job.

The junior officers were interrogated first. When their interviews were over, some of them were sent to Harvey. Ahl and von Gosseln were kept in solitary confinement at Fremantle because it was thought they were valuable witnesses to the action. The remainder stayed at Swanbourne Barracks and were relatively free to speak with each other, and with Detmers, who was the last to be interviewed on 2 December.

Although they were interviewed at Swanbourne, Detmers and Foerster were accommodated separately at the local police station. Detmers added little to the brief account he had given Rycroft two days earlier. However, he did mention that the first salvo from *Kormoran* had struck the cruiser amidships and caused a fire. He claimed that he still did not know her identity. Foerster recalled that when those on the raider's bridge had positively identified the ship as a British 6-inch cruiser, Detmers turned to him and asked: 'Shall we scuttle or fight?'; to which Foerster allegedly replied, 'We can only die once captain.'

Two days after the Japanese attack on Pearl Harbor, the

interrogations were finally completed and all of the *Kormoran* survivors were despatched to the Murchison POW Camp. The officers were conveyed in the coastal liner *Duntroon*, which sailed for Melbourne on 13 December, while the sailors made their way by train in two groups. The first departed in late December and the second in early January. Soon after their arrival at Murchison, the officers were kept separate and later moved to 'Dhurringile', a large homestead that had been taken over by the Commonwealth government and set up as a detention camp, ten miles away. Here, the officers from *Kormoran* joined 50 Wehrmacht and Luftwaffe officers. At Murchison, the sailors had the company of 1200 men from the Afrika Corps.

On 7 January, Detmers was interrogated for the third time at Dhurringile. On this occasion it was the Army and not the Navy which conducted the proceedings. The next day, Detmers was permitted to visit his men at Murchison. He informed them that he had been awarded the Knight's Cross of the Iron Cross, Skeries had received the Iron Cross (First Class) and Foerster had received a Bar to his Iron Cross (First Class). Jakob Fend, who operated the starboard 3.7-centimetre anti-tank gun, was the only sailor awarded the Iron Cross (First Class). Hitler had directed that the remainder of the crew were to receive the Iron Cross (Second Class).[4] Detmers was proud of his achievement and made no secret of his delight. He had been decorated with a high honour and, although he had not sunk 100 000 tons of shipping, would certainly achieve a place in history. After being reunited with his officers, Detmers produced a composite account of the action, which included a narrative of events with courses, speeds and times. This report was subsequently confiscated by the Australian authorities.[5]

By this time, nearly two months had passed since the loss of *Sydney*. The Naval Board had gradually obtained a vast amount of information about the action. The earliest account of the action had come from Radio Operator Hans Linke on 26 November. He stated that at 1700 on 19 November a lookout sighted a convoy of 5–7 ships escorted by a *Perth* Class cruiser. Thinking her to be part of the convoy, the cruiser approached signalling with flags to within half a mile. At 6.40 [pm] *Kormoran* opened fire, silencing the cruiser's guns with her first salvo; she continued until 8pm, by which time she [*Kormoran*] was burning fiercely amidships.

Linke's impression that they had sighted a convoy was probably created by the initial reporting of the cruiser's masts as two sailing vessels. As Linke was not an eye-witness to the action, he had evidently been told some of the detail he repeated to Wing Commander McLean and did not report *Kormoran*'s replies to the cruiser's flag-hoists. Admiral Royle's remark that Linke was lying was unfair. Linke did not say that *Sydney* was with a convoy. He said that through the haze it appeared as though there was a convoy.

Rycroft used Linke's account together with the little he could obtain from Detmers in his first brief to the Naval Board on 28 November.

Raider captain can confirm previous report with addition [that] action took place [at] latitude 26 degrees 32 minutes, longitude 111 degrees. Raider torpedo hit forward and salvo amidships [with] HMAS *Sydney* badly on fire. Action began 19th at 1600 [and] broke off 1830. Raider struck in engineroom and on fire. HMAS *Sydney* last seen turning behind smoke screen bearing 153 degrees 5 miles from raider and steering south 5 knots. Raider had 25 killed, remainder of 400 in boats and rafts experienced bad weather. Endeavouring [to] obtain further information.

Linke had not known that one of the German boats had capsized and many more men had died.

A further update was sent from Fremantle on 30 November. After the officers from *Kormoran* had been interrogated, the Acting Chief of Naval Staff, Commodore Durnford, presented the following summary to the War Cabinet on 4 December:

The engagement took place in position 25 degrees S 111 degrees E on 19 November. HMAS *Sydney* made the first sighting at a range of 15 miles. The raider altered course from 000 degrees to 025 degrees and made no reply. At closer range the raider, which was flying the Dutch flag, made *Straat Malakka* by light.

At 1650 [time zone H] the ships were on a parallel course, speed 15 knots. *Sydney* which was abaft the raider's beam, distance less than two miles, was at action stations and made 'Make your signal letters'. *Steiermark* immediately opened fire with guns and torpedoes, her first salvo hitting *Sydney*'s bridge and starting a fire forward. *Sydney* opened fire simultaneously but her first salvo was over. Early in the action the cruiser was hit by a torpedo under A turret, resulting in A and B turrets being jammed. *Sydney*'s torpedo tubes were hit by a further salvo, and a bad fire was started resulting in the destruction of her aircraft.

The action was broken off after about half an hour and *Sydney*, burning fiercely and down by the bows, proceeded at five knots. The raider, which had received a vital hit, was now on fire amidships, with her engineroom out of action. At about 1815H the raider's crew abandoned ship, and at midnight the vessel, which was scuttled, blew up.

It is believed that *Sydney* sank at 2300 [on 19 November].[6]

In the discussion that followed, Durnford told the War Cabinet that the Naval Staff did not believe 'a second German ship . . . was present at the action'.[7] It appears that the Naval Board had earlier kept open the possibility that two raiders may have been involved as the sinking of *Sydney* appeared beyond the capacity of one. In a letter to the Prime Minister's Private Secretary dated 1 December, the Assistant Secretary of the Department of Defence Coordination stated that 'the Naval Board have continuously under review the possibility of two raiders'.[8]

Detmers' interrogation on 30 November, 2 December and 7 January, and the contents of his confiscated 'action report', provided a comprehensive description of the action. On the afternoon of 19 November, *Kormoran* was proceeding on a course of 025 degrees at 11 knots at a position 26 degrees 34 minutes S, 111 degrees E. The sea was moderate, the swell was from the south-west, the weather was fine and visibility was very good. At 1555, a report was received from Sub-Lieutenant Rudolf Jansen that a sailing vessel was visible off the port bow.[9] Directed to make constant reports, Jansen's relief, Sub-Lieutenant Bunjes, said he could see two sailing vessels. This was altered to several ships when two smoke trails were visible. The next report was what Detmers had hoped to avoid. The contact on the horizon appeared to be a 'British' cruiser.

Detmers had the action alarm sounded as the raider altered course to port to 260 degrees with the main engines ordered full ahead. As *Kormoran* started to swing towards the west, the cruiser was identified as being of the '*Perth*' class. After ascertaining that the cruiser was heading in a south-westerly direction towards him, Detmers had *Kormoran* steady on a course of 250 degrees. This course took the raider into the setting sun. The raider made thick smoke as she gained speed. The engine room then reported that No. 4 engine was unavailable owing to one of the pistons running hot. This would restrict *Kormoran* to a maximum speed of 14 knots. With the knowledge that dusk was not for another three hours, Detmers realised he could not run from the cruiser and would probably have to fight. He still wanted to avoid this and hoped the enemy cruiser would lose interest. At 1605, the cruiser altered towards the raider at a range of approximately 20 000 yards and slowly closed *Kormoran* while allegedly signalling the letters 'NNP' with signal light. Detmers claimed that he could not understand this signal and did not respond. The cruiser then signalled *Kormoran* to stop. Detmers responded by ordering the signal letters for the Dutch merchantman *Straat Malakka* to be hoisted. With the cruiser drawing nearer to *Kormoran* over the next thirty minutes, No. 4 engine was available again and a speed of 14 knots could be maintained with less strain on the engines.

At 10 000 yards, the main rangefinder in *Kormoran* was retracted to maintain her identity as an innocent merchant ship. At 1645, the cruiser was visible off *Kormoran*'s starboard quarter and the range continued to close. At 1700, Detmers ordered the radio room to signal 'QQQ *Straat Malakka* 115-1-26S'. Fifteen minutes later, the cruiser appeared to alter course to place herself broad on *Kormoran*'s starboard beam. At 1725, the Allied ship signalled 'Hoist your secret callsign'. While the chief signals yeoman on the raider's flag deck fumbled with the signal pennants, the cruiser may have stopped. According to Detmers, she seemed completely unsuspecting of *Kormoran*'s true identity.

At 1730 with the cruiser 'somewhat more than a mile' away, that is, in excess of 2000 yards, *Kormoran* revealed her identity. The Dutch flag was struck and a German battle ensign hoisted in its place. The time taken for the raider to reveal her identity was six seconds as the crew were earlier ordered to stand-by to fire their guns and torpedoes. As the cruiser appeared to drift astern, the engine in her aircraft running, the raider slowly turned to 260 degrees to improve the angle of fire for her torpedoes while not interfering with the firing arcs of her guns. The point of aim for the torpedoes was the cruiser's stem and stern.

With her camouflage removed, *Kormoran* opened fire with a salvo that fell short of the cruiser. Detmers could not recall which ship fired first but believed it may have been the cruiser by half a second. The second salvo from the raider was also unsuccessful. However, salvoes three, four and five struck the cruiser's bridge and gunnery director tower. *Kormoran*'s anti-aircraft and starboard 3.7-centimetre guns directed accurate fire onto the cruiser's bridge, her torpedo-tube space and aircraft. It was not until *Kormoran*'s fifth salvo that the cruiser returned fire from X turret.[10] The two forward turrets (A and B) did not fire at all while the two or three salvoes from the after-most turret (Y) passed over the raider. *Kormoran* was hit on her funnel and in the engine rooms.

Kormoran fired her first pattern of torpedoes towards the cruiser after the eighth or ninth salvo. At least one of the torpedoes struck under the cruiser's forecastle, 'about 20 metres from the bow', which was almost submerged by the blast. With *Kormoran* maintaining her course of 260 degrees, the Australian cruiser veered hard to port and it appeared she was trying to ram the raider. The cruiser crossed the wake of the raider which had maintained her course and speed to avoid a collision. *Kormoran* was then fired upon by the cruiser's after turrets and a pattern of four torpedoes. Detmers stated that he turned towards the torpedoes which passed ahead and astern of his ship. Five minutes after the first shots were fired, *Kormoran* altered course to port to open the firing arcs of her guns to ensure the cruiser's destruction. However, the engine revolutions in the raider fell rapidly before the engines failed completely and *Kormoran* lost way. At 1745, the engine room reported that the engines and the raider's fire-fighting equipment were out of order.

With the engineers struggling to get *Kormoran* underway again, *Kormoran* again fired at the cruiser, which was maintaining a steady course to the south at slow speed. The cruiser was burning fiercely between the bridge and the forward funnel. The engagement ended at 1825 when Detmers ordered his guns to cease fire. By this time, the cruiser was about 12000 yards distant.

After surveying the damage to his ship and being unable to communicate with the badly damaged engine room, Detmers ordered his men to begin scuttling action. The cruiser was visible to the south-east at about 20000 yards with a heading of approximately 150 degrees when she disappeared over the horizon. By 2100, all but two lifeboats had been lowered, manned and cast off while 124 men, among them almost all the officers, remained on board. If the cruiser returned or they were joined by another Allied warship, Detmers would order the officers to man the raider's guns. At 2330, after giving the order to abandon ship at 2300, a boat with 57 men on board cast off from the raider. With the quantity of smoke coming from the mine deck increasing, a charge was set in the forward port oil tank. The timer was activated for midnight and the last boat cast off from the raider. At 0100, the charge exploded; 25 minutes later, the mines exploded and *Kormoran* sank slowly by the stern.

There were four significant differences between the information Detmers had given under interrogation at Swanbourne Barracks, and in the action report which was later confiscated. First, Detmers stated that *Kormoran* was ordered to stop before the cruiser signalled in plain language for the secret callsign of the *Straat Malakka* to be hoisted. Second, that *Sydney* was preparing to lower a boat. Third, that the cruiser had fired first.

Fourth, that *Kormoran*'s first salvo fell short of *Sydney*. Detmers' later descriptions were inconsistent with these statements.

Detmers' second-in-command followed his captain's example and said very little when interrogated. Foerster recalled that he was 'very astonished' that the cruiser came so near to *Kormoran*. During the engagement, Foerster was concerned with fire-fighting and emergency equipment and tended to confine his statements to these areas. He said that soon after the firing started and *Kormoran* was hit, it became apparent that the ship was in danger of exploding.

The navigator, Henry Meyer, a merchant service officer, was another vital source of information. At the time of the action he was aged 40. He had joined the Hamburg–Amerika line in 1922 and had been to North and South America with the company. In 1938 he spent a short period in Australia in the merchant vessel *Reliance*, before being conscripted for naval service in 1939. He had been a member of the Nazi Party since 1934. At the outbreak of the war, Meyer was serving in the pocket battleship *Deutschland* as First Officer.

During the final action, Meyer moved between *Kormoran*'s bridge and navigation room. Meyer states that when *Kormoran* was sighted by the cruiser she was steering 024, not 025 degrees as mentioned by Detmers. According to Meyer, it was not until the vessel on the horizon was identified at 1630 as a '*Perth*' class cruiser, that the raider increased speed and turned towards the sun on a course of 250 degrees. After being asked to 'Hoist your signal letters', Meyer recalled that they gave the name *Straat Malakka*. When asked for *Straat Malakka*'s secret callsign, *Kormoran* did not reply. The only method of signalling used by *Kormoran*, according to Meyer, was signal flag. Meyer stated that the firing started six to seven minutes after the raider failed to hoist the secret callsign. He did not say which ship was the first to fire.

During the engagement, which by his estimate lasted until 1900, Meyer was wounded and did not play a major role. However, he was able to state that *Kormoran*'s fire was very accurate and that the distance between the two ships during the entire action ranged from one mile to four miles. The latter was the distance when the raider ceased firing. By this time, he noticed that the cruiser was burning amidships. In the period before sunset, Meyer did not see any boats lowered from the cruiser. Had there been any survivors from the Allied ship, he said he would have expected them to drift towards *Kormoran*. He was adamant that the only ruse used by *Kormoran* was the Dutch flag; he would not disclose the name of the ship the raider was disguised as.[11]

While Meyer's recollections varied from that of his captain on several points, those of the 1st Division Artillery Officer, Fritz Skeries, were more consistent. Skeries, of Prussian descent, was 26 years old at the time of the action. He had joined the German Navy in 1935 and was promoted lieutenant on 1 October 1939. On the afternoon of the final action, Skeries assumed his action station above the bridge at 1600 where he started taking ranges of the cruiser. He believed the action started between 1730 and 1745 with the cruiser 1500 yards away. Confirming Detmers' recollection, rounds from *Kormoran*'s first salvo fell short or were too high. The second salvo struck the cruiser near the after part of her bridge. The third salvo hit the gunnery director tower; the fourth struck the engine room; the fifth crashed into the cruiser's aircraft, which had earlier been running and was later shut down.

Skeries stated that during the action, *Kormoran* fired 450 rounds from her 5.9-inch guns and used her anti-aircraft guns to destroy the cruiser's port torpedo space. After eight to ten salvoes had been fired from the raider, X turret in the cruiser fired several rounds. Skeries recalled that Y turret also fired but he could not say where its rounds had landed. It was during this exchange that *Kormoran* was hit. A torpedo from *Kormoran* struck the cruiser between her two forward turrets. When the cruiser turned towards the raider, Skeries remarked that *Kormoran* turned to avoid salvoes from her after turrets which were still capable of firing. When *Kormoran* fired her last round, the cruiser was approximately 12000 yards away. Skeries was in the last boat with Detmers, which cast off from *Kormoran* apparently about 0100. He recalled that they lost sight of the cruiser at about midnight.

It became apparent from Skeries' interrogation that Detmers told his subordinates very little about the ship's activities. Skeries stated that Detmers never discussed such matters with him; that officers seldom went into the chartroom; and that during night watches only the navigator, Meyer, determined the ship's position. This was consistent with Foerster's evidence, which stated that Detmers never spoke with him about the ship's planned movements and kept all secret papers in a cupboard in his cabin. Foerster said he had never seen anything from inside the cupboard and was given only eight to ten days notice of a rendezvous with a supply ship.

Another officer well placed to describe the action was the battle watch officer, Lieutenant Joachim von Gosseln, who was among the group recovered by *Yandra*. In his report, the captain of *Yandra*, Lieutenant James Taplin RANR(S), stated that 'although very weak and suffering from exposure', von Gosseln 'skilfully evaded answering any question whatever, and politely refuses to give any relevant information. This officer was Anti-Aircraft Officer in the pocket-battleship *Deutschland* and is fanatically Nazi-minded'.

Aged 29 at the time of the action, von Gosseln had been an officer in the Merchant Navy and had joined the Nazi Party in 1934. He was on *Kormoran*'s bridge during the engagement. He stated that the raider was disguised as *Straat Malakka* and flew the Dutch flag. When the distance between the two ships was 1400 yards, the Dutch flag was hauled down and the German ensign hoisted. Von Gosseln was unwilling to provide any information about the action, other than to say that both ships fired torpedoes and that the cruiser was at a range of 12000 yards when the order to cease fire was given. Contrary to the picture of orderliness that was painted by Detmers, von Gosseln said he could not reach his lifeboat owing to flames and the prospect of an explosion. He claimed he had no option but to jump into the water and a boat later picked him up.

Heinz Messerschmidt, a 26-year-old specialist in underwater

weapons and Detmers' secretary, was also of little help. There was no question in his mind that *Kormoran* had to fight. She was a warship and could not be scuttled. He recalled that the first salvo was fired at 1800 yards. He prepared the explosive charges and used the mines carried by *Kormoran* to blow up the ship.

Of greater assistance was Wilhelm Brinkman, another former merchant service officer. Brinkman was born in Westphalia in 1912 and lived there for 15 years before moving to Nassau. He had also joined the Hamburg–Amerika line and visited North and South America. He entered the German Navy in 1937. Brinkman remarked that for his anti-aircraft weapons, range was not as important as it was for the 5.9-inch guns. He said that before the action no-one was visible on *Kormoran*'s upper decks but all had assumed their action stations. When the range closed to 1800 yards and the first of *Kormoran*'s salvoes were fired, Brinkman ordered the anti-aircraft guns to open fire. Although he was to bring down the cruiser's aircraft if it were launched, he was able to concentrate on her torpedo space and upper decks. He stated that one of *Kormoran*'s torpedoes struck directly under A turret in the cruiser and he confirmed that the cruiser did fire her torpedoes when astern of the raider. He was also able to state that the four Chinese laundrymen remained in the ship's laundry, one deck below the upper deck, throughout the action. They had no action station but one was killed when *Kormoran* sustained damage during the engagement.

Brinkman was in the last boat with Detmers, the last man to leave *Kormoran*, and mentioned that the cruiser was last seen at 2300. Contrary to a statement made by Chief Engineer Rudolf Lensch while in the sickbay of *Trocas*, Brinkman denied that anyone jumped overboard and said that both he and von Gosseln, the other officer accused of hastily leaping over the side, left the ship before Lensch had. Lensch also told the 3rd Engineer in *Trocas* that he had heard that *Kormoran* had been ordered to stop and that the 'cruiser lowered a boat before fire was opened. He, Lensch, refused to repeat this when visited in hospital by 3rd Engineer and Intelligence Clerk on 28 [November]'.[12]

The key officer to give evidence of the action was Sub-Lieutenant Wilhelm Bunjes, who was recovered by *Yandra* whose captain reported that Bunjes was a German Naval Reserve officer, 38 years old, and formerly Chief Officer in the German liner *Pretoria,* which had engaged in passenger and cargo trade between Germany and Africa. Bunjes was conscripted into naval service soon after the war began and, despite his considerable civil experience, was the junior of five 'prize' officers carried in *Kormoran*. Bunjes was thought to be

> quite unenthusiastic regarding the war and is quite willing to pass on any knowledge at his disposal, his only concern being the possible disclosure of his name to German authorities in connection with information given, the welfare of his family in Germany being foremost in his mind. These prize officers, one of whom was sent to Bordeaux in the British prize ship *Canadolite*, were evidently treated as the 'dogs-bodies' of the mess, and life onboard the ship for them was not very congenial.

Bunjes opened his account by mentioning that 19 November was 'a day of penance and prayers [and] consequently a holiday routine'. Late in the afternoon, the bridge estimated that *Kormoran* was 150 nautical miles from the coast of Western Australia. After Petty Officer Jansen's original report, Bunjes relieved

> the watch in the lookout at 4pm. The supposed masts became so broad that one is bound to believe it is a sailing vessel. Soon, however, I report that it may be a coastal patrol boat, as I think I can see a funnel. On our bridge suspicions have been aroused. We proceed at full speed and change course.

After the ship was identified as a cruiser, Bunjes noted that she positioned herself on the starboard quarter of the raider and closed at 28 to 30 knots. At this point she was 14 000 yards distant.

> She starts signalling with helio lamps. We do not answer but maintain our speed and course 250 degrees. Steadily nearer comes our doom

and we distinctly recognise the vessel as an Australian cruiser of the *Sydney* class. Fight is out of the question, but maybe we can deceive her somehow. Our ship with a wooden gun covered with brass and mounted on the stern, strikingly resembles the Dutch steamer, *Straat Malakka*. At 1635 hrs. Engine No. 4 starts working again, but it is too late now. The cruiser keeps on asking us for our name. She is so close that it is impossible to overlook her helio signals. We answer *Straat Malakka* and hoist the Dutch ensign astern. All [sailors] disappear from deck, but behind the camouflage flag shutters everyone stands in feverish excitement and holds his breath.

At a range of four miles, Bunjes was aware that the cruiser had not been satisfied with the raider's replies and that by 1700, the two ships were 1.5 nautical miles apart. The nearness of the cruiser was unexpected.

We can distinguish every single man on board; the bridge is full of officers. She is now travelling parallel to us on our starboard side at the same speed as ours. She wants to know more and asks for our destination and cargo. We are flag-signalling the answers. The tension is reaching boiling-point; what will she do now? We observe that the engine of her plane which has been running, is stopped, and the aircraft replaced under cover. Her eight 6-inch guns, however, still point threateningly at us.

When *Kormoran* was unable to hoist her secret callsign letters, Bunjes records that Detmers had no option but 'to attack and gain the advantage of surprise and swiftness of action. Orders are flashed: Hoist German Flag—Reveal Identity—All Weapons Fire'. Six seconds after revealing her identity at 1730, *Kormoran* opened fire. He had earlier stated the raider opened the covering plates and fired the first shots in 'less than a minute'. The raider was, according to Bunjes, immediately on target, with *Kormoran*'s 5.9-inch guns, 3.7-centimetre guns and machine guns all scoring hits on the cruiser's superstructure. The cruiser's first salvo, which seemed from this account to follow *Kormoran*'s second salvo, 'falls wide'. After the cruiser's B turret took a direct hit, the other turrets ceased firing. Bunjes suggested they may have been 'waiting for orders from the control room'. After the fifth salvo from *Kormoran*, X turret in the cruiser began to fire again with rounds crashing into the raider's funnel and boat deck.

> Splinters cause several dead and wounded on our bridge. Another hit on our third gun pierces the armour, causes some casualties but explodes in the water behind us. All our guns are firing rapidly. The enemy answers with No. 3 [X turret] and No. 4 [Y turret] but the remaining two turrets are silent. We are hit by several shells. The deck where the officers' quarters are situated is ablaze and the engine room is also hit.

Bunjes stated that two torpedoes were fired but that only one hit its target, exploding somewhere under A or B turret in the cruiser. As the cruiser swung around to port, *Kormoran*'s engines failed. The distance between the two ships was now 4500 yards. At 1735, a pattern of torpedoes was fired from the starboard side of the cruiser but all four torpedoes passed astern *of Kormoran*. By 1745, the raider had practically lost all way while the cruiser was on fire from stem to stern about 6700 yards distant. Fifteen minutes later, *Kormoran* fired one torpedo in an effort to sink the cruiser. With the cruiser slowly moving away from the raider with a steady course of 120 degrees, the torpedo missed. At 1825, *Kormoran* fired her last salvo when the range was approaching 10 000 yards. Bunjes' account, in dramatic prose, ended with vigour.

> The sea battle has lasted about an hour. We know that our time as an auxiliary cruiser has come to an end. A glorious end, nevertheless, as the victory of an auxiliary cruiser over a cruiser is unique in the history of modern warfare. During the battle the *Kormoran* fired about 600 [5.9]-inch shells and 3 torpedoes and sank a far more powerful opponent, of whose crew of 645 not one was rescued.

As the starboard boats were badly damaged, only those from the port side could be used. Bunjes cast off from *Kormoran* and saw the raider explode shortly after midnight.

The sailors from *Kormoran* did not offer anything particularly noteworthy. One of the radio operators, Pachmann, after a night spent in a cell, stated that *Kormoran* sent two messages when she sighted the cruiser. On both occasions the message was 'QQQ 111 E, 26S 1100 GMT *Straat Malakka*'. During his interrogation, Hans Linke confirmed that *Kormoran* sent out two 'Q' signals before engaging the cruiser after 1600. The position given was 26 degrees S and 111 degrees E. The 'Q' signals were meant to distract the cruiser and were intended to be received in the Dutch East Indies. According to Linke, the first shots were fired three or four minutes after the 'Q' signals were sent. Neither 'Q' signal was acknowledged by a shore station. Linke was adamant that *Kormoran* never sent out SOS or distress signals to lure other ships as a warship might reply. This practice was considered too risky. Linke also stated that no signal had been sent to Germany regarding the action.

When *Kormoran*'s radio equipment was damaged during the engagement, no message could be relayed to SKL. However, the *Beobachtungs-Dienst* (Observation Service), which was part of the German naval intelligence service, had been reading British naval ciphers at the time and was able to pick up details of the action. On 5 December 1941, a *B-Dienst* report revealed that the Germans were aware that *Sydney* had been sunk by one of their auxiliary cruisers off the west coast of Australia around 18 November. On 12 December, *B-Dienst* read a report on the German auxiliary cruiser and the action.

> According to a report by the Australia Admiralty [i.e. Naval Board], the battle between the *Sydney* and the German merchant raider took place 300 nautical miles west of Carnarvon (Western Australia). According to an Admiralty report of 30 November, an extensive search for survivors of *Sydney* was unsuccessful. According to statements by survivors of the merchant raider, the battle lasted two hours.[13]

It appears that the German authorities knew almost as much as the Australians about the action.

While the sailors from *Kormoran* had not expanded on what

the officers were prepared to reveal, their accounts did include some contrasting and conflicting information. The Chief Signalman, Erich Ahlbach, thought that the cruiser had initially signalled 'NNF' or 'NNP'. This occurred when the entire superstructure of the cruiser was visible on the horizon. The cruiser then asked *Straat Malakka*' where she was bound. This signal was sent by light and flag-hoist. The answer given was 'Batavia'—signal letters 'ABKU'. The cruiser then gave a two-flag signal which, according to the 1931 *International Signal Book*, meant 'Have you suffered damage from cyclone, typhoon or tempest?' When no answer was given by *Kormoran*, the action commenced. Ahlbach stated that on the command 'Drop Screens', the German flag was hoisted. This took 'ten to fifteen seconds' while the whole manoeuvre took less than one minute. The statements made by the survivors in *Trocas* made no mention of *Kormoran* making any reply to the cruiser's signals.

Other statements varied in minor respects. For example: Heinz Paul thought that the cruiser was 3500–5000 yards away because he could see people on her upper decks. Tymmers recalled that the cruiser began signalling when the range was 18 miles and took one hour steaming at 30 knots to close *Kormoran*. He thought the action took place when the range was 6000–8000 yards and that the cruiser sank at about 1930. He could not tell who fired first but thought that salvoes were exchanged at 1700. Robert Brune thought that both ships opened fire together. Ehrhardt Otte stated that *Sydney* was slightly aft of *Kormoran* when the gun camouflage screens were lowered. One of the Chinese laundrymen, Shu Ah Fah, stated that *Kormoran* fired three torpedoes and that the torpedoes and rounds from the main armament appeared to hit at the same time. Two other sailors, Hans Bohm and Fritz Noll, and the survivors in *Trocas*, all said that *Kormoran* had fired three torpedoes.

It was difficult to know whom to believe. The information which was obtained before the *Kormoran* survivors were reunited was an obvious means of separating recollections of the action from subsequent reconstructions in the minds of the survivors. A summary of the information obtained from the survivors recovered by *Trocas* was provided to Commander Dechaineux, who bore responsibility for drafting the Naval Intelligence report, as background notes to assist in his preparation of a report for the Naval Board. This group of survivors had had little opportunity to embellish their accounts with details from survivors in other boats. After outlining the genesis of the action, the report noted that the cruiser

> altered course to the westward, closed rapidly, challenging with daylight lamp. Raider made no reply but opened fire when cruiser was within comparatively short range. Estimated range varies from about 1 to 5 or 6 miles. One survivor stated that he could see men on deck of cruiser. First shot from raider hit cruiser's bridge and started fire. Cruiser altered course to port. Survivors stated that it appeared that he intended to ram. Passed close around stern of raider and proceeded on parallel course, gradually drawing ahead on port side of the raider. Cruiser was now heavily on fire in bridge and midships section. Raider also badly damaged and on fire in engineroom area. Hit in engine room, put electrical controls out of action. Literally all electrical equipment, including fire-fighting inoperative. Action commenced at about 1730 and lasted for about one hour.
>
> Raider abandoned ship at about 1900, her reason that fire could not be put out, and it was certain that fire would reach ammunition stowage. Survivors stated that captain and officers were on board when they abandoned ship at about 1900. At this time, cruiser was seen still heavily on fire and shortly afterwards disappeared. No violent explosion was seen or heard. They believe she [was] torpedoed.

Dechaineux accepted the broad details of the accounts given by the *Kormoran* survivors, most notably including Detmers' statement that *Sydney* ordered *Kormoran* to stop. Regarding the signals, he noted that

> *Kormoran* on purpose made a great display of endeavouring to reply and also to comply with the instructions from the *Sydney*. It is reasonable to suppose that this apparent inefficiency in signalling by the

Kormoran was a *ruse de guerre*, in the hope that the *Sydney* would close to investigate.

Dechaineux recorded that the cruiser came 'up on the starboard quarter of *Kormoran* to a distance of about 1,500 yards when the *Kormoran* opened fire, the first salvo hitting the *Sydney*'s bridge'. He accepted that the *Kormoran* did fire two torpedoes but this took place 'shortly after the first salvo', rather than after the eighth or ninth as reported by Detmers. He believed one of these torpedoes probably hit *Sydney*. As for the actions of the Australian ship, Dechaineux explained that '*Sydney*'s first salvo, fired after she was hit, missed the *Kormoran*. The second salvo hit the *Kormoran*'s bridge'.

Of events after the action, Dechaineux stated that 'most evidence seems to show that the cruiser disappeared suddenly and most prisoners believe that she sank before midnight'. The initial order to abandon *Kormoran* was given 'about 1810, when the engineroom personnel got away' rather than between 2000 and 2100 as stated by Detmers. Further, Dechaineux concluded that 'the personnel had ample time to equip the boats very thoroughly' and that *Kormoran* sank around midnight. As the raider's radio had been damaged early in the action, 'no signal was sent to any German authority'. A rubber lifeboat, containing approximately 60 of the men who had survived the action, sank without warning. All were drowned. The remaining two steel lifeboats, located in No. 2 hatch, were difficult to launch because of damaged hydraulic equipment. The raider's final position was 25 degrees 34 minutes S, 111 degrees E. In all, 314 German officers and men, and three Chinese were recovered.

Dechaineux had produced an admirable report which attempted to draw together into a coherent narrative all that the Germans had said. It was completed on 16 January 1942.[14] In reading the final document, one would be inclined to think that there was little variation in the German accounts, such was the certainty with which Dechaineux argued his conclusions. The report did not reveal the deficiency of the interrogations, which were not conducted with a great deal of skill or cunning; furthermore, the report did not attempt to explain *Sydney*'s actions. As a good staff officer, Dechaineux understood that the Naval Board wanted his best assessment of the action and not an admission that little could be proved with any certainty. In fact, the inconsistency of the German accounts left a great deal unexplained.

8

Reservations and Doubts

The *Sydney–Kormoran* engagement won Detmers the coveted Knight's Cross of the Iron Cross but it was an action he would always have wished to avoid. Once his ship was sighted by the more heavily armed Australian cruiser he was left without any choice. Everyone on board was always aware that the raider had to avoid Allied warships at all cost. On the occasions when Detmers believed he had been sighted by British armed merchant cruisers, he fled at speed. *Kormoran*'s assistant surgeon and makeshift dentist, Dr Habben, captured within his diary[1] the feeling of doom which prevailed within the raider when the crew were informed that a cruiser was closing *Kormoran* at high speed:

> First Officer Foerster went through the ship with the hard news that it was a cruiser. The one thought was in every mind, but speaking for myself, I simply could not believe that I was now about to say goodbye to life. All the same, two friends—Engineer Lensch and Medical Mate von der Twer—and I exchanged addresses and last messages to those at home. Von der Twer was lost in subsequent action.
>
> Next thing was to pick up some emergency drugs, and then go back to my cabin, where I pocketed my watch, took off my collar and tie, and put on my white pullover and blue jacket. Having a look through my starboard side porthole window I could just see the approaching cruiser, and that she was repeatedly flashing signals.[2]

Although Detmers wanted to avoid any fight with a warship in which he would have little chance of surviving, he achieved a stunning triumph in sinking *Sydney*. The problem he now faced was convincing the Australian naval authorities that he had observed the rules of war throughout the engagement.

This would not be readily achieved because there were major inconsistencies between the substantial action report prepared by Detmers as a POW and, for instance, the earliest account given by Bunjes. Whereas Detmers stated that *Sydney* turned towards *Kormoran* five minutes after she sighted the raider and approached slowly, Bunjes had claimed that *Sydney* closed *Kormoran* at a speed of 'between 28 to 30 knots'. Bunjes stated that the signal letters for *Straat Malakka* were shown at the same time as the Dutch flag was hoisted although Detmers stated that the Dutch flag was raised approximately one hour after the signal letters at the time *Kormoran* sent the QQQ signal.

There is also disagreement about when and where (relative to the raider) *Sydney* readied her aircraft for launching.

Detmers stated initially that *Sydney* had made the signal 'NNP' by light and that he did not understand the signal. Ahlbach thought it might have been 'NNF'. Neither signal existed. On subsequent interrogation he stated that *Sydney* signalled 'NNJ' but that he could not understand its meaning. It is extremely hard to believe that a raider captain did not know the letters 'NNJ' stood for 'Hoist your signal letters'. Later, Detmers said that he responded immediately to the signal 'NNJ' by hoisting the letters for *Straat Malakka*. Detmers stated in his action report that *Sydney* shut down her aircraft 'and thus had not the least suspicion'. As Montgomery rightly points out, if *Sydney* was not suspicious, there was 'no reason to ask for the secret callsign'.

The suggestion that *Kormoran* was not disguised as *Straat Malakka* but as a Norwegian ship was a curious element in the story. It should be noted that Prime Minister Curtin's statement, which was drafted by the Naval Board,[3] made no mention of *Kormoran* flying any flag. The suggestion that she was, or may have been, flying the Norwegian flag was carried in contemporary newspaper reports. The source appeared to be a 3 December report in the Melbourne *Herald* which was based on information from the newspaper's 'Special Correspondent in Carnarvon'. The *Herald* correspondent, who was not named, stated that the information had come from a similarly unidentified *Kormoran* survivor. The *Age* evidently realised that this information was not correct.

> It is believed that the raider, when approached by *Sydney*, was flying the Dutch flag, and not the Norwegian flag as previously reported. There is no conclusive evidence as to whether the German flag was flown at any time during the action.[4]

However, a *Sydney Morning Herald* leading article on the loss of *Sydney* gave its readers the impression that Curtin had mentioned the Norwegian flag.

The alleged use of the Norwegian flag was later repeated in an article published on 1 January 1942 by journalist Robert Close in *Digest of World Reading*. When asked by Montgomery for the source of this information, Close told Montgomery that he had 'overheard it in a conversation between two military intelligence officers on a bus'. After publication of the article, Close claims he was placed under the *Official Secrets Act*. The fact that civilians in private employment cannot be made subject to the Act seems to have escaped both Montgomery and Close. It is also a pity that Montgomery failed to check whether Close was actually interviewed by military intelligence staff after the publication of the article. It is more likely that, as a hack journalist, Close merely accepted the substance of earlier newspaper reports. The overheard bus conversation was surely not meant to be taken seriously.

The statements by the prisoners from *Mareeba* and *Velebit*, provided later in the war, that *Kormoran* constantly changed her disguise should also be treated with caution. The men from these ships were not in a position to observe the essential elements of *Kormoran*'s disguise and seemed to forget that the raider only flew the Dutch flag during attacks on merchant ships. As the prisoners were held below decks when these attacks were taking place, it is not surprising they did not see the Dutch flag being flown. One of the *Kormoran* survivors, Tymmers, stated that although equipment for disguising *Kormoran* was stowed around the ship, 'they have not been used'.

It was not surprising that most of *Kormoran*'s crew did not know her disguise or, at least, could not be certain about which merchant ship *Kormoran* was meant to be on the day of the action with *Sydney*. One of the few who seemed to know was one of the raider's bosun's mates, Gerhardt Grossman. In his interrogation notes, Captain Farncomb recorded that the disguised *Kormoran* was 'asked her nationality. German replied "Holland" whereupon English ship opened fire'.[5] Of the group of survivors recovered by *Aquitania*, Grossman was the only one to volunteer this information. Most of them did not need to know and, given Detmers' near obsession with secrecy, it is likely that they did not know. Paul Heinz told his interrogators that he did not even know where the ship was at the time of the action.

According to Winter, the allegation of a Norwegian disguise was

> a fabrication by an Australian citizen, based probably on the fact that *Pinguin*, sunk in May 1941, had a Norwegian disguise. No member of the *Kormoran* crew said she was; in fact, there was no Norwegian ship as which she could credibly have been disguised, by reason of appearance, or usual route.[6]

The Australian citizen referred to was Pat Young, the manager of the Gascoyne Trading Company, which provided vehicles to transport the *Kormoran* survivors from the beaches north of Carnarvon. Whereas Young told Montgomery that he had been told by a *Kormoran* survivor that a large painted board bearing the name 'Norge' was hung over the side of the ship as part of the Norwegian disguise, he told Winter that the flag was painted on the *Kormoran*'s hull. Young told Winter in an initial interview that 'he drove up to 27-Mile Well [sic] and Red Bluff alone. Since then he has changed that story too and says he drove up with a companion who fortuitously is dead and can't confirm it either way'. In a letter to West Australian state parliamentarian Ross Lightfoot, Gordon Laffer stated that Young 'has threatened to sue any person who uses his name, particularly Barbara Winter'.[7] It would seem that Pat Young is a rather sensitive individual.

There was no corroborative evidence for the statements made by Young. It is also curious that none of the other *Kormoran* survivors who gave statements prior to being reunited with their officers mentioned the Norwegian disguise or the painted board. The fact that the survivors did not mention the Dutch disguise until later in their interrogation is not evidence that *Kormoran* was at any time flying the Norwegian flag. It is also significant that Norwegian ships were not issued with secret callsigns in November 1941. Burnett would hardly have asked a Norwegian ship to show a callsign he would know she did not have.

Montgomery argues that because *Straat Malakka* had a counter stern and a straight stem and *Kormoran* had a cruiser stern and a curved stem, the raider would obviously not have adopted the disguise of *Straat Malakka*. Instead, she would have adopted the disguise of the Norwegian ship, such as the *Tai Yin*, although that ship bore less resemblance to *Kormoran* than *Straat Malakka*. This is not a realistic objection. These features in *Kormoran*'s design would not have been apparent to another ship until the raider was either in a position to attack, or to be attacked. In the case of her final action, Detmers would have been aware that sailing into the sun with *Sydney* on her starboard quarter would have obscured the fact that *Kormoran* and *Straat Malakka* had dissimilar stern and stem features, and that this would not have been evident until *Sydney* approached the raider's beam. Until then, *Kormoran* would have fitted the general description of *Straat Malakka*. Raider disguises were intended for long-range rather than short-range deception. Detmers could also rely on the shortcomings in Allied shipping intelligence. He could not be sure that his ship had actually been photographed from such a position and with sufficient clarity for all the features of her hull to be readily discernible. Indeed, the appearance of the stern was obscured in a photograph of

Steiermark distributed by the Admiralty in the latter half of 1941. The photograph also showed *Steiermark* with two sets of samson posts fore and aft.

The Australian interrogators considered the possibility that *Kormoran* had used an illegal ploy to sink *Sydney*. Commander Victor Ramage, who was evidently unconvinced by the German accounts, suggested that *Kormoran* may have signalled that her engines were unserviceable or sent an emergency signal for medical assistance. The fact that a *Kormoran* survivor mentioned 'that a boat was seen to be lowered from the cruiser would, if believed, indicate that the cruiser's suspicions had been allayed'.

I believe it is unlikely that on sighting the Australian cruiser *Kormoran* indicated some form of general distress. A vessel seeking assistance would not have continued to sail away from assistance. It is also reasonable to assume that Burnett would have seen such a distress message as an attempt to draw *Sydney* into a gun battle and he would not have suspended the usual challenge procedures.

According to Montgomery, the role of the QQQ signal was also allegedly open to various interpretations.

> In the form that it was picked up in Geraldton, it read '[Begins unintelligible then] 7C 111, 15E 1000 GMT [Greenwich Mean Time]'; if we assume that the figure before the 7 was a 2 and the C was a misreading for an S, then we are given a longitude of 27 degrees south. Such a position compares with the 26 degrees south 111 degrees east which everyone but Linke onwards claimed . . . this very unanimity might be thought suspect, because with the exception of those on the bridge very few of the crew would have had any reason to know the ship's position . . . the most noticeable feature of the QQQ signal position is that it lies at least 30 miles west of the *Sydney*'s usual course to and from Sunda Strait, and the fact that she had been a day late for her rendezvous there leaves no room for thinking that she was taking any but the most direct route back to Fremantle.

Noting that Detmers allegedly waited for some time before he sent the QQQ signal, Montgomery conjectured that *Kormoran* was attempting to have *Sydney* believe that the QQQ signal had come from another ship, not *Kormoran*, and that the primary purpose of the QQQ signal was to 'distract the *Sydney*'s attention from the *Kormoran*'. This possibility had also been suggested by Linke's evidence. It was the possibility, according to Montgomery, that another ship had reported a raider that led Burnett to order the Walrus prepared for launching. This is reflected in Detmers' statement that at 1815, *Sydney* hauled out onto *Kormoran*'s starboard beam, to turn across the wind to launch the Walrus. Her range at this point was about 11 000 yards.

It is possible that the Naval Board initially believed that the QQQ signal was from another ship because of the comment relayed to the Prime Minister on 1 December that two raiders were involved. Although this was discounted on 4 December, the Board may have initially been deceived intentionally by Detmers.

There are objections to the contention that the QQQ signal contained a false position. First, *Sydney*'s direction-finding equipment would have indicated that the signal came from *Kormoran*. Second, it is not surprising that most of the crew were able to cite the position 26 degrees S 111 degrees E because the men in charge of each lifeboat would have been advised of this position when they abandoned *Kormoran* to enable them to judge the general direction in which they needed to proceed, and to give them some idea of the distance they had to travel in order to reach Western Australia. It seems reasonable to believe that they would have repeatedly discussed their whereabouts during the passage from the scene of the action to the coast and that the position they later gave for the action would have been firmly in their minds. Whether or not it was a correct position is another matter.

The fact that the position stated in the QQQ signal was at least 30 miles west of *Sydney*'s 'usual' route, and was therefore a deception can also be given an alternative explanation. It is possible that Burnett may have investigated an unidentified object to the west earlier in the day and *Sydney* was still regaining her track in the late afternoon. He could have had a temporary machinery breakdown and drifted towards the west, or perhaps he wanted to exercise the Walrus aircraft and headed towards the west in the hope of finding some wind.

As *Sydney* was not due in Fremantle until the following day when tugs and support services would be available and there was plenty of time during the night of 19–20 November to make up any distance lost during the day with exercises or other ship's activities, it is quite possible that *Sydney* was to the west of the shortest route from Sunda Strait to Fremantle and possibly steering a zig-zag plan. However, Montgomery is correct when he says that if *Sydney* altered away to starboard at a range of 11 000 yards at 1815, it is not possible for the action to have begun at 1830.

The statement in Detmers' account which provokes the strongest reservation is that it took just six seconds from the time the order to decamouflage was given until the first shot was fired at *Sydney*. While the crew of the *Kormoran* were very efficient in raider operations, they were not as good as that. According to Detmers, on the order to decamouflage:

> The ship's rails folded down, the heavy camouflage covers fore and aft were whisked away, hatches 2 and 4 opened to reveal their guns, the 2-cm anti-aircraft guns were raised, the torpedo flaps opened, and all barrels and torpedo tubes swung onto the target.

Conceding that every preparation had been made before the order to decamouflage was given, it is difficult to believe that the Dutch flag was lowered and the German battle ensign was hoisted by one man, and that this was reported by the same individual to Detmers; and that the ship was decamouflaged and the guns were trained and fired, all within six seconds. Paul Kobelt, who manned the midships 5.9-inch gun on the starboard side, said that 'there was an error in transmission of order [to fire] and he received order to fire on the port side'. Bunjes stated during interrogation the sequence of events described by Detmers took something nearer to one minute to complete while von Gosseln stated that it took nearer to 45 seconds for the heavier guns to be trained outboard from their position fore and after behind the camouflage.

The claim that decamouflage action took six seconds, and that *Sydney* did not seem to be at action stations, far too conveniently explains how *Kormoran* was able to decamouflage and fire on *Sydney* without it resulting in any action from *Sydney*. It was standard procedure for warships to go to action stations whenever a suspicious ship was sighted. Indeed, this was shown to be Burnett's practice. Under this regime, all of the ship's weapon systems are fully manned by specialised personnel. The main and after director towers are operational. The range of *Kormoran* would have been called and the raider placed in the centre of the master gun-sight operated by the Chief Gunner's Mate. The turrets would have been manned and personnel closed up in the shell rooms and magazines. The crews of the secondary armament would have readied their guns for firing. A well-trained and worked-up ship's company would take only a few minutes to man action stations. When this state of readiness was achieved, the Gunnery Officer would be closed up at his action station, while the Navigator and Captain would be on the bridge.

Given the earlier sequence of events and the suspicion Burnett would have had of the unidentified ship, it is to be expected that *Sydney* would have been closed up at action stations with guns loaded, cocked and ready to fire on *Kormoran* at the order from Burnett relayed through the Gunnery Officer, Lieutenant Commander Singer. Through the high-power optics used in *Sydney*'s gunnery control system, the gunnery staff would have been able to see practically every movement on board *Kormoran* that was not obscured by her superstructure.

However, it appears that despite the Australian cruiser's high level of readiness, *Kormoran* was able to decamouflage in six seconds, apparently without provoking any reaction in *Sydney*. But the first salvo at least failed to reach its target. Thus, by the time the gun's crews in *Kormoran* were able to assess the fall of shot, reload and adjust their fire, the elapsed time would have been approaching thirty seconds. And yet, Detmers claimed that there was no answer from *Sydney*'s guns. Detmers' statement that he could see the 'pantrymen in their white coats' walking along *Sydney*'s deck for a look at *Straat Malakka* and that the scene was a particularly peaceful one suggests a conscious desire to create the mood in which his unlikely account could be accepted. The innocence with which Detmers attempts to portray this mood appears too deliberate and too necessary to the rest of his story to be accepted as fact.

Perhaps unexpectedly, there is little consistency in statements about where *Kormoran*'s first salvo landed, when she fired her torpedoes, and when *Sydney* finally returned fire. One of the survivors recovered by *Koolinda* stated while the ship was proceeding to Carnarvon that 'the cruiser [*Sydney*] opened fire first and we retaliated'. Other survivors made the same statement.

The other major problem in Detmers' account is reconciling the various statements about how many torpedoes were fired at *Sydney*. Opinion was evenly divided between two and three. In its signal to the Admiralty in London on 27 November, the Naval Board had concluded that three were fired. If it were two, it is probable that both were fired from the above-water tubes. If three were fired, it is almost certain that the third came from the starboard underwater tube. The use of this tube is not inconsistent with the available evidence. Detmers stated in a later account that for the underwater tubes to be used with any accuracy, *Kormoran* had to be nearly stationary. How, then, could he fire successfully at *Sydney* if his ship was steaming at 14 knots? The strong evidence that *Sydney* was torpedoed below her two forward turrets suggests that *Kormoran* was stopped in the water by the time *Sydney* was abeam at 1200 yards.

The claim that it took six seconds for *Kormoran* to fire guns *and* torpedoes is also inconsistent with other evidence concerning the moment during the action when a torpedo from *Kormoran* struck *Sydney*. If it took six seconds to fire the guns, and Dechaineux is correct that the torpedo hit *Sydney* between the first and second salvoes rather than after the eighth as claimed by Detmers, the torpedo must have struck *Sydney* no more than thirty seconds after Detmers gave the order to fire. However, at a range of 1200 yards the torpedo would take approximately one minute to hit its target. Therefore, it must have been fired before the order was given to the main armament to fire, and while the Dutch flag was still flying. The Admiralty thought 'it was possible that the *Kormoran* opened fire with an underwater torpedo before declaring herself'.[8]

There was a paucity of detail in Detmers' accounts about how *Kormoran* was sunk. It appears from a general reading that one shell hit the after end of *Kormoran*'s bridge and another the engine room near the waterline, and that these were largely responsible for the loss of the ship. However, in an engineroom log which was taken to Germany by Dr Habben when he was repatriated in 1943, it appeared that there were:

Several hits in main engine room. One shell tore the forward tank bulkhead badly open. A thick jet of burning fuel oil poured into the room, which was rapidly filled with dense smoke. The main fire extinguisher pipe was punctured on either side of the room, and the same time the whole foam extinguisher plant which had been transferred to the starboard side went out of action. An explosion on the starboard side rendered the transformers unserviceable, thereby putting the electrical drive for the main generators and propulsion motors, and thus the whole of the main engine installation, out of action.

The post-action sequence of events was also the subject of considerable variation. The times given for the abandonment of *Kormoran* range from around 2000, which approximated to sunset, and midnight. Linke stated that the order to abandon ship was given at around 2000 when *Sydney*, by his estimation, was 8000 yards away. When the ship was abandoned, 'the boats rowed towards the cruiser in the hope of being picked up; she was on fire amidships and astern, and disappeared so suddenly that she was believed sunk'. It is possible that Linke's latter observation was of *Sydney* passing over the horizon beyond view although another survivor spoke of the cruiser exploding as they rowed towards her in the hope of being picked up. It appeared as though there was no aspect of the engagement on which the *Kormoran* survivors were in complete agreement.

Attempts by the Australian naval authorities to reconcile the many conflicting statements in the German accounts could not be considered successful. The first Admiralty account of the action was Battle Summary No. 13, entitled Actions with Enemy Disguised Raiders. It was produced by the Historical Section of the Admiralty in 1942 from information provided by the RAN. For the benefit of the Fleet, the publication included a detailed discussion of the *Sydney–Kormoran* action (the information being derived solely from signal M.05540/42) as an illustration of how raiders should not be approached.

The Summary stated that the version of action provided by the Germans bears all the marks of a bona fide account. However, the Admiralty conceded that the Germans could not explain 'why the *Sydney* came so close before opening fire or attempting to launch her aircraft'. It went on to state that after sighting *Kormoran, Sydney*

for half an hour, as she approached, repeatedly signalled NNJ, but Commander Detmers had no idea what NNJ meant and did not reply . . . When the range had closed to 7 miles the *Sydney* ordered the *Kormoran* in plain language to hoist her signal letters and the raider hoisted PKQJ, the letters of the *Straat Malakka* . . .

The *Sydney* had all guns and tubes trained when she came up with the *Kormoran*. In reply to her signal 'Where bound?' the *Kormoran* replied: 'Batavia'. The *Sydney* then apparently hoisted the letters IK, which the raider was unable to understand as in the International Code they mean 'You should prepare for a cyclone, hurricane or typhoon'. They were, in fact, the second and third letters of the *Straat Malakka*'s secret callsign IIKP. The *Sydney* then ordered the *Kormoran* to show her secret letters.

The significance of the two-flag hoist 'IK' will be considered later in this book. The Admiralty evidently accepted that *Sydney* was on the raider's starboard beam and that the two ships were on parallel courses separated by 2000 yards. But again the question must be asked, was the Admiralty justified in attributing so much reliability to potentially misleading evidence from an enemy?

When considering the German accounts in their entirety, one is struck by two things. First, that many of the German survivors had stated during interrogation that they saw things which they could not and did not actually observe. Even the account of Bunjes, which appears to have been offered in the hope of courting favour with his captors, includes such selective detail that one must conclude that Bunjes was relaying what he had been told in addition to what he had seen.

It has been alleged that Bunjes was nominated by *Kormoran*'s officers to provide a detailed, concocted account. But the arguments for this are thin. Bunjes provided his account while he was in *Yandra* and could not assume that he would have an opportunity, if reunited with his fellow officers prior to interrogation, to make certain they all gave the same information. Indeed, Rycroft noted that he was kept alone while on board *Yandra*. If Bunjes was nominated to give a false account the morning after the engagement when his boat met the lifeboat carrying most of *Kormoran*'s officers, the other survivors in Bunjes' boat would have overheard the details of the false account and their statements would have been more consistent with Bunjes' account than they were.

His willingness to give evidence should also be considered in the context in which it was made. He was conscripted into the *Kriegsmarine*; he had spent nearly one year at sea; he had been treated with some disdain on board the raider; he had probably been accused of responsibility for the wire hawser wrapping around *Kormoran*'s propellers in Stavanger; he had been relieved in command of the lifeboat by the much younger von Gosseln whom he did not like. If von Gosseln did jump overboard from the burning *Kormoran* out of fear rather than as a last resort as Lensch alleged, Bunjes would not have held von Gosseln in very high regard. It is also possible that von Gosseln's enthusiasm for Nazism had worn Bunjes down during the days they had spent together in the lifeboat. While Bunjes' account was not completely reliable, it was probably a truthful statement of what Bunjes thought or was told had happened.

Hearsay was apparent elsewhere. Some of the statements made by the *Kormoran* survivors, especially the sailors, suggest that some of them were 'fed' information which they assumed was factual and which they later repeated as incontestable fact. Some suspicion of the reliability of the German accounts is therefore justified. It is likely, however, that the true circumstances of the loss of *Sydney* are contained within the statements provided by the Germans. There is sufficient consistency in the broad details of their accounts to make them generally reliable while there is sufficient inconsistency in minor details to suggest that their recollections are not wholesale fabrications or entirely reliant upon a single source.

Yet it would be very easy for one or two key events in the action to be absent from the composite account prepared from all the German statements. These events could have been observed by as few as four or five individuals in *Kormoran* and could be the key in making *Sydney*'s actions explicable. This possibility has to be admitted and kept open until positively excluded by evidence or analysis. If, for instance, a key element in the action was known only by Detmers and von Gosseln, and they chose to conceal this element during interrogation, the extent of German deception was minor although its consequences were major. Indeed, von Gosseln later stated that only he, as Battle Watch Officer, and Detmers were on the bridge as *Sydney* approached. Thus, a major conspiracy among the *Kormoran* survivors to conceal the true circumstances was unnecessary. Detmers was a secretive captain who told his men only what they needed to know. He could rely on the ignorance of most of them about a key detail and the discretion of the very small number who did know, to ensure this element remained concealed.

There is no clearly evident *pattern* of deception in the German accounts. This is confirmed by the same general inconsistency of statements offered by the group of German sailors who were recovered by *Aquitania* and interrogated on two occasions by Farncomb with those offered by sailors who had been reunited

with the raider's officers. The *Aquitania* group, who had no further contact with their shipmates after the action, stated that the
firing began when the two ships were between 1500 and 3000
yards apart, and that the first salvo from *Kormoran* hit *Sydney*'s
bridge. According to evidence obtained from Fritz Treber who
manned one of the 5.9-inch guns, *Sydney* opened fire 15 seconds
after *Kormoran*. This was possibly after the raider's 'second
salvo, although there was some doubt on this latter point'.[10] The
doubt had come from the account of Eugen Frohlich who thought
that *Sydney* fired first. According to the information Farncomb
obtained, 'on about *Kormoran*'s fifteenth salvo, *Sydney* ceased
fire, but opened up again shortly afterwards, apparently firing
two salvoes. The action with *Sydney* lasted about an hour'.[11]
Hans Hess thought that the action started at 1600 and ended at
1700 but the others felt it was nearer to 1830 when the order
was given to abandon ship. Farncomb was led to believe *Kormoran* exploded three hours after her men had taken to lifeboats
and rafts although Max Hahnert stated that the raider sank at
1800. He was also able to confirm that the raider had not rendezvoused with either Vichy French or Japanese merchant ships
since leaving Germany.

Edgar Blau,[12] who served as a midshipman in *Canberra* under
Farncomb in late 1941, acted as an interpreter during the interrogations because the RAN had only one other officer who had
been trained as a German linguist.

There were about ten men, none of whom appeared to be officers.
This is what they revealed: *Sydney* steamed to within one mile of *Kormoran* and kept station on her and commenced signalling. *Kormoran*
simultaneously opened fire with her camouflaged guns and submerged
torpedo tubes. As *Sydney* was virtually at point blank range, the gun
and torpedo crews could choose at will the most effective targets with
no risk of missing ... The guns destroyed the compass platform, all
but one of the gun turrets and main director, and the torpedoes struck
the engine room, boiler room and fuel tanks, rendering *Sydney* virtually immobile, disarmed and devoid of command.[13]

Blau was also able to describe the circumstances and spirit in which this information was given.

> I would like to emphasise that the evidence was given reasonably will-ingly except for one man who was obviously a political appointee, who saluted Captain Farncomb with a 'Heil Hitler' and refused to give any information apart from his name, service number and home address. To my mind there was no sign of pre-arranged and misleading answers, and some of the seamen showed symptoms of distress and sympathy for the victims of the *Sydney*.[14]

In his first interrogation report, which was forwarded to the Naval Board on 8 December, Farncomb stated that

> several of them were inclined to talk a lot about the action, but it was considered that most of their information was hearsay. Their morale appeared to be good; one or two of them were obviously strongly Nazi. One stated that he was a member of the SS.[15]

After the second interviews, Farncomb found that the *Kormoran* survivors were even more willing to discuss the action, 'although some were very surly. One, Fritz Treber, was particularly loqua-cious on the subject. He also seemed fairly intelligent'.[16] The evidence of these survivors who were not reunited with their countrymen was sufficiently varied to discount the suggestion that all of *Kormoran*'s crew had been coached into giving the 'right' answers. Indeed, Farncomb later wrote that: 'In view of their dispersion, the possibility of collusion among them to fake the account of the action can be ruled out entirely.'[17]

The statements made by the vast majority of survivors were not offered with the discernible intention of deceiving the Aus-tralian authorities or persuading them to believe a massive lie. However, many of the *Kormoran* survivors were unable or unwilling to separate recollection from post-action reconstruc-tion. In this vital respect, their evidence was flawed.

Indeed, it is likely that Detmers and von Gosseln were probably the crew's source of much information about the engagement in the hours before they were separated. If they chose not to reveal one key element, and if those whose knowledge was second-hand or hearsay spoke and relayed it as if it were a first-hand eye-witness account, a composite account which was substantially correct in all its details—with the possible notable exception of the key detail—would be accepted by the Australian interrogators. Thus, if the German accounts do not seem to provide any logic for *Sydney*'s movements or if the accounts are not entirely factual, the suspect area is likely to be minor and in the form of an omitted detail.

But by mid-1942, the RAN had both the European and Pacific Wars to fight and had to scale down its inquiries into the loss of *Sydney*. While the broad details of the German accounts seem to have been accepted by the Naval Board in early 1942, they obviously felt that the entire story might not have been told. Listening devices were placed in the POW quarters while attempts were made to infiltrate the camps with Australian agents. Neither method obtained any useful information. At any rate, there were no new avenues to explore. The enemy governments were certainly giving nothing away. Accounts of the action appeared in the Axis press; first in the Vichy *De Jour* in September 1942 and in the *Voelkischer Beobachter* on 10 August 1944. They added nothing new.

In 1943, Detmers learned that he had been promoted to the rank of captain. This made him the senior officer in the Dhurringile camp, although he had already been elected Camp Leader. It was acting in this capacity that he probably planned the escape attempt on 11 January 1945. With 19 other officers, Detmers broke out of the camp through a tunnel which had taken the German officers seven months to construct. All of the POWs were recovered within 50 miles of the camp. Detmers was one of the least successful escapees. When he was recaptured 20 miles from the camp 12 days after his escape, a coded diary was found in his possession. Neither Australian nor British analysts to whom it was subsequently passed could decipher the code. However, Detmers was given 28 days detention at the rather inhospitable Old Melbourne Gaol. Shortly after his return to

Dhurringile, Detmers suffered a stroke that left him partly paralysed. As strokes are not common in men aged 42, the otherwise healthy Detmers was evidently under some stress. He was taken to Heidelberg Military Hospital in Melbourne and spent three and a half months regaining the use of his body.

There were, however, several new developments when the war ended. On 2 February 1945, Detmers revealed that Dr List had taken a series of photographs of the *Sydney–Kormoran* action in progress but had buried his camera with the film still inside in a cave near Red Bluff. A search for the camera was unsuccessful. In 1947, shortly before the *Kormoran* survivors were to be repatriated to Germany, the Australian guards at Dhurringile discovered a diary referring to the *Sydney–Kormoran* action written by the raider's Administrative Officer, Lieutenant Commander Bretschneider. It was an interesting account which showed the hallmarks of being largely a composite account produced from evidence gleaned from the survivors to whom Bretschneider had access.

Bretschneider stated that *Sydney* started signalling immediately after she appeared to turn towards *Kormoran*, and that once identified as an Australian cruiser, there was 'no escape for us, and only a faint hope that we shall be able to deceive her'.[18] This conflicted with Ahlbach's statement that *Sydney* waited until she was seven miles from *Kormoran* before signalling 'NNJ'. The diary stated that at some point between 20 000 yards and 8000 yards, *Sydney* apparently signalled 'What ship?' and was given the reply '*Straat Malakka*'. This suggests that *Sydney* was possibly making some other signal before she started sending 'NNJ'. At 1700 with *Sydney* at 1000 yards abeam travelling on a parallel course, the cruiser 'demand[ed] information regarding destination and cargo'. After answering by flag, Bretschneider stated that

> we think our replies must be satisfactory for the cruiser's seaplane is swung inboard, although the muzzles of four 6-inch turrets still point in our direction. But when figures were observed onboard *Sydney*, von Gosseln waved his cap from *Kormoran*'s bridge in deceptive greeting.

Just when it seemed as though the cruiser might turn away, there came a final order at 1725 for us to hoist our Code or Secret Call Sign. This, of course, we could not do, so fate took a hand. Using surprise and speed our commander decided to attack.

There was no prize for guessing the alleged period of time Bretschneider stated that it took *Kormoran* to decamouflage—six seconds! Bretschneider also claimed: 'the first salvo scores all hits; and is followed by another and another. The opponent answers with a full salvo, which, however, misses us'. This is inconsistent with earlier evidence in three respects. First, that every shot fired in the first salvo struck *Sydney*. Second, that *Sydney* fired a full salvo. Third, there is no mention of the successful torpedo strike, which is curious given its dramatic effect on *Sydney*'s movement. The remainder of the account added little to what was known of post-action events.

In anticipation of the departure of the Germans from Australia in January 1947, the Director of Naval Intelligence in Melbourne asked his equivalent at the Admiralty to have the *Kormoran* survivors searched on their arrival in Germany. It appeared the Australian naval authorities were still hopeful of uncovering new revelations about the action.

From reports received from POW camps in Australia where survivors from the raider *Kormoran* were held, it is understood that the above survivors produced a secret official report regarding the *Sydney–Kormoran* action. It is believed that this report is being transmitted to Germany, and it would appear probable that attempts will be made to turn it over to the German Admiralty, or such skeleton organisation as is in existence.[19]

The *Kormoran* survivors boarded the steamer *Orontes* in Port Phillip Bay on 21 January 1947. In what must have seemed ironic even to the Germans, the ship at the adjacent pier was the Dutch freighter *Straat Malakka*. When the survivors arrived in Cuxhaven in Germany, the temperature was well below zero. One of the Australian soldiers who guarded the large group of

Italian and German POWs during the passage recalled that on arriving at Cuxhaven, 'the sea was absolutely frozen and ice-breakers were being used to clear the harbour'.[20] The Germans were thoroughly searched on arrival.

A selection of papers was seized and forwarded to Melbourne. It included a typewritten report on the 19 November action by Petty Officer Otto Jurgensen; diaries written by Lieutenant Commanders von Malapert and Diebitsch,[21] and accounts written by Detmers, Bunjes and Karl Heinz.[22] After having the German accounts translated and assessed, the Australian naval intelligence concluded that 'whilst no new information has resulted from research carried out on the documents, they have confirmed previous information held'.[23]

This marked the end of Australian hopes of obtaining any further information on the loss of *Sydney*. The mystery loss of Australia's best-known and most-loved warship was to pass into the hands of historians.

9

The Post-Mortem

Kormoran's success against Sydney and presence in Australian waters were not entirely unexpected. Before the war began in September 1939, the Naval Board recognised that Australia would have to deal with the threat of German raiders. Within the first 12 months of the war, there was no doubt that protection was needed for shipping around the Australian coastline, and in the littoral waters of the two adjacent ocean basins. However, the number of ships and maritime reconnaissance aircraft available to patrol the shipping lanes was extremely limited. Throughout most of 1940, only four ships remained on the Australian and New Zealand Stations—the cruisers HMAS Hobart and HMS Achilles, the obsolete Australian cruiser Adelaide and the armed merchant cruiser HMAS Manoora.[1]

It did not take long for the German raiders to start their campaign. The liner SS Niagara was sunk by a mine laid by Ship 36, also known as Orion (7800 tons), four hours out of Auckland on 18 June 1940. The mines had been laid three to four days earlier.[2] Also on 18 June, Orion had another success, capturing the Norwegian Tropic Sea. The Free French collier SS Notou was sunk off Moreton Island, east of Brisbane, on 16 August. The large freighter SS Turakina sent a raider report four days later from a position 900 miles to the south. Turakina refused to stop when ordered and was fired on by the main armament of Orion. This short action in which the freighter was sunk and 36 people were killed was the first recorded naval action in the

Tasman Sea. The cruisers HMS *Achilles* and HMAS *Perth* were despatched to locate the raider, which managed to elude them. The worst was yet to come.

There was constant raider activity in Australian waters from October 1940 until the end of the year. In addition to *Orion*, the Naval Board suspected that Ship 45, also known as *Komet* (3287 tons), was operating in the Australian Station with the supply ship *Kulmerland*.

Komet entered the Pacific from the Arctic Sea through the Bering Strait in August 1940 and sank SS *Ringwood* two months later near Nauru. In a memorandum to the Minister for the Navy, Billy Hughes, the Naval Board stated that Nauru was remote from Australia and undefended. To avoid making shipping anchored off the island attractive to raider captains, the Board had earlier tried to regulate shipping movements to avoid any concentration of shipping in and around Nauru. These instructions were evidently not implemented adequately. The Chief of Naval Staff, Admiral Colvin, considered that:

> In view of the importance of trade to Australia and New Zealand, sufficient protection must be given to the Islands and the route to enable this trade to continue. As the trade concerns Australia and New Zealand equally, arrangements are being made between [the Australian] Naval Board and the New Zealand Naval Board for an armed merchant cruiser to be made available in the vicinity for the immediate future. Sailings which have been temporarily suspended will be resumed as soon as detailed movements of this armed merchant cruiser can be arranged.[3]

On being joined by *Orion*, *Komet* and *Kulmerland* sailed south and sank *Holmwood* and the 16 000-ton liner *Rangitane* in late November in New Zealand waters. The three ships returned to Nauru and sank five ships—the British *Triona*, *Triadic*, *Triaster* and *Komata*, and the Norwegian *Vinni*—over a two-day period in early December. The armed merchant cruiser that Colvin had mentioned was not yet available. These merchant ships had provided a tempting target as they anchored off Nauru waiting for favourable weather to come alongside. The raiders landed 343 European and 171 Chinese and native prisoners at Emirau Island in the Bismarck Archipelago. On 27 December, the phosphate plant and jetties at Nauru were shelled; this destroyed a stock-pile of phosphate belonging to Japan. Loading of phosphate was disrupted for the next ten weeks.

Komet then headed for the New Zealand–Panama trade route and went within sight of Antarctica. She met with *Pinguin* and her consort tender, *Adjutant*, and the supply ship *Alstertor* at the Kerguelen Islands before a fruitless cruise into the Indian Ocean which lasted until May 1941. *Komet* and *Adjutant* returned to the Pacific where, on 14 August, *Komet* sank the *Australind* north-east of Wellington. This was the raider's first victim in eight months. In the five days that followed, *Komet* captured the Dutch *Kota Nopan* and sank *Devon*. To avoid encounter-ing a warship, *Komet* turned to the south and rendezvoused with *Atlantis* which had returned to the Pacific. After this great success, *Komet* sailed for the South Atlantic without mounting any further attacks. She arrived in Hamburg on 30 November. *Orion* had departed from the Marianas in February 1941 bound for the Indian Ocean. After several months without success, she was ordered back to Germany and sank one ship in transit. This had been her only success in nine months.

Ship 33, also known as *Pinguin* (7766 tons), had entered the Indian Ocean in August 1940 and quickly sank four ships—*Filefjell*, *British Commander*, *Morviken* and *Benavon*—near Madagascar. MS *Nordvard* and SS *Storstad* were taken as prize vessels on 15 September and 7 October respectively, the latter off Exmouth Gulf, Western Australia. Moving south of the Aus-tralian continent into coastal transit waters *Pinguin* laid mines and succeeded in sinking another four ships—*Nimbin*, *Hertford*, *Cambridge* and *City of Rayville*. Returning to the central Indian Ocean, the raider sank a further four ships—*Nowshera*, *Mai-moa*, *Port Brisbane* and *Port Wellington*—before disappearing into the South Atlantic. Three months later, *Pinguin* returned to the Indian Ocean but remained in the Arabian Sea where she sank three ships—*Empire Light*, *Clan Buchanan* and *British*

Emperor—before being sunk by the heavy cruiser HMS *Cornwall* on 8 May 1941 north-east of the Seychelles. *Pinguin* had sunk 31 ships totalling 156,000 tons.

A second raider was operating in the Indian Ocean during *Pinguin*'s successful deployment. Ship 16, known as *Atlantis*, entered the Indian Ocean in May 1940 after passing the Cape of Good Hope. For the next ten months, *Atlantis* operated in the approaches to the Sunda Strait in the Dutch East Indies, and in the southern half of the Indian Ocean sinking thirteen ships— *Tirranna, City of Bagdad, Kemmendine, Talleyrand, King City, Athelking, Benarty, Commissaire Ramel, Durmitor, Teddy, Ole Jacob, Automedon* and *Mandasor*—between 10 June 1940 and 24 January 1941. Two ships, *Speybank* and *Ketty Brovig*, were taken as prize vessels on 31 January and 2 February respectively, with *Ketty Brovig* remaining in the Indian Ocean as a supply vessel for raider operations. After a rendezvous to the east of Madagascar with the pocket battleship *Admiral Scheer* on 16 February 1941, *Atlantis* returned to the Atlantic where she was sunk nine months later by the heavy cruiser HMS *Devonshire*. *Admiral Scheer* re-fuelled from *Ketty Brovig* during the February 1941 rendezvous with *Atlantis* near Seychelles. Four days later she captured the tanker *British Advocate*. After sinking another three ships—*Grigorios C. II, Canadian Cruiser* and *Rantau Pandang*—the pocket battleship made for the Atlantic three days later.

Admiral Scheer had earlier become the focus of Allied attention in the western Indian Ocean when an intelligence report indicated on 3 February that she had entered the ocean basin. Although a flotilla of Allied ships, including *Canberra*, rapidly closed her last known position, the pocket battleship managed to elude them and returned to the South Atlantic. However, it was believed that a supply ship and a raider were probably still in the northern Indian Ocean. On 4 March while patrolling to the north of the Saya de Malha Banks near Seychelles, *Canberra* launched her Walrus aircraft to make an aerial search for German ships. Just before 1700, the aircraft reported sighting a tanker with what appeared to be a raider in company.

On being sighted, the two ships separated. The suspected raider, *Coburg*, moved to the north while the tanker, *Ketty Brovig*, headed south. *Coburg* was a 7400-ton German supply ship.[4] Her consort on this occasion, *Ketty Brovig*, was a prize vessel captured by *Atlantis* mentioned earlier. Captain Farncomb in *Canberra* altered course towards the two suspect ships and increased speed to 25 knots. He ordered both ships to stop but this was ignored even after warning shots from the heavy cruiser's 8-inch guns were fired. Being unsure as to the maximum range of the suspected raider's armament and fearing a torpedo attack, *Canberra* opened fire on *Coburg* at 21 000 yards. The Australian cruiser kept beyond 19 000 yards until *Coburg* was seen to be on fire. Even after her fate seemed assured, Farncomb kept his distance from *Coburg* because he was 'still suspicious of a "booby trap" in the merchant ship in the shape of a couple of torpedoes'.[5]

While this surface action was taking place, *Canberra*'s Walrus aircraft was attempting to make *Ketty Brovig* stop by dropping bombs close to the tanker. When *Ketty Brovig* did heave to, scuttling action was well underway and the tanker was being abandoned. To prevent her loss, the Walrus landed on the sea and its observer, Lieutenant Malleson, jumped into the water and boarded the ship despite the presence of sharks. After making a quick search for code books and ciphers, Malleson believed the tanker could be saved and requested a salvage party. They faced a daunting task with little hope of success. Deciding that the ship was a lost cause, *Canberra* hastened the end *of Ketty Brovig* with several 4-inch rounds after her composite German, Norwegian and Chinese crew were recovered. Survivors from *Coburg* were rescued earlier by the light cruiser HMS *Leander*, which had arrived in the area.

The action had been an important one for the Australian ship because it was, in the words of her captain, 'an excellent rehearsal for the real thing, with the added advantage that the enemy was unable to profit by our errors'. These errors, consisting of various minor mistakes in gunnery drills, resulted in *Canberra* firing 215 8-inch rounds at the hapless enemy ships which it was later

learned had started scuttling action when *Canberra* fired her
warning shots. Despite the hollowness of her success, the sinking of *Ketty Brovig* was achieved without her loss being known
to the Germans for over two months. With one less tanker and
one less supply ship, German raider operations were curtailed
for the next few months. However, the auxiliary cruisers had
already achieved great success.

In 1940 alone, German raiders had sunk 54 ships totalling
366,644 tons. In the first two years of the war, German raiders had sunk one cruiser (*Sydney*), one armed merchant cruiser
(*Alcantara*) and 98 ships totalling over 620,000 tons. This was
an improvement on the performance of German raiders in the
1914–18 war in which ten armed merchant raiders sank 427,433
tons. Much of this total had been due to the success of *Emden*.
Of the eleven raiders that put to sea in World War I, four were
sunk, three were interned, one was wrecked and the other three
managed to return to Germany.

The number of ships sunk by raiders in 1941 also exceeded
the tonnage sunk by mines and other surface combatant ships.
However, it was well behind the submarine figure of 2,172,000
tons and of aircraft, 1,017,400 tons. There were other measures of success. Of the seven raiders the Allies had identified,
only three had been sunk. Therefore, the German capacity for
raider warfare was still intact although altered shipping patterns changed the scope of operations. By the end of 1940, the
Naval Board believed that the threat of German raider operations was more serious in the Atlantic than in the Pacific and
Indian Oceans:

> In general, their policy has been to attack unescorted shipping on the
> trade routes well away from terminal ports and focal areas. By so
> doing, they avoid our naval forces guarding such areas and also air
> force reconnaissance and striking forces which are only able to oper-
> ate for a limited distance from their aerodromes. Their policy has the
> grave disadvantage from the German point of view that our ships are
> scattered over wide expanses of ocean and difficult to find, and their
> victims are thus less frequent. They have endeavoured to meet this

difficulty to some extent by the use of aircraft by raiding ship to locate and report our merchant ships.[6]

The Naval Board did not believe that raiders posed any threat to Australian ports or troop convoys. Both were too well protected to attract raiders. General shipping provided a different problem:

No ships have been lost due to raider action (not mine-laying) within air striking distance of the Australian coast. Evasive routing and dispersal of shipping across the Indian and Pacific Oceans is employed. Air and naval cover is given on the coast and within the focal areas. The problem of protection on the trade routes outside coastal and focal areas is largely outside Australian naval responsibility—the Admiralty are tackling this problem as they can make ships available for hunting, and the Naval Board propose carrying out patrols in trade routes outside air striking distance on the Australian Station.[7]

By this time, the Admiralty had achieved great success in combating the raiders. The key in removing this threat was exemplified in the theoretical writings of the great American naval strategist, Admiral Alfred Mahan. Before World War I Mahan stated that 'When the enemy confines himself to commerce destroying . . . then the true military policy is to stamp out the nest where they [in this case German raiders] swarm.' When this principle was applied in 1941, the official British naval historian, Captain Stephen Roskill, remarked

we caught no less than ten German supply ships in the Atlantic, and that drastically curtailed the raiders' operations. Though the last disguised raider was not accounted for until October 1943, they did not cause us serious concerns after the end of 1941.[8]

However, the Admiralty did not know that the raider threat was going to decline after 1941.

In addition to being a vitally important matter for the Australian people, the unlikely loss of *Sydney* forced the Naval Board to re-examine the threat of German auxiliary cruisers. It also prompted a reconsideration of Admiralty operational policy. As the threat of German raiders was a continuing one, the Admiralty needed to re-state and re-define its strategy while advising seagoing captains on the approach to be taken in sinking these ships.

Of course, raiders were not a new problem. During World War I, the Allied navies had numerous encounters with German raiders. One action, involving the converted British armed merchant cruiser HMAS (formerly SS) *Alcantara* and the German commerce raider *Greif* in the North Sea on 28 February 1916, appeared to be very similar to the *Sydney–Kormoran* action. After approaching within torpedo range of a suspicious contact, *Alcantara* was torpedoed but managed to fire on *Greif* before she sank. The German ship was later sunk by the armed merchant cruiser *Andes*. The immediate lesson to be drawn from this action was the necessity of remaining beyond torpedo range. Earlier in the war (8 August 1915), the armed boarding steamer *Ramsey* was torpedoed in the Moray Firth by the disguised German minelayer *Meteor*. This prompted the Commander-in-Chief of the Grand Fleet, Admiral Sir John Jellicoe, to issue special instructions for the handling of suspicious vessels. They were to approach on the quarter, avoid bearings on which torpedoes could be fired, and to direct the master of a suspected vessel to bring his ship's papers to the interrogating warship in his own boat. The general practice was revived in World War II and required very few alterations.

There were five major actions involving Allied warships and German raiders in the period before *Sydney* encountered *Kormoran*. Each was significant in establishing the possible actions taken by Burnett on sighting *Kormoran*, and in passing judgment on his actions, assuming the main facts of the German accounts.

In July 1940, intelligence was relayed to Rear Admiral Sir Henry Harwood, commanding the South America Division with his flag flying in HMS *Hawkins*, that a German raider was sighted in the North Atlantic and was possibly bound for the

South Atlantic. When direction-finder (D/F) bearings of the raider's radio transmissions indicating a position to the west of the Cape Verde Islands were obtained on 15 July, Admiral Harwood despatched the armed merchant cruiser (AMC) HMS *Alcantara* (the second converted merchant ship to serve in the Royal Navy with that name and not be confused with her Great War namesake) from her patrol in the Rio de Janeiro–Santos area to the waters off Pernambuco while *Hawkins* would occupy the AMC's former station. By the time Harwood estimated the raider would have passed Pernambuco, the two ships would return to their respective former stations. This would provide adequate protection for the shipping focal area adjacent to the Plate River.

The following day, Harwood learned that two British merchantmen, *Davisian* and *King John*, had been sunk by a German raider in the Caribbean, probably on 13 July. When coupled with the news that the German tanker *Rekum* had sailed from Teneriffe on 17 July, Harwood had good reason to believe that the raider was heading towards his station. Assuming the D/F bearings received on 15 July were correct, the raider should have been to the south of Pernambuco by late 22 July. Accordingly, he signalled to *Alcantara* at 1630 that she should patrol the waters to the south-west of Trinidad Island, 250 miles off the South American coast. After re-fuelling on 23 July, *Hawkins* patrolled the shipping routes between Rio de Janeiro and the River Plate. Two days later, the tactical appreciation changed completely when news was received that a U-boat had sunk a Norwegian tanker near the Cape Verde Islands on 18 July. This suggested that the D/F bearing obtained on 15 July was probably a U-Boat and that the raider was still undetected. Further intelligence advised that there were probably two raiders at sea, one in the West Indies and the other in, or heading for, the South Atlantic.

With *Hawkins* continuing her patrol to the south, *Alcantara* patrolled around Trinidad Island from the morning of 26 July. Two days later, the AMC sighted two masts on the horizon to the east and closed to intercept the ship. When the range had closed to 23 000 yards, the unidentified ship altered course briefly towards and then away from *Alcantara*. For more than three hours, *Alcantara* gathered speed and closed the range on the suspected raider. When the ships were 16 000 yards apart, the unidentified ship raised the German battle ensign and fired with a two-gun salvo at the AMC.

Despite the incoming salvoes *Alcantara* had no choice but to press on and close the German ship until she was within maximum range (14 000 yards) of the AMC's 6-inch guns. Several shells struck the deck of *Alcantara* disabling her gunnery control system and main aerial. When the raider was at maximum range, several salvoes were fired without success. A shell then exploded on the waterline of the British ship, piercing the engine room, which flooded. The AMC gradually slowed down from over 20 knots to ten. However, when the range between the two ships had been reduced to 9800 yards, one round from *Alcantara* appeared to strike a gun mounting in the German ship and her fire became erratic. As the range opened again, the two ships continued to exchange fire with *Alcantara* scoring a hit on the raider's stern. After laying a smoke screen, the German ship escaped over the horizon.

In this short action, the Germans did not even attempt to disguise their ship as an Allied or neutral merchant ship or try to lure the British ship closer by prolonging interrogation. They chose instead to engage the British ship at the maximum range of the raider's armament with a display of long-range gunnery and fire control which was accurate and effective. These decisions were probably prompted by the fear that other British ships were in the area and would also close the raider once her interrogation by *Alcantara* began. Once the British ship was identified as a possible AMC, the Germans would have also considered their chances in a gunfight would have been greater at longer range. It is also noteworthy that the Germans hoisted a battle ensign before firing.

Four and a half months later in adjacent waters, the AMC *Carnarvon Castle* sighted a suspicious ship on the horizon. The range was 19 000 yards with the unidentified vessel steaming away from the British ship. After increasing speed, *Carnarvon*

Castle ordered the fleeing vessel to stop. When she did not heave to, the AMC fired a single round which fell well short. When the range had closed to 17 000, still 3000 yards beyond the maximum range of *Carnarvon Castle*'s 6-inch guns, a salvo was fired at the unidentified ship. In reply, *Carnarvon Castle* was fired upon by the suspect ship which was obviously a raider. Twenty minutes later when the range was 14 000 yards, a salvo from the AMC appeared to hit the raider, later identified as Raider 'E'—*Thor* (formerly *Santa Cruz*), which was set on fire both fore and aft. After laying a smoke screen and returning fire, *Carnarvon Castle* was also subjected to an unsuccessful torpedo attack. With the two ships now only 8000 yards apart, several salvoes from *Thor* crashed into the British ship damaging her fire control communications and setting her ablaze. With the range opening again, the two ships exchanged fire until both were out of range and the German ship fled at approximately 18 knots.

Once again, *Thor* had shown a German preference for a long-range duel rather than a fight at close quarters. The action also confirmed that raider long-range gunnery was effective and well controlled.

A duel more closely resembling the *Sydney–Kormoran* action was fought by the light cruiser HMS *Leander* on 27 February 1942.[9] During a routine patrol in waters off the Maldive Islands in the northern Indian Ocean, *Leander* noticed a suspicious vessel heading towards the east at an unexpectedly high speed. The cruiser increased speed and made a preliminary identification of the ship as an Italian *Ramb* Class freighter.[10] The presence of a gun on the forecastle only added to suspicions. After closing to 11 000 yards with her 6-inch guns trained fore and aft, Captain R.M. Bevan in *Leander* ordered the suspicious vessel to hoist her colours. The red ensign was hoisted four minutes later. When ordered to display her signal letters, the suspected Italian raider took five minutes to hoist 'GJYD'. These letters did not appear in either the *Signal Letters of British Ships* or the *Signal Letter Index* although it was thought she may have been trying to pass herself off as the British merchant ship *Grosmont Castle*.[11]

Finally, to confirm their suspicions, *Leander* made the secret challenge. When there was no reply, Bevan decided to board the unidentified ship and ordered her by flag and signal lamp to stop. After five minutes elapsed and no reply had been received, *Leander* was preparing to fire a single shot across the bows of the suspected raider when she hoisted either the Italian naval or merchant ensign, there is some dispute about which, and trained her gun on *Leander,* which was just forward of the raider's quarter at a range of 3000 yards. When the Italian ship fired and failed to hit *Leander* even at such close range, the British cruiser responded with five rapid salvoes which devastated the Italian ship. By the time Bevan asked the Italians whether they surrendered, the raider was on fire and men were abandoning ship. Her gunners had left their positions and the ensign had been struck. Hoping to capture the Italian ship, Bevan despatched a prize crew in one of the ship's boats. When warned by one of the Italian officers that the raider was carrying ammunition, *Leander*'s boat stood off while several explosions broke her apart.

As *Ramb 1* had the potential to cause serious disruption to Allied shipping movements, her sinking was considered by the Commander-in-Chief East Indies, Vice Admiral Ralph Leatham, to be a highly commendable action on the part of Captain Bevan and *Leander*. However, Bevan had unnecessarily hazarded his ship by bringing *Leander* into a position where *Ramb 1* could have inflicted serious damage on her had the Italian gunnery been accurate. Given his initial suspicions and the raider's consistent failure to reply rapidly and accurately to *Leander*'s challenges, Bevan should have remained abaft the raider's quarters and outside, or at the extremity of, her arcs of fire. Bevan and *Leander* had been fortunate.

Six weeks later, the AMC *Voltaire* set out from Trinidad bound for Freetown via the west of the Cape Verde Islands. When she failed to arrive at Freetown on 9 April, the Commander-in-Chief South Atlantic, Vice Admiral Sir Robert Raikes, signalled to the Admiralty that she was overdue and that nothing had been heard. Prompted by a German report that *Voltaire* had been sunk by a German cruiser, the Canadian AMC *Prince David* had earlier been directed to search along *Voltaire*'s intended track. On 7 April, the Canadian ship discovered wreckage from *Voltaire*, half-way between the West Indies and the Cape Verde Islands. This was where the British ship had been expected to be on 4 April. No survivors were recovered from *Voltaire* and the Admiralty was left to conjecture about the circumstances.

The tentative conclusion was that she had been severely damaged by enemy fire, probably from *Thor*, beyond the maximum range of her own armaments. It was not until 1943 when there was an exchange of prisoners that the Admiralty learned that *Voltaire* had indeed been attacked by *Thor*. The first long-range salvo from the raider crippled the AMC, which sank three hours later. A number of survivors from *Voltaire* were recovered by the Germans. However, as nothing was known of the action at that time, very little could be learned from it in 1941.

In stark contrast, the engagement of a German raider by the 8-inch heavy cruiser HMS *Cornwall*, commanded by Captain P.C.W. Mainwaring, on 8 May 1941 was fully documented and provided many object lessons on anti-raider warfare. The genesis of the action was a raider report from SS *British Emperor* in the early morning of 7 May. At that time, *Cornwall* was proceeding north towards Seychelles to refuel. After increasing speed, the cruiser turned north-north-west towards the position reported by *British Emperor* 500 miles away. *Cornwall*'s course and speed were altered shortly when a signal was received from the Commander-in-Chief East Indies, Admiral Leatham, ordering her to close the gap between Seychelles and the Chagos Archipelago to the east.

At 0330 on 8 May, *Cornwall* was allegedly sighted by the raider as the cruiser turned against the setting moon. Shortly after dawn, both of *Cornwall*'s aircraft were launched to search for the raider, which was observed by one of the aircraft 65 miles to the west of the cruiser and heading to the south-west. When the aircraft returned to the ship and made their sighting report slightly less than one hour later, *Cornwall* increased speed and steered a converging course with the raider. The second of the ship's aircraft was launched mid-morning with instructions to ascertain whether or not the suspect ship was a raider. On its

return shortly after midday, the aircrew reported that the ship
had hoisted signal letters identifying her as the Norwegian ship
Tamerlane. Although the suspect ship resembled *Tamerlane* in
appearance, she was not among the list of expected ships held
in *Cornwall*.

Although running short on fuel, *Cornwall* had to increase
speed to 26 knots, and then to 28 knots, to ensure she was in
visual contact with the raider before sunset. At 1607, the raider
was finally observed from the bridge of *Cornwall*. As the British cruiser altered course to close, the raider turned away and
presented her stern as she fled. Keeping the raider fine on her
starboard bow and avoiding crossing her track and the possibility of hitting mines, *Cornwall* continued to close when the raider
signalled that she was the Norwegian *Tamerlane* and was being
attacked by a raider. The cruiser's aircraft was ordered to inform
the alleged *Tamerlane* that she was being followed by a British
cruiser, after which *Cornwall* altered course to expose her profile to the fleeing ship before returning to a parallel course. The
cruiser ordered the raider to stop or she would be fired upon
when the range had been reduced to 19000 yards. This was
reinforced with an 8-inch round which was fired ahead of the
raider.

Because of the possibility that the suspect ship might be a
neutral, *Cornwall*'s captain was not prepared to open direct
fire. Instead, he ordered one of his aircraft to drop a 250-pound
bomb close to the raider as a final incentive for her to stop. If this
was unsuccessful, a second 250-pound bomb was to be dropped
onto her forecastle. But there was a delay in passing this message to the aircraft and *Cornwall* needed to take action herself.
Fourteen minutes after the first 8-inch warning round was fired,
the raider was again directed to heave to and another shot was
fired. By this time, the distance between the two ships was less
than 12000 yards. As *Cornwall* turned to port to increase the
range, the raider believed she was manoeuvring to fire a broadside salvo. When the raider, known as Ship 33 or *Pinguin*, also
made a sharp turn to port, *Pinguin* was presented with a large
target area and opened fire with five guns.

Disastrously for *Cornwall*, there was a failure in the electrical circuits that did not allow the guns to be trained after the second warning shot was fired. With the range closing to 10 500 yards, the British ship had to continue with her turn to port to open the range and minimise the torpedo target area. It was extremely fortunate for *Cornwall* that she was not hit during the turn. When alternative control had been ordered, the two forward turrets trained on the raider and fired two salvoes before a 5.9-inch round from *Pinguin* disabled *Cornwall*'s forward steering gear. When after steering was rigged, all of *Cornwall*'s turrets were trained and fired at the raider whose guns seemed unable to range on the cruiser. Several minutes after *Cornwall* manoeuvred to put the two ships on parallel course, a salvo from the British ship exploded in the raider which quickly disappeared from view. A number of survivors, both British and German, were later recovered from the sea and landed on the cruiser's return to the Seychelles.

There was a thorough critique of the action by the Admiralty and criticism of *Cornwall*'s performance was wide-ranging. Members of the aircrew were criticised for not relaying immediately the initial sighting of the suspicious merchant vessel. The cruiser's captain was criticised for failing to keep the Commander-in-Chief informed of the situation, especially since his staff could have advised *Cornwall* that no neutral merchant shipping was in the area. The Admiralty also believed that the concerns of the captain of *Cornwall* that his signals could be detected by D/F in *Pinguin* were excessive. It was considered that he should also have informed the Commander-in-Chief when *Tamerlane*'s signal letters were hoisted. The major criticism was kept until last.

Throughout the period between the surface sighting of the raider and the time when she opened fire, the *Cornwall* held on to the idea that the suspect might still prove to be a friendly neutral although in view of her suspicious behaviour all the evidence was very much against it. The Admiralty considered that the *Cornwall*, by allowing herself to close to a range under 12,000 yards contrary to her expressed intentions, showed a lack of attention to the changing situation. It is quite clear from her report [M.012944/41] that this was fully appreciated at the time. The error of closing a very suspicious ship was intensified by her temporary inability to open fire, which left no alternative but to turn away and close 'A' arcs at a critical moment, which might easily have resulted in the raider's escape and in much more serious damage to herself than she actually suffered.

Three days after *Sydney* was lost, the heavy cruiser HMS *Devonshire* engaged a German raider in the South Atlantic. The first sighting of the German vessel was by the Allied cruiser's Walrus aircraft, which was sent ahead of the ship to conduct an anti-submarine sweep and surface search. On its return shortly after dawn, the aircrew reported a suspicious merchant ship and *Devonshire* closed the contact to investigate. One hour later the suspect ship was sighted from the cruiser's bridge and the aircraft relaunched in an effort to identify her. However, Captain Oliver in *Devonshire* suspected from her appearance that the ship was Ship 16, which had been described in a supplement to *Weekly Intelligence Report* No. 65. With the cruiser kept between 12 000–18 000 yards to avoid torpedo attack, the suspect completed a full turn to starboard before heading towards the south-east. Oliver tried to avoid firing on the ship, which he believed was carrying a number of British prisoners. When a warning shot was fired, the ship stopped and turned towards *Devonshire* as she sent a raider report with the letter groups 'RRR RRR RRR' claiming to be the merchantman *Polyphemus*. This left Oliver pondering whether the suspect ship might not be *Polyphemus* as this vessel had been recorded at Bilbao two months earlier and could well have reached the South Atlantic by this time.

To identify the suspect positively, Oliver signalled Commander-in-Chief South Atlantic, Vice Admiral Algernon Willis, asking whether the ship he had interrogated could possibly be *Polyphemus* while despatching his own aircraft to make a closer observation of the ship's hull. When the aircrew reported that her hull was similar to that of raider *Atlantis* and Admiral Willis signalled that this ship could not be *Polyphemus*,

Devonshire fired a salvo at the raider from a distance of 17 500 yards. The German ship, later confirmed to be *Atlantis*, had by this time sunk or captured 22 ships since leaving Kiel in March 1940. *Atlantis* laid a smoke screen but did not exchange fire with *Devonshire*, which fired 30 salvoes in four minutes. After a short respite of several minutes, the raider was fired upon again until fires raged on the upper deck and she was down by the stern. The fourth salvo fired by *Devonshire* had actually inflicted mortal damage. It started a major fire on board which spread to the raider's magazines and a massive explosion resulted. The fear of submarine attack prevented Oliver from stopping and rescuing survivors.

In the post-action analysis, there was no criticism of Oliver's handling of *Devonshire* during the action. The raider was sunk without any risk to the heavy cruiser, which made the most of her superior gunnery.

Several days later, the heavy cruiser *Dorsetshire* was searching for German shipping to the south-west of St Helena when the masts of a ship were sighted on the horizon. The cruiser turned towards the contact, increased speed and prepared to recover her Walrus aircraft, which had been patrolling further to the south. The suspicious ship made smoke and appeared to gather speed as Captain Augustine Agar VC in *Dorsetshire* tried unsuccessfully to recall his aircraft. While on a converging course with the unidentified ship, several small oil slicks were observed from the cruiser's bridge and the presence of a submarine which may have been refuelling had to be assumed. Agar believed the suspect ship was either a raider or a supply ship although the possibility that she was a British ship fleeing from a German cruiser could not be discounted.

Still suspecting the presence of a submarine, *Dorsetshire* remained at 16 000 yards from the contact and operated at high speed. Agar was aware that in these circumstances he could not prevent the suspect ship from scuttling if she were a raider or supply ship. After *Dorsetshire* fired two warning shots from 24 000 yards, the suspect ship stopped and lowered boats. There was very little that Agar could do to stop her scuttling. There was also the concern that if *Dorsetshire* commenced firing, any British seamen imprisoned on board might be injured. As the cruiser circled the suspect ship and maintained a range of around 17 000 yards, several boats moved away from the ship, which was listing to port and appeared to be on fire. Fifteen minutes later, as the sun started to set, scuttling charges were detonated and the German submarine supply ship *Python* started to sink. With the ever-present fear of a U-boat attack, *Dorsetshire* cleared the area and left behind about 500 survivors in 14 boats and two large rafts. It was later learned that *Python* had met *U-126* on 23 November and had received several crew members from *Atlantis* before steaming south for another rendezvous with a U-boat. Several boats despatched from *Python* before she was sighted by *Dorsetshire* were probably resupplying a submarine.

By this time, the first news of the loss of *Sydney* during an action with a German raider was being received by the Naval Board. It appeared, from the *Dorsetshire* action alone, that Burnett had blundered badly and should never have lost his ship. But a number of points ought to be made. The first is the dissimilarity of the action fought between *Sydney* and *Kormoran* as it was relayed in the German accounts. Even by comparative standards, Burnett's purported actions were exceptional. The captains of the other Allied ships which had engaged raiders had all acted quite differently from Burnett, and none with anywhere near as much carelessness as allegedly displayed by the Australian captain.

The assertion that all of the cruiser captains were being less than prudent in their approach to suspected raiders, and that Burnett was no less so than the others, is far too general to be accepted. It also fails to account for the actions of Oliver in *Devonshire* who engaged *Atlantis* without any knowledge of the *Sydney–Kormoran* action. In fact, the *Devonshire–Atlantis* action suggests that this approach to raiders was indicative of accepted practice within the Allied fleets at that time. There were also many differences in the respective situations faced by the captains of *Leander* and *Cornwall*, and neither gives any clear indication of how Burnett might have acted when he encountered

Kormoran. The force and effect of comparable actions does not make the *Sydney–Kormoran* action any more explicable. In fact, it makes it inexplicable.

Similarly, the suggestion that Burnett may have thought he had sighted an unarmed German supply ship would not mean an end to caution. As the existence of a supply ship might mean that a raider was also in the area, Burnett had to assume the worst case and act as though the suspect ship was the raider. In the event that it was a supply ship, Burnett was still not entitled to assume she was unarmed.

Neither was he entitled to assume that this ship could not be the elusive Raider G. In May 1941, the Admiralty knew very little about Raider G. In the *Weekly Intelligence Report* dated 26 September, the Admiralty thought that Raider G might be known by the Germans as Ship 41, formerly the 9400 ton *Steiermark*. In the narrative that followed, the Admiralty advised that 'very little is known about this raider, but she may have sunk two or three ships in the North Atlantic in January and February 1941 and was reported in the Indian Ocean in March'. The same report advised caution.

> Armed raiders have not been very active during the past two months. There has been no activity in the Indian Ocean since June, possibly none since the beginning of May. It is probable, however, that a raider is in this area and will soon resume operations.

There was, therefore, nothing which precluded the suspicious ship encountered by *Sydney* on 19 November from being Ship 41.

In fact, there was every reason for Burnett to believe that the suspicious ship was a raider. She altered away from *Sydney* and increased speed as soon as she was sighted. Given that *Sydney* was readily observed to be a warship and looked nothing like a raider, that she made no attempt to jam *Kormoran*'s QQQ signal, that merchantmen in these waters adjacent to a major port and shipping route should have been expecting to encounter RAN ships, and that other merchant ships in these waters in recent months had not diverted from their course as *Kormoran* had done, Burnett would reasonably have expected he had caught a raider or a German supply ship.

There is no doubt that Burnett knew the details of the earlier actions and was aware of the practice endorsed by the Admiralty for approaching such ships. Thus, there is no immediately apparent reason why he would have acted contrary to all the principles of anti-raider warfare, which had been practically demonstrated over the past two years, and highlighted by the errors of the *Devonshire–Atlantis* action.

On 16 December 1941, prompted it would appear solely by the *Sydney–Kormoran* action as the *Cornwall–Pinguin* engagement had occurred seven months earlier, the Admiralty issued a 'Most Secret' message regarding raider operations. After analysing the actions involving *Cornwall*, *Sydney* and *Devonshire*, the Admiralty referred to four aspects of raider and anti-raider warfare: recognition, challenge procedure, tactics and U-boats. After pointing out that in each of these engagements the ships whose names were being used as a disguise were actually some considerable distance away, the Admiralty commented that:

> Enemy raiders will always disguise themselves and use the appropriate name in any signal whether by an RRRR message on 500 k/cs or the reply to challenge.
>
> In no case so far has the disguise adopted been such as should have deceived commanding officers had they trusted the negative intelligence that information of the ship's movements had not been reported to them.
>
> Positive information of British, Allied and US Merchantmen from Admiralty or Shipping Intelligence Officers is sufficiently accurate, and positive information of neutral vessels by local War Trade Reporting Officers should be sufficiently accurate to enable commanding officers to be kept informed of the position of all non-enemy ships that they may meet. Commanders-in-Chief should ensure that their information and plotting organisations can achieve this.

The Admiralty believed that warships were not using the merchant ship challenge procedure set out in the *Recognition Manual* and in *Naval Control of Shipping Instruction* (NCSI) No. 371. Although the application of the procedures was limited to British ships, and notably 'some Dutch ships', the Admiralty was hoping to extend its use to all Allied shipping and American ships as well. In the issue of tactics, the Admiralty felt:

> There is a possibility that commanding officers under-estimate the offensive power of raiders. They should be warned that enemy raiders are often powerfully armed with guns and torpedoes and if fitted with modern RDF (Radar Direction Finding) may be able to open fire even at long range with great accuracy.

The Admiralty concluded its message by reminding commanding officers of the constant threat of U-boats that could be operating with the raiders or with merchant ships, which would attempt to lead the warship towards the waiting submarine.

In sum, this could be taken as a damning criticism of Burnett's action by the Admiralty. By inference, he was criticised for not confirming with shore authorities the expected location of *Straat Malakka* on that day; that he failed to follow laid-down procedures in both the *Recognition Manual* and NCSI No. 371; that he should not have been deceived by *Kormoran*'s disguise or her 'QQQ' signal; that he came far too close to *Kormoran*; and that he severely under-estimated her armaments. The Admiralty's assessment of raider disguises was obviously not shared by Roskill who stated in the official British naval history that 'granted the difficulties of piercing raiders' disguises, the very close approach made by *Sydney* during the exchange of signals was certainly injudicious'.[12] The Admiralty was of the view that flaws in the disguises should have been apparent before warships came into the range of the raiders' guns.

It appeared that Burnett had, in fact, done nothing right and that his actions amounted to gross professional incompetence and culpable negligence. The Admiralty seemed prepared to apportion all of this blame and to attribute all of this responsibility onto Burnett on the basis that the accounts of Detmers and his crew possessed 'all the marks of a bona fide account'.

However, the Admiralty conceded that *Kormoran* survivors 'could not explain why the *Sydney* came so close before opening fire or attempting to launch her aircraft'.

The suggestion that *Leander*'s action in coming to 3000 yards showed that *Sydney*'s 'mistake' was not unique fails to consider the vast differences between the two actions and the two enemy ships involved. *Ramb 1*, overtly poorly armed, and *Kormoran*, covertly heavily armed, presented dissimilar problems to the captains of *Leander* and *Sydney*. The actions of *Leander*'s captain were comparatively prudent when one considers *Sydney*'s movements. *Leander* also remained on the quarter of the Italian ship at a range of 3000 yards. This was relatively risky but not suicidal as *Sydney*'s position was, abeam of *Kormoran* on a parallel course at less than half that distance. At any rate, *Leander*'s experience with *Ramb 1* was a warning to other ships that under-estimated any would-be raider.

There were enough doubts about what might have happened between *Sydney* and *Kormoran* to raise the possibility that Burnett might have been the victim of an unfortunate injustice that warranted deeper investigation.

The Genesis of a Controversy

Owing to wartime secrecy, very little could be added during the war to what was known about the loss of *Sydney*. Volume II of BR 1738, the Admiralty's preliminary narrative of the war at sea between January and December 1941, was produced by the Historical Section in the Admiralty in 1944.[1] Item No. 493 dealt with the *Sydney–Kormoran* action. The narrative simply repeated the German accounts of the action. It stated that *Kormoran* was disguised as the *Straat Malakka* and that *Sydney* had closed the raider to 1.25 miles on a course of 250 degrees at about 15 knots.

The first non-official accounts of the loss of *Sydney* were *Prisoner of the Kormoran*[2] produced by W.A. (Syd) Jones, the 3rd Cook in *Mareeba* at the time of her sinking, and *Stormy Petrel*, published by Paymaster Lieutenant W.H. (John) Ross in 1943. The volume by Jones, which was actually written by James Taylor, is a superficial and anecdotal account of the *Mareeba* action and Jones's experiences as a German POW. It also differed from the report Jones submitted to the Navy after his repatriation in 1943.

Prisoner of the Kormoran contains a very brief description of *Sydney*'s final engagement and Jones's reaction to hearing of her loss without trace. The value of the book lies in Jones's allegation that *Kormoran* fired at *Mareeba* under Japanese colours. When the crew of the Australian ship rowed towards the raider after *Mareeba* was abandoned, Jones says that the survivors found 'that [*Kormoran*] had not only fought under false colours but under a false name'.[3] It appears it was only when the boarding party was despatched from *Kormoran* that the Australians realised they had been attacked by a German raider. This significant statement was later referred to the War Crimes Commission although no action against the *Kormoran* crew resulted. In a note to the Commission, the Naval Board did, however, state that the matter of which flag *Kormoran* was flying at the time of the action against *Mareeba* 'remains open to doubt'.

In describing his time in *Kormoran*, the only noteworthy recollection that Jones recorded was that Detmers appeared to several of the prisoners to be heavily intoxicated on his birthday.

> There could be no mistake. The captain of the *Kormoran* had been celebrating, and celebrating hard. But he was not so far gone that he did not realise the unflattering attention he had attracted. Straightening himself, he shot a burning glance at us and staggered towards his cabin.[4]

Later in the same day after Detmers had apparently recovered from this drinking bout, he shared six bottles of rum with the crew of *Mareeba* and started to reminisce about his trip to Australia in *Koln* in the early 1930s. Apparently Detmers drank a great deal of alcohol during the cruiser's visit to Sydney and recalled waking up one morning on Bondi Beach with a woman he could not remember meeting.

Other than first-hand observations, this is a generally unreliable book. Jones reports that several days after *Mareeba* was sunk *Kormoran* met

> a Japanese freighter from which rubber boats were dropped. Attached to these floats—and remember Japan was still not at war with us—were cases of whisky, tins of cigarettes and bundles of English and Australian newspapers! [original exclamation retained]

The alleged encounter, for which there is no evidence, suggests the author has either a very fertile imagination or was taken in by information or rumours which no doubt circulated among the prisoners. Another member of *Mareeba*'s crew, Trimmer Jack Bottomley, in a letter published in 1991[5] describing his experiences on board *Kormoran*, made no mention of a Japanese supply ship. Other than the sinking of the *Embiricos*, he stated that *Kormoran* did not meet another ship until the rendezvous with *Kulmerland*.

Jones evidently lost track of time while in *Kormoran* because he dated her rendezvous with *Kulmerland*, and his transfer to the supply ship, as occurring on 5 November, rather than on the correct date of 16 October. Of the *Sydney–Kormoran* action Jones stated that

> the raider was probably flying the Norwegian flag. Personally, I should say *certainly* flying the Norwegian or some other neutral flag, for she always, to my knowledge, had neutral colours ready for instant use.[6]

Jones incorrectly states that 291 Germans and three Chinese were recovered—the accepted number was 314 Germans and three Chinese—and that *Sydney*'s ship's company was 550 whereas it was actually 645. Jones also alleged that *Kormoran* operated in company with another raider to sink *Eurylochus*, and that the two raiders proceeded together to rendezvous with *Nordmark*. Other than Jones's description of Detmers' drunkenness, which was a first-hand observation, *Prisoner of the Kormoran* cannot be relied upon for accuracy and for the *Sydney–Kormoran* engagement it is practically a useless account.

Stormy Petrel, by John Ross, needs to be considered differently. It is a book with great historiographical significance in that Ross was assisted by 'Lieutenant Commander G.H. Gill of the Naval Intelligence Department for access to parts of *Sydney*'s War Diary' and by Lieutenant Commander Rycroft's 'continued assistance, advice and encouragement'.[7] Ross was posted to HMAS *Canberra* before *Sydney* sailed with *Zealandia*. He had served in *Sydney* since her commissioning in 1935. After being sunk in *Canberra* during the Battle of Savo Island on the night of 8–9 August 1942, Ross later served as secretary to Captain John Collins when he was Naval-Officer-in-Charge in Fremantle. He was promoted to Lieutenant Commander and retired in that rank in 1951.

Perhaps unintentionally, *Stormy Petrel* reveals what people within the Navy believed had occurred during the war off Carnarvon. Although Ross's primary purpose was to describe *Sydney*'s five years of service, which he does with many anecdotes and in great detail, it is only the last three pages that mention the cruiser's action with *Kormoran*. Some of the details provided by Ross, such as the flag flown by *Kormoran* at the time of the action, appeared to contradict other evidence:

> The survivors, obviously well coached, told conflicting stories so that on piecing them together very little fact could be garnered except that it seems certain the engagement took place at point blank range, the raider having the advantage of surprise, being disguised as a freighter and *flying the Norwegian flag*, and that both ships were seriously damaged within the first few moments. The Germans were forced to abandon their vessel which sank soon after and they stated that when last seen *Sydney* was badly on fire in three places and disappearing slowly over the horizon in the dusk. As no trace of any survivor or wreckage large enough to be identified could be found it can only be assumed that she must have suddenly blown up, taking all hands with her . . .
>
> One point which seems very difficult to decide upon is the date of the sinking. Officially it is recorded as 19th November and although some of the Germans gave that date, others gave November 22nd. This latter date seems more likely the correct one and is to a point confirmed by personnel of the liner [*Aquitania*] which picked up one boat load of the Germans on the 23rd. They stated that the men rescued had practically no growth of beard and therefore could not have been adrift in an open boat for four days (19th to 23rd), whereas if the action had taken place in the evening of 22nd they would have little, if any, growth of beard—and this was the case. [emphasis added]

Ross based his account of *Sydney*'s final action on wartime newspaper reports which, as was shown earlier, were the only source of the statement that *Kormoran* was flying the Norwegian flag.[8] However, it is surprising that this statement was allowed to stand given that Ross was aided by Rycroft and Gill, the latter vetting the manuscript in accordance with wartime secrecy requirements. The nature of their assistance was not specified by Ross in his acknowledgments although he told me in 1993 that Gill did not give him access to any official records.[8a] One suspects that Ross's comment about the German accounts probably originated with Rycroft who was involved in the interrogations from the outset and who was in the best position to make such a judgment on the German accounts.

With the official files from the wartime period closed for thirty years, there was little that other writers could add to the *Sydney* story. Access to records held by the Navy was needed for anything new to be revealed.

After years of research and writing, George Hermon Gill published the first of two official volumes on the history of the RAN in World War II in 1957. Gill's account covers 12 pages of his first volume or about 5000 words of text and a reconstruction. It is told in a bland and unemotional manner and is devoid of any speculation in the absence of corroborated evidence. Given the amount of activity that Gill attempts to describe, commencing with the German raiders in the second half of 1940 and ending with the repatriation of the *Kormoran* survivors in 1947, the narrative is necessarily superficial and covers only the main aspects of the story.

There were two significant features in Gill's account. The first is that his veiled criticisms of Burnett were, if properly understood, severe and well beyond the usual apportionment of responsibility to warship captains. Gill attributes personal blame to *Sydney*'s captain. The second significant feature is the list of mitigating circumstances which Gill offers on Burnett's behalf. While he is prepared to concede to Burnett a range of possible defences to a charge of negligence, the force of Gill's criticisms remains.

Two years after Gill's first volume was released, Detmers published his book, *Hilfskreuzer Kormoran*.[9] It was an unremarkable book with many inaccuracies and the absence of any analysis.

The raider's action with *Sydney* ran for about nine pages of the 159-page paperback edition, and Detmers recounted in it his version of events much as he had done during the war, albeit with less detail. Detmers, who during the war had suffered a stroke which had left him partly paralysed, seems wisely to have based his narrative on reconstructions of the action, principally the ship's war diary, rather than on his, presumably, incomplete and suspect recollections. However, on three separate occasions Detmers mentioned his fears of being court martialled by Australian naval authorities. In effect, he implied that he was worried by the possibility of a war crimes tribunal charging him for violations of international law. These statements are considered more fully in a later chapter when the possibility that illegalities were committed during the raider's action with *Sydney* will be assessed in detail. Detmers' book sold a large number of copies and was reprinted numerous times.

Geoffrey Scott, a popular writer, published a chatty and anecdotal account of the cruiser's five years in commission in a mass-produced paperback, *HMAS Sydney*,[10] released in 1962. The book has not a single reference to either primary or secondary sources. From a close reading of the narrative it is obvious that Scott's book is merely an amalgam of material previously published by Ross, Gill and Detmers. It certainly added nothing factual to the *Sydney* story. In rather melodramatic prose, Scott stated that 'the gallant *Sydney* was tricked to destruction and mortally wounded before she had a chance to hit back' and asked 'what was the real fate of HMAS *Sydney*?'[11] Scott concluded that 'how the cruiser *Sydney* died has been fairly well established' as he merely repeated Gill's opinion that the German accounts were accurate.[12]

As for Burnett, Scott restated the argument that criticisms of Farncomb about the sinking of *Coburg* and *Ketty Brovig* prompted Burnett to close *Kormoran* to a very short distance to prevent her scuttling. He conceded, that 'no-one, of course, can say what impression the criticisms of Farncomb made on Burnett'. But, according to Scott, it is just possible that it flashed before his mind when *Sydney*'s lookout reported *Kormoran* in the distance. That theory, however, would still leave unanswered the question of why Burnett did not fire a warning shot to force the supposed Dutchman to heave-to. But Scott left Burnett's professional reputation in tatters by contrasting the *Sydney–Kormoran* action with the *Devonshire–Atlantis* action and pointing out that 'the *Devonshire*'s action was a textbook lesson in correct naval procedure'.[13] His closing paragraph was lame.

The loss of the cruiser *Sydney* can also be seen as a cold, academic question of naval tactics. Or can it be regarded as one of those appalling tragedies always liable to flow from sudden, unaccountable frailties of human judgment.[14]

Vice Admiral Sir John Collins, Burnett's predecessor in command of *Sydney*, took a similar line to Gill and Scott in his short monograph published in 1971.[15] Collins described briefly the career of the ship he commanded for two years and ended his account of *Sydney*'s service on 18 November. He concluded by quoting a statement from the Naval Historical Officer, John Ware, which passed several questionable judgments on the action.

It is easy to be wise after the event but having said that, it remains difficult to escape the conclusion that *Sydney* was lost because she failed to observe prudent tactics in the situation that arose . . .

The lessons of history pointed clearly to a need for extreme caution in dealing with an unidentified merchantman as witnessed by a warning issued by the Commodore Commanding the Australian Squadron shortly after the outbreak of war in 1939. A pamphlet dated 7 October 1939 warned that 'months, and even years of immunity were no guarantee that the next vessel is not the disguised raider and vigilance can never be relaxed'. The fact that 'a vessel's description agrees with her name is no guarantee that she is not a raider so that precautions must always be taken when approaching a suspicious vessel. It can be expected that raiders will have powerful gun armament and also torpedo tubes and be well and carefully disguised'.

This order is very much to the point. However, most patrolling

British cruisers found that many merchant ships did not respond correctly to repeated signals. According to a report from one Commanding Officer of a cruiser not more than 25 per cent of merchant ships replied to the signal 'NNJ' ('You should make your secret letters') correctly. The failure to make the correct reply, therefore, gave little indication of the true nature of the vessel. Despite the Commodore's order there may have been a tendency, after many such experiences, to assume the suspect was just another friendly ship which did not know the procedure.

Whatever the reason, there were several examples before *Sydney*'s action of failure to appreciate that the suspect might, in fact, be a formidable enemy.

On 27 February 1941, HMS *Leander* approached the Italian raider *Ramb 1* to within 3,000 yards though her suspicions had been well aroused at a safe distance. She was fortunate that the enemy's fire was brief and erratic otherwise she may well have suffered the fate of *Sydney*.

The fact that only 25 per cent of merchant ships replied with their secret callsign when challenged is irrelevant to Burnett's alleged decision to bring his ship to within 1500 yards before making the challenge. At that range the challenge was useless because the suspect ship would have been in a position to fire on the ship demanding to know its identity. The challenge should, of course, have been made at 14000 yards and, if then the merchant ship did not reply correctly or reply at all, Burnett would have had plenty of time to use other methods to establish the ship's identity.

While Collins wisely and graciously resisted the temptation to describe what he would have done had he been in Burnett's position on 19 November 1941, he leaves his readers in little doubt of his opinion that Burnett had been in error, however understandable his error of judgment might have been. It is significant that he did not say Burnett had been either incompetent or negligent.

Shortly after Collins's monograph appeared, Commander Patrick Burnett, the elder of Burnett's two sons, both of whom joined the Naval College as cadet midshipmen soon after their father's death, published a biographical article on his father. Regarding *Sydney*'s final action he wrote:

> The reasons behind *Sydney*'s close approach to *Kormoran* before the action started will never be known, but it seems in the light of events that my father in this instance was too confident of his ability to handle any eventuality that might arise.[16]

This statement of his son's recollections of him has since been used unfairly by others to imply that Burnett was, in fact, over-confident.

An article published by Heinrich Ahl, the pilot of *Kormoran*'s aircraft, in the Australian *Naval Historical Review* in December 1979 was the first German contribution to the subject for 20 years.[17] Ahl attempted to explain some of the thoughts which ran through the minds of the raider's crew as *Kormoran* was closed by *Sydney*. He mentioned that Detmers had been ordered to avoid engaging a warship at all costs 'because this would mean surely the loss of the auxiliary cruiser. As it would take a considerable time to replace the ship, there would be neither direct nor indirect losses of enemy tonnage for a considerable time.'[18] But as *Kormoran* was a warship

> it was impossible just to surrender. We had now to make the most of it, that is, to sell ourselves as dearly as possible. For this we had fully to utilise our legal camouflage as a merchantman according to international sea-convention, in order to decoy the cruiser as close to us as possible and to get her into the most favourable position for our weapons.[19]

Ahl stated that *Sydney* did not launch her aircraft 'when she saw we could not escape' and then, by light signal, asked 'for our ship's name, where we came from and where we were bound for'. As the cruiser drew near, she began to interrogate by signal flags. Ahl stated that this was *Kormoran*'s first reply. After fumbling with signal flags, the answer given was '*Straat Malakka* from Fremantle to Batavia'. By this time, Ahl claimed, *Sydney* had closed to 1200 yards on the raider's beam rather than quarter and asked for the raider's secret callsign.

Having been forced into an engagement

> Detmers informed the *Kormoran* crew of this fact . . . At the order 'Decamouflage' the guns were made free for action. At the same time the Dutch colours were lowered and simultaneously the German ensign was hoisted. It takes a very short time. Only after the report by the signalman: 'Ensign is fluttering', the order 'Fire' followed. All targets were hit besides the rear turrets.

The remainder of the article was full of platitudes and generally conformed to most other post-engagement accounts.

By 1980 it seemed that this is where the assessment of *Sydney*'s loss would end. What else could be said? A host of secondary accounts simply repeated what had been published elsewhere and there is no hint that additional primary research was undertaken in the first 30 years after World War II which might have challenged the prevailing conclusions. Put simply, conventional interpretations of the action concluded that Burnett was to blame for the loss of *Sydney*. But the conventional view of the action had been privately challenged in the mid-1970s by Michael Montgomery, the English son of *Sydney*'s Royal Navy navigator at the time of the sinking.

Montgomery was four years old when his father was lost in *Sydney*. He left Australia and returned to Britain with his mother in 1944. He was educated at Harrow and Oxford and completed National Service before working as a financial journalist and teacher. Montgomery did not return to Australia until 1973.

> It was only then that I read for the first time the full official account . . . Up to that point I knew very little more than that both ships had succeeded in sinking each other . . . Gill's account . . . fell short of satisfying the whole of my curiosity . . . To make any attempt to answer [the questions raised by Gill about Burnett's actions] I had

to wait first for the release of the whole body of official war records, which under the 30-year Rule was not due to take place until 1976. It was therefore not until I returned to Australia again in 1977 that I began to pursue the subject in earnest. My first step on arrival was to make contact with a number of RAN officers, both serving and retired, but they all assured me that the whole episode had been exhaustively investigated at the time and that there would be no prospect of my being able to reveal anything new.[20]

After gathering 'a mass of material that has taken . . . the best part of three years to accumulate and assimilate . . . includ[ing] evidence for the very strong motives that the navy has for not wishing to see the subject resurrected', Montgomery published *Who Sank the Sydney?*[21] in 1981.

The title and the approach were deliberately provocative. Montgomery claimed a long-running conspiracy was preventing vital information about the loss of *Sydney* being made public. At the heart of this contention was the inference that Gill and the Naval Board closely colluded in that part of the official volume which deals with the loss of *Sydney*. Montgomery alleged that an elaborate and hitherto successful cover-up had prevented the 'facts' from being publicly known.

There are curious omissions in the recorded evidence as it now exists in naval archives and other official sources[22] . . . Everything thus points to the Navy having been in possession of all the essential facts, but having been equally determined to pretend otherwise. Little, if anything, has happened since the war to contradict such an inference.[23]

Montgomery's allegation of a cover-up was founded on the basis of a mere inference. It was curious that Montgomery should make such allegations when his acknowledgments mention the assistance he had received from the Naval Historical Officer in Navy Office, and from a number of senior officers, including Commodore Rory Burnett, the younger of Joseph Burnett's two sons, who was still serving in the Navy at that time.

Montgomery's starting point was the German accounts. After

perusing the interrogation records, Montgomery quite rightly believed that the German accounts were unreliable. Some of them contained more truth than others which, he argued, were offered to deceive. Those which seemed to challenge the conventional accounts he tended to accept, on the grounds that they were given by men who had not been influenced by Detmers or the other officers. One such account was contained in a diary allegedly written by Petty Officer Heinz Kitsche

> which was discovered after the war hidden in the false back of a box under a house in New South Wales belonging to a German expatriate; it seems that it was smuggled there by a sympathiser following an escape that Kitsche made from Murchison.[24]

However, the alleged diary was merely a German translation of an English magazine article written by the journalist Robert Close. As mentioned earlier in relation to Close's repetition of the allegation that *Kormoran* was flying the Norwegian flag at the time of the action with *Sydney*, Close had no special access to naval records or officials, or the *Kormoran* survivors. When the President of the *Kormoran* Survivors' Association, ex-Petty Officer Otto Jurgensen, showed Kitsche a copied page from the hand-written diary he was alleged to have written, Kitsche said he was not the author.

Although he failed to explore the questionable origins of the alleged diary, Montgomery was not put off by the grandiose and florid style of the prose. He used the 'Kitsche diary' as the basis for his contention that *Kormoran* had been flying the Norwegian flag, and for a range of other allegations. The following quotation covering the period before the engagement is a sample of the diary's style and Montgomery's regard for its historical veracity.

> [Detmers] put his glasses to his eyes and recognised the increasing silhouette of the warship. He said, 'If it wasn't for the fact that they haven't launched their aircraft, I would say that it was the *Sydney*'. The First Officer [Foerster] replied 'Eight fifteen millimetre guns; it is

the *Sydney*, Herr Kapitan.' [So much for Detmers' pretence that it was not until he was landed at Carnarvon that he established this; several others of his crew also admitted under interrogation that they had known her identity all along.][25] (Montgomery's brackets)

Three points can be made in reply. First, it is not clear why Detmers thought the approaching ship was *Sydney* or why he rejected the possibility simply because she had not launched her aircraft. Second, the RAN had, of course, three light cruisers armed with eight 6-inch guns. If the basis of his identification was a description of her main armament, the ship allegedly identified by Foerster could, for all he knew, just as easily have been *Hobart* or *Perth*. Third, there is no direct reference to *Sydney* in the interrogation reports. Montgomery has failed to provide a reference for his claim that they did. However, the episode of the 'Kitsche diary' demonstrates the extent to which Montgomery was determined to attribute every conceivable form of guilt on the part of *Kormoran*'s crew.

Unfortunately for Montgomery, the accounts of several men in *Aquitania* who had not been influenced by the *Kormoran*'s officers also upheld the broad details contained in the conventional view of the action. Whereas Montgomery might have concluded from these conflicting accounts that the conventional description of the action was open to challenge, and that the truth was probably contained somewhere within all of the accounts which had been given, he showed as much selectivity in accepting some accounts and rejecting others as had those he had criticised for producing the conventional description.

In rejecting most of the conventional descriptions of the action, Montgomery alleged that *Kormoran* had engaged *Sydney* with gunfire and torpedoes under the flag of a neutral nation, that of Norway rather than the Netherlands; that a Japanese submarine acted in concert with *Kormoran* to sink *Sydney*; that the Australian cruiser was not sunk where the circumstantial evidence suggested she was lost; and that Australian survivors from the engagement were machine-gunned in the water to prevent them from reporting the involvement of a Japanese submarine. To establish a wider significance for the loss of *Sydney* and, one suspects, to reach a larger market for his book, Montgomery asserts that the commission by Japan of an act of war three weeks before the attack on Pearl Harbor was concealed as part of a wider Allied effort involving Australia and Britain to force the United States into the war.

An examination of Montgomery's sources, in the instances where references were given, revealed that most of these claims were little more than deliberate speculation designed to create controversy. There was no pretence of balance or careful scholarship in *Who Sank the Sydney?* It was a polemical, finger-pointing, brawling account which offered conclusions that were either inadequately supported by evidence or were based on evidence consciously distorted to suit the author's purpose. This is despite Montgomery's statement that

> it is no part of my purpose to stir up recriminations among parties to an event which took place all of forty years ago, either over simple errors of judgment, or over actions committed by men of an impressionable age and under influence of philosophies that their countries have long since renounced.[26]

One could be excused for thinking otherwise given the obvious public reaction that Montgomery should have expected from his vigorous claims that survivors from *Sydney* were machine-gunned as they sought assistance from the crew of *Kormoran*.

Montgomery thought it was likely that the ship's company from *Sydney* had met this fate because *Kormoran* had earlier allegedly fired on a lifeboat from *British Union*. Commander Irwin Chapman RAN, the intelligence officer in HMS *Arawa*, stated that the survivors recovered by *Arawa* claimed that *Kormoran* had fired on one of the other lifeboats from *British Union* while it was in the water, and that in their lifeboat they lay down to avoid being detected by *Kormoran*'s sweeping searchlight.[27] Montgomery also misquoted a letter from Harold Hearne, another member of *Arawa*'s ship's company, to the Naval Board in December 1941. According to Montgomery, Hearne stated that while 'lowering the lifeboats they were machine-gunned; all except one were wounded . . . ' This suggests that the crew of the *British Union* were wounded while they lowered the boats. However, Hearne's letter actually stated: 'whilst lowering the lifeboats they [i.e. the lifeboats] were machine-gunned, consequently all the contents of one of the boats was lost, such as lamp, water, compass etc, if we had not found them they would certainly have died of thirst'. The letter did not include the statement 'all except one were wounded'. Hearne recalled that several of the survivors were wounded but did not say they received their injuries while lowering the boat. In reply to Hearne's letter, the Secretary to the Naval Board advised that the 'information supplied by you has been substantiated by the evidence of the prisoners, who, of course, deny having machine-gunned the boats'.[28]

None of the survivors from *British Union* embarked in the lifeboat allegedly machine-gunned later reported this incident. Winter also claims that Montgomery was told by a survivor from the tanker *Alexander Bandeen* that they had not been fired upon by *Kormoran*. In sum, the evidence supporting this allegation is highly questionable. In such circumstances, Montgomery should have raised the incident with caution, rather than with outrage.

Equally contestable is Montgomery's claim that he had

> done enough to demonstrate, to those of the bereaved, that their menfolk's lives were not needlessly sacrificed as they have been led to believe all these years by a conspiracy of silence surrounding what has been described as 'the most monumental bloomer in our navy's history'.[29]

Montgomery's investigative method and literary style were better described as tabloid journalism than serious history. If Montgomery's aim was to create sensation, he achieved his objective. The only drawback was that his conclusions were so outrageous that even the most populist sections of the media found difficulty in accepting them without some reservations.

But some reviewers, such as Arthur King in the *Journal of the Australian Naval Institute*,[30] were persuaded by some of his conclusions, particularly those relating to *Kormoran*'s alleged Norwegian disguise, the purpose of the QQQ signal and the 'real' location of the action. King also said that the submarine and machine-gunning theories 'may seem far-fetched, but there is some evidence to support both and such possibilities should not be discarded lightly'. However, Captain Sam Bateman RAN was critical of Montgomery's methodology.

> Montgomery's analysis shows some evidence of considerable research and is full of 'plausible' ideas but there is little real 'meat'. While some of the scenarios he conjures up are feasible, albeit remotely so, there is scant explanation of why the incident should have occurred in the way he appears to be suggesting . . . It is a pity that Montgomery did not get to grips with some hard historical research rather than letting his imagination run riot with circumstantial evidence and wild conjecture.[31]

In addition to creating a public controversy where none existed previously, the foremost effect of Montgomery's book for Australian naval history was to complicate the issues about which there could be doubt. Consequently, another two contentious issues were added to the already open-ended debate: when did the Naval Board learn about the loss of *Sydney* and what exactly was it told? And second, was there ever an elaborate attempt to conceal the true circumstances of the ship being lost, a cover-up which allegedly continues?

Not surprisingly, Montgomery had no positive evidence that a massive cover-up was ever in progress. He relied, as most conspiracy theorists do, on the argument of silence. Because the official files did not contain the information Montgomery believed they should have contained, there must have been a cover-up and records destroyed. Of course, one could contend that the more successful the cover-up the better the conspirators have managed to conceal their tracks—a very convenient defence for Montgomery. However, there is little circumstantial evidence to support his allegations of a cover-up, and even less evidence of a motive for such a conspiracy.

Without proving that a substantial motive or motives did exist, Montgomery's claims of a cover-up cannot be sustained. His assertion that the involvement of a Japanese submarine constituted such a motive is open to challenge, especially since the involvement of a Japanese submarine cannot be proved with primary evidence. Of course, if the involvement of the Japanese could be positively disproved, Montgomery's motive for the cover-up would collapse as well. The possible involvement of the Imperial Japanese Navy is considered in detail in a later chapter. All that needs to be said here is that the basis on which Montgomery claims a conspiratorial motive existed is highly suspect.

After Montgomery's book was released, Barbara Winter published what was in effect, although not totally in intention, a reply to Montgomery in *HMAS Sydney: Fact, Fantasy and Fraud* in 1984.[32] Winter, whose maiden name was Till and whose married name is Poniewierski, lived near the Great Northern Highway between Perth and Carnarvon at the time *Sydney* was lost. She studied modern languages at the University of Western Australia and the Karl-Ruprecht University in Heidelberg. She later moved to Queensland where she has lived ever since. Having spent a large part of her working life as a secondary school teacher specialising in foreign languages, Winter made use of overseas archives in her first book, *Atlantis is Missing*, which concerned the experiences of two German fliers lost in the Kimberley Ranges in 1932, and in her study of the *Sydney–Kormoran* action. Since completing her book on *Sydney*, Winter has published *Stalag Australia*, a volume describing the experiences of German POWs in Australia, and *The Intrigue Master*, a major study of Commander R.B.M. Long RAN and Australian naval intelligence during World War II.

Winter began her formal research into the loss of *Sydney* shortly after Montgomery had started but did not know of his work until some time later. Winter's book is very different in style and tone from *Who Sank the Sydney?* It is written in a conversational style with a sprinkling of anecdotal material to season the narrative. Although the flow of the book was disrupted by her attempts to weave the activities of *Sydney* and *Kormoran* together, it is a much better organised book than *Who Sank the Sydney?* Whereas Montgomery concentrated on Australian and British sources, Winter undertook detailed research into German and American material while making much better use of Australian wartime intelligence records.

HMAS Sydney: Fact, Fantasy and Fraud is a reasonable and persuasive account, and Winter deserved the complimentary reviews the book received. However, she tried too hard to defend the crew of the *Kormoran*, and Detmers in particular, at the expense of *Sydney* and Burnett. She was also too ready to overlook the many variations in the accounts given by the Germans after the action.

In effect, Winter upheld the general thrust of Gill's account that Burnett was at fault. She attempted to explain the action largely in terms of the relative competence of the two ships' captains, and seemed unwilling to admit other factors into her explanation of a naval engagement which should have been one-sided. According to Winter, *Sydney* was lost primarily because Burnett was inexperienced in wartime and professionally deficient.

> There were a number of Australians whose first command was a cruiser. It was absolutely unthinkable [in the Royal Navy] but it was Australian practice at that time. Burnett had to have command of a ship in order to be promoted to rear admiral. That was why they gave him a cruiser. They gave it to him in what they thought was a quiet area so that he could get in his sea time without doing any damage.

She thus infers that Burnett was less than fully competent. However, it needs to be remembered that the Australian Navy took great care to keep officer employment policies in line with those pursued by the Royal Navy; it was on the professional judgment of British officers that Burnett was appointed in command of *Sydney*; that a number of British officers were in fact appointed to cruisers as their first command; that the size of an officer's first command was of less relevance to his professional development than Winter suggests; that Burnett had considerable experience as an executive officer when his captains would have delegated command responsibility to him in preparation for his own command; that Burnett was appointed in command with the expectation that *Sydney* would be deployed into demanding operations including direct combat with enemy units; and, that Burnett was by that time fitted by training and character to command a cruiser. It should not be held against Burnett, indeed it was not important, that the RAN had an insufficient number of smaller ships in which he could have exercised command earlier in his career.

As for Winter's statement that appointing an officer to a cruiser as his first command was unthinkable in the Royal Navy, one has only to point to the career of Admiral of the Fleet Sir Bruce Fraser to show that this statement is incorrect.

Lord Fraser commanded the Home Fleet in 1942–3, the British Pacific Fleet in 1945 and served as First Sea Lord between 1948 and 1951. His first command was the cruiser HMS *Effingham*, flagship of the East Indies Station, from 1929 to 1932. He then had a short period in command of the newly commissioning cruiser HMS *Leander*. The same was true of Fraser's successor, Admiral Sir Rhoderick McGrigor, whose first command was the battlecruiser HMS *Renown* in 1940–41.[32a]

It is also wrong to claim that Burnett's appointment was simply a prerequisite for promotion to flag rank. Following his time in *Sydney*, Burnett would, in the normal course of events, have been posted to sea again in the rank of captain before the end of the war. He would have probably commanded the flagship *Australia* or the replacement for the lost HMAS *Canberra*, the heavy cruiser *Shropshire*. Burnett's time in command of *Sydney* was preparation for this higher level of command. If Burnett had not been suitable for the command of *Sydney*, it would have been given to another RAN captain who would make the most of the opportunity. Given the career progression of Collins and Farncomb, it was unlikely that Burnett would have been promoted to flag rank much before 1949, eight years after he was appointed in command of *Sydney*.

In contrast to the 'inexperienced' Burnett, Detmers is portrayed by Winter as a seagoing captain accomplished and highly experienced in battle.

There is an arrogant assurance that Australians could not have been beaten in a fair fight, so something was wrong. Indeed there was. *Kormoran*'s captain had wide experience in battle; *Sydney*'s had none. *Kormoran*'s crew had trained and fought together for a year; a high proportion of *Sydney*'s crew had less than three months seagoing experience, and had never been in battle. And *Kormoran*'s firepower was not as inferior to *Sydney*'s as many people think.[33]

But it should be remembered that the essence of this engagement was not the relative merits of the two captains. In fact, it had very little to do with seagoing or battle experience until Burnett allegedly manoeuvred his ship into a position where both *Sydney* and *Kormoran* would certainly be lost. As for the issue of gunnery raised by Winter, the pertinent comparison was not firepower but fire control.

Winter is unable to provide any evidence, other than that which was implicit in the German accounts of *Sydney*'s final action, that Burnett was anything other than a very competent officer. The mitigation she offers on Burnett's behalf is unconvincing. Winter suggests that Burnett may have thought that the unidentified ship off Carnarvon was the unarmed supply ship *Kulmerland* but she does not adequately explain why Burnett might have thought this. At any rate, the fact that Burnett *thought* the unidentified ship *might* have been unarmed does not explain why he would risk the safety of his ship by approaching her without caution. Nor does this apparent mitigation diminish his culpability for *Sydney*'s loss. Winter suggests that Burnett's approach to *Kormoran* was not surprising as

another British ship . . . went to four hundred yards of an unidentified ship. Everybody was doing it . . . Burnett was the poor bunny who got caught.

This is going too far. There is no evidence that 'everybody' was doing what Burnett was alleged to have done.

Winter's view of Burnett's abilities runs parallel to the recollections of Alastair Templeton, who served as a very junior sailor in *Sydney* from July to October 1941. Templeton—a man with a well-developed self-view, an acerbic personality and a grandiose writing style—offered his own account of the loss of *Sydney* 'written at sea level, as it were'. In a letter to me, Templeton stated: 'please take it from me that there is no mystery about the loss of *Sydney*'.[34] In a later letter he stated in clumsy prose that

> It has been induced to believe that there is a mystery, that there is complexity, when, to my 'certain' knowledge, the mystery and complexity are only the creations of ignorance and opportunistic journalism, cemented together by those Araldite-like qualities of self-importance and self-interest.[35]

Templeton claimed, as a raw and inexperienced sailor, that while he was not 'in a position to see and hear everything that went on on every occasion, there were times when significant events occurred and gave an insight into the workings of the captain's mind'. Templeton claimed that on two occasions, Burnett came alongside two unidentified merchant ships and, had they been armed, *Sydney* would have been lost. Further, he claimed that a proportion of the ship's company believed that Burnett's recklessness would eventually have them all killed.

On this basis, it has been suggested that consideration may have been given at Fleet Headquarters in Sydney to relieving Burnett of his command. The termination of Burnett's command may not have resulted, it has been posited, because at that time the office of Chief of Naval Staff was effectively vacant as Colvin had returned to Britain and Royle was yet to commence his duties. However, *Sydney*'s letters of proceedings for the period in which Burnett was in command do not give rise to any suggestion that he was negligent in any approach that he made to any ship. These reports were submitted in the first instance to the RACAS, Rear Admiral Crace, who could, and would if it were justified, have initiated action to remove Burnett from *Sydney*.

Removing commanding officers was an operational matter over which Crace exercised authority from his headquarters in Sydney. He and his staff were ideally placed to intercept any rumours about Burnett's competency should they have been circulating. One suspects that Crace would not have missed the opportunity of commenting adversely on Burnett in his diary if such rumours had been current. During his time as RACAS, Crace showed a willingness to make hard decisions and would have had no hesitation in removing Burnett had he even the slightest doubt about his competence. Had the exercise and termination of command been an administrative matter, which it was not, the Chief of Naval Staff would have initiated action. Thus, the absence of a substantive incumbent in that position is irrelevant.

These suggestions that Burnett was incompetent, albeit expressed tentatively, place more reliance on Templeton's judgments than they can properly bear. One is bound to say that the judgments of Templeton, about the actions and decisions of an experienced seagoing captain possess no historical value. Although Templeton later became a junior officer, his recollections and opinions of Burnett were formed in the mind of a junior sailor who could not, and did not, have the experience and the wherewithal to assess the performance of his captain in any situation. I would doubt Templeton's interpretation and assessment of any event which he might cite in support of his contention that the loss of *Sydney* was in any respect an inevitable or certain occurrence.

There is little support elsewhere for Templeton's views. Lieutenant Commander John Ross, who served in *Sydney* for much longer than Templeton and who was a keen observer of people and events, was dismissive of his allegations:

I am rather baffled about Templeton. His claim that Burnett had 'come alongside' two unidentified merchant-ships during the period of July–October, 1941 is not supported by my memory. Of course, it could be a case either that my memory is failing or that he has a very fertile imagination. I cannot believe, however, that if these incidents did occur (we investigated very few ships during that year, as far as I recall, and certainly would not have come *right alongside* any) there would have been some discussion about them in the Wardroom that I would have heard even if I had not seen the event itself. Such 'recklessness' would most certainly have caused some comment in the Mess. If such a view about Burnett was held onboard it didn't surface in the Mess even though Templeton claims that it was widespread on the lower deck.[35a]

One can also cite the completely contradictory views held of Burnett by another sailor, Tom Fisher, who also served with Burnett in *Sydney*. Fisher, who spent a much longer period in the cruiser and whose action station was on the bridge of *Sydney* where he was the searchlight control operator, thought that Burnett was a 'very alert man' and 'was well thought of by the older crew as a very able and competent captain'. Another ex-*Sydney* sailor, Stoker Ken Holt, told Montgomery that 'there was no lack of confidence in Burnett on the lower deck, and that morale continued to be high and discipline tight'.[36] Albert Putman, who served in *Sydney* during Burnett's command, wrote a number of letters to his aunt about the ship's activities. These letters, which make no mention of Burnett being considered incompetent by anyone on the lower deck, are held in the Australian War Memorial.[37] Fisher also recalls that on 5 October 1941, Burnett addressed the ship's company after Sunday-morning divisions and told them 'there was a raider about, and that he intended to get it'.[38] His evidence is also relevant in assessing Burnett's approach to unidentified contacts at sea.

During the trip back to Fremantle from Sunda Strait (in October 1941) . . . we sighted an object on the sea. [There was] no reply to [*Sydney*'s] challenge, so Captain Burnett stood approximately six miles off with the ship closed up at action stations, and sent a motor boat away to examine [the] object. It turned out to be a target consisting of four 44-gallon drums, a platform and a mast. The target was picked up by the ship's crane and hoisted inboard at the port waist. It was dismantled and landed at Fremantle on 7 October 1941.[39]

Chaplain Norman Symes, who wanted to embark in the investigating motor boat, was told by Burnett that this was not wise. In recalling the incident, Symes said, 'I saw that day how cautiously Captain Burnett did his job; he was always a safety-first man and not one to take risks.'[40] If one is to believe the evidence of the *Kormoran* survivors, these descriptions of Burnett and his conduct are plainly inconsistent with his actions six weeks later off Carnarvon. Who, then, is to be believed?

In my view, Winter relies far too heavily on the need for Burnett to be seen as professionally incompetent for the German accounts to be accepted without serious reservations. But Winter readily acknowledged that her book was far from being the final word. As she stated at the beginning of her book, 'The history without error or omission has yet to be written.'[41]

There was no doubt, however, that both Montgomery and Winter had shown that Gill's account was suspect despite the comments of Associate Professor John Robertson in his introduction to the 1985 reprint of Gill's volume. Robertson comments that the debate over the loss of *Sydney*

has attracted the attention of amateur historians, resulting in a misleading version of *Sydney*'s loss. [Footnote: Many of the questionable assertions in Michael Montgomery, *Who Sank the Sydney?* are convincingly refuted in the more thorough *HMAS Sydney: Fact, Fantasy and Fraud* by Barbara Winter.] The best, most polished account we have of this encounter with *Kormoran* is still Gill's gripping story.[42]

It would be difficult to describe Gill's account as 'gripping'. It was fanciful to suggest that an account of 12 pages was to be preferred in an absolute sense to two major works on the subject, notwithstanding their flaws. Gill no longer had the final word.

The ship laid down as HMS Phaeton is launched as HMAS *Sydney* on 22 December 1934. (*WA Newspapers*)

Sydney berthing at Fremantle in August 1936. (*WA Newspapers*)

A view of *Sydney* looking aft. The Walrus amphibian and catapult are visible in the middle ground. (*WA Newspapers*)

The *Bartolomeo Colleoni* ablaze after her engagement with *Sydney* on 19 July 1940. (*WA Newspapers*)

Sailors in Alexandria surround the hole in *Sydney*'s funnel caused by the only direct hit scored by the enemy during the Cape Spada action. (*RAN Historical Section*)

Sydney's command team in February 1941. *From left*: Lieutenant Commander Michael Singer, Commander Thomas Hilken, Captain John Collins, Engineer Commander Lionel Dalton, Lieutenant Commander Edmund Thruston. (*WA Newspapers*)

Captain Joseph Burnett RAN, commanding officer of HMAS *Sydney* from May 1941. (*WA Newspapers*)

Sydney's Communications Department photographed in 1941. In the centre of the front row is the navigator, Lieutenant Commander Clive Montgomery, and (to his left) Chief Officer Telegraphist David Shepherd. (*Joan Dent*)

Sydney as she appeared on 1 August 1941. Note the carley floats on the stern deck.
(*AWM 301407*)

The troopship *Aquitania* photographed in Gage Roads, Fremantle, in December 1945.
Also visible is the tug *Wyola*. (*WA Newspapers*)

HSK *Kormoran*. (*RAN Historical Section*)

Commander Theodor Detmers in the rose garden outside his home in Hamburg shortly before he died. (*WA Newspapers*)

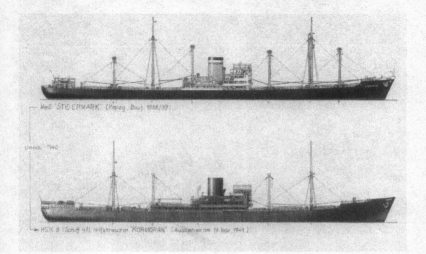

MoS "STEIERMARK" (Hapag, Bauj. 1938/39)

Umbau 1940

HSK 8 (Schiff 41) Hilfskreuzer "KORMORAN" (Aussehen am 19. Nov. 1941)

Die Tarnung: MS "STRAAT MALAKKA" (KPM, Bauj. 1939)

HMAS "SYDNEY" (Aussehen 1941)

Jochen Mühle
1988

Three carley floats are visible on the stern deck of Sydney. Astern of Sydney are the transport ships *Queen Mary* and *Queen Elizabeth*. This photograph was taken on 4 September 1941. (*AWM 128904*)

Painting of the engagement between HSK *Kormoran* and HMAS *Sydney*. (*Jochin Sachse*)

The Navy and the 'Official' History

The account of the *Sydney–Kormoran* action published by George Hermon Gill in 1957 seems to have played a major role in creating the unfolding controversy surrounding the events of 19 November 1941. An inability to accept the truthfulness of Gill's account and a suspicion that its publication was part of an elaborate official program of disinformation have led to the denunciation of Gill and doubts about the integrity of his work. This has also fuelled suggestions that the Naval Board was an active and long-term participant in a conspiracy to conceal what was known about the loss of *Sydney*. Gill's critics and detractors do not appear to know much about the man who was appointed the official historian of the RAN in World War II.

Gill was one of a long line of Australian naval officers who, although acting in a private capacity, have taken a leading role in shaping what is known of the RAN's past. Naval officers such as William Creswell, Herbert Feakes, John Collins, James Goldrick, Bob Nicholls, Peter Jones, David Stevens, John Pengman and Greg Swinden, and Navy civil servants such as George Macandie and Robert Hyslop ISO, have made substantial contributions to the extant body of knowledge. They have all been unashamed polemicists believing that the strongest argument for the continued development of the RAN was its history. Gill was foremost among them as I explained in the short biographical essay I produced for the *Australian Dictionary of Biography* in 1995.

In his introduction to the 1985 reprint of the official history of the RAN in World War II, Associate Professor John Robertson commented that Gill 'stresses the importance of seapower. His argument is not special pleading, but he is more concerned than the other historians to write as an advocate for his service'. Gill was born in 1895 and served for most of the 1914–18 war as a young officer in the British merchant service. After the war he worked as a journalist before serving for the duration of World War II at Navy Office. He died in 1973. The two volumes he produced as official historian were the only major literary works he ever published.

Gill was not the subject of any personal derision and criticism until 1981. As noted in a previous chapter, Montgomery began his research into the loss of *Sydney* because Gill's account 'fell short of satisfying my curiosity'[1] and he doubted Gill's claim that 'no room was left for doubt as to the accuracy of the German accounts'. As Gill's account covered just 12 pages that was hardly surprising. But his remark that he was persuaded to research the matter more fully by the families and friends of those lost in *Sydney* 'who have felt unable to accept the official account of her loss' suggests a predilection to reject this view not on the balance of available evidence or its plausibility, but on the basis of preferring one view over another. This is a flawed basis for approaching any topic in history. It is also unfair.

As noted in a previous chapter, Gill's account of the *Sydney–Kormoran* action was brief, only 12 of the 689 pages of the first volume in his two-part official history.[2] Many of the criticisms of Gill's account are directed at what he did not write. But Gill cannot be fairly criticised for the brevity of his account of the loss of *Sydney*. As the official historian his task was to record and describe a vast body of history covering naval administration, policy and operations. The same editorial limitations which affected all the authors of the history of World War II also applied to Gill and these prevented him from treating any subject exhaustively. The depth of his discussion of *Sydney* was consistent enough with his treatment of subjects of similar significance.

His account was based primarily on a 1942 report prepared by the Directorate of Naval Intelligence. His discussion of the *Sydney–Kormoran* action was placed in the wider context of the raider problem facing Australia at that time. Following a brief discussion of the activities of the raiders *Komet*, *Orion* and *Atlantis*, Gill outlined the origins of *Kormoran* and her successes in the period to October 1941. He then introduced Burnett and commented that he was marked early as an officer of 'professional achievement and promise' who later 'shone as a staff officer'. Gill commented that the first months of Burnett's command were filled with escort duties, culminating in the delivery of *Zealandia* to HMS *Durban* in the Sunda Strait. Gill stated that *Sydney* sailed with the transport and that her expected return to Fremantle was advised as pm 19 November, later amended to 20 November, and that this was the last that was ever heard from *Sydney*.

He then explained that her failure to arrive on time would not initially have caused too much concern. But by 23 November, anxiety about *Sydney*'s safety was such that she was ordered to break radio silence. After a brief account of the recovery of the *Kormoran* survivors and the search for *Sydney*, Gill began his account of the engagement with a rather remarkable preamble.

> From *Sydney* herself no word was ever received, and only one small shell-torn float was found as tangible evidence of her loss, in spite of wide and thorough searching. The story of her last action was pieced together through exhaustive interrogation of *Kormoran*'s survivors. No room was left for doubt as to its accuracy.[3]

It is questionable whether Gill was entitled to say that the interrogation was exhaustive, and that no room for doubt about the German accounts existed. A critical observer of the interrogations might have said that their conduct had left plenty of room for doubt.

In describing the action, Gill stated that at about 1600 on 19 November, *Kormoran* sighted *Sydney* and turned towards the sun at best possible speed. At 20 000 yards, *Sydney* altered towards *Kormoran* and closed on the raider's starboard quarter, signalling 'NNJ' by flashing light as she went. *Kormoran* made no reply until *Sydney* was 14 000 yards away when she signalled by light to hoist her signal letters. *Kormoran* flew the Dutch flag and hoisted the letters 'PKQ1' for *Straat Malakka*. At 1700, Gill accepts that *Kormoran* sent a QQQ signal which 'was picked up, faint and in mutilated form, by the tug *Uco*, and by Geraldton wireless station'.[4] The portion of the signal received by Geraldton gave no indication that it was a distress signal. When there was a request from Geraldton to all ships to report if necessary, there was no reply. The Naval Board, according to Gill, did not learn of the 'Q' signal's receipt by Geraldton radio until 27 November.

Despite the existence of conflicting evidence from the German survivors, Gill states that *Sydney* was alongside *Kormoran* at 1715 at a range of less than 2000 yards and that both ships were steering 'WSW at about 15 knots. The cruiser was at action stations with all guns and torpedo tubes bearing'.[5] With her aircraft running and mounted on the catapult, the reason for which Gill does not explain, *Sydney* signalled by flag and light: 'Where bound?', to which the raider replied 'Batavia'. The following passage of events is proof in Gill's mind that the German accounts were accurate.

> The crucial moment was approaching. *Sydney* made a two flag hoist, the letters IK, which the raider could not interpret. They were in fact (and their being quoted correctly under interrogation is corroboration of the German story) the secret letters of *Straat Malakka*'s secret identification signal, which was unknown to the Germans. They made no reply.[6]

The official historian accepted that on being directed to show her secret sign, Detmers ordered the Dutch flag to be struck, the German battle ensign to be hoisted and the raider's guns to be fired at 1730. Based on Skeries' evidence, Gill accepted that the first two shots from *Kormoran* ranged short at 1400 yards then above the cruiser at 1700 yards. Thus, *Sydney* must have been about 1500 yards from *Kormoran*. Within four seconds of firing, *Kormoran* had scored hits on *Sydney*'s bridge and gunnery director tower. Gill states that *Sydney*'s first salvo went over the raider and that her forward turrets did not engage. However, the after turrets fired on *Kormoran* hitting the raider in the funnel and in the engine room. It was at this point that one of the two torpedoes from *Kormoran*, launched at the time of the initial salvo, struck the cruiser under A and B turrets. *Sydney* then veered to port under the stern of the raider. As the cruiser slowly headed towards the south, *Kormoran* continued to fire. At 1745, *Sydney* fired a pattern of four torpedoes, all of which failed to hit their target. At 1825 when *Sydney* was at a range of 11 000 yards, *Kormoran* ceased fire. Gill seems to have preferred Detmers' recollection of the post-engagement events as his account conforms most closely with Detmers' evidence.

Having made the surprising judgment that the German accounts were entirely accurate and having completely neglected their inconsistency, Gill suggested that 'the story of how *Sydney* was lost would appear to be straightforward'. Yet in the very next sentence, he stated: 'What induced Burnett to place her in the position where her loss in such a way was possible, must remain conjecture'.[7] Given that Gill could not account for Burnett's reasons in approaching *Kormoran* as he did, and that within that reasoning the conduct of the *Sydney*'s engagement with *Kormoran* had its origins and essential form, this was a confusing, if not contradictory, statement. He then tried, unsuccessfully, to find mitigation for what was either poor judgment or negligence on the part of Burnett. It is not clear from the official history whether even Gill is convinced by his defence of *Sydney*'s captain.

Gill mentions that Burnett had peacetime experience comparable with his contemporaries but that his wartime employment in Navy Office, and 'the employment of his first wartime sea command in routine duties in an area which for nearly twelve months had known no enemy action', appeared to leave him deficient in wartime experience. Consequently, 'he lacked that experience which, gained in a recognised war zone, sharpens suspicion and counsels caution on all chance meetings'. It was arguable whether the area in which *Sydney* was steaming had not known enemy action, at least in the absolute sense implied by Gill, or that Burnett would not have utilised the vast wartime operational experience of his command team to complement his own limited experience in war. Good captains rely on the officers in their ship who have been trained thoroughly, and who possess experience and judgment. When they show trust, they are more likely to be regarded as outstanding captains. There is nothing to suggest that Burnett would not have been open to the advice and counsel of his senior officers, or that these officers would not have felt able to approach Burnett to offer their advice or express their opinions. An earlier chapter in this book demonstrates this.

Having hinted that Burnett was ill-prepared for this 'chance meeting', Gill then seems to doubt his previous assertion by reflecting on the fact that as the Deputy Chief of Naval Staff

> he had participated as a behind the scenes operator in the earlier raider attacks on or near the Australia Station. He would have realised that a repetition was always possible. From the fact that he went to action stations and approached *Kormoran* with his main armament and torpedo tubes bearing, it would seem that he had suspicions of her *bona fides*. If it were just a routine measure, other routine measures of greater importance in such a situation were neglected.[8]

Perhaps in an effort to show an even hand, Gill then tried to alleviate some of the blame borne by Burnett. This was done by concluding that the action was, from the Allied viewpoint, inexplicable.

> Why Burnett did not use his aircraft, did not keep his distance and use his superior speed and armament, did not confirm his suspicions by asking Navy Office by wireless if *Straat Malakka* was in the area, are questions that can never be answered.

And because these questions could never be answered, Burnett had to enjoy the benefit of at least some doubt. However, Gill's attempts to use similar Allied encounters with German raiders to explain Burnett's actions strain credibility and fail to convince. While noting that *Devonshire*'s actions in sinking *Atlantis* were entirely correct, Gill attempts to imply that very minor criticisms of Farncomb's performance while in command of *Canberra* during the sinking of *Coburg* and *Ketty Brovig* may have caused Burnett to hazard his ship.

In his post-action report on the sinking of the two enemy ships, Farncomb did not justify the large amount of ammunition that was expended in destroying them. As the Acting Chief of Naval Staff, Commodore Durnford (the Second Naval Member) asked whether any further official action was suggested in relation to the ammunition used by Farncomb. As the Deputy Chief of Naval Staff, Burnett read Farncomb's report and saw Durnford's comments on the Navy Office file. However, he merely initialled the file and did not suggest any action despite Durnford's invitation. Gill notes that several weeks later a letter was received in Navy Office from the Commander-in-Chief East Indies, Vice Admiral Leatham, regarding the action. On the subject of ammunition expended, Leatham commented:

> It was correct that *Canberra* should have taken precautions against the possibility of the supposed raider firing torpedoes, but I think it was being over cautious to avoid approaching nearer than 19,000 yards on this account. Had a more effective range been attained quickly the enemy might have been identified sooner and much ammunition saved.

As Burnett had already joined *Sydney* in command, Gill could only assume that the copy of Leatham's letter which was forwarded to Admiral Crace was also shown to Burnett. There is no evidence that Burnett did see the letter. Consequently, there was no way Gill could know what reaction it might have evoked from Burnett. Leatham's letter was, in any event, unclear. What precisely was Leatham's 'more effective range'? The answer would depend on each ship's gunnery system, the state of training and the weather. For *Sydney*'s 6-inch system, at a mid-point in her commission and with fine weather, the range would have been between 12 000 and 14 000 yards. It was certainly not 1500 yards. To suggest, as Gill does, that Burnett's possibly extreme reaction to Leatham's comments contributed to the loss of *Sydney* is conjectural and illogical.

Gill's suggestion that Burnett was concerned about the approach of sunset and wanted to remove all doubt about the identity of the suspect ship before darkness is also untenable as an explanation. Burnett had at least two and a half hours from the time he could send a visual signal to the suspect ship to the moment when sunset became a pertinent factor. He also had ample time to signal Navy Office when the suspect ship claimed it was *Straat Malakka*.

Gill also fails to explain why the need to have the interrogation completed by sunset would have 'swayed [Burnett] to over-confidence'. If anything, it would have prompted carelessness. But having opted for the theory that Farncomb's experience was the key to understanding Burnett's actions, Gill was left with no choice but to state that 'to act as Burnett did was to court disaster should a trap exist'. Thus, he assumed that Burnett was trying consciously to avoid the criticisms made of Farncomb for wasting ammunition by firing at a target that was at excessive range. As has already been stated, there is no evidence that this was in Burnett's mind.

But the official historian did not believe that Burnett's actions would have been wise in any event

> for even had *Sydney* triumphed in an action it is improbable that it would have been without damage and casualties, and Burnett would have been unable to explain the risks he ran.

In other words, all that Burnett would have achieved, aside from a court martial, was a reduced expenditure of ammunition.

Gill is right when he says, according to his own theory, that the element of surprise would have remained with Detmers until 'Burnett's suspicions deepened into absolute certainty. In the circumstances Burnett created, he could not have reached such certainty until Detmers abandoned all disguise and struck'. In effect, there was no mitigation for Burnett.

This created a strange situation. Gill offered a theory to explain *Sydney*'s actions but readily conceded that the theory was full of objections and improbabilities. Yet he expected the reader to believe that these objections and improbabilities were not similarly apparent to Burnett who was actually a witness to the whole event. Why then would Burnett have been so negligent—for this is what Gill is alleging—in placing his ship in such a dangerous position? Perhaps Gill does not realise the sheer gravity of his allegations for the professional reputation of Burnett. This possibility is reflected in Gill's failure to answer the questions begged by his own conclusions. However, the post-action sequence of events proved less vexing for the official historian.

Gill is able to accept that *Sydney* sustained mortal damage from *Kormoran*'s gunfire and torpedoes. As the cruiser was on fire for at least five hours after the action:

> It is not surprising that there were no survivors, for after the punishment she received from shells and bullets, and the ravages of fires on board, it is unlikely that much that could float remained.[9]

The Naval Board was not completely exonerated by Gill. He was critical of the Board for failing to request an appropriate censorship instruction when concerns about *Sydney*'s fate arose on 23 November. Gill was also critical of the Commonwealth government, which had the Chief Publicity Censor, Edmund Bonney, issue a censorship instruction on 25 November which read, 'No reference press or radio to HMAS *Sydney*'. As *Sydney* was widely rumoured to be overdue in Fremantle, this instruction implied that *Sydney* had been involved in an action and further speculation in the absence of factual information resulted.

Gill's conclusions are seriously flawed, inconsistent and contradictory. In parts of his account, Gill tried to be declarative. He accepted substantial elements of the German accounts but tried to argue that Burnett's actions remained inexplicable to the extent that Gill had some reservation about attributing complete and absolute blame to *Sydney*'s captain. Gill tried in his account to gain the trust of his readers with an almost patronising tone of reassurance. He sought to convince them that, as a professional historian, he had undertaken comprehensive research into the loss of *Sydney* and that no piece of evidence remained unexamined. There was, of course, a great deal of material that he had not seen.

In other places, Gill made statements and drew conclusions that went well beyond the reliable and corroborated evidence which was available to him. In attempting to exclude doubt where it continued to exist, Gill showed that he was susceptible to a temptation to which many good historians succumb. He tried to offer firm and incontestable conclusions, and expected to have the last word on the matter. However, his narrative did not justify such conclusions nor did his research entitle him to close this chapter of Australian naval history. Although Gill's account of *Sydney*'s loss can be described as poor history, it was nothing more than that. By being so 'matter of fact' about the loss of *Sydney*, Gill raised many more questions than he answered. But there is no evidence to suggest, as Montgomery does, that his account was part of a grand conspiracy of deception within officialdom. Furthermore, it is most unlikely that the Naval Board at the time Gill produced his account would have been behind the criticisms of Burnett contained in the official account. This would also have been contrary to the mind-set of the senior officers serving in the Navy at that time. I observed similar attitudes during another similar research project.

Very early in my research into the loss of HMAS *Voyager* in equally controversial circumstances in 1964, I realised that naval officers were extremely loath to criticise their colleagues publicly, or to see them criticised by others in public. They hold this view notwithstanding their own views of the conduct of the individual who is the subject of comment, or their personal regard for the individual. In other words, even if their fellow officers are guilty of some offence, they do not gain any pleasure from seeing them suffer publicly. This is consistent with the 'tribal' nature of professional groups who see a criticism of one of their number as criticism of their profession. If anything, this attitude would have been more strongly held in the mid-1950s when Gill came to complete his first volume. Furthermore, most of the members of the Naval Board at that time either had been at the Naval College when Burnett was there, or had served with him during the 1930s. If they had been able to influence Gill in any way they would, if anything, have tried to have him dilute his criticisms of Burnett.

It is also apparent that many self-styled revisionist historians, such as Montgomery, fail to understand the status of Australia's official war histories. Montgomery told the 1991 *Sydney* Forum in Fremantle:

> In talking about 'the official accounts', I should perhaps begin by defining my terms. For the purposes of this paper, the official English-language account of the action will be taken as that contained in Hermon Gill's *Royal Australian Navy 1939–42*, which was published in 1957 . . . On the German side, the official history may be said to be that embodied in Captain Detmers' book *Hilfskreuzer Kormoran* published in 1959.

It is strange that Montgomery should describe Detmers' work as in any sense 'official' when it was written and published by a commercial publisher when Detmers was a civilian. Detmers sought no assistance from the German Navy in producing his book and included no disclaimer as one would expect in an 'official' account. Detmers' account of the *Sydney–Kormoran* engagement is no more official than that produced by Ahl for the *Naval Historical Review* in 1979.

What Montgomery and some other writers fail to appreciate about official history is that the statements in Gill's account are not supported, sanctioned or endorsed by the Navy. What he has written is not, and never has been, the 'official' view of the RAN. All of the official histories of Australia at war in the twentieth century, from World War I to Vietnam and more recent minor operations and peacekeeping missions, were commissioned by the Commonwealth government. However, they do not represent the views of the government, or any government agency, including the Navy. The official historians themselves are at pains to emphasise that the views expressed in their work are personal and do not represent the views of ministers, the Service Boards or the Chiefs of Staff. In fact, the Chief of Naval Staff and the Naval Board at the time when Gill's first volume was released might have had completely different views. This crucial point has not been understood properly.

There are several reasons for the official historians being independent from the Services about which they are writing. In the first instance it has to do with historiography. At the heart of history are the judgments of the historian. An institution is unable, because of the diversity of views, attitudes and values held by its constituents, to make judgments in the same way that an individual can. Thus, the Navy cannot properly have an endorsed historical view of its own. The Navy could state that the majority within the Service held one view over and above another. But this is a collective view rather than an institutional view with the former only having significance because it is the sum total of a number of individual views.

For an institution such as the Navy to hold, endorse or propagate a particular view of history would be wrong. It would also be to interfere improperly in what is a historical matter which history and its practitioners must judge. If the Navy insisted on advocating and pressing a particular corporate view, it would be on dangerous ground. The most the Navy can do is to point to the views of competent historians and the reasons for which their views might or might not appear convincing. There should be little need to say that retired naval officers, however senior or distinguished, do not speak for the RAN; they speak only for themselves. I have found no evidence to suggest that the Navy has ever tried to develop, propagate or defend as history any official view of any naval event, including the loss of *Sydney*.

In Australia, the independence of the official histories has been strongly defended since the idea for a 'National Histories of the War' series was proposed by the former war correspondent Charles Bean in 1919.[10] Bean emphasised that the crucial condition was that the volumes be free from censorship and he felt there would be no point in producing a history 'if it were not a book in which one could tell the people of Australia anything which one is convinced they should be told'.[11] From that time, a tradition was established that official historians would not be subject to censorship.

In the preface to the first volume of his official history of Australia in the Korean War, Robert O'Neill states:

> My predecessors as Australian official war historians have been proud to claim that their works have been official only in the sense that the Australian Government opened its records for their examination and provided the essential financial support for the completion and publication of the volumes. In the present case the claim can be no different. I have been subject to no censorship and have been given full access to all relevant materials. The necessary judgments taken regarding the shape of the work and its overall content, and on individual episodes and persons, are entirely my own based as rigorously as possible on the firm evidence available at the time of research and writing.

The official historian of Australia in the Vietnam Conflict, Peter Edwards, concluded after a detailed study of official history in Australia that

> generally speaking the record of Governments with respect to official histories is a credible and honourable one. As far as I am aware, Ministers refrained from exercising the opportunities to intervene with Bean and Long on the histories of the two wars.[12]

By way of example, Edwards states that Sir Wilfred Kent Hughes as Minister for the Interior might have had reason to influence the writing in the official history of the role of General Gordon Bennett in the fall of Singapore and the capture of the Australian 8th Division, given that he was a former staff officer to Bennett. That he kept a proper distance from the official history was as much a reflection of the standing of the official history in Australia as it was of the integrity of Sir Wilfred.[13]

The only documented attempt by the Naval Board to sanitise or, more properly put, to control history, was in the writing of the Official History of the RAN in World War I.[14] In this instance, the Naval Board, made up predominantly of British officers seconded to Australia, did everything it could to frustrate the author, Arthur Jose, who was critical of some British officers and the Admiralty in the opening stages of the war in 1914.

This was the only volume of the series to have met with such interference. In the middle of the long-running controversy in the 1920s, Jose wrote to Charles Bean, the General Editor: 'I know that pukka Australian naval officers have read and approved of my work; it is the imported element that is trying to suppress it.' The difficulties encountered by Jose were not lost on the Australian officers who later commanded the RAN.[15]

There was a similar tension in Britain where the Admiralty strongly disagreed with Sir Julian Corbett's views in the first volume of his official history of the 1914–18 war at sea.[16] The disclaimer that was included at the beginning of that volume publicised the dispute and brought little credit to the Admiralty.

Both Gill and the Naval Board were only too well aware of the widely publicised problems associated with the official histories of both the RAN and the Royal Navy in World War I, and this would have worked against any interference in the World War II naval volumes. Certainly, there is no evidence that there was a repeat performance of Jose's experience when the history of the RAN in the 1939–45 war came to be written. An examination of the Gill papers at the War Memorial justifies such a conclusion. Gill himself also stated: 'The author has been untrammelled by censorship, and given complete freedom in comment and the expression of opinion, for which he alone is responsible.'[17] The only restriction placed upon Gill was that applied to every volume of the World War II series:

> The exercise of censorship by the Government is to be limited to the prevention of disclosure of technical secrets of the three services which it is to preserve in the post-war period.

But remembering that Gill was an RAN Volunteer Reserve (RANVR) officer and that during the war he was employed in Navy Office as Publicity Censorship Liaison Officer, did he have undisclosed motives for distorting the truth or feel any complicity in the events he was describing? It is known, for instance, that Gill was involved in attempts to contain the initial release of information to the Australian press. Gill also maintained a close working relationship with Commander Long and the Directorate of Naval Intelligence (DNI). Was there, then, the tension described by Sir Keith Hancock between 'the historian's loyalty to the standards of his profession and the civil servant's loyalty to the state?'[18]

Gill's departmental action in suppressing any mention of *Sydney* in 1941 was intended to avoid the prospect of the inconclusive information being published in the press. Motives were different four years later: 'Long and Gill refused in 1945 to release information on the loss of *Sydney*'[19] and this led to 'ill-informed, emotional and extravagant rumours spread[ing] unchecked, [and] later publication of the facts could not stamp them out'.[20] With hindsight, withholding information after the war was probably an error of judgment on the part of Gill. While naval inquiries about *Sydney* were continuing and Long remained unconvinced that all that was known about the action had been disclosed, there should have been a full public statement of what was known in 1945. However, there is nothing to suggest that Gill was party to any deception or cover-up, either in 1945 or later.

There is no evidence to show that Gill was anything other than the man of integrity that others believed him to be. He remained throughout his life a journalist and one committed to the ideals of a free press. He would not have continued as official historian had he felt any pressure from the Naval Board on his freedom of expression. His working notes which are preserved at the War Memorial reveal that as an historian, his judgments were prompted solely by the historical evidence available to him and that his conclusions were published without fear or favour. It is for those who allege that Gill's account was consciously fabricated to present evidence that this was the case. They must also show that Gill was susceptible to, and in fact was, pressured by the Naval Board.

Of course, if Gill was directed to prepare a sanitised or 'approved' version of the *Sydney–Kormoran* action, his entire two-volume work is effectively worthless. If the Naval Board did exert editorial influence on Gill, it is impossible to know when and where this influence was represented in the completed narrative, and the whole history is potentially flawed. This is the conclusion that Gill's detractors must be prepared to accept unless they can also demonstrate that the Naval Board's improper interference was limited to the *Sydney* narrative, or other selective sensitive incidents during the war. To date, Gill's critics and detractors have not been able to do that.

Speculation and History:
HMAS Sydney *and the Japanese*

The *Sydney–Kormoran* action should have been a one-sided contest. *Sydney* should have sunk *Kormoran* without any risk of damage to herself. This made the loss of *Sydney* inexplicable. Was there, then, another player in the action whose presence accounts for what cannot otherwise be adequately explained?

During World War II, Japanese radio propaganda claimed that the Japanese had been party to the loss of *Sydney*. These claims, together with the Italian boast that its aircraft had sunk *Sydney* in the Mediterranean, were rightly dismissed during the war as enemy disinformation. Both the Australian and the British governments maintained resolutely throughout the war that there was nothing to suggest the Japanese were involved. However, in answering the principal question raised by his book *Who Sank the Sydney?*, Montgomery claimed that a Japanese submarine was party to the loss of the Australian cruiser and that this complicity was known in Australia and in Britain.

This claim is based on information allegedly contained in sketches drawn on toilet paper by Dr Fritz List, the 'war reporter' in *Kormoran*, after his capture by Australian authorities. These almost child-like sketches of no artistic merit were apparently prepared by List during his time at Carnarvon but were discovered in early 1942 at the POW camp in Murchison in the possession of Dr Habben, the raider's surgeon. It is possible that they were to be conveyed to Germany by Habben who was repatriated to Germany in 1943. Soon after their discovery

they came into the possession of Captain John Hehir of Australian Military Intelligence. The original sketches are preserved at
the Australian War Memorial.

At first glance, these sketches in green ink attempt to depict
a burning ship *(Kormoran)*; a small sailing craft *(Kormoran's*
lifeboats under sail at sea); a boat approaching a shoreline
showing a number of caves (the successful arrival of one of *Kor-*
moran's lifeboats on the West Australian coast); a cave with two
arched entrances (possibly the place where List buried his Leica
camera); a figure wearing a hat (possibly the local Australian
military authorities); a group of people inside a building (possibly the interrogation of the *Kormoran* survivors); and a number
of people in various positions around another building (presumably the POW camps). A separate sheet bears three dates, 17 or
27, 28 and 29 November, and a description of events.

As Hehir believed that the sketches *might* have contained
shorthand messages—what other purpose would they possibly serve as Habben could verbally relay this basic sequence
of events on his return to Germany—they were referred to an
expert in German shorthand within Australian Military Intelligence. This expert, referred to as Mr H. Kevin by Montgomery,
was actually Ms H. Kevin. Her identity, including her first name,
remains something of a mystery. However, she believed that the
sketches did contain shorthand passages written in the *Deutsche*
Einheitskurzschrift. The report on the sketches was signed by
Kevin and (Sergeant) E. Caminer.

Winter, who doubted that the *Einheitskurzschrift* was used,
was advised by the German Shorthand Writers' Guild that 'there
was nothing which resembled any shorthand system known to
them'. In papers belonging to a former member of Australian
Military Intelligence and amateur historian of the *Sydney–*
Kormoran engagement, Jonathan Robotham, Winter also found
'a declaration from a W. Tauss, who was an expert shorthand
writer, and he specifically stated that there were no *Einheit-*
skurzschrift symbols in the sketches'.

An examination of Kevin's working notes, which are held at
the Australian War Memorial, further undermines any confidence

that one might have in her interpretation of the sketches. There were two alleged references to Japan in the shorthand script. By a process of deduction, one refers to two Japanese aircraft carriers, and the other to a 'sudden gunfire attack from Japan itself'. Kevin stated that she found the words 'two' and 'carriers' in the sketches. As the letter 'p' apparently appeared between the two sets of shorthand characters, she took this to mean 'plane' although the German word for aircraft, *flugzeug*, was not present. One assumes that this word would have been used if List was trying to relay some information specifically about aircraft carriers rather than seaplane carriers or plane carriers (a special class of transport vessel). There is nothing to suggest that this might have been a reference to Japanese submarines carrying aircraft.

Kevin's notes show that she did not find the word 'Japan'. When she apparently found a 'j' and an 'n', she added the letter 'p' in the middle to form 'Japan'. Neither was Kevin certain that the word 'gunfire' appeared. She was able to distinguish the three letters 'knn'. With further interpolation, she concluded that this might be the German word for gun, 'Kanone'. The uncertainty evident in the working notes on all of the sketches is not reflected in the final report, which was examined and assessed by intelligence analysts.

Montgomery establishes his case that a submarine was involved by citing the shorthand analysis of List's sketches of the two caves which allegedly state:

> Short honour conferred on *Kormoran* for working according to ideals of unity of the German people . . . until reinforcements arrived when . . . in the evening conquered their victim. A Japanese gunfire attack from Japan itself.

This suggests to Montgomery that '*Kormoran* first engaged *Sydney* on her own, but then at some stage was reinforced by a Japanese unit of some kind whose armament finally accounted for the *Sydney*'.[1] While this interpretation goes well beyond the literal meaning of the words, Montgomery's next assertion is even harder to accept. As the Japanese would not have risked one of their surface units being observed so far from home, and he is able to discount the possibility that the vessel concerned might have sailed 'from Japan itself',[2] the '*most natural interpretation* of Dr List's words . . . refer to a conventional Japanese submarine acting in liaison with the *Kormoran*' (emphasis added).[3]

The alleged sighting of aircraft originating from Japanese submarines was apparently further proof. Montgomery cites a letter 'posted at Townsville on 28 October 1941' in which a civilian (presumably a fisherman) claimed to have observed an aircraft which probably originated from a submarine. The writer, a Mr E. Dodd, stated:

> Myself and two crew saw six strange boats like submarines come to the surface, then wings shot out to the sides and after cruising about for an hour and a half they took to the air and flew in a north-westerly direction towards the coast . . . these boat planes may be ours, I don't know, but it's up to you people to find out if they are not.

Montgomery is critical of the staff officer who suggested on the official file that it was probably flying fish that Dodd had observed. However, Montgomery believes these 'submarines' could have sailed from the Townsville area in time to rendezvous with *Kormoran* off Carnarvon. As the time taken to travel 3000 miles is considerable, he suggests without the slightest evidence to support his assertion, that as the letter 'was *posted* on 28 October, and it had presumably taken him a few days at least to put into Townsville (and a few more to put pen to paper?)' (original emphasis retained), there was plenty of time for the long passage to be completed.

The sighting of several unidentified aircraft in the airspace above Geraldton is cited as further evidence that a Japanese submarine was involved. Noting that *Kormoran*'s aircraft had not been deployed since September, and given that there were no other raiders operating in waters off Western Australia at the time, 'the only possible source would therefore seem to be an I-Class submarine'.[4] Of course, the aircraft could just as easily have come from anywhere else. Winter claims to have been told that RAAF flying instructors 'occasionally engaged in some unauthorised flying'. This would seem infinitely more likely than the bold assertion that they were from a Japanese submarine.

One of Montgomery's defenders, the late Gordon Laffer, cited Lew Lind's coffee table volume, *The RAN: Historic Naval Events Year by Year*, to support the case that the aircraft were Japanese. Lind stated that 'post-war research into enemy records suggests that the aircraft [reported over Pearce and Geraldton on 7 November] could have been launched from Japanese submarines known to have operated in the area at that time'. However, Lind does not provide any detail of the supposed 'post-war research' nor does he provide any source for his statement that Japanese submarines were known to be in the area where *Sydney* was lost. To seek support, as Laffer does, from a populist book produced entirely from secondary sources to substantiate what is a highly controversial assertion suggests a complete lack of evidence and little proficiency in historical analysis.

Although Montgomery is not sure which Japanese submarine was the culprit, he mentions the locations of a number of submarines in October and November 1941 and infers that one of the boats in waters closer to Australia could have been involved. At the time of the action with *Sydney*, allegedly according to one *Kormoran* survivor, the raider was re-supplying the submarine. According to Montgomery, this accounts for Detmers' decision to return to an area he had vacated three months earlier because it had offered little scope for successful raider operations. As each entry in Dr List's diary for the period 13–18 November contains the word 'Manilfahrt', translated by Montgomery, almost certainly incorrectly, as 'Manila-bound', the rendezvous must have been code-named 'Manila'. It was unlikely that Detmers would sail for the port of Manila in the American protectorate of the Philippines. It should be pointed out, however, that the only evidence that any German ever mentioned a Japanese submarine originated with the same Pat Young who claimed that a *Kormoran* survivor told him the raider was operating under a Norwegian disguise.

The possibility that *Kormoran* may have been resupplying a Japanese submarine with water is allegedly strengthened by a *Northern Times* news report of 6 December.

On November 30th Mr M.M. McBolt of Ningaloo Station reported seeing the footprints of four adults and two children emerging from the sea at the abandoned whaling station at Port Cloates, 180 miles north of Carnarvon. They led to a derelict house, where *all the taps had been turned on in a fruitless search for water* [Montgomery's emphasis] and an empty medicine chest inspected. The tracks led back again to the sea; natives considered that they were a week old. Apart from Ningaloo itself which is three miles away, the coast is uninhabited for many miles.[5]

Montgomery accounts for two of the prints being described as those of children by pointing out that 'the average Japanese foot . . . is proverbially small'.[6] But if the two smaller footprints are Japanese, who owned the larger four? Or are we to believe that some adult Japanese have feet the same size as European children while others have feet of a size comparable with European adults? Montgomery cannot have it both ways.

The tracks were presumably noticed on sand. Given tidal variations and wind, it is difficult to believe that these tracks could be reliably dated as one week old. And can Maurice McBolt be certain that the taps in the derelict house had not been turned on some time well before November 1941? And what of the possibility that a fishing boat or a yacht did not heave to off Ningaloo Station at sunset in search of water and depart the next morning unnoticed?

Yet, not all of McBolt's alleged revelations were reported in the *Northern Times*. He 'conveyed to Jim Sullivan of Carnarvon Police, that he had previously heard during the night the sound nearby of *a submarine recharging its batteries*' (Montgomery's emphasis retained).[7] One assumes, of course, that McBolt well knew the various sounds which emanate from a submarine; that he was able to explain how he knew that this particular submarine was recharging its batteries; and, that he actually investigated the sound to confirm that it was indeed a submarine. Montgomery apparently assumes that he did. Although these are extremely dangerous assumptions on which to base or support any historical argument, Montgomery has absolutely no hesitation in accepting at face value whatever evidence is available to support his case.

He then returns to Dr List's cave sketch, which allegedly concealed the following phrases: 'Two aircraft carriers . . . German transports . . . unselfishness is everything . . . a cell or transport to Wyndham'.[8] Montgomery states that this was taken by the highly imaginative shorthand interpreter, H. Kevin, to

indicate a joint plan of invasion via Wyndham (joint, because only the Japanese possessed aircraft carriers) and he adduced further evidence for this from a remark by one of the *Kormoran* officers, which was picked up by a hidden microphone to the effect that 'half a dozen transports could take Australia'.[9]

This is another highly ambitious interpolation of the alleged message contained in List's sketches but it is nonetheless crucial to Montgomery in that the Japanese can again be implicated. The alleged phrase could be interpreted to mean practically anything. Noting the method by which Kevin 'found' the word 'Japan', it could mean that two Allied aircraft carriers could be brought against the German transports. Furthermore, there is no documentary evidence to support the shorthand interpreter's wild conclusion that a joint Axis invasion of Australia was ever considered or planned. As for the remark made by a *Kormoran* survivor which was overheard by microphones hidden in their accommodation that 'half a dozen transports could take Australia', this was more probably the kind of derisive remark a captured German sailor would make about the state of Australia's defences given their successful operations in the Indian Ocean and what had happened with *Sydney*, than a disclosure of secret Axis war plans.

Despite serious objections to the arguments on which he bases his submarine allegation, Montgomery believed the site of the alleged rendezvous between *Kormoran* and a Japanese submarine had broader significance.

> The very fact that the rendezvous was set in the main shipping lane would seem to point to this having been its main purpose, and it is confirmed by the following entry in the diary of W. Grun for the 17th: 'If it were not for this boredom . . . Sea-going liner must soon be met'. Four days later just such a liner did, as we already know, pass that very spot; none other than the four-funnelled *Aquitania*, whose capacity for over 3,500 troops must have made her a tempting target for both Germans and Japanese alike—but particularly for the latter.[10]

According to Montgomery, as *Aquitania* was much faster than both *Kormoran* and a Japanese submarine, and neither could hope to sink the liner independently, 'together they were capable of preparing a trap which might considerably shorten the odds'.[11] However, Montgomery fails to provide positive evidence to show how Detmers, or Grun for that matter, could have known that *Aquitania* would be transiting down the West Australian coast at that time; that Detmers, did, in fact, know that she was in the area; when the Germans' information about *Aquitania*'s movements was acquired to allow such a rendezvous to be planned; and how the raider knew that *Aquitania* would not be escorted by the size of warship that *Kormoran* would wish at all costs to avoid.

It is also of interest to Montgomery that the *Kormoran* survivors picked up by *Aquitania* on 23 November displayed a 'lack of distress . . . having ostensibly spent three and a half days tossing about in heavy seas'. He asserts that 'the destruction of *Kormoran* would not automatically have spelt an end to Japanese designs on the liner', the raft could have been used as a trap.

> An I Class unit would certainly have been able, if not to accommodate all twenty-six of the raft's occupants at once (and even the biggest of these submarines were notoriously short of living space), then at least offer them the facilities to wash, shave, eat and rest in turns. That the

Aquitania managed to escape such a trap may be put down to the combination of her speed and the haste with which Captain Gibbons got her underway again, which would not have allowed the submarine enough time to manoeuvre (under water) for a shot.[13]

This is extraordinarily difficult to believe. Notwithstanding the unlikelihood of a Japanese submarine, already short on water and supplies by Montgomery's own reckoning, acting as a floating hotel for 26 German sailors, there is no reason to believe that this same submarine could possibly miss the opportunity to torpedo *Aquitania*. When the liner was observed on the horizon, all the submarine needed to do was stand off the German raft several hundred yards and wait until the liner, which would take about a mile to stop, was no longer making way through the water and then fire its torpedoes. A submarine captain could wish for no more straightforward target.

But why was Detmers' lifeboat not the one that remained to trap *Aquitania*? After all, Detmers would have received preferential treatment, according to Montgomery, because he was the commanding officer of the raider. Montgomery has no shortage of answers.

That might indeed have been their intention, but it would have been easier said than done to locate in darkness and heavy seas one particular lifeboat or raft out of seven that were launched, and which had been so widely dispersed by daybreak that only two of them were still within sight of one another; it can also hardly be a coincidence the raft was apparently the only one of the seven to carry a radio set.[14]

Persisting in the absence of any proof that the alleged submarine even existed, Montgomery believes the submarine's role in sinking *Sydney* would have been to inflict the *coup de grace*. Upon sighting *Sydney*, the submarine operating with *Kormoran* would have dived and sailed away from her consort to avoid sonar detection. By the time *Kormoran* engaged *Sydney*, the Australian cruiser's sonar would have been out of action and the submarine could close the *Sydney* and fire its torpedoes. As it would be dark, the submarine could also surface and fire at will. Montgomery believed that this 'appears to be indicated by the words' (in the cave sketch) 'until reinforcements arrived when . . . in the evening conquered the victim'.[15]

Detmers' decision to remain in the area of the action with *Sydney* thus contributes to Montgomery's submarine theory. When his lifeboat sighted *Aquitania*, he refused permission for a flare to be fired because, he later wrote, 'I was hoping to fall in with a neutral steamer, of course, and I had the impression that we were gradually approaching more frequented shipping lanes'.[16] As Detmers allegedly gave the impression that it was the Japanese he was hoping would arrive (Montgomery provides no evidence of the source of such an impression), and the Fremantle Harbour logbook shows that the last Japanese ship to have berthed there was the *Takunama Maru* on 9 December 1940 (a document to which one presumes German agents had access before they passed the information to Detmers), Montgomery not surprisingly concludes, 'it was a submarine rather than a ship he was expecting'.[17] But when Detmers was asked during interrogation on 7 January 1942 to comment on rumours that survivors from *Sydney* might have been taken to Japan, he stated, 'I do not think so at all. I do not think there was a Japanese ship within six days sail of where the action took place.'[18]

Yet Montgomery is still able to suggest that survivors from *Sydney* did become Japanese POWs. After citing a private letter dated March 1942, which mentioned that several Australian women had received letters from their sons who were presumed lost in *Sydney*, and mentioning that Japanese POW Camp commandants were directed shortly before their nation's surrender to kill prisoners and destroy sensitive documents, Montgomery infers that *Sydney* may have been captured while still afloat and some of the survivors taken to Japan. The factual basis for such a suggestion is non-existent and Montgomery must be condemned for what is complete speculation and callous sensationalism. In his review of *Who Sank the Sydney?*, Dr L.H. Pyke thought that 'such mischievous fantasia can only be excused if they are based on sound documentary evidence which, unfortunately, is lacking in this part of Montgomery's book'.[19] Perhaps mindful of the paucity of evidence, Montgomery is more inclined to believe that 'the Japanese either assisted in, or were even wholly responsible for, the disposal of Sydney's survivors in the water'. In Montgomery's view, this 'has an altogether greater probability'.[20]

Although sparing his readers the trauma of recounting the atrocities committed by the Japanese at sea during the Pacific War, Montgomery argues that the 'temptation to completely destroy' the crew of the Sydney would have been overwhelming among the Japanese and would have been undertaken in compliance with Admiral Yamamoto's General Order to the Combined Japanese Fleets of 7 November:

> In the case of discovery within 600 miles of the objective against which war is to be declared, make immediate preparations to attack and destroy the unit responsible.[21]

The submarine's need to conceal its role in the loss of Sydney also accounts, in Montgomery's view, for the lack of wreckage recovered from the area of the action.

> An I Class submarine may have had a minimal capacity for storing wreckage onboard, but there was nothing to prevent it making a sweep of the area and sinking the larger items with its machine gun.[22]

But there seems to be no good reason why the submarine captain thought gathering or sinking wreckage would have helped him to 'cover his tracks'. A machine-gun would hardly have been much use in sinking solid objects such as deck planks or lifesaving equipment, had any such items remained afloat—something which Montgomery, in any event, cannot prove.

Those who allege that the Australian survivors were machine-gunned are more inclined to believe that it was done by the Germans rather than the elusive Japanese. In the absence of anything Australian surviving from the battle, Laffer assumed that 'if some agency had got rid of the Sydney crew and most of the wreckage, was it von Gosseln [*Kormoran*'s battle watch officer] and Jurgensen [the senior petty officer]? Why has this question not been asked?' In a letter which Laffer sent to West Australian state parliamentarian Ross Lightfoot he seemed almost certain of the culprit.

We think that because von Gosseln was still in the flotsam area at [0700 on 25 November] when the other boats had either landed at Quobba or were close to landfall that it indicates that he was the executioner who murdered the *Sydney* crew. He may have had an outboard motor or even a regular motorboat equipped with machine guns. The captain's boat was also close by at the time.[23]

It appeared that Montgomery still preferred to blame the Japanese.

The final three items of 'evidence' offered by Montgomery of Japanese complicity cannot be described as anything but bizarre. In the first he mentions that a survivor from HMAS *Perth* often had discussions with his Japanese captors about naval matters 'but as soon as the name *Sydney* was mentioned the Japanese would abruptly break off and take their leave'. One would have to think that if military guards in isolated POW camps knew 'the truth' about the loss of *Sydney*, it was the worst-kept Japanese naval secret of the war. If the military guards did 'break off and leave' at the mention of *Sydney*, it is more likely that they felt they were being manipulated into disclosing information on the course of the war.

In the second item, Montgomery has no objection to repeating dubious evidence. He states:

In a similar conversation in the Petty Officers Club at Kure [in Japan] where he was serving in 1950, L. Fitzgerald was describing how the *Sydney* was sunk by a raider when an ex-naval steward intervened and corrected him with 'No, it was with torpedoes'; the man was overheard by the ex-Captain managing the club and removed from his job the same day.[24]

The inference of this statement is that the steward was disclosing something that was meant to be kept secret. How and why this man acquired this information is not made clear. Why it should remain secret among men who were now Japanese civilians, five years after the war, is not explained. As for the steward's dismissal, it is more likely that he lost his job because he interrupted a private conversation and this was seen by the manager of the club as inappropriate behaviour for a steward. Montgomery's efforts to give this uncorroborated incident a sinister overtone are comical. It is also notable that no reference is given for this incident. Did 'L. Fitzgerald' relay the incident to Montgomery directly or did it come second- or third-hand?

The final item of evidence is the strangest of all. Montgomery states:

> In October 1967 an abalone diver named Jim Lester discovered a sunken submarine off the coast of New South Wales 20 miles south of Eden, which bore the still legible name *He-Toi* on the hull; the Japanese Embassy, however, denied all knowledge of it—and there the matter rested because a week later Jim Lester disappeared and was never seen again.

A number of comments can be made about this 'evidence'. First, there is no proof that Lester saw anything. This would not have been the first time in Australian history that someone became a public nuisance. Second, Japanese submarines were not given names, but numbers. Third, the actual written reply by the Japanese Embassy to a report of such a submarine should have been reproduced for the sake of fairness and historical clarity. Fourth, the disappearance of Lester is yet another attempt by Montgomery to inject a sinister and conspiratorial element into his *Sydney* story. Are readers to believe that Lester was murdered by a Japanese military intelligence hit squad or was ASIO perhaps responsible? Or was Lester a fraud who moved whenever detection seemed apparent?

In his cutely titled book *Imperialist Japan: The Yen to Dominate*, published in 1987, Montgomery added further to his submarine theory.

[A]s early as November 24th—that is, before any of the German survivors had been recovered and interrogated—the Admiral Commanding the Australian Squadron had recorded in his diary that 'the Naval Board are very worried about *Sydney* . . . they think there is a possibility that a Vichy submarine escorting a Vichy ship has torpedoed her'. It would have taken the Naval Board only a few hours to establish with the Admiralty in London that there was no Vichy (or German) submarine nearer to Australia than the Mediterranean at that time, and that if indeed a submarine had been responsible for her loss it could only have been from Japan.[25]

Montgomery has actually misquoted the diary entry. Crace wrote that 'N' Branch at Navy Office was 'very worried about *Sydney* . . . Naval Board think there is a . . . '

The contents of Crace's diary need to be properly understood. In the first instance, a careful examination of all of Crace's diary shows that it is full of speculation, hearsay, wild assertion and scathing criticism of others. None of this is particularly surprising as most diaries are usually reserved for private thoughts and private expressions of opinion.

Montgomery suggests that there may have been a feud between Crace and the Naval Board, and that it might have had some bearing on the loss of *Sydney*. After mentioning several disputes between Crace and the Naval Board, Montgomery states that:

[Crace's] complaints to successive First Members continued to fall on deaf ears, until finally (in October 1941) he was driven to consider submitting his resignation. Happily, however, he stopped short of such a step, staying on to lead his Squadron with considerable distinction in the vital battle of the Coral Sea, which has gone down in history as 'the battle which saved Australia'. Some may even conclude that had he been allowed his say in the Naval Board's counsels, the *Sydney* might never have been lost.[26]

I have written in detail elsewhere[27] about Crace's shortcomings as RACAS, particularly his inability to understand the Australian political system and the need to keep operational and administrative matters separate. His proper role in naval affairs ought to be made clear.

The Naval Board had responsibility for the overall administration of the RAN. RACAS bore responsibility for the operational command of the Fleet. As RACAS was not responsible for administration, Crace did not have any 'say in the Naval Board's counsels'. The disputes between Crace and the Naval Board related to administration and not operations. It clearly was Crace who was 'out of line'.

Montgomery is also wrong when he says that Crace was driven to resign in October 1941. By way of background: after the outbreak of World War II in Europe and the detachment of a number of RAN ships to the Mediterranean, few ships remained in Australian waters and Crace felt he was under-employed. By October 1941, Crace told Royle that he no longer wanted to serve as RACAS. As Crace was a British officer on secondment to the RAN, he would revert to service in the Royal Navy. Crace served as RACAS until May 1942 when he returned to Britain. And as I argued in my book *Pacific Partners: A History of Australian–American Naval Relations*, the description of the Battle of the Coral Sea as 'the battle that saved Australia' is quite erroneous.[28]

Contrary to the portrait painted by Montgomery, Crace performed adequately as RACAS but little more. He was a 'second eleven' officer of average ability who tended to jump hastily to conclusions. He was inclined to be mean-spirited and had a rather sullen outlook on life. Crace's diary cannot be properly evaluated without an understanding of Crace and his standing in Australian naval affairs at the end of 1941.

So when Crace says that the *Naval Board* thought a Vichy French unit was involved, to whom exactly was he referring? Was this the collective view of the Board or one or more of its members? As the Board did not officially endorse such a view by way of a Naval Board minute, how was it communicated to Crace? Was it first-hand from one of the Board members, or their staffs, or was it hearsay? It is also important to notice that the Crace diary says the Board 'think there is a possibility'.

There is no evidence to show why they thought this was a possibility. Similarly, there is no evidence to reveal other possibilities that Board members might have had in mind because certainly a number of possibilities did exist. Given that it had no evidence of what had occurred, the reference in Crace's diary is useful only in that it discloses what *some* members of the Board *might* have been thinking on 24 November. Of course, they could, and apparently did, change their views when some information was received. It may have been Crace's imagination at work. As Hyslop has commented: 'A fleet commander needs to keep his emotions to himself so that to keep a diary may bring some relief and be persisted with in spite of its being officially discouraged. I see some of Crace's comments in his diaries as his letting off steam rather than making considered observations!'[28a]

The lack of clarity in this single statement in Crace's diary has not prevented Laffer from offering an explanation for its origins.

> The only discovery that we know prior to the morning of 24 [November] was the *Aquitania* rescue at 6am on 23rd which was not reported, therefore that particular submarine story did not come from the *Kormoran* crew, and therefore it must have come from the *Sydney*, probably as a radio signal, either directly or through Singapore Radio . . . Now if the *Sydney* could not see the submarine, she would not know its nationality, and if she signalled the Board to that effect, they would not know either. In the event, they told Admiral Crace that they thought it was a Vichy submarine.

One suspects that Laffer, obviously a man who possessed a fertile imagination, believed that this signal from *Sydney* was probably destroyed with her other alleged post-action communications. Equally astonishing is the statement by McDonald, who was evidently unfamiliar with the primary source, who stated that 'Admiral Crace had his thoughts about a submarine involvement but nobody seemed to want to listen'. This really is taking things too far. There is no evidence that Crace had any view of the possibility of a Vichy submarine being involved. Neither is there any evidence that Crace discussed this possibility with anyone. Consequently, it is sheer invention for McDonald to say that 'nobody seemed to want to listen'. It should also be noted that there is no subsequent mention in Crace's diary of a submarine being involved in the loss of Sydney.

It should have been obvious to Montgomery, Laffer and McDonald that the mere fact of the Board mentioning a Vichy submarine did not mean the Board was convinced that a submarine was, or could have been, involved in the loss of Sydney. It is illogical to say, as Montgomery does, that because the submarine could not have been Vichy it must have been Japanese. And it is entirely illogical to contend that because the Board thought a submarine might have been involved, then its involvement is accepted. Thus, in Montgomery's hands the notion that a *Vichy* submarine *might* have been involved becomes: a *Japanese* submarine *was* involved in the sinking of Sydney.

In a paper delivered at the 1991 HMAS Sydney Forum, Montgomery claims that Australian naval authorities continued to believe throughout the war that the Japanese were involved. This, he alleges, is

> shown by this entry in the *Seekriegsleitung* War Diary following Doctor Habben's return to Germany in 1943: 'In the opinion of Australian specialists the *Kormoran* was co-operating with a submarine, and it was the latter which was responsible for sinking the cruiser'.[29]

Three points can be made in reply. First, how could Habben have possibly known what Australian 'specialists' thought in 1943? Second, the War Diary was merely stating what some Germans *believed* the RAN *believed*. Third, the more probable intention of this entry in the War Diary would be to ridicule Australia for thinking that the Japanese were involved.

Montgomery claimed that the RAN believed as late as 1945 that the Japanese were involved because it specifically sent the then Commodore John Collins to Japan to investigate the loss of Sydney. This is one example of the compounding confusion created by Montgomery's shoddy research. Although his statement about Collins being sent to Japan for this purpose is without any factual foundation, it was accepted without question by McCarthy and repeated as fact. Inasmuch as Collins was despatched to Japan 'to investigate HMAS *Sydney* related matters', McCarthy is curious to know the grounds of suspicion on which Collins was sent to Japan, and why Collins evidently rejected the possibility of Japanese involvement. Indeed, one could ask whether Collins was part of the Naval Board conspiracy?

Collins was posted to Japan in 1945 for command duties with the British Commonwealth Occupation Force (BCOF). He was neither briefed nor authorised by the Naval Board on his departure from Australia to investigate any matter relating to the loss of *Sydney*. There is no evidence that Collins initiated any inquiries on his own behalf about *Sydney* or that he believed there was any point in conducting such an investigation. It is not surprising then that Montgomery provides no source or reference for this baseless assertion. However, given the speculation and the fact that he was already in Japan, Collins was later asked to 'make inquiries' about the loss of *Sydney*. This was a pre-emptive measure designed to rebut any suggestion that the government had not been diligent in examining fully the reason for the ship's loss. Makin, the Navy Minister, later stated in Parliament that:

> Unfortunately, Commodore Collins has replied that no information on the subject is available in Tokyo. As HMAS *Sydney* is thought to have been engaged in battle with a German raider, it is probably correct that particulars of the battle are not known in Tokyo. Every effort has been made to obtain authentic information regarding the fate of the vessel, but so far without success.

There is no suggestion in Collins' autobiography, *As Luck Would Have It: The Reminiscences of an Australian Sailor,* that he even took the request to obtain evidence in Japan seriously.

Contrary to Montgomery's statement that 'all records of Japanese submarine movements were among the casualties of the post-surrender bonfire',[30] positive proof does exist that a Japanese submarine could not have been involved in the sinking of *Sydney*.

Shortly after *Sydney Morning Herald* journalist David Jenkins published *Battle Surface! Japan's Submarine War Against Australia, 1942–44*,[31] I suggested that he publish an article on the possibility that a Japanese submarine had been involved in the loss of *Sydney*. As he had not commented on this controversy in his book, I believed his primary research in the area would be of great value to the *Sydney* debate. The article was published on 17 September 1992 and should have brought speculation about Japanese involvement to an end.

Jenkins concluded that archival material held at the Military History Department of the National Institute for Defence Studies in Tokyo 'establishes beyond doubt that none of Japan's 46 I-Class submarines could have been off Carnarvon on 19 November. At the time, Japan also had 15 smaller RO-Class submarines. But they were in home ports preparing for operations in the South China Sea and the Pacific'.[32] He was also critical of Montgomery.

> Despite the gravity of his charge, Montgomery offers only disappointing scraps of evidence, presented in a narrative which moves effortlessly from speculation to allegation. He is unable to identify the alleged Japanese attacker, beyond suggesting that it was a long-range submarine equipped with a reconnaissance floatplane. Unfortunately, this hasn't stopped his claims being taken at face value by prominent British and American historians.[33]

Of the 46 submarines operated by Japan at the time of *Sydney*'s sinking, 28 were in Japanese waters on their way to, or preparing to depart for, Pearl Harbor in the Hawaiian Islands. *I-2*, *I-3*, *I-4*, *I-5*, *I-6* and *I-7*, the Second Submarine Group commanded by Rear Admiral Yamazaki Shigeteru, departed from Yokosuka on 16 November. *I-1* followed five days later. *I-9*, *I-15*, *I-17* and *I-25*, the First Submarine Group commanded by Rear Admiral Sato Tsutomu, also sailed on 21 November from Kure. The Third Submarine Group under Rear Admiral Shigeyoshi Miwa, consisting of *I-8*, *I-68*, *I-69*, *I-70*, *I-71*, *I-72*, *I-73*, *I-74* and *I-75*, set out from the Inland Sea in the early part of

November for Kwajalein, and then Hawaii. On 18 November, the Special Attack Force led by Captain Hankyu Sasaki departed Kure with each boat carrying a 46-ton midget submarine. This accounted for *I-16*, *I-18*, *I-20*, *I-22* and *I-24*. Three reconnaissance boats, *I-19*, *I-21* and *I-23*, left the Kurile Islands on 26 November with the main Japanese battle fleet. I-10, fitted out as a headquarters submarine and equipped with a surveillance floatplane, sailed from Yokosuka bound for the South Pacific on 16 November. It is noteworthy that before the Pearl Harbor attack she sighted, but did not sink, the American heavy cruiser USS *Astoria*. Setting out at the same time in the opposite direction was I-26 which sailed for the Aleutian Islands from Yokosuka on 19 November.

This accounts for the movements of 30 Japanese submarines and all 12 boats that were equipped with aircraft. As Montgomery's story depends on the submarine operating an aircraft, there is really no need for the other 16 boats to be accounted for. However, this can be done to exclude all other possibilities. All four mine-laying submarines, *I-121*, *I-122*, *I-123* and *I-124*, were in Japanese ports in early November preparing for operations in the South China Sea. *I-52* was in home waters 'assigned to headquarters'. Another five submarines, *I-53*, *I-54*, *I-55*, *I-56* and *I-58*, arrived at Hainan Island on 27 November from Japan. *I-62*, *I-64*, *I-65* and *I-66* arrived at Hainan from Japan on December 2. For these two groups of submarines to have been at Hainan Island on 27 November and 2 December respectively, they could not have been off Carnarvon on 19 November. The distance they would have been required to cover would not have been possible in the time available.

The remaining two submarines, *I-59* and *I-60*, were the subject of a special inquiry by Jenkins.

According to Professor Teruaki Kawano of the [Military History Department in Tokyo], they, along with all other operational submarines, were at their home ports preparing for major operations. No one has questioned the accuracy of the relevant Japanese log books and patrol reports.[34]

I-124 has been mentioned as a possible accomplice for *Kormoran* because she was sunk by HMAS *Deloraine* near Darwin on 29 January 1942.[35] Laffer thought it 'interesting that the Minister for Arts [etc] has made a protected zone of 797 metres radius around the *I-124*'. *I-124* was attached to Submarine Division 9 of Submarine Squadron 6 in the Japanese 3rd Fleet which was to capture the Netherlands East Indies, the Philippines and Malaya. In mid-December 1941, Submarine Squadron 9 relocated from Cam Ranh Bay on the South Vietnamese coast to Davao in the Philippines with its flagship, the light cruiser *Chogei*. *I-124* sailed from Davao on her final mission. Although fitted with aviation gasoline tanks, she did not embark any aircraft.

Jim Davies, a supporter of the *Sydney* Research Group, asked the Japanese naval authorities whether *I-124* could have been involved. He was told:

> The *I-124* was involved in preparations for the Philippines invasion on 8 October 1941 at Hainan Island, and didn't go near the west coast of Australia. It was active around the Philippines until it went to Port Darwin in January 1942.[36]

Davies is prepared to accept the information supplied by the Japanese.

> I have had a lot of correspondence in recent years with the Historical Section of the Japanese Defence Department in Tokyo regarding the activities of Japanese submarines along the WA coast in World War II. I have never had any reason not to believe the answers they have given me.

This information is consistent with that provided by Japanese authorities to David Stevens, who had also undertaken major research into Japanese submarine operations within Australian waters and is presently Director of Naval History in the Navy Seapower Centre.[37]

Despite the lack of any evidence for Japanese involvement, Montgomery builds upon it an edifice of international intrigue and conspiracy, personally involving Churchill and Roosevelt, to account for the commencement of the Pacific War. Montgomery is, not surprisingly, a fully fledged member of the antiquarian Pearl Harbor conspiracy club; a loose alliance of writers who believe broadly that both Britain and the United States were aware that Japan was intending to declare war on the Allies on or about 7 December, and that the attack on Pearl Harbor was expected because the American aircraft carriers were withdrawn from the island of Oahu before the attack.

The key date in this developing conspiracy for Montgomery is 26 November 1941 when he alleges Roosevelt changed his attitude towards negotiating with Japan to avert a war. The reason usually given to explain the American president's decision to close off options for negotiation is that it was reported to him that a convoy of between 30 and 50 Japanese troop transports had been sighted south of Formosa (Taiwan). This news, received by Secretary for War Henry Stimson late on 25 November, when coupled with a telegram from Churchill early the following day, was apparently enough to change Roosevelt's mind about the prospects of peace. This is challenged by Montgomery. He states that parts of a declassified file of Stimson's correspondence (reproduced in John Costello's book *The Pacific War*,[38] published in 1981)[39] revealed that the reported sighting was not of 30–50 ships but of 10–30, and that the force was not at sea but assembling in the mouth of the Yangtse River. This was considered to be a routine movement of Japanese forces around China. What, then, of the telegram from Churchill?

Montgomery shows, and most scholars would agree, that there was very little in this communication to have concerned Roosevelt. However, it is marked in the main Churchill–Roosevelt correspondence file as having been despatched at 3.20 a.m. on 26 November. As he does not provide any details of the administrative processes which were associated with handling such high-level correspondence, it is difficult to be certain about what actually happened at 3.20 a.m. and the extent to which the handling of this telegram varied from occurrences at other times. But, Montgomery contends, there exists other evidence to suggest that a *second* message was indeed received from Churchill during the early hours of the 26th and that it was subsequently expunged from the files both in London and Washington. Tucked away in another file in the London Public Records Office and bearing the much less conspicuous title of 'Far East—General: US Policy vis-a-vis Japan' can be found the following cover note from Churchill's Secretary to the Third Secretary at the US Embassy: 'Dear Mr Beam, I enclose a telegram from the Former Naval Person [Churchill] to the President for dispatch as soon as possible. I am sorry to trouble you at this hour'. Notwithstanding the irregularity of Churchill's working hours, even he would have felt bound to apologise for disturbing the Embassy's slumbers at 3.20 in the morning. What could it have contained to have justified such a disturbance—and to have caused such a momentous reaction when it reached Washington?[40]

Montgomery claimed that the 'submarine possibility' entry in Crace's diary on 24 November was the answer.

Australia then being 11 hours GMT ahead of London, there would thus have been ample time to convey to Churchill, and for him to pass it on to Roosevelt by 3.20 am London time on the 26th, the stunning conclusion that Japan had already in effect entered the war.

This, claims Montgomery, led Roosevelt to authorise a new document, 'Proposed Basis for Agreement', 'whose terms were altogether less accommodating'.[41] It comes as no surprise, therefore, that the involvement of a Japanese submarine in the loss of *Sydney* has since been used by others in the Pearl Harbor 'conspiracy club'. In 1986, James Rusbridger quoted Montgomery as his authority that:

By November 24 the Australian Navy was convinced that the *Sydney* had been sunk by a Japanese I-Class submarine operating in conjunction with the *Kormoran*, which machine-gunned the survivors. If, as seems likely, Churchill told Roosevelt that the Japanese had already attacked and sunk an Allied warship, then the President would have been in no doubt as to their future intentions. What is unclear, however, is whether Roosevelt passed on Churchill's information about the *Sydney* to his Chiefs of Staff so that they could warn Admiral Kimmel and General MacArthur.[42]

It is noteworthy that Rusbridger claimed that the Naval Board also knew that the survivors from *Sydney* had been machine-gunned.

In their book, *Betrayal at Pearl Harbour*,[43] Rusbridger and Nave state as *fact* that the Japanese were party to sinking the Australian cruiser. Rusbridger also claimed that Britain had broken the Japanese naval code JN25. If this were so, the British would have been aware of the rendezvous between *Kormoran* and the Japanese submarine. He has, however, not made this claim. And in an article published in 1991, Rusbridger led *Sun-Herald* London correspondent Matt Condon to state, as *fact*, that:

> The two ships fired at each other and both were badly damaged. While the *Kormoran* crew surrendered, the *Sydney* was suddenly hit by a single torpedo, believed to be from a Japanese I-Class submarine . . . This was a very significant turning point in the war because the Australian Naval Board [sic] told Winston Churchill they suspected a Japanese submarine had been working with the German vessel to sink the *Sydney*. Churchill then told Roosevelt that Japan was not to be trusted. That showed the West that Japan was prepared to go to war. At the time Roosevelt was reconsidering an oil embargo on Japan, so this incident involving the *Sydney* may have led to the unavoidability of war.

It is far-fetched to say that Roosevelt needed to be convinced as late as 26 November 1941 that Japan had aggressive intentions. The Japanese had invaded Manchuria in 1931. They had captured most of central China by 1937 and Indochina by mid-1941. The Japanese 'Purple' Diplomatic Code was being read in Washington and also in London after the Americans provided a copy. The exchange of telegrams on 26 November did not relate to Japanese submarines but the possibility that Japan was preparing for an air-sea offensive in South-East Asia to secure oil in the Dutch East Indies. An intercepted encrypted Japanese diplomatic telegram sent on 25–26 November informed Japanese negotiators that if an agreement were not reached by 29 November, there would be no point persisting with diplomatic efforts. This was tantamount to advising that war was imminent. Both Washington and London fully expected Japanese aggression before long but not in the form of a massive pre-emptive strike by naval airpower on the US Pacific Fleet based on Pearl Harbor.

In addition to the physical impossibility of Japanese involvement, there are several other serious operational flaws in Montgomery's account. Foremost was the Japanese fear of detection before the Pearl Harbor operation. The crucial element of surprise in the Japanese offensive against the US Navy would have been affected by even the faintest suspicion that Japan had committed a warlike act elsewhere. Japan had too much to lose and too little to gain in going after Australian shipping, or in directly supporting a German operation. This is reflected in a document which was recovered from the Japanese cruiser *Nachi* which was sunk in the Philippines in early 1945.

The use of military power before the opening of hostilities affects greatly the conduct of the whole operation. Crews of the small ships and airplanes may be impetuous and, urged on by their feelings, intentionally attack the enemy (patrol craft, reconnaissance planes, etc.) and draw him into battle. Such incidents must be prevented. Moreover, because an unexpected defeat may result from losing opportunities for defence, the principal aims set forth in the orders must be adhered to completely.[44]

Although Montgomery has suggested that the Japanese would have been attracted to the prospect of sinking *Sydney* or *Aquitania*, this is not sufficient motive. Japan wanted to concentrate her forces for the Pearl Harbor attack and would not have weakened herself with a highly speculative operation in waters off Western Australia. Sinking *Sydney* might have been a major setback for Australia but it would mean little for Japan.

The possibility that a Japanese submarine acting without specific orders could have sunk *Sydney* is also unlikely. It is reasonable to believe no Japanese submarine captain would have undertaken such an action without express approval from Tokyo, and for this approval to have been administratively recorded. When Admiral Yamamoto promulgated General Order No. 1 on 7 November 1941 (not 5 November as stated by Montgomery) it did not authorise submarine operations against Australia. A submarine attack against *Sydney* on 19 November was most unlikely on that date in particular because the following morning the First and Second Submarine Groups carrying five midget submarines for the Pearl Harbor operations sailed under tight security from Kure and Yokosuka.

Furthermore, there is no mention in the diaries[45] of the German naval attache in Tokyo, Admiral Paul Wenneker, of Japanese involvement in the loss of *Sydney*. In the rank of captain, Wenneker was German naval attache in Tokyo from 1933 to 1937. After a period in command of the battleship *Deutschland*, Wenneker was promoted to rear admiral and returned to Tokyo in 1940 where he remained until the end of the war.

Wenneker's diaries reveal how reluctant the Japanese were to assist Germany in the Indian Ocean. After allowing German raiders and supply ships to use Japanese anchorages from July 1940, the Japanese were much less co-operative in 1941 although relations between the two navies remained friendly.[46] During the visit of the Japanese Navy Mission to Germany between March and May 1941, Commander Menzel, the head of the Navy Group in Abwehr, impressed on the Japanese the importance of them passing on as much information as they could obtain about Allied naval and shipping movements in the Indian Ocean. By late May, Menzel informed the German Naval War Staff that

> the supply of information from [Japanese] consular posts at Cape Town and Suez was not coming in sufficient quantity and information urgently needed from Singapore was not coming at all. His view was

that the Japanese were not being deliberately obstructive or that they were lacking in goodwill, but that it was simply a fact that they were not in a position to organise their intelligence service tightly enough and especially they lacked a ship inquiry service, which would have been of great value to the Germans.[47]

As 1941 progressed, Wenneker found it increasingly difficult to secure Japanese co-operation in obtaining stores and equipment for German supply ships and blockade runners ported in Japan. Given the prevailing attitudes of caution among the Japanese who did not want to go to war at any moment other than at the time of their choosing, there was no scope for Wenneker to arrange co-operation between German raiders and Japanese submarines. There is no suggestion that such co-operation was possible nor that it ever occurred. And as Winter has pointed out,

> there was at that time no mechanism by which German and Japanese units could have identified each other. They had no common codes, ciphers or identification signals. Nor, when naval ciphers were read retrospectively, was any signal found between Germany and Japan which would have authorised such contact. And Germany and Japan were as uneasy allies as Russia and America; they did not trust each other.[48]

Furthermore, Patrick Beesley, who drew on his experience in the Operational Intelligence Centre in Britain in writing the authoritative *Very Special Intelligence*, told Montgomery before his book was released that: 'Cooperation in the operational sense between Germans and Japanese both with raiders and U-boats was non-existent . . . The two navies did not . . . coordinate plans and never worked together on operations'.[49]

Montgomery is also unable to account for the decision of the Australian government to authorise the despatch of additional Australian troops for Middle East Service on 26 November—the day on which the Naval Board allegedly advised the British Prime Minister that Japan had committed an act of war. Given Curtin's determination to match the Japanese threat with an appropriate level of Australian defence despite the European situation, and that he had to assume that Japanese acts of war would occur around the Australian coast, it is extremely difficult to believe that Australian troops would not be withdrawn from the Middle East, let alone that their numbers would be substantially increased. There is no doubt that Curtin would have used any evidence of Japanese involvement in his disputes with Churchill over Australia's contribution to the European theatre to argue for a strengthened Allied force in the Pacific.

It is also important to remember that it was not until *after* the loss of *Sydney* that the Japanese and the Germans finally agreed on a no-separate-peace agreement. And although Hitler agreed after a meeting with Admiral Raeder to loosen the rules of engagement for raider operations in the Atlantic on 13 November in the belief that Japan would enter the war, it was not until 6 December that both the German Naval War Staff and General Staff began to formulate war plans which took into account the involvement of Japan and the United States. By this time, both the German and Italian leaderships were becoming more strident in pressing Japan to enter the war following the British and Soviet counter-offensives in November. What they did not know was that on 30 November 1941, Japan made an irrevocable decision to resort to war. It is worthy of mention that there was apparently no mention of German–Japanese collusion in the sinking of *Sydney* at the conferences between Hitler and Raeder, nor was there any discussion of practical Japanese assistance for German naval operations beyond intelligence and port access.

The allegation that a Japanese submarine was involved in the sinking of *Sydney* should never have been taken seriously. It explained nothing and only added to the confusion and the controversy which obscured the most pertinent unanswered questions. However, it revealed Montgomery's ineptitude as an historian, and the willingness of some Australians to recast the historical record regardless of evidence and the principles governing the practice of history.

13

Defying the Unknown

For some, the almost total mystery surrounding the loss of *Sydney* was the greatest attraction of the story. For others, it was an unsatisfying dimension that either needs to be overcome or defied. For both groups, there was the undiminished hope that incontrovertible evidence to explain the *Sydney–Kormoran* action still existed but was yet to be found. It appeared in the early 1980s that such evidence had finally been uncovered.

On Remembrance Day 1981, a former merchant marine captain, Sam Benson, passed a set of papers and some historical relics allegedly originating from *Sydney*, to the Naval Officer Commanding, Victoria, Commodore Tony Miller RAN. Benson was known within naval circles. He had served at sea with the RAN in the latter part of World War II and commanded the corvette HMAS *Kiama*. In the early 1960s he was active in politics and in 1963 became Labor member for the Federal seat of Batman until becoming an independent in 1966. He was an uncharitable critic of the Navy in the parliamentary debate which followed the first HMAS *Voyager* Royal Commission in 1964 but spoke strongly in the Navy's favour in the parliamentary debate in 1968 which followed the second *Voyager* Royal Commission.[1]

The material had come from Wilson Percy Evans, an amateur historian of Williamstown in Victoria. Evans was the author of a historical work on the Victorian Colonial Navy, *Deeds not Words*.[1a] He claimed to have located the material wrapped in a canvas bag on a beach near Kalbarri in Western Australia. The bag itself was stamped 'COIC for HMAS *Sydney*'. The bag

would have been used for the delivery of signals and confidential
material from the Combined Operational Intelligence Centre
(COIC) for *Sydney*. Among the items found by Evans—which
included a highly varied assortment of small naval stores items
such as some Service manuals, a flask, a life preserver, some
photographs and Captain Burnett's cap badge—was a 'Letter
of Proceedings' and a casualty list which had been cast adrift by
its author, the allegedly senior surviving officer, Sub-Lieutenant
Elder RAN Reserve. The Letter was signed with an 'X' and not
a signature.

According to Benson, who seemed to think the papers were
authentic, Evans wanted the items to be passed to the Australian
War Memorial. However, Evans was concerned that the existence of the material might distress Captain Burnett's younger
son, Rory, who was then a serving commodore in the Navy. Was
this to be the breakthrough in the *Sydney* story? For the first
time, historians would be able to interpret the action from the
Australian side.

The Letter of Proceedings (reproduced in full in Appendix
I) is a typed narrative of the events occurring off Carnarvon,
commencing at 1400 on 19 November. It records that *Sydney*
suffered a small engine room fire at 1442 which disabled the
ship's telegraphy equipment, and then sighted a Japanese submarine, later confirmed as an I-Class submarine, which dived
on being observed by the Australian ship. About an hour later,
with *Sydney* attempting to send a submarine sighting report,
'a suspicious merchant vessel was sighted'. *Sydney* closed the
merchant ship and exchanged identities before requesting the
display of her secret callsign because Burnett believed the ship
might have been 'Raider G'. Receiving no reply, *Sydney* ordered
the vessel to stop engines. A white flag was hoisted by 'Raider
G' as *Sydney* came alongside and prepared to lower a boat. At
this point, *Sydney* was suddenly struck by a torpedo and fired
upon by *Kormoran*, which was still flying the Dutch flag and
a white flag. The cruiser's bridge was badly damaged, most of
the officers were killed and Elder took command. Final gunfire
was exchanged at 1926, after which *Sydney* turned towards the

coast. With the ship's company fighting fires, tending the sick and keeping the cruiser mobile, Elder produced his report of proceedings which was thrown overboard some time after 0300 on 20 November.

Two questions need to be answered. Was Elder capable of producing the Letter of Proceedings? Did he have sufficient time and facilities to do so?

The alleged author of the 'Letter of Proceedings', Sub-Lieutenant Bruce Alfred Elder, was an unremarkable officer. He was mobilised for naval war service on 3 September 1939, the date of his 21st birthday, as an ordinary seaman. He served initially in the Sydney shore establishment HMAS *Penguin* and was advanced to able seaman on 17 February 1940. Elder was then accepted for officer training and, after completing Officer Training Course No. 4 in HMAS *Cerberus* at Western Port in Victoria, was appointed a probationary sub-lieutenant on 9 March 1941. He was promoted provisional sub-lieutenant on 3 September 1941 while posted to *Sydney*. His training to that time had been in naval gunnery although his duties in *Sydney* are likely to have been in a gun turret during action stations and on the bridge as a trainee watchkeeper at other times. Certainly, he was no 'old salt'. He was very young and had little seagoing experience. Other than his five months in *Sydney*, his only other sea service was a fortnight in the auxiliary minesweeper HMAS *Bombo*.

Elder was a very unlikely, although not inconceivable, author of the Letter of Proceedings. He had completed only a small part of his training and was inexperienced at sea. However, in handling the situation and producing a report, prompted by damage to *Sydney*'s telegraphy equipment and inability to send any signals, he could have been guided by the surviving senior sailors on whose experience he could have drawn. Other than his decision to write a formal and rather stilted report of the engagement, Elder seems to have acted with a fair amount of commonsense given the cataclysmic events of that day. As Stephen Allen has commented in his analysis of the Letter for the War Memorial:

Elder's previous experience and training could not have prepared him for the demands he now faced. We may indeed be surprised that he achieved what he did. That errors, such as collecting [personal identity] discs, were made, should not really surprise. Under the circumstances the absence of such mistakes would be surprising. Posting lookouts for shorelights that had to be at least twelve hours away can be seen to have been a very logical motive indeed. 'Idle hands are the devil's work', and with a disaster to contemplate some logical activity would be necessary to distract the survivors from their plight. Re-establishing a routine and, if necessary, making 'work' would be an immediate priority for the maintenance of discipline.[1b]

Thus, the Letter contains some of the illogicalities, inconsistencies and inaccuracies which would emanate from such a tense situation and its handling by a young man. The Letter states that *Sydney* was keeping Golf Time (GMT + 7 hours), when she always kept Hotel Time (GMT + 8 hours) when off the west coast of Australia. The Letter stated that *Sydney* was steaming south-east at 23 knots when she usually steamed at 18 or 19 knots on two boilers. Twenty-three knots was beyond the capacity of two boilers but insufficient use of the three that were necessary to exceed 19 knots. The use of non-nautical terms and nomenclature to identify parts of the ship, such as referring to the after gun turrets as the 'rear turrets', suggested that the author was not familiar with seagoing. However, some of these shortcomings tend to strengthen its claim to authenticity. If the Letter were to show the situation on board *Sydney* being handled in a perfectly efficient and effective manner, it would seem more like a later concoction.

But did Elder have the time to compose the Letter? It would certainly have been possible for it to have been written following the action given the time that Elder had available after the fires were brought under control at 2200. With the ship's company fully organised in damage control or in providing medical care, a junior officer may have felt it necessary to record the sequence of events before and after the engagement. He could have gathered together a selection of personnel from the various departments in the ship and asked them for information, provided either verbally or in writing, which was coordinated into a consolidated account. Although he was injured, Elder could at least rely on the recollection of his typist. In sum, it was quite possible that the Letter was authentic.

But Commodore Miller was cautious in receiving the material on behalf of the Navy and made no comment on its authenticity. He decided to pass the material to the Chief of Naval Staff, Vice Admiral Sir James Willis, under a covering letter which expressed his concerns.

> While there is much about the material which has an air of authenticity, one aspect of this matter raises a question mark in my mind: Dr Evans' war diary entry for 20 August 1942 concludes with the entry, 'Last letter box has not been found . . . ' It is a remarkable coincidence that the same Dr Evans could, 40 years later, find such a box on the coast of Western Australia.[2]

On arrival in Navy Office in Canberra during late November 1981, the material was given detailed examination by Commodore Ian Richards who, noting the origins of the material, was somewhat sceptical.[3] The Naval Historical Officer, John Mackenzie, remarked on 23 November that 'from my examination of the material so far, I am reasonably sure that a most elaborate hoax is involved'.[4] Admiral Willis declared on 15 December that, after further analysis, 'it has been concluded that there is very little likelihood that they originated from HMAS *Sydney*'.[5]

In August 1982, the Navy passed the material and an opinion on its authenticity to the Minister for Home Affairs. Other than an assessment by Barbara Winter, which was submitted to the Department on 20 September 1982 (and later published in her book), it appears that no further action was taken for nearly six years. In June 1988, the 'Evans' material was passed to the Australian War Memorial by the Commonwealth Department of Arts, Sport, the Environment, Tourism and Territories (DASETT) for detailed analysis.[6] Rather than relying on the piecemeal and circumstantial approach adopted by the Navy in the early 1980s

which *suggested*, albeit strongly, that the material was fake, the
Memorial was asked to *prove* the authenticity or otherwise of
the material by whatever means possible. The specific aim of the
Memorial's analysis was to assess the purported relics forensi-
cally to determine the period of manufacture and proof of any
connection with *Sydney*, and to subject the alleged 'Letter of
Proceedings' to rigorous historical analysis.[7]

On 9 September 1988, the Memorial convened a panel of historians and members of its own senior staff to discuss the Letter. I
was invited to be a member of the panel. Stephen Allen, research
officer in the Memorial's Historical Research Section, presented
a 'case for the defence' of the Letter. The panel considered issues
relating to textual analysis, such as the reports of Richards and
Winter, historical provenance and material analysis.

Allen has argued persuasively that it was unreasonable to
discount the contents of the Letter because it contradicted the
German accounts, which he describes as a 'curious mix of statement, supposition and inference—not a reliable primary source.
Many of the reservations that apply to the Elder Letter apply
in turn to the *Kormoran* evidence'. He is also correct when he
remarks that Richards and Winter have not handled the material with pure historical objectivity.

> The real reason for the shabby treatment accorded this document
> is that it challenges the accepted interpretations of a historical inci-
> dent. The assessments have been attempts to discredit not efforts to
> evaluate.

The panel agreed that while there was doubt about the origins
of the material and believed 'it highly improbable that the Elder
documents and relics are authentic, the textual analysis had not
been conclusive'. In a report prepared for the War Memorial
by the Navigation School at HMAS *Watson*, Lieutenant Commander Peter Leschen conceded that 'some basic errors were
made in the navigational record of the *Sydney*. It is, however,
not inconceivable that these errors could be made by inexperienced personnel'. On the basis of the Letter,

no clear conclusion can be made as to the authenticity of the document from my analysis. It is not, even in very favourable circumstances, possible to pin navigational information down to the nearest millimetre in the way that the Winter analysis attempted. Errors, sometime gross errors, occur particularly when the originator is inexperienced. Particularly if the original navigational data has been destroyed and you are relying on memory, circumstances suggested by the 'letter of proceedings'.

As there was no definitive proof arising from either textual analysis or a consideration of the historical provenance of the collection as a whole that the Letter was a forgery, the Memorial agreed to undertake material analysis of the individual items.

There were some obstacles to conducting a conclusive material analysis. Evans was believed to have subjected the collection to various corrosive and abrasive tests while it was in his possession. It was thought that he also washed out the box in which the relics were held. However, the Memorial asked its curators and conservators to examine the paper on which the Letter was typed; the typewriter and ribbon ink that had been used; whether the condition of the material was consistent with exposure to the physical elements; and whether the material had been subjected to any previous testing.

The findings of the analysis were conclusive. The prime observation of the Memorial's conservation staff

> was that the condition of the collection was not consistent with a long period of burial within an inter-tidal zone and/or exposure to a marine environment. Water damage was limited and this was not consistent with the supposed age of the collection and its mode of arrival on the beach.[8]

Although the individual items within the collection did not obviously date from the period after 1941, there was nothing to prove that they originated from *Sydney* on 19 November 1941. It was first thought that the existence of several ballpoint pen entries on pages in an address book contained in the collection would prove post-war origins. However, the Biro patent was taken out in 1937 and ball-point pens were in very limited use by this time. The key finding was the canvas bag, which was thickly encrusted with salt, in which the collection had been wrapped.

The bag was examined closely after it was discovered that it fluoresced on exposure to ultra-violet light. The phenomenon was reproduced when calico washed in a modern laundry detergent was exposed to the same wavelength of light but did not occur in samples of calico from the 1940s.

The bag was subjected to more extensive tests.

The bag was examined under long-wave and short-wave ultra-violet light. Under this light the bag fluoresced a fairly patchy light blue colour. The fluorescence was on the cords as well. The inside of the bag fluoresced more than the outside. Natural cotton does not fluoresce a light blue, it fluoresces dull cream to fawn colour . . . The brightness and the fluorescence of the bag appear to be the optical brighteners similar to those used in 'OMO' and other modern soap powder. Optical brighteners were not in common use until the mid-1980s.[9]

Laundry blues used before the introduction of modern optical brighteners fluoresce a very dark blue. Therefore, the bag had been tampered with between 1941 and when the last layer of salt adhered to the canvas.

In a paper delivered to the Memorial's 50th anniversary history conference in November 1991, Stephen Allen revealed that

the finder of the collection [Evans] now knows the results of the Memorial's investigation. He now 'recalls' washing the bag after retrieving it—for what earthly purpose I cannot understand. Perhaps he would say that he was attempting to decipher the markings on the bag by cleaning off the surface grit and salt.

The Memorial claimed that 'the finder' had washed the bag in salt water with 'OMO' soap powder, and demonstrated that the bag and its contents were not from *Sydney*. Although the Memorial's staff emphasised that their tests were general and not exhaustive, and DASETT indicated that they did not constitute a thorough scientific assessment, they were sufficient to give a reliable result and sufficient to cast further, and probably final, doubt on the historical provenance of the 'Evans' collection.

Given that the Letter of Proceedings was faked, who was its author? Or were there several authors or participants to the fraud? Winter believes it was Robotham.

> His friends have taken this rather amiss, saying that Robotham was a nice old gentleman who would never have done anything like that. Since my book was published, I have found out that Robotham was a nice old gentleman most of the time, but as a result of experiences in World War I, he suffered from psychotic episodes in which he was anything but a gentleman, and that his military discharge was on psychotic grounds. I feel very sorry for Robotham; he was basically a decent chap, but could not be responsible for what he did at times. I should be perfectly happy if anyone can prove that someone else forged this document, but it could not have been done without access to material which Robotham alone possessed.[10]

Although the obvious candidate is Robotham, his unofficial biographer, journalist Bryan Clark, does not agree. Clark believes that Robotham 'was not in any way a deceitful person or devious in any manner or degree; he was a decent man of independent character with a lone and simple spirit'.[11]

In a photocopy of Robotham's unpublished history of the *Sydney–Kormoran* action, entitled 'Eagle in the Crow's Nest', which I was given in 1991,[12] one page is a copy of a 'Government of Victoria' official telephone message form. The message on the form appears to have come from Sam Benson and was recorded by Evans in his distinctive handwriting. The message read: 'Letter of Proceedings shown to Bracegirdle and Showers. Both consider it accurate and can see nothing wrong with it'. The two names mentioned were almost certainly those of two retired RAN officers, Commander Warwick Bracegirdle and Rear Admiral Harry Showers. It is surprising that they were selected to comment on the Letter. Showers was 80 years old, Bracegirdle was 70, and neither was noted for any expertise in naval history. In the same manuscript there was a copy of a rather rough certificate recognising the contribution of an Australian to the Polish Resistance. The form was dated 1979 and was made out to His Excellency General Wilson P. Evans.

There is no doubt that the Letter is a forgery. Had its contents been slightly less sensational and a little more consistent with the broad outline of the German accounts, the forger might have been more successful. Fortunately, the Letter's origins and claims to authenticity were rigorously scrutinised before it received any publicity and very few people seem to have been taken in by it. Archival institutions in Australia were apparently already sufficiently suspicious of old documents purportedly 'found' long after the passing of events they described, especially when they claimed to present an altogether different view of history. The situation was apparently different in Germany where several German institutions were forced to learn hard lessons about documentary evidence after the fiasco of *Stern* magazine and the forged Hitler diaries in 1984.

It is difficult to be positive about the identity of the forger and the date of his work. I am inclined to believe that the forger was indeed Jonathan Robotham; that the letter was forged in the 1960s; and that he received some assistance in his forgery although the people assisting Robotham may not have known that their efforts were being exploited to perpetrate a forgery.

I suspect that the bag and the Letter may have passed into the hands of another person after Robotham's death in 1978, and that this person either passed them to Evans without disclosing their connection with Robotham or 'assisted' Evans in recovering them from the beach at Kalbarri. This gave Evans a period of one to two years in which he could make discreet inquiries, with retired officers such as Harry Showers and Warwick Bracegirdle, about the Letter and its contents. Having satisfied himself that the Letter and the other items recovered from Kalbarri were authentic, Evans tried to give his 'find' greater standing in the eyes of the Navy by asking Benson to act as his intermediary. The announcement of the *Sydney* 'find' was probably also timed to coincide with the release of Montgomery's book in the hope that this publication might serve to make the contents of the Letter more believable. It must be emphasised that there is no evidence directly linking Montgomery and the Letter. Once Evans became aware that the Navy and the War Memorial were able to highlight its many deficiencies, and that the Letter was being openly regarded by both institutions as a forgery, he tried to distance himself from the entire collection.

There have been few recorded instances in Australia of historical fraud. The case of the HMAS *Sydney* 'Letter of Proceedings' ought to be remembered for the skill displayed by the War Memorial in its exposure, and as a warning that other documents purportedly relating to the *Sydney–Kormoran* action may still be waiting to be 'found'.

14

Stirring the Pot
or Whipping Up Ill-will?

The controversy created by Montgomery in 1981 was perpetuated by a small informal association of elderly men who formed the *Sydney* Research Group in the mid-1980s. Most had had some involvement with the armed forces during World War II, and nearly all had some connection with the aftermath of the loss of *Sydney*. Although the group's initial aim was to provide alternative theories to explain the loss of *Sydney* based on different interpretations of available evidence, the group began to argue that the tragedy has been obscured by a massive cover-up. In a story which was based on the Group's allegations, the Perth tabloid, *Sunday Times*, stated defiantly in October 1991 that:

> For almost 50 years successive federal governments and the navy have kept the truth about the 1941 sinking of HMAS *Sydney* from the Australian people. For all that time they have had us believe that the *Sydney* vanished with all 645 men aboard without a sound or a trace. It has been the greatest cover-up in Australian history.[1]

The cover-up theory has been adopted by overseas conspiracy theorists. An article published in the *Sun-Herald* several months earlier by London correspondent Matt Condon used the prospect of a search for HMAS *Sydney* by the Woods Hole Oceanographic Institute to give James Rusbridger his chance to enliven the controversy. Rusbridger, who obviously fed the story to Condon, stated that the sinking of *Sydney* was a highly controversial issue and the RAN has done everything possible to prevent people from finding the wreck. Many documents and files have gone missing and the Australian Government has even prevented divers from inspecting a wreck in the general area off Geraldton. There has also been dead silence from the Japanese ever since the incident . . . It will be interesting to see the Australian Government's reaction to the search for *Sydney*, whether they say it should be stopped because it is a wartime burial ground or some other excuse.

The suggestion of a cover-up did not originate with the Group. It will be remembered that Montgomery used a cover-up to explain deficiencies in his research. However, the Group repeatedly alleged that the RAN consistently sought to prevent a full flow of information to the Australian people about the action between *Sydney* and *Kormoran*, and that this active concealment continued. Proving these changes became the principal focus of its activities.

The virulent expression of the *Sydney* Research Group's views reached a climax with the 50th anniversary of the loss of *Sydney* in November 1991. The *Sunday Times* played a leading role in giving a host of unsubstantiated allegations from the Group a major public airing. In its 27 October 1991 edition, the paper carried a two-page article in its features section headed 'Australia's shame—*Sydney* secret was hidden for 50 years'. The story was accompanied by photographs of *Sydney* and *Kormoran* and another of the article's author, Jim Davies, a retired journalist.

The article, drawing upon information provided by the *Sydney* Research Group, alleged that signals from *Sydney* reporting the action were heard ashore, 'and the navy ignored them'. Apparently, the *Sydney* Research Group had been able to ascertain (although the source is unknown) that Farquhar-Smith stated: 'The *Sydney*'s not overdue. The messages must be connected with something else.' Had the RAN responded to these signals as Davies evidently believes it could and should have done, 'survivors would have been found'. Furthermore, he claimed the RAAF sighted the *Kormoran* and took photographs of her. Unfortunately, 'for some unknown reason, Fremantle didn't tell

[*Sydney*] about the *Kormoran*' or Montgomery's alleged enemy aircraft flying over Pearce and Geraldton. Consequently, 'when the truth was revealed secretly in government and navy circles, [Farquhar-Smith] was kicked out of Fremantle'. As for the action, 'an engagement signal from the *Sydney* was received at Fremantle [at 2045]. The signal said that the *Sydney* was about to open fire on the *Kormoran*'. It was alleged that at least twenty people were aware of the signal sent by *Sydney* including

> a group of off-duty airmen [who] were having a party in the lounge of the Esplanade Hotel [in Geraldton]. When the local radio station closed for the night at 10.30, they switched on the short wave. They could all read morse and they picked up a message from the *Sydney* saying she was on fire fore and aft and preparing to abandon ship.[2]

It was alleged by *Sydney* Research Group Convenor Ean McDonald that these signals could have been re-transmitted on 25 November in an attempt to create the impression that this is when the action occurred. Another *Sydney* Research Group member, Gordon Laffer, claimed to have seen an official file during the war which included

> a message written in red pencil which began: Sydney calling Darwin, Sydney calling Darwin. On fire fore and aft. Preparing to abandon ship. The next page was the start of interviews with people who had heard the message over short wave radio. (All the airmen at the Geraldton party were interviewed).[3]

Laffer was told by the RAAF officer who showed him the file that 'the navy had been told of the distress signal but had replied that the *Sydney* was not overdue'. Unfortunately for Laffer, the file was allegedly sent to Canberra after the war. '[As] part of the navy and government cover-up, it is now not available to the public.' The article closed with some further details on the sighting of an alleged foreign-cum-enemy plane observed over Geraldton.

In the news section of the same paper, another article on the action was headed 'Navy's snobs could have saved *Sydney*'. This piece, which was devoid of a by-line, claimed that professional jealousy 'between the RAN and the RAAF was to blame for the loss of HMAS *Sydney*'. This article, using Davies' unpublished manuscript on wartime activities on the West Australian coast as its focus, cited Davies' belief that troublesome inter-service rivalry

> started in the ranks of both the RAN and the RAAF early in the war. Many permanent pre-war officers in the two services were 'so full of their own importance' they would not talk to their junior officers unless they had to. At one eastern States base shared by the two services, the men would not talk to each other. The RAN was blamed for most of the antagonism between the two in WA.[4]

When, according to Davies, the apparently snobbish RAN did ask the RAAF for assistance in investigating a suspicious merchant vessel on 11 November 1941, and the ship was observed to be *Kormoran*, the Navy was unable to intercept the ship because 'there wasn't anything bigger than a corvette in Fremantle'. Of course, 'the alternative was to ask the air force to bomb the enemy ship. But it appears that it was too much for the Navy's pride'. The astonishing revelations from Davies' unpublished manuscript went even further:

> The *Kormoran* met two Japanese submarines and gave them provisions.
> The submarines were submerged when the *Sydney* came along and when they saw the *Kormoran* was in trouble, they repaid a favour and torpedoed the Australian ship.
> Instead of trying to reach the coast, two boatloads of German survivors spent more than five days following the *Sydney*'s wreckage, shooting Australian survivors to make sure there would be nobody to tell the world that Japan was in the war—eighteen days before Pearl Harbor.

Five months later, the *Sunday Times* published yet another article alleging a grand conspiracy to conceal the 'truth' about the loss of *Sydney*. The subject for this article was Maureen Moylan, the daughter of a senior sailor lost with the ship, who

has written to State and Federal authorities urging a police inquiry or public inquest into the sinking ... She said this week she was convinced of a cover-up at higher levels because of sensitivity with Australia's wartime enemies and allies.[5]

It was evidently for people such as Moylan that Montgomery had written. In a letter to the Police Minister in Western Australia she stated:

From early adulthood, piece by piece, emerging contradictions in the official story of the *Sydney* and the German raider became known to me. I began to seriously doubt the claimed circumstances of the obviously violent deaths of my father and his 644 shipmates.

This doubt increased after the 50th anniversary of the sinking because she was now convinced that 'the circumstances and true nature of my father's death in service to his country have been deliberately falsified by successive Australian governments, and others'. Regrettably, Moylan was unable to cite any of the evidence that had led her to this conviction. But this did not prevent her from claiming that the *Sydney–Kormoran* action was

a war crime that hasn't been recognised as a war crime. But I don't want retribution. It's too late for any of that. It's just for the truth to be told, for the country to know what happened, and the *Sydney*'s end to be set straight.

To this end, Moylan placed a public announcement headed 'HMAS *Sydney*' in the 14 September 1992 edition of the *West Australian*.

Family members and friends of naval personnel lost on [sic] HMAS *Sydney* in November 1941 are invited to contact Mrs Maureen Moylan (daughter of the late petty officer Harry Tassell 'End the Secrecy on *Sydney*' (ESOS) group) so they may become aware of the efforts and progress being made to determine the true circumstances of the *Sydney's* loss.

The basis of this unfortunate, and entirely unproductive, agitation was an unwillingness to accept that nothing was heard of or from *Sydney* after she handed *Zealandia* over to *Durban*. It needs to be stated categorically that no documentary evidence has ever been produced to show that any RAN administrative authority ever received any signal from HMAS *Sydney* during or after her action with *Kormoran*. No evidence has ever been produced to show that the Navy acted as though it had received a signal from *Sydney*, or that it ever had any reason to conduct a major conspiracy to conceal a signal from *Sydney*. While it is possible that the District Naval Officer in Fremantle may have received information from other sources which should have given him reason to believe that *Sydney* was involved in some action, it has not been shown that he obtained any such information by the usual methods of naval communications. It is also possible, and one suspects probable, that some individual on board *Sydney* would have attempted to send some signal during the action if the ship's communications equipment was operational. If this individual was not a specialist radio operator, or if some or all of the ship's communications equipment was damaged, and both situations must be deemed possible, it is likely that signal transmissions from *Sydney* could have been totally unsuccessful, broken and incoherent, difficult to decipher, or sent on inappropriate frequencies or by suspect methods in the hope of raising some alarm ashore.

Sydney Research Group member John McArthur claimed that a plain language message was received at the Applecross Wireless Station shortly after 2000 on 19 November. This station relayed messages from ships at sea to the District Naval Office in Fremantle. These were usually encrypted except in emergencies. The signal allegedly received at Applecross indicated that *Sydney* 'was engaging'.

Other signals were also received at Geraldton and relayed to Perth [I assume by Perth he means the District Naval Office in Fremantle] by RAAF personnel. In addition, the OTC station at Geraldton received similar messages and informed Perth that *Sydney* was in trouble but no response, no acknowledgment was ever received. On the morning of 20 November, messages were relayed along the landline through Marble Bar. They stated that *Sydney* was in trouble, on fire and abandoning ship . . . And now there is a real possibility that they were picked up on [sic] HMAS *Nizam* in Alexandria. The Navy's position has been to deny the existence of any signals.[6]

The Navy had, in fact, denied nothing. It had simply stated that copies of such signals cannot be found, while there is nothing to suggest that they even exist. McArthur has been unable to produce, for instance, a copy of the signal received by the Applecross teleprinter, which one assumes would also have been relayed to the District Naval Office in Fremantle. As McArthur was unable to provide Date-Time-Groups for any of the transmissions to which he makes reference, and failed to provide any footnote references to the paper he presented at the 1991 *Sydney* Forum in Fremantle, the Navy's task in finding any such signals was not straightforward. Given that so many people allegedly heard signals from *Sydney*, it was surprising that McArthur has been unable to turn up a contemporaneous record from 1941 to prove that such signals were received and to show if action was taken upon their receipt.

But why would the Navy decide against investigating any information about *Sydney* after she failed to arrive as expected on 20 November? According to McArthur:

Flight Lieutenant Len Harrop, the RAAF intelligence officer at Pearce learned of the loss of *Sydney* in the early hours of 20 November. He contacted the District Naval Officer offering to put planes into the air at first light to search for *Sydney* and survivors. He received a curt reply that *Sydney* was not overdue.[7]

The problem with this assertion is that we do not know what Harrop told the District Naval Office or to whom he spoke.

(I doubt that he would actually have spoken with Farquhar-Smith.) Did Harrop advise the Navy of how he knew that *Sydney* had engaged an enemy the previous evening? Did Harrop say who the enemy was? Did Harrop say when he was told and what other action the RAAF was planning? Are junior RAAF officers authorised to make aircraft available to another Service for operational sorties? If not, who authorised Harrop to make the offer? Did he make any contemporaneous record to show that his offer of aircraft was declined? Did Harrop inform his commanding officer that he had spoken to the District Naval Office about *Sydney* and been ignored? If the RAAF was convinced that *Sydney* had suffered some calamity, why did they fail to act on their conviction and deploy their aircraft regardless of the Navy's attitude? How does Harrop account for the Navy's allegedly cavalier attitude towards its own ship? What would it have taken for the Navy to have initiated action on 20 November? The greatest problem with recollections such as those offered by Harrop is that they are notoriously unreliable and cannot be independently corroborated.

The action signal, or signals, which McArthur and Laffer allege were sent by *Sydney* and picked up in Geraldton and in Perth are recorded in the South West Area Combined Headquarters (SWACH) log. This signal was received in Darwin as 'Sydney Calling Darwin' and was sent in plain language (unencrypted). The signal was re-transmitted from Darwin to Perth on a Postmaster-General (PMG) circuit via Marble Bar, and was queried by RAAF Pearce. This would appear to explain the RAAF involvement. While it is extremely unlikely that *Sydney* would have sent an action signal in plain voice on an unguarded frequency that could, and probably was, monitored by *Kormoran*, and that the apparent signal destination was not the standard addressee for such a signal, the signal recorded in the SWACH log was actually transmitted on 4 December and is positively identified as PMG Sydney calling PMG Darwin.

The log entry at 1520 on 4 December stated: 'Geraldton heard a call on 24.50 metres possibly from HMAS *Sydney* and requested Pearce call Darwin for bearing.' Twenty-three minutes later:

Squadron Leader Cooper at Geraldton reports one of his operators
listening on 24.5 metres heard R/T [voice] telephone signal calling
Darwin or technical telegraph operator. Signals weak and operator thought it may be from HMAS *Sydney*. Radio Geraldton report
strength of signal increasing.[8]

There were a further two entries in the log regarding the signal
allegedly transmitted by *Sydney*. Its actual origin was recorded
in a log dated 6 December.

Signalled [Central War Room]: information received from Darwin
that short wave broadcast overheard on 4 December was from PMG
Sydney to PMG Darwin. In view of confusion caused, request information [on] whether this is [a] regular and authorised channel.[9]

McArthur based other claims on the SWACH log. According
to McArthur:

There can be no doubt that there was concern about raiders and this concern was not the sole preoccupation of the RAAF. In a letter written to
[Montgomery] in 1978, Flight Lieutenant H.W. Foord (Rtd) stated that
in 1941 he was a member of the City of Perth Squadron and during the
period under discussion 'we at the time knew that a raider ship in operation was working somewhere along the West Australian coastline. But
the general impression was that it was somewhere down on the lower
South West coast'. Foord corroborated independently information given
by Group Captain C.A. Bourne (Rtd). Bourne stated that he was involved
in searches operating off the coast to a depth of 250 miles looking for a
suspected commerce raider. 'On two occasions a ship was sighted creep-
ing in towards the coast, when this was reported to the Navy, I was
informed that one was positively identified as the *Kormoran*'.[10]

However, the entry in the SWACH log for 11 November 1941,
an entry which Montgomery cites as corroboration for the statements of Foord and Bourne, does not substantiate their claim
about sighting *Kormoran*. The log entry that Montgomery quotes
for 11 November, 'an unidentified merchant ship, believed to be

a raider', was actually entered into the log on 15 November and referred to a sighting on 11 November. The delay of four days in making the entry in the log denotes that the information was received from another source and was to be understood as a background report of a sighting outside the SWACH area. The position cited was BCNA 9990. This is a grid reference and seems to indicate that the unidentified ship was sighted in the South-West Pacific.

It is also reasonable to ask how Foord or Bourne could know the ship they sighted was *Kormoran* when that name was not yet known to the Allies. *Kulmerland* was known; *Kormoran* was not. And how could they have seen *Kormoran* when in the few days before the action with *Sydney* she was in the western Indian Ocean making her way towards the West Australian coast on a steady north-easterly course. As Winter points out, they may have seen *Orion*, which was sighted off Albany in September 1940.

Bourne's recollections become especially doubtful when he claims that during a flight around the time *Sydney* was lost, his aircraft came out of heavy fog and nearly struck a ship that he was adamant resembled a Japanese *Nagami* Class cruiser. 'He described the vessel as camouflaged in light and dark green. It was fitted with a three-gun turret aft and two three-gun turrets forward. As well it had a raked bow and a truncated funnel.' Although Bourne was advised that the Dutch cruiser *Tromp* had sailed down *Sydney*'s track from the Sunda Strait and was probably the ship sighted by Bourne, McArthur was absolutely convinced by this uncorroborated recollection that a major Japanese combatant had been sighted in a major shipping route adjacent to Australian territorial waters:

> Given the presence of a heavy Japanese cruiser in the area, something which has not attracted any interest whatsoever, concern must be raised about the relationship of the *Kormoran* to the Japanese. And there is indisputable evidence of its association with them.[11]

Although there was no evidence to support this claim, and ample evidence to discount it, McArthur again demonstrated his characteristic attraction for sensation and his dislike for the more obvious of contesting conclusions.

A number of conclusions could, however, be drawn from the South West Area Combined Headquarters (SWACH) log. The first was that the log recorded all reconnaissance flights and none was recorded by any aircraft type for 11 November 1941 when it was alleged that *Kormoran* was sighted. Second, the signals which are alleged to have been sent several hours after the *Sydney–Kormoran* action were actually sent on 4 December. It should also be noted that the Naval Board sent a signal to the Admiralty on 25 November 1941 regarding the action. It is quite possible that confused recollections of this particular signal have led some people to think it was sent during the action.

It was also difficult to accept McArthur's allegations that signals were received from *Sydney* when he was unable to state whether they were transmitted in plain voice, morse or encrypted morse. If he was so certain that the signals exist, why was he unable to describe them more fully? Other than some vague references in several operational logbooks which could be interpreted in a number of ways, McArthur built his case on recollections which were more than 50 years old. While he might have been convinced by the truthfulness and the sincerity of the individuals offering their recollections, as primary historical sources they were of extremely dubious value.

McArthur also drew the most sinister conclusions from every piece of evidence. By way of example: he stated that while the search for *Sydney* was underway, the Naval Board 'sent urgent telegrams to the next of kin of all *Sydney*'s crew. The date was the 26th November, the time lodged was 1745 (Time Zone Hotel) at Melbourne GPO. The funereal tone was clear to the recipient'. These circumstances led McArthur to believe that the Naval Board must have known that *Sydney* was lost for some considerable time.

Yet McArthur did not cite the contents of the telegrams; he could not prove that telegrams for the entire ship's company had been prepared by that time; and he could not be sure when the telegrams were actually despatched. They may have been lodged with the Post Office at Melbourne at 1745 on 26 November in readiness for their immediate despatch when the apparent loss of *Sydney* with all hands was confirmed. Their prompt transmission and delivery to next-of-kin would need to be achieved before a public statement could be made to the nation. The Navy was directed by the government to prepare casualty lists and telegrams for possible despatch at short notice in the event, for instance, that Berlin may have announced the sinking of *Sydney* as part of a propaganda broadcast. At any rate, by the time the telegrams were lodged, the Naval Board held little real hope of finding *Sydney* or any of her ship's company alive. Such a gesture was far from premature.

It has been alleged that logs belonging to the merchant ships involved in recovering the *Kormoran* survivors have been tampered with as part of the grand cover-up. While it is true that the logs of ships like *Centaur* and *Koolinda* are bland and provide little detail of their involvement in the aftermath of the *Sydney–Kormoran* action, it needs to be remembered that wartime regulations prevented the inclusion of information such as position, course, speed and local defence procedures in ships' logs to avoid their being of any use if captured by enemy raiders. As laid down by the Admiralty in *AMSI 221*, the information excluded from the logs was kept in a notebook maintained and retained by the ship's master. Thus, if the ship were captured the master could easily throw the notebook over the ship's side. It has also been alleged that the log of the tug *Uco* has been 'forged' in that there is no reference to the distorted QQQ signal intercepted by the tug.[12] This is entirely a matter of opinion.

In the first instance, it was the signal pad from *Uco* that was taken by the Navy. The word 'confiscated' has been used to describe its removal but this is much too strong a word for what actually happened. There is no reliable evidence to prove the log is suspect or that it was ever rewritten for the purpose of deleting information that was formerly included in it. It is noteworthy that the *Uco* log does not include any signals of an operational nature, either before or after she intercepted the garbled QQQ signal from *Kormoran*. In several instances it would appear that pages were removed from the logs of ships involved in the recovery of the *Kormoran* survivors by naval staff shortly after the loss of *Sydney* became known. Those pages of these logs were then re-written with exactly the same information to ensure that the ship's records remained complete. There is nothing to prove that the contents of the re-written pages varied from the original pages removed by naval staff.

Neither should sinister undertones be attributed to the collection of this material. The Navy was investigating the loss of *Sydney* and the circumstances surrounding the recovery of the *Kormoran* survivors. In the absence of photocopiers, the only way for the Navy to obtain the required information quickly was to obtain the original documents. This is what occurred. There is nothing to suggest that the information was seized as part of an elaborate cover-up.

It would be stating the obvious to say that the members of the *Sydney* Research Group were enthralled with their conspiracy theories. Laffer, who referred to a mysterious 'they' when describing the forces behind the cover-up, addressed the 1991 *Sydney* Forum and spoke

> with a sense of outrage and bitterness, because history has been so unfair. Several bloody minded people, in high places, have perverted and suppressed the real story of HMAS *Sydney*, and this I know without recourse to other people, because I was in the right place at the right time.

Such an outlook ruled out open-mindedness and the chance of dispassionate critique. Those who do not share the views of the *Sydney* Research Group were seen as willing dupes. McArthur claimed that the work of Winter and Clark, the Naval Historical Association [sic] and other 'so called naval histories which are no more than unquestioning chronicles' had ensured that

> the only account to be told is that now enshrined as the conventional wisdom—an unchallengeable doctrine . . . It is time to pose some of the questions and to expand upon the limited framework which has persisted for the telling of the story.[13]

This appeared to be McArthur's long-winded way of revealing that he was a revisionist, and a conspiracy theorist.

The greatest failing of the *Sydney* Research Group was its understanding of what constituted historical evidence. Most of the purported evidence gathered by the Group was practically worthless in such a controversial debate. Signals allegedly seen by McDonald; the file allegedly read by Laffer; and the recollections from 1941 of Mrs Betty Mack at the Marble Bar Post Office, were, as personal recollections with little or practically no independent or documentary corroboration, all unreliable sources. By way of example, the Group brought no credibility to its case when McDonald stated that Signalman Wally Holt, who served with him in *Sydney* and who later became a customs officer, told McDonald that 'two Germans migrating after the war told [Holt] that when *Sydney* came nearby . . . they were waiting . . . But when we saw her lowering a boat, we knew our number was up, and then we opened fire'. What was to be made of this? When did the conversation take place and where? How long and detailed was the conversation? Could Holt state the names of the Germans, where they were situated in *Kormoran* at the time of the action, whether they spoke from first- or second-hand information, and why they had volunteered the information? Why was this subject raised and did the Germans know that Holt had served in the Navy? Of course, one needs to ask whether Holt could be believed. Winter pointed out that none of the *Kormoran* survivors who later migrated to Australia ever settled in Western Australia. An historian is, of course, not required to believe that any conversation took place simply because one of the parties to it said it took place. However, McDonald did not seem able to countenance all of these objections to his 'evidence'.

The Group also appeared to think that because an alleged witness to a certain event records his recollection under a statutory declaration, that the event actually took place. All a statutory declaration indicates is that the individual actually and sincerely believed that this is what he can recall. As most of the recollections cited by the Group in support of their allegations were 50 years old, they needed to be treated with great caution. They deserved little credence.

There was also the Group's continuing lament about the *Official Secrets Act* and their claim that a great deal of information would emerge if a large number of people able to give evidence were to be freed from any obligations under the Act. Although I doubt that as many people as they believe feel so constrained by the Act and information relating to events occurring over 50 years ago, McArthur asserted that there is no doubt

> that many of the people involved in this story were approached by authorities and warned against ever disclosing information. Notwithstanding the passage of half a century they are restrained from being whistleblowers regardless of the morality of the position.[14]

There was also the allegation that files are presently being withheld from the public. Despite repeated assurances that government departments and Australian Archives have made all available files available to researchers, and do not seek to withhold any information about the action, McArthur nonetheless asserted that classified files might still be held in the 'Navy Signals Directorate' (which does not exist) and 'Australian Archives and various parts of the Defence Departments'. There is, of course, only one Defence Department, and it had made several thorough searches for files still in its possession which might be even vaguely relevant to the loss of *Sydney*. But it appeared that a refusal to accept such assurances was ineradicably within the psyche of the hardened conspiracy theorist. This characteristic of the *Sydney* Research Group was destructive and counterproductive. Its members were unwilling to accept evidence which challenged their views while they held resolutely to theories which were demonstrably false. They also refused to accept any statement made by Gill or any other historian that tended to uphold the conventional view of the action.

The allegation that files relating to *Sydney* have not been released was answered adequately some time ago. Montgomery's book prompted a number of letters to the then Minister for

Defence, Sir James Killen, doubting the Navy's honesty and asking whether it still had any files locked away in its vaults relating
to *Sydney*. Killen stated more than a decade earlier that all
relevant records were available at the War Memorial and ended
by noting: 'I doubt that additional incontrovertible evidence will
emerge, and so questions are likely to remain unanswered'.[15]
More recently, the then Defence Minister Kim Beazley again
confirmed that all documents held by the Navy had been made
available to researchers.

Despite some suggestions to the contrary, I can confirm from
firsthand experience that Navy Office does not maintain filing
cabinets of secret or embarrassing documents from World War
II. During my two years as Research Officer to the Chief of Naval
Staff, I did not encounter one document relating to events occurring during World War II within the private vault attached to that
office. If there are documents in existence which relate to the loss
of *Sydney* which have not been made available to any researcher
into this subject, it is only because their incorrect location on an
official file has obscured their presence. Although this possibility
cannot be discounted, two points should be made. First, there
is nothing sinister in this. Documents were sometimes placed on
incorrect or inappropriate files by inexperienced staff. Second, it
is highly unlikely that anything of real historical import relating
to *Sydney* would have been placed on an obscure file and left
there unnoticed. While this does not discount the possibility, the
effort involved in searching every file possessing even the most
tenuous link with *Sydney* would not be time well spent.

The Group also lacked a sense of perspective. They had
no detailed knowledge of naval operations, administration or
record-keeping beyond that associated with the loss of *Sydney*.
In discussing information relating to a carley float alleged to
have originated from *Sydney*, Laffer spoke of another researcher
running 'into the usual dead ends with RAN history'. This was
an extraordinary remark for Laffer to make. There was no evidence that he had ever conducted any research into any matter
within Australian naval history unconnected with *Sydney*. From
his meagre published work dealing with the sinking of *Sydney*,

there is nothing to suggest that he had any naval historiographical experience which allows him to make any comparative judgment. While it is very true that naval records relating to *Sydney* were not created, managed or passed by the Navy to Australian Archives in an orderly fashion, the particular shortcomings he observed were not restricted to *Sydney* or record-keeping in World War II.

Correspondence records in the Navy Department were always kept well enough for the conduct of naval business. As part of moves by the Commonwealth government to improve the archival quality of records from the point of view of future historians, naval records were better organised and maintained after the war of 1939–45 under the guidance of Commonwealth Archivists and with the appointment at Navy Office of a Registrar, Ira Menear.

If Laffer had, for instance, to research the loss of the stores carrier HMAS *Matafele* in June 1944, he would find some 'notable absences in the official records'. If its members decided to conduct research into the RAN's wartime fuel stocks policy the *Sydney* Research Group would find that naval records were not as complete or as comprehensive as they seem to expect. Another example that could have been cited is the mistaken attack made on HMAS *Hobart* by an American F-4 fighter off the coast of Vietnam in June 1968. The report of the American inquiry into the attack, which left two Australian sailors dead and another five wounded, and the notes made by the Australian officers seconded to Subic Bay for the inquiry, cannot be found within Navy Office. In government administration, it is an unfortunate fact from the viewpoint of historical research that sometimes records, the raw stuff from which history is made, are deficient, lost or non-existent.

But when the Group requested official records from government agencies and was told that a document cannot be found in the relevant records searched, they claimed that the government agency has 'denied' that the document exists. Of course, as they were the ones bringing allegations against the government, the prime burden of responsibility rested with the *Sydney* Research

Group to substantiate its claims with concrete evidence. It needed to show that the Navy had, and continued to have, a substantial motive for covering up the 'truth'.

Official cover-ups are designed to serve a purpose. No author has yet been able to identify any substantial reason for the Navy wanting to conceal anything about the loss of *Sydney*. What would be gained by such action? What of the consequences of the cover-up being exposed? It would appear that, if anything, the Navy stood to lose by having rumours circulating unchecked and unrestrained across the country during the war. There is every indication that the Navy would have revealed the 'truth' about the loss of *Sydney* if it believed it had found the 'truth'. But what of the suggestion of a continuing cover-up?

Of course, the Navy is not an inchoate entity. Those who serve today are not accountable for the actions of those who served in 1941. They do not feel obliged to defend the actions of those who administered or operated the RAN during World War II; nor should they feel so obliged. At any rate, the loss of *Sydney* is regarded by most officers and sailors within the Navy rather as a matter of antiquarian interest.

The modern Navy has a very mature attitude towards its traditions and heritage. Many things have contributed to its evolution and the development of its professional ethos. There is a willingness to accept the entire corpus of RAN history; the successes and failures; the good and the bad. It is for this reason that I cannot accept the view that a cover-up is in progress or that it has ever been attempted. If pressed, I would be inclined to agree that the efforts to locate *Sydney* in the few days after the action and the interrogations which followed seem to have been poorly handled and that some effort was made to conceal some personal shortcomings. But the 'concealing' was only from the public and was limited to the duration of the war. There does not seem to have been an effort to expunge every mention of the search or the interrogations from official records where the deficiencies of what did take place were apparent.

There is always the tendentious argument that the disclosure of previously withheld facts relating to historical events involving Australia and another nation might adversely affect current diplomatic ties. This is an entirely specious argument. Such assertions have been made in connection with the release of files relating to the loss of USS *Frank E. Evans* after a collision with the aircraft carrier and RAN flagship, HMAS *Melbourne*, on 3 June 1969, or the mistaken attack by the American F-4 fighter on HMAS *Hobart* on 17 June 1968.[16] Of course, there is a world of difference between an academic treatment of these matters by non-polemical and disinterested historians, and their use by journalists to create controversy or polemicists to stir up sentiment.

The *Sydney* Research Group's lack of restraint and balance attracted the tabloid media and caused speculation where none should have existed. They based their allegations on potentially faulty personal recollections or on speculation and assertion, and they have then demanded that evidence be produced to rebut their claims. It is said that one fool can ask more questions than a thousand sages can ever hope to answer. Had the Group prepared a well-documented and soundly argued account before it 'went public', unnecessary controversy might have been avoided and the matters in dispute resolved in a more scholarly manner than the reckless form of virtual street-fighting which has characterised the *Sydney* debate. Montgomery and the *Sydney* Research Group were together solely responsible for the mishandling of the historical record relating to the loss of HMAS *Sydney* and the animosity and discord it has caused in relations between the Navy and the civil community, and within the naval historical community. Although the Group has 'stirred the pot', which is not a bad thing *per se*, they also created a great deal of unnecessary ill-will.

The Carley Float
and Forensic Analysis

The only trace of *Sydney* found after the 19 November action was the carley float recovered by *Heros* on 27 November and the lifebelts found by *Evagoras* and *Wyrallah*. In the absence of identifying marks, the splinter-marked lifebelts appeared to have little real significance in explaining the loss of *Sydney*. That only two lifebelts were found is sufficient mystery in itself. The German lifebelt recovered by *Wyrallah* was in a slightly more damaged condition than the Australian belts. The carley float, which was given to the War Memorial during the war as an historical relic, appeared to offer more scope.[1]

Carley floats were used in RAN vessels as part of the ship's lifesaving equipment; they came in two sizes. The smaller size, ten feet long and five feet wide, fitted inside the larger version. They were stored either vertically or horizontally around warships. The floats were constructed principally of canvas and cork built around a steel tube frame which also formed watertight compartments. The floor of the float was made of New Zealand kauri suspended by rope netting when the float was in use. Carley floats were, in effect, large lifebuoys.

In addition to the ship's boats which would be the principal means of conveying personnel away from a ship if she were being abandoned, the carley floats played an important secondary and emergency role. Floats were evidently rotated around the Fleet and were not issued specifically to one ship. It was normal for a ship undertaking a refit to have her lifesaving equipment landed ashore and surveyed before being returned to the ship. As this surveying was done on a pool arrangement, from which replacements for damaged equipment were drawn, the vessel might not receive back the equipment she had landed. Thus, it is not surprising that only the circumstances of its recovery establish any definite link between the carley float recovered by *Heros* and HMAS *Sydney*. However, this has not stopped the float being the source of much speculation about the *Sydney–Kormoran* action.

Montgomery stated that

the five or six larger holes caused by shrapnel are spread haphazardly over its circumference, but there is a much greater number of machine-gun perforations, and these are noticeably concentrated on the sides. The length of the holes, one of which is a 6-inch strip torn across the top of one side, their proximity to each other (one machine-gun expert who examined the float stated that 'he doubted if with 100 or more rounds he could have put more than a dozen bullets into a raft at a range of 1,000 yards from a moving ship') and the depth of penetration all point to their having been inflicted at a much closer range than the consensus figure of 1,200 yards for the opening of the action; in other words, they suggest that the float was fired on not while it was still onboard the *Sydney* but after it had been launched into the water.[2]

Gordon Laffer of the *Sydney* Research Group suggested that after the sinking, a motor boat from *Kormoran*

could have been used with mounted machine guns to mop up the *Sydney* survivors, and this would account for the bullet holes in the [carley float], and the absence of survivors. If this did in fact happen, and the motor boat was scuttled afterwards then it would explain why the two boats commanded by Detmers and von Gosseln were so grossly overloaded.

In an article in the *Sun-Herald* which made exclusive use of information from British writer James Rusbridger, the reporter stated:

Only one of the *Sydney*'s life rafts was ever found. It is now displayed in the Canberra War Museum. It is riddled with bullets and suggests that any survivors were machine-gunned in the water to ensure there were no witnesses to [the involvement of a Japanese submarine].

In the wake of growing allegations that the float was 'riddled with bullets' because the *Sydney* survivors who had taken to the water in it were machine-gunned by *Kormoran*, the War Memorial conducted a thorough examination of the float by industrial X-radiography, videoimagescope and mechanical probing in 1992 to determine whether 'it did contain evidence supporting or denying the machine gun theory'.

The investigation revealed that the float had been subjected to

multiple strikes by pieces of both high-explosive and, perhaps, solid projectiles of varying calibres. Other damage has been caused by early investigative techniques and as a result of being on 'open' display from 1942 to 1960.[3]

It appeared that during this period parts of the float's canvas covering were breached to allow internal probing and that souvenir hunters tore small strips off the float. There was no evidence 'of burning or heat damage to the painted surface or to the canvas or rope fibres. This tends to prove the damage was done to the float before the ship was engulfed in flames'.[4]

The projectiles within the float had struck predominantly what is presumed to be its port side. There were:

339 disruptions of the canvas likely to have been caused by the projectiles. 222 are entries into the canvas and cork only. 63 are entries into the canvas, cork and steel body. 26 are exit holes from cork and canvas. 28 are exit holes from the steel, cork and canvas . . . The wooden platform received 14 hits, probably contributing greatly to the loss of about 17 per cent of the timber. The netting suffered 13 hits that resulted in loss of substantial areas of cordage and five hits that have only grazed the fibres.[5]

The angles of trajectory of the projectiles range 'from 5 degrees to 33 degrees above the horizontal. The divergence angle (from 90 degrees abeam) ranges from −17 degrees to +23 degrees'.[6] The projectiles 'were removed and analysed by scanning electron microscopy and X-ray fluorescence'. The Memorial's technicians then concluded that:

> The analyses of the samples chosen from the projectiles indicated that they were only partly similar to pieces of exploded, large calibre munitions consistent with the types carried by *Kormoran*.[7]
>
> Nothing discovered and removed from the carley float has any morphological or metallurgical resemblance to the type of machine-gun bullets that would have been used during the naval action in November 1941.[8]

These conclusions certainly made Montgomery's allegations of concentrated machine-gun fire at close range look foolish.

The War Memorial's examination of the carley float raised more questions than it answered. As the Memorial's float is the smaller of the two types, and noting that the smaller floats were usually fitted inside the larger version to save deck space, where is the larger float in which it was fitted? Or does the fact that it suffered direct damage from a high explosive shell mean that it was dislodged from a position within a larger float before being damaged by gunfire? How was this float set free from the deck of *Sydney* when there is no evidence of fire or shock damage? Why was this the only float to have survived? Perhaps the only thing that could be concluded from the Memorial's thorough examination of the float was that it had definitely not been 'riddled with bullets' from a machine-gun in or from *Kormoran*. As this was considered unlikely by most researchers at the outset, the Memorial's efforts were unfortunately disappointing.

The carley float found by *Heros* on 27 November may not have been the only item recovered from the Australian cruiser. In the early evening of 6 February 1942, some Chinese and Malay coastwatchers on the Australian territory of Christmas Island in the Indian Ocean noticed that a raft bearing a body was floating towards the island. A pilot vessel took the raft, initially identified as a naval carley float, in tow. The man in the float had been dead for some time. The Christmas Island Harbour Master, Captain J. Reginald Smith, stated that

> the . . . float . . . was undoubtedly of Naval pattern. The wooden decking was branded with the word 'patent', and one hole, apparently caused by a bullet, was found in this decking. The outer covering . . . was damaged in several places, a few pieces of metal being found embedded in the kapok filling. One of these pieces according to the gun's crew on the island, was what remained of a bullet.
>
> The inside framework, also the divisions between the buoyancy tanks, were branded as follows: 'Lysaght Dua-anneal Zinc. Made in Australia' inside. All the roping attached to the float had a red yarn running through the strands. The canvas shoe found on the float was branded either McCowan or McEwen, also Pty, followed by a crown and/or a broad arrow.
>
> The corpse was clothed in a boiler suit which had originally been blue, but was bleached white by exposure. There were four plain press buttons from neck to waist . . .[9]

The Christmas Island residents had already been touched by the war. The previous month, a U-boat had sunk the Norwegian phosphate ship *Eidsvold*, some 120 yards from the shoreline. It appeared to them that the carley float had been in the water for some time as weed had grown both inside and outside the rim of the float while the body had been attacked by birds. The shoe found in the float was apparently Australian government issue although, in the opinion of the local medical officer, it did not belong to the body.

When the lining of the raft was opened, Joseph Baker, an operator at the Christmas Island radio station, recalled that 'the raft showed damage from gunfire' and 'several expended bullets' were found. After a medical examination, the results of which cannot be located, the body was buried in the small cemetery on the island. It is likely that any records relating to the float and the corpse produced on Christmas Island were destroyed by the

Japanese who occupied the island on 31 March, 53 days after the float was first sighted.

But from where did the carley float and the dead man originate? There were no marks on the float which linked it to *Sydney*; its association with *Sydney* from the outset was only circumstantial. The Navy conducted a limited inquiry into the Christmas Island discovery after a memorandum about the matter was received in Navy Office from NOIC Fremantle. The Director of Naval Intelligence, Captain George Oldham, commented in a subsequent minute dated 23 April 1949 that this memo 'resuscitates a matter which was brought under notice during the war and which is believed to have been investigated at the time, although no records can be found'. A fresh inquiry was apparently commenced at the direction of the Deputy CNS. Although the shoe described by Captain Smith 'definitely correspond with supplies from our stock', Oldham was persuaded by other evidence which he outlined in his report dated 2 August 1949.

> I have carried out detailed investigations for the purpose of assessing the possibility whether the carley float, with the corpse on board . . . could have been from . . . *Sydney*. Identification particulars set out in some detail in Shipping Intelligence Report No. 137/1942 . . . assisted those investigations. While these show that the clothing found on the corpse could possibly have been that of an RAN rating, it seems reasonably certain from the particulars given of the covering of the carley float that the float did not belong to an HMA ship. My conclusion, therefore, is that the carley float sighted . . . off Christmas Island was not ex HMAS *Sydney*.

Not surprisingly, Gill made only passing mention of the Christmas Island carley float.

> It was at first thought that this might be from *Sydney*, but in the early post-war years, and after detailed investigation of all reports and descriptions of the float and its occupant, [Captain Oldham RAN] concluded that this could not be so.

When Bryan Clark asked BHP Steel for more information about its involvement in wartime projects, particularly the supply of Dua-anneal zinc, he was advised that

> although the company [formerly John Lysaght (Australia) Limited] manufactured a sheet steel with an annealed zinc coating, it was called Zincanneal and we cannot find Dua-anneal listed as a trade mark for annealed zinc coated steel.

The War Memorial's analysis of the carley float also casts doubt on the RAN origins of the Christmas Island carley float. There was no red yarn running through the cordage of the float recovered by *Heros*. In one of the ropes there is a single blue strand but nothing resembling a red yarn. Neither was the float made of kapok. One could also reasonably ask why Captain Smith thought it was of naval design. Was his knowledge of lifesaving equipment such that he could distinguish a civilian float from a naval float? Sceptics were also entitled to have doubts about the descriptions of battle damage offered by the local Christmas Island militia. The alleged 'machine-gun expert' mentioned by Montgomery who examined the War Memorial's float had also given a completely inaccurate assessment of its battle damage—and he was an 'expert'!

As for the overalls and the shoe, they could well have come from Australian government stores but this did not mean the wearer was a naval person. It was also noteworthy that the description of the shoe, which was canvas, was consistent with Navy issue shoes except for the fact that the Navy shoes were usually leather. Similar leather shoes and overalls were provided to a range of occupational groups and were possibly available for private purchase. Alternatively, the items could have been given to the wearer by a sailor or anyone else in government service.

The condition of the items also raised doubts. No evidence had been provided to show that the state of the overalls, the shoe, or the float was consistent with two and a half months exposure to the elements. The float and its occupant could have been adrift for six months to a year. It remained the responsibility of those who asserted that the float originated from *Sydney* to prove conclusively that this factor is consistent with its purported origins and that, furthermore, it discounts other possibilities. Given that the float was destroyed and statements about its appearance and condition were very brief, it was unlikely that conclusive proof could ever be established.

Yet Winter was prepared to state that she 'firmly believes that the unidentified sailor came from HMAS *Sydney*' because, Clark relays,

> summer currents from the battle site were to the north-north-west at half a knot. Accordingly, a raft from the *Sydney* could have been within 100 kilometres of Christmas Island by 6 February 1942.

In other words, by a process of elimination, Winter believes it must have come from *Sydney*. She writes:

> I think it really should be recognised that the body definitely came from *Sydney*. To me, that is the important thing. What should jump up and hit people on the head is this: there was no other ship from which [the body] could possibly have come. Public servants handling this matter seem to have been concerned mainly with dodging anything which would make them think or work . . . So far, all anyone has done is bleat that they don't think it came from *Sydney*.

Putting aside her unfortunate stereotyping of public officials who are not, contrary to her understanding, obliged to investigate exhaustively every claim made by a member of the public, her logic was not good enough. It was insufficient to say that simply because the carley float could have come from *Sydney* that it was from *Sydney*. It is equally illogical for Laffer to use the 'fact that the carley float did emanate from *Sydney* . . . to establish the velocity of the current and hence the wreck positions of *Sydney* and *Kormoran*'. Having glibly accepted all that was stated about the Christmas Island float because it was consistent with his other arguments, Laffer challenged Winter to explain the bullet holes in the . . . carley float found at Christmas Island? Having made that explanation, could she then explain the presence of footwear in that float, which did not fit the corpse? More likely that the owner of the footwear preferred to take his chance in the water, rather than be shot to death in the float, as was probably the case of the corpse.

These inflammatory statements did not sit easily with Laffer's claim that he did not 'seek to run a hate campaign against any other nation'.

Neither Laffer nor Clark demonstrated any special expertise in the meteorological factors relevant to their assertion that the float had to come from *Sydney* and I was not prepared to put faith in their calculations. They also failed to explore the existence of other weather patterns which might have brought the float from elsewhere. A sceptic could reasonably argue that for the float to have drifted from the south-west Australian coast all the way to Christmas Island where it turned due west off North East Point towards the island's main jetty was practically a fluke. It would be manifestly more likely for the float to miss washing up on the tiny island completely.

That the Navy would mount yet another cover-up in destroying records relating to the Christmas Island float was without a convincing motive. Why would the Navy deny it held a report of the examination of the corpse if it did? What purpose would this achieve? Even if the body did contain small arms fire, why would the Navy want to conceal this information? The comments made by *Kormoran* survivor Otto Jurgensen were inflammatory, totally unnecessary and in any event superfluous as there was never any suggestion that the float or the corpse came from *Kormoran*.

There is no *Kormoran* survivor who can say that the unidentified sailor on Christmas Island was one of our men. He must have been a HMAS *Sydney* man. We had no floats made by Lysaght. I cannot understand the Australian authorities' attempts to cover up the truth.

Equally gratuitous were Clark's remarks about the attitude of
the Navy and the Commonwealth War Graves Commission
towards the Christmas island float and corpse:

> Australian officialdom do not know the actual location of the unknown
> seamen's [sic] last resting place and seem disinterested in locating it,
> much less marking the site with a commemorative headstone or iden-
> tifying plaque. This is, indeed, a sad indictment against our public
> service's apathetic mentality, reinforcing the legend: 'There are none so
> blind as those who do not wish to see'. Nor as ignorant as those who
> do not want to know.

Laffer asked, 'How could they disown the young man's remains,
when the *Sydney* was the only possible source? Why has no post
mortem ever been published? Why have these terrified gormless
people tried to cover up the whole story?'

The comments by Clark and Laffer were most unfair and
insulting to officers in both organisations who have tried, apparently without success, to point out that the available evidence
was thin and inconclusive. Furthermore, it was unreasonable to
expect either the Navy or the Commission to expend their limited resources on trying to prove that the float and the corpse,
which was lying in an unmarked grave and which could not be
positively identified, originated from *Sydney*. However, Clark
was right when he asked, 'if the unidentified corpse was not an
HMAS *Sydney* crewman, where did he come from?' It is a pity
that he did not expend as much effort exploring the possibility
that it did not than in simply declaring that it did.

In sum, I felt that Clark had not demonstrated that all of the
alternative origins of the float, a number of which he mentioned,
could be reasonably discounted. Certainly, neither Laffer nor
Clark has been able to overcome the substantial material differences in the construction of the two carley floats. Therefore,
I concluded in 1993 that Oldham's conclusion of 1949 that the
float did not come from *Sydney* was a more reasonable conclusion than that which holds that it did.

16

An Autopsy Without a Body

In chapters seven and eight, dealing with the German accounts of the *Sydney–Kormoran* action, mention was made of the more obvious inconsistencies and contradictions in their statements. These chapters did not discuss whether *all* of the Germans revealed *all* that they knew about the action, but they suggested that *some* of the Germans may have withheld *some* information. These omissions may have contained the key to understanding *Sydney*'s otherwise inexplicable manoeuvres. If any such key does exist, it is most likely to be found in the early phases of the action when *Sydney* allegedly departed from established procedures.

The crucial moment in the encounter occurred when Burnett took his ship within 14 000 yards of *Kormoran*. At that point, the character of the engagement changed dramatically. At or beyond 14 000 yards, *Sydney* was definitely safe and *Kormoran* was certainly doomed. The only undetermined factor at this range for Burnett was whether or not the suspicious ship, which might have been a German tanker or supply ship, could be prevented from scuttling. There was no other need for Burnett to close the suspect ship any further than 14 000 yards. At that range, he could and should have undertaken the interrogation, principally with the assistance of his Walrus aircraft. This would have obviated the need for him to close the suspicious ship to read her signal flags.

Sydney's previous encounters with merchant ships after Burnett took command in May 1941 also show that Burnett

regarded 14 000 yards as a 'satisfactory distance' from which
to identify suspicious ships.[1] In addition to the observations he
made during the board of inquiry into the alleged sighting of
Salland by *Yandra* in early October 1941, Burnett submitted a
report to RACAS regarding merchant ship identification on 7
September which explained his approach to the task. During a
short convoy escort passage in early September, Burnett reported
that three merchant ships had failed to observe the Admiralty
procedure for challenge and reply. 'On two occasions, owing to
good visibility, it was possible to establish the friendly nature of
the ship with reasonable confidence at a satisfactory range [i.e.
approximately 14 000 yards], but on one occasion it was considered prudent to alter the course of the convoy away until the
identified ship was at a safe range'.[2]

The German accounts leave no doubt that Burnett had
intended using his aircraft during the interrogation. For some
reason not made evident by the German accounts, the Walrus
was not launched and its engine was shut down. It is of course
conceivable that the aircraft had become unserviceable. There is
nothing in the German descriptions of *Kormoran*'s actions prior
to the aircraft being shut down which would have induced Burnett's decision not to use the aircraft. Nor did *Kormoran* take
any action which would have reduced his suspicions about her
identity. Why, then, did Burnett change his mind and not keep
to his standard procedure, which would have been a plainly prudent measure in the circumstances?

When *Sydney* came within 14 000 yards of *Kormoran*, she
was inside the maximum effective range of the raider's guns.
After coming within 14 000 yards, there was little effective
alteration in the tactical situation until the range was only 5000
yards. Between 5000 and 14 000 yards, *Sydney* was always in
danger of being hit by *Kormoran*'s guns; the probability of the
Australian ship sustaining damage increased slowly with the
steadily decreasing range. At 5000 yards, *Sydney* had become
an easy target for *Kormoran*. However, Burnett's decision to
proceed within 5000 yards involved less additional risk than his
decision to come within 14 000 yards. Once *Sydney* was within

5000 yards, she advanced from a moderate level of risk of being hit by *Kormoran*'s poorly directed and controlled guns to a substantial risk. Within 5000 yards, there was a high probability that *Kormoran* would be able to inflict serious damage on the Australian ship.

When the range was further reduced to between 1200–1500 yards and *Sydney* appeared to move from a position on *Kormoran*'s quarter, where she was within the firing arc of one or possibly two of the raider's guns, to the beam, where she was within the firing arcs of four 5.9-inch guns and within range of the 3.7-centimetre and anti-aircraft mountings (which had a maximum effective range of about 3000 yards), *Sydney* had become a simple target and could not avoid being hit and badly damaged by *Kormoran*'s guns. But once again, Burnett's decision to proceed from 5000 to 1200 yards involved a lesser amount of additional risk than his earlier decision to come within 14000 yards. All of this suggests that the key to understanding Burnett's actions is most likely to be found by establishing what *Kormoran* may have done when *Sydney* was at a range of 14000 yards.

In reconstructing the action from the German accounts, Burnett's decision to close *Kormoran* almost exclusively determined the course of subsequent events and the likelihood that *Sydney* would be lost. In the 30 minutes after being sighted by *Sydney*, according to Detmers, the raider had acted entirely as if she were a disguised enemy raider fleeing from a warship. Burnett had not established the identity of the suspicious ship nor had anything occurred which would have allayed any of the concern in his mind. Within the next 30 minutes when the range was 14000 yards, it seems that *Kormoran* must have done something to allay or confirm Burnett's fears about the identity of the suspect ship. It is much more likely, given his subsequent actions, that his fears were at least partially allayed by *Kormoran*'s actions.

The evidence suggests that *Sydney* ordered *Kormoran* to stop when the range was more than 14000 yards. It will be recalled that Detmers made a statement to this effect at Swanbourne Barracks on 2 December. As he never repeated the statement, he probably learned from his officers that they had not included this crucial detail in their accounts. Indeed, other than von Gosseln who was the only other commissioned officer on the bridge with Detmers (Petty Officer Otto Jurgensen was also apparently on the bridge), it is likely that no-one else in *Kormoran* was aware that *Sydney* had ordered *Kormoran* to stop. This same observation can be made of all the signals from *Sydney* of which the German officers made reference in their later accounts. Apart from Detmers and von Gosseln, none of the German officers was in a position to see *Sydney*'s signals or to interpret them. The wide variation in their description of the signals points to their reliance on Detmers and von Gosseln for the information.

Stopping the unidentified ship would have been Burnett's first priority. In addition to reducing the time taken to identify the ship, he would not want to chase a merchant ship for several hours in a westerly direction when his destination—Fremantle— was to the south-east. The evidence of Detmers and Ahlbach that *Sydney* repeatedly signalled to *Kormoran* before she sent the letters 'NNJ' is probably a reference to the 'heave to' order. Alternatively, as the letters 'NNJ' were normally sent by flag, it is also possible that the letters 'PRB' preceded 'NNJ' to signify that the flag hoist was being sent by light using morse.

Detmers was confronted with two choices when *Sydney* ordered *Kormoran* to stop. The first was to ignore the order in the hope that the cruiser would lose interest. As this was extremely unlikely, Detmers would have expected *Sydney* to fire a warning shot if the order were not obeyed. And if the warning shot went unheeded, *Sydney* would fire for effect at long range. *Kormoran* would doubtless be sunk without putting up a fight. This is exactly what had happened to *Pinguin*. Detmers would have known that there was nothing to be gained from continuing to flee.

It is reasonable to assume that *Kormoran* obeyed *Sydney*'s order to stop because there is no evidence to suggest that *Sydney* fired a warning shot at or beyond 14 000 yards. Neither would Burnett have tried to hit the unidentified ship as he would not have had sufficient information to warrant such action. He did not know that the suspect ship was Raider G or that she definitely was not *Straat Malakka*. It can be accepted that had either a warning shot or a ranging shot been fired at *Kormoran*, it would have been heard or seen by some of the raider's crew or the Chinese laundrymen. No *Kormoran* survivor ever mentioned an incoming Australian round at that range.

It is also likely that *Sydney* stood off the raider at 14 000 yards for some time. The evidence of the survivors is quite clear on this point. At least one hour elapsed from the time that *Sydney* was sighted by *Kormoran* until the engagement. With *Kormoran* cruising at 14 knots and *Sydney* closing at nearer to 30 knots, *Sydney* should have covered the distance of seven to nine miles between the two ships in 30 minutes.[3] However, at 1715, Detmers claimed that *Sydney* was still 9000 yards distant. Five minutes later, he claimed the range was 1200 yards. As the Australian interrogators noted, the Germans wanted to get rid of half an hour. As identification of merchant vessels usually took about 30 minutes to complete, it is very likely that both *Sydney* and *Kormoran* either stopped or slowed considerably before *Sydney* closed to less than 14 000 yards, possibly to board *Kormoran*.

Having been ordered to stop, *Kormoran* then hoisted the Dutch flag. This is consistent with the evidence of Bunjes who said that the Dutch flag was hoisted some time before the signal letters were given for *Straat Malakka*. Detmers' strategy was to prolong the identification by whatever means to ensure that *Sydney*'s suspicions were not aroused until he was in a position to fight. The QQQ signal was one such ploy and was consistent with *Kormoran* having stopped. Burnett was justified in approaching the Dutch ship because she had obeyed his orders, and because he would need to board the ship if she were unable to prove her identity.

The possibility that *Kormoran* may have sent a medical distress or general emergency signal at this point can also be dismissed. A ship genuinely seeking medical attention would hardly have proceeded towards the south-west away from the coast and away from the approaching *Sydney*. A general emergency would also have attracted far too much interest and the possibility of drawing the attention of another warship. Indeed, in his book Detmers said, 'what I didn't understand was why he didn't signal me to heave to. That would have been very disagreeable'.[4]

While appearing to comply with *Sydney*'s order to stop, *Kormoran* would need to proceed very slowly through the water at two or three knots, both to prevent her bow from swinging around across the swell and exposing her entire profile and to help her to maintain her westerly course into the sun. The reduction in speed, possibly achieved by the use of only one engine, would not have been completely apparent to the German crew as *Kormoran* was already heading into the wind and swell which gave the appearance of additional speed. A substantial drop in the raider's speed would also explain why *Sydney* was later able to cover so much distance in such a short period of time.

The suggestion that *Kormoran* had either slowed down or, more likely in my view, ceased making headway has support in some German accounts. Indeed, sketches prepared by Fritz Treber for Captain Farncomb of the engagement seemed to show that *Kormoran* was not underway as *Sydney* approached. In his book, Detmers says that he watched the compass bearing until *Sydney* 'had come practically to a standstill'. Although the reference to a compass bearing would normally mean that *Sydney*'s bearing from *Kormoran* was steady, his choice of words suggests that the Australian ship was not underway or making way. There is also a reference to *Sydney* stopping in Detmers' action report, although its meaning is debatable. It is unclear from the original German version of the decrypted action report whether Detmers was recording that the *Sydney* stopped main engines, or that the aircraft's engine was shut down. Both interpretations of this entry in the report are possible.

With *Kormoran* having obeyed the order to stop, it is likely that *Sydney* continued the interrogation as she approached from a position of safety, astern of the unidentified ship. As the purported Dutch merchantman had stopped and *Sydney* was making rapid progress towards her in the hope of preventing her from scuttling if she were an enemy ship, the Walrus was not needed and could be shut down. In accordance with Admiralty procedure, Burnett then ordered the 'Dutch' ship to hoist her international signal letters. It is most likely that Ahlbach did fumble with the signal letters as Detmers suggested. Detmers' statement that *Sydney* hauled away to starboard at about 9000 yards was probably an attempt by the Australian ship to read the signal letters.

Having ascertained that the ship claimed to be *Straat Malakka*, Burnett would have consulted the latest edition of 'Vessels in the Area' which was transmitted to all warships at sea every 12 hours. This would have told him that *Straat Malakka* was not expected in that area. As *Straat Malakka* could have been left off the latest report in the same way that the British freighter *Cyclops* was not on the list when she was challenged by *Yandra* on 2 November, it appears that Burnett asked '*Straat Malakka*' for her destination and cargo. Detmers states in his book that, 'trusting to luck I replied "Batavia"'.[5] Much later, *Sydney* asked for a description of her cargo, to which Detmers 'vaguely replied, "piece goods"'.[6] However, other versions of the exchange of signals are different. Von Gosseln stated that *Sydney* asked 'From where, bound to?' and soon after the nature of her cargo.

Regardless of whether one accepts the evidence of Detmers or von Gosseln, the answer given by the bogus '*Straat Malakka*' was reasonable. This information could have been compared with previous editions of 'Vessels in the Area' and the possibility that *Straat Malakka* could be in the area after being delayed or diverted during a mid-ocean passage assessed. It is at this point that Burnett may have erred and could be criticised. Had he sought information from the naval intelligence staff ashore, he would have been told that *Straat Malakka* could not be off Carnarvon as she had left the port of Beira on the Portuguese East African coast earlier that day.

However, if Burnett believed that the unidentified ship was a German supply ship, such as *Kulmerland* which had an appearance similar to *Kormoran*, in transit to a rendezvous with a raider, sending a signal ashore would have been detected by the auxiliary cruiser and prompted her to flee the area. If he was able to sink or capture the supply ship without sending any signal, he might have been able to track down the raider and sink her also. If the unidentified ship were a raider rather than a supply ship, he would sink it anyway and nothing would be lost. The evidence of the W/T operators from *Kormoran* who were recovered by *Aquitania* and interrogated by Captain Farncomb was emphatic. *Sydney* did not send any signal. Had she sent a signal, they were ready to jam it.

Even if this additional information about destination and cargo were of no assistance to Burnett in establishing whether or not this ship could have been *Straat Malakka*, his next action in accordance with the Admiralty procedure was to demand that she hoist her secret callsign. This was probably done when *Sydney* was at between 5000 and 7000 yards, and not at 1200 yards as contended by Detmers.

There is some speculation about the manner in which *Sydney* asked '*Straat Malakka*' for her secret callsign. According to Admiralty procedures, *Sydney* should have signalled the letters 'IK'—the middle two letters of *Straat Malakka*'s secret callsign 'IIKP'. Gill states that:

> *Sydney* made a two flag hoist, the letters 'IK', which the raider could not interpret. They were in fact (and their being quoted correctly under interrogation is corroboration of the German story) the centre letters of *Straat Malakka*'s secret callsign, which was unknown to the Germans. They made no reply.[7]

This was a slight misrepresentation of what had occurred during the interrogation. During his interrogation, Chief Yeoman Ahlbach stated that *Sydney* made a two-flag signal after she asked *Kormoran* where she was bound. Ahlbach did not actually say that *Sydney* hoisted the letters 'IK'. What he said was that the two-flag hoist from *Sydney* meant, according to the 1931 *International Signal Book*, 'Have you suffered damage from cyclone, typhoon or tempest?' As this seemed a ridiculous question for an approaching warship to ask in the circumstances, Detmers also checked the interpretation of the signal in the *International Signal Book*. The Australian naval intelligence staff subsequently found that the signal letters used to ascertain whether a ship had 'suffered damage from cyclone, typhoon or tempest' were 'IK'. This was reflected in the statement in their report that 'Sydney apparently made "IK"'.

However, Montgomery claimed that

> there is no mention of the Sydney having signalled the letters 'IK' in the interrogation evidence, or even in Detmers' book . . . furthermore, Herr Ahlbach stated categorically in a recent interview that he knew nothing of them, and if they were unknown to his Chief Yeoman of Signals it must be presumed that they were unknown to Detmers also.[8]

It would appear that when Montgomery examined the interrogation reports, he did not check the duplicate set of reports which was included in the same file. The duplicate pack contained a report on Ahlbach's interrogation and included the information cited above. It is more likely that Ahlbach told Montgomery he could not remember the letters 'IK'. Indeed he was unable to remember them two weeks after the action. It is not clear whether Montgomery asked Ahlbach if he could remember a two-flag hoist that referred to a 'cyclone, typhoon or tempest'. Montgomery's suggestion that the letters 'IK' were 'planted' by naval intelligence staff in their report can be disregarded.

Having a punt each way, Montgomery argued that if Detmers did know the secret callsign for Straat Malakka it was probably obtained from the documents captured by the raider Atlantis in April. As Winter has pointed out, Dutch ships had not received secret callsigns by the time Atlantis had seized the documents. Of course, if Detmers had the secret callsign, he could have replied to Sydney's request for Straat Malakka's secret callsign and the action might have been avoided.

The evidence that Sydney signalled in plain language to 'Straat Malakka' to hoist her secret callsign was widely corroborated, although the distance between Sydney and Kormoran when this occurred was not. If the Dutch ship did not hoist the callsign, what options were available to Burnett? He could not order the ship to stop or fire a warning shot because she was already practically stopped. Although Burnett could fire on the 'Straat Malakka' if she failed to hoist the secret callsign, he could not rule out the possibility that the master of the Dutch ship did not know how to reply. Dutch ships were issued with secret callsigns after 1 June 1941. Although some had not received them by 19 November, they were nonetheless listed in Admiralty publications for each Dutch ship. As mentioned previously, Burnett had complained in September that three merchant ships failed to observe Admiralty procedure on being challenged.

This presented Burnett with a dilemma. Prudence dictated that he should have fired at 'Straat Malakka' and forced the ship to surrender. However, the fear of killing innocent people and sinking an innocent ship would have weighed heavily on Burnett's mind. Were the suspect vessel a German prison ship, Burnett needed to think of the hundreds of Allied sailors that might be drowned if he fired. This had occurred when Pinguin was sunk and more than 200 Allied men were lost. Of the first three RAN College graduates to reach captain—Burnett, Collins and Farncomb—Burnett would have suffered most from personal anguish in deciding whether or not to shoot. Whereas Collins and Farncomb would have been fortified with their own bravado, Burnett would have been more concerned with the human consequences of any decision he made. In the absence of positive proof that the ship on his port bow was not Straat Malakka, Burnett would more likely have decided not to fire.

By this stage, the Germans stated that Sydney was still on Kormoran's starboard quarter. In other words, Sydney was still in the safest position that was available to her given that the need to read 'Straat Malakka's' flag hoists prevented her from being dead astern. As Kormoran was unable to reply and the range had closed to 5000 yards, Sydney prepared to board the Dutch merchantman from a distance of 1200 yards. In the prevailing seas, this was the optimal distance from which to despatch a boat. Any closer would have given Sydney no room to manoeuvre. Any further away would have possibly endangered the boarding party. It is noteworthy that the German accounts included a description of a boat being swung outboard from its davits and made ready for launching. Having decided to board the 'Straat Malakka', Sydney would then try to remain bows-on to the raider so as to present the smallest possible target area. However, with moderate winds and swell, it was possible that the ship would swing with the wind and the swell. At the same time, a signal would have been sent to 'Straat Malakka' advising that she would be boarded. This is probably the signal that Detmers tried to suggest was the order from Sydney demanding the hoist of her secret callsign.

With Sydney close enough for the raider's guns to have some chance of success, Kormoran's engines would be providing just enough revolutions to keep the ship heading towards the west without making any headway. However, if the ship's head were to drift slightly towards the south-west, Kormoran would be able to decamouflage the guns and torpedo tubes on the starboard side without this being noticed by Sydney. As Kormoran was heading into the sun, the shadow created by the raider's superstructure would have made it a little more difficult for Sydney to observe her decamouflaged guns as she swung slowly around to starboard. If Sydney were unable to keep bows-on to Kormoran, and the raider's engines and rudder were used in conjunction with the prevailing wind to swing the ship's head, Kormoran could quickly manoeuvre herself into a position parallel with Sydney with her guns cleared to fire. It was argued earlier that there would be no point in Sydney manoeuvring to Kormoran's beam. There is no good reason why Burnett would have continued to close Kormoran and place his ship in even greater danger when 'Straat Malakka' failed to be aware that two letters in her secret callsign had been hoisted. If Sydney were in a position abeam of Kormoran, it was likely to have been achieved by manoeuvres undertaken by the raider.

Alternatively, if Kormoran were unable to manoeuvre to decamouflage her guns undetected before swinging around to starboard to be parallel with Sydney, she could have waited until she had swung to starboard, possibly with the aid of the port main engines, and then fired one of her underwater torpedoes while the Dutch flag was still flying. This possibility was considered earlier. Detmers stated that he altered course shortly before opening fire to improve the angle for a torpedo shot. Whereas he claimed that his alteration was of some ten degrees, it could have been in the nature of 80 to 90 degrees. In all of this, his crew were not in a good position to see or to assess correctly the overall progress of events. The underwater torpedo crew could have been directed to fire their weapon without knowing which flag was flying from *Kormoran*'s mainmast. Karl-Heinz Knag stated that the Dutch flag was flying at the stern before the action; Ehrhardt Otte recalled that he hoisted the German ensign from the mainmast before the action. From their respective positions in the ship, neither could have known the position of the other's flag at the time the torpedoes or main armament started firing.

As *Kormoran*'s four 3.7-centimetre guns and five anti-aircraft guns were easier to decamouflage and were less obvious than her 5.9-inch guns, it is possible that these weapons were fired just prior to the underwater torpedo exploding under *Sydney*'s two forward turrets. This might explain the sharp disagreements in the German accounts about the result of her first salvo. The first rounds from the 3.7-centimetre and anti-aircraft guns may have been responsible for the initial hits on the bridge and the director tower of *Sydney*. It is possibly for this reason that Detmers awarded the Iron Cross (First Class) to the sailor manning that starboard 3.7-centimetre mounting, Jakob Fend. As mentioned earlier, he was the only sailor to receive this superior decoration.

If *Sydney* were hit by a torpedo, it is likely that the hydraulics in the gunnery systems would have failed. This would have affected the ability of each turret to train and elevate. If the gunnery director tower were also struck, each turret would have to go into local control. Both sources of damage would have delayed *Sydney*'s ability to return fire. Alternatively, there is evidence that the two ships may have fired simultaneously. This would have resulted from *Sydney* noticing movement on *Kormoran*'s deck as weapons were cleared to fire. The extent of the variation in statements made by the *Kormoran*'s crew makes it almost impossible to establish the correct sequence of events.

However, my purpose is to show that the accepted account is less likely than this alternative reconstruction.

Firing first from the 3.7-centimetre mounting would have given the crews of the 5.9-inch guns time to decamouflage, train and fire their weapons. Whereas the first two salvoes from the main armament may not have been on target, the 3.7-centimetre guns and the torpedoes would have created havoc on board *Sydney*. There is support for this in an interview given by Gustav Albers to the *Daily Telegraph*.

> Suddenly Captain Detmers orders 'Open Fire'. Whoosh! We launch two big torpedoes. One hits the *Sydney*'s bows ... Our small-calibre quick-firing guns hammer at *Sydney*'s bridge, pumping in many shells as the Australians see the Dutch flag struck and the German ensign rising to the mast. Then our big guns open fire.[9]

It is difficult to determine whether *Kormoran* initially fired under the Dutch flag, the German ensign, or no flag at all. It is doubtful whether this aspect of the engagement occupied as much of Detmers' attention as he later claimed. His foremost priority was to hit *Sydney* first. However, this reconstruction does not depend on the country-of-origin flag-hoists in *Kormoran*.

It is, of course, vital to Detmers' reconstruction of the engagement that *Kormoran* took only six seconds to decamouflage and fire. Had the period been any longer, *Sydney*, whose gun crews were closed-up and ready to fire, would have ended any chance that the raider had of inflicting damage.

An alternative reconstruction involves the possibility that Detmers may have indicated to *Sydney* that he either surrendered or did not intend to fight. This interpretation requires a slight change in the sequence of events outlined above. The surrender would logically follow immediately after *Sydney*'s order to '*Straat Malakka*' to hoist her secret callsign. At this moment Detmers would have realised that *Kormoran*'s disguise had been penetrated.

While Detmers might have been persuaded to surrender earlier when he was forced to give international signal letters, expecting that *Sydney* would have quickly established that *Straat Malakka* was not expected in the area, it was possible that *Straat Malakka* was in the area and his disguise might have succeeded. As *Sydney* had not sent any signals seeking confirmation on the whereabouts of *Straat Malakka*, Detmers could stall for more time gambling on Burnett thinking that the information he had received was inaccurate. Thus, it is more likely that any surrender would not have been indicated until after the demand was made for the secret callsign.

Faced with the prospect of being fired upon without further warning because he was unable to hoist the secret callsign, Detmers' decision to surrender would have avoided a gun battle and perhaps make Burnett think that *Kormoran* was unarmed. Working on the principle that raider captains never surrendered, Burnett may have thought that he had captured a German supply ship, possibly *Kulmerland*. As the enemy ship was not about to fight, Burnett's attention was focused on preventing the ship from scuttling. There was no longer any need for a pre-emptive salvo. He would also have believed that the legalities associated with the act of surrender would be observed. When the two ships were practically stopped in the water, *Kormoran* would have been directed to abandon ship while a boat from *Sydney* would have been despatched to capture her code books and prevent her from scuttling. Of course, *Kormoran* could have indicated an intention to surrender with very few members of her crew being aware of such a signal being sent. As the signal could have been sent by light, there being no hesitation in using a naval signal-light once *Kormoran* revealed her identity as a German ship, it is possible that this information was restricted to Detmers, von Gosseln and Ahlbach.

There are two main objections to these reconstructions, and it should be emphasised that they are possible accounts of the action which are not inconsistent with the evidence, particularly those aspects which involve firing under a neutral flag or an indication to surrender. The first objection is that the assertions that *Kormoran* may have stopped or indicated an intention to surrender are not supported by evidence. Second, the suggestion that

Detmers may have ordered his gun crews and torpedo crews to engage *Sydney* when the German ensign was not flying at the head of the mast involved conduct that was completely contrary to Detmers' personal ethical code.

The first objection can be overcome by a resort to the first principles of historical method. It must be conceded that there is no positive evidence of a surrender signal. For this reason, this reconstruction is an alternative. However, other than the statements of those Germans who were in a position to observe and interpret all the communications between the two ships, the possibility remains open. If Detmers did signal to *Sydney* that he intended to surrender, and those in the *Kormoran*'s crew who were aware of it later made no mention of such a signal being sent, it could be successfully and permanently concealed. Likewise, if *Kormoran* fired without the German ensign flying at the mast and if other circumstantial evidence including eye-witness accounts did not allude to this key detail, the historical record would be distorted. Yet, there is no positive evidence which proves either that such a signal was not sent or that *Kormoran* did fire under the German ensign. To suggest that a surrender signal may have been sent or to contend that *Kormoran* might not have fired under the German ensign is not speculation. It is a function of regarding the German accounts with proper reservations about their reliability and their truthfulness. It is simply to leave open a possibility that is not closed off by the evidence or its proper handling by the historian. Other reconstructions are possible but, in my view, they are much less convincing.

They include the curious report published on 1 December 1941 in London's *Daily Express* by naval reporter Bernard Hall. Under the heading, 'Sydney Was Sunk By Torpedo In Saving Raider's Crew', Hall stated

> it was a torpedo which sank the cruiser *Sydney*. In one of the strangest actions of the sea, it was fired at the first moment of the Australian warship's triumph. By gunfire she had shattered a powerful armed raider, and she was closing the range to sink her and pick up survivors when she was hit, and both victor and vanquished went to the bottom.

Whether the torpedo was fired by the Nazi vessel or by an attendant submarine is uncertain.

Montgomery claimed that this information would have come to Hall from the Far Eastern Communications Bureau (FECB) based in Singapore. Montgomery claimed that it was 'evident elsewhere that Bernard Hall enjoyed an inside track with the FECB' although he does not substantiate this claim with any evidence. When Montgomery contacted Hall, he considered himself bound by the *Official Secrets Act*. When Hall was asked in 1991 for the source of his information by Associate Professor Kim Kirsner of the University of Western Australia, Hall stated that he could not recall writing the article. It is surprising that Montgomery is prepared to credit the *Daily Express* with a degree of accuracy in 1941 that one doubts he would accord such a newspaper today.

Although it is very difficult to surmise Hall's source without his assistance, it is just as likely that Hall obtained the information from either a serviceman or a civilian involved in, or aware of, the interrogations in Western Australia. Hall could have gathered one or two snippets of information and built an elaborate story around them. That his 'line' was not taken by any other British or Australian newspaper can be cited as evidence that the story was either not true, or that Hall's 'informed source' had not fed him the facts and that newspaper editors were aware of this. However, part of the *Daily Express* article contributes to the strength of the reconstruction that *Kormoran* either stopped before the engagement or fired after indicating an intention to surrender.

The second objection to this reconstruction of the action—that Detmers would not have acted in such a manner—is much weaker than the first objection because it is based entirely on the purely subjective judgments of those who have a not-unexpected bias in their attitude towards the action. The key issue is whether Detmers is capable of deception and whether his evidence is truthful.

It is not being mean-spirited to assume nothing good about

Detmers. He was just as disposed to committing a war crime as any other professional German naval officer—and some did commit war crimes for which they were later prosecuted and punished.[10] Of all the World War II raider captains, only von Ruckteschell was later called to account for his actions. He was charged with prolonged firing on *Davisian*, failing to rescue men from *Anglo Saxon* and *Beaulieu*, and continuing to shell *Empire Dawn* after she surrendered. On 21 May 1947, a British Military Court found von Ruckteschell guilty of the first three charges. His sentence of ten years imprisonment with hard labour was commuted to seven years as the officer confirming the sentence would not uphold the *Beaulieu* conviction. However, von Ruckteschell died the following month while in the Hamburg-Fuhlbuttel prison. Muggenthaler claims that the trial was an act of revenge 'for Ruckteschell's escape from prosecution for the part he played as one of the U-boat commanders the Allies hoped to bring to trial for war crimes after World War I'.[11]

Vice Admiral Friedrich von Ruge considered that the British had been unfair on von Ruckteschell because it was difficult 'for a raider to decide at what point in an engagement it would be safe to cease firing, and it was certainly impossible to do so in any subsequent reconstruction in a court of law'.[12]

Detmers has been accused of a similar crime concerning the *Kormoran*'s action with *Eurylochus*. It is alleged that he fired at *Eurylochus* longer than was necessary to secure her capture. Whatever way one looks at Detmers' actions, it is difficult to judge their legality. It is almost impossible to reconstruct the action as it appeared to Detmers. It is doubtful whether a war crimes tribunal would have found against him if he were tried for the *Eurylochus* action given the provocative actions of some of the merchant ship's crew. Of more doubtful legality was his assault on the first officer from *Eurylochus* after he came on board *Kormoran*.[13]

Regardless of whether Detmers was guilty of any war crime, the historian is not obliged to accept that Detmers was honourable or law-abiding simply because others, who are clearly partisans to his cause, assert that he was. It is also illogical to say that Detmers' actions during previous encounters proved that he would always be honourable and law-abiding in the conduct of naval operations. The circumstances of previous engagements did not require him to be dishonourable or to violate international law. However, and by his own admission, the encounter with *Sydney* could not be compared with previous engagements in which *Kormoran* had fired her weapons. Thus, in his fight with *Sydney* Detmers was presented with a new set of circumstances and his previous behaviour is not a sure guide. In the fight with *Sydney* Detmers expected to lose his ship.

What Winter and others do not seem to realise is that Detmers is an advocate in his own cause and that his word cannot be accepted as truthful at face value. This is not an insult to Detmers' character and integrity. It is simply to observe the historian's obligation to test and scrutinise historical evidence thoroughly before deciding that it is, or is not, acceptable. A historian should always have reservations about the standing of evidence obtained from an individual with a vested interest. Such an approach is mandatory in the case of evidence derived from Detmers.

Yet Winter has rejected outright the possibility that Detmers may have violated international law because she has been persuaded by positive affirmations about his conduct and character. She asks her readers to accept that Detmers invariably acted according to the highest standards of moral conduct while thousands of his countrymen were carrying out horrendous crimes against humanity. While Detmers should not be damned simply because he was a German naval officer, deserving to be judged independently for his own conduct, he suffers from being a member of an officer group whose individual standards of honour and integrity need to be proved rather than assumed.

Consequently, Detmers' evidence cannot be accepted without substantial corroboration because of his involvement in the action and his liability for moral sanction arising out of its conduct, and because his credibility as a witness of history is suspect.

Winter seems to have applied neither reservation in her

treatment of Detmers' evidence. She never met Detmers but she accepts his evidence because she cannot see any reason to doubt its reliability. Her understanding of Detmers' character does not admit the possibility that international law was violated, so that to her, this could not, and did not, happen. She also appears to assume that there was little difference in the standing of his evidence during the war and later after his repatriation in 1947.

It can be assumed that Detmers was concerned during the war to give no material assistance to his captors. He had justifiable reasons for concealing the details of the engagement until the German capitulation in May 1945. However, the Australian view of the action and his part in it had not changed substantially since early 1942. After his return to Germany, Detmers' sense of history and his own vanity gave him sufficient reason to produce a version of the action from which he emerged in the best possible light while concealing anything which may have suggested he violated international law.

That Detmers was concerned that he might be accused of war crimes is apparent in his book. Before he was made a POW, he thought about the action, *Sydney*'s fate and his anxieties:

> She had been terribly battered, but she might have managed to stay afloat. How many of her crew had been saved, and what would they have said about me and my conduct of the engagement? I might easily find myself before a court martial.[14]

Why? If *Kormoran* had done everything Detmers had stated, what charge would he be asked to defend? And why would a court martial have so 'easily' happened? Later in his book, Detmers triumphantly stated that:

> Never before in naval history had an armed merchant ship defeated a cruiser in open battle; but we had proved that the presumed impossible was possible. I felt sure that I should have to face an enemy court martial over the business, but I was not disturbed; come what may I looked forward to standing at the head of my men in the face of the enemy once again.

But again one would ask, why should he face a court martial? And why was Detmers able to prove that the impossible was possible? What made this engagement different? Was Theodor Detmers the most capable of all raider captains? Detmers' account raises the very questions one would assume that he would not want asked if he were certain about the morality or legality of his conduct or if he were trying to avoid speculation and controversy.

In the second-last paragraph of his book, in which Detmers very briefly describes his time as a POW, failing to mention in the narrative that he suffered a stroke and made an unsuccessful escape attempt, he comments that:

> There was never at any time the slightest suggestion that I was to be brought before a court martial, so obviously my conduct had been accepted as within the laws of naval warfare.

This passage suggests that Detmers' mention of a court martial was probably a reference to the form of war crimes tribunals rather than purely naval proceedings. One cannot help but speculate on the charge that could have been brought against him based on the evidence of himself and his crew. However, the repeated denial of any war crime stands out and leads the reader to think that he was either afraid of some damning evidence emerging at a later date, or that history would infer some guilt of that nature. There is an overly defensive tone about Detmers' writing that makes an informed reader suspicious of his conduct.

Was Detmers capable of knowingly violating international law and lying to conceal the fact if the operational demands were necessary? Being mindful of his ruthless determination to achieve his objectives and the need to avoid ignominious defeat, one must conclude that Detmers had the capability and probably the willingness to violate international law and, later, to deceive his captors. He could do this by justifying any technically illegal conduct in terms of the imperatives of Germany's war aims and by rationalising his subsequent concealing of the truth in the context of his understanding of naval professionalism. By these standards, Detmers did not believe he acted wrongly.

When Detmers realised after the war that the version of events he had relayed in late 1941 and early 1942 had been accepted by the RAN and seemed unlikely to be challenged seriously in the future in the absence of any new evidence, there was no need for him to make any contradictory post-war statement on the action. Had he made any statement suggesting that an illegal ruse was used to sink *Sydney*, it would have had the effect of diminishing the magnitude of his success off Carnarvon and the reverence in which he was held in naval circles in post-war Germany. Detmers had achieved a place alongside the heroes of raider operations in World War I. He had been promoted and decorated because he sank *Sydney*. His name would be remembered before and above the other raider captains in World War II because he had the unique achievement of having sunk an enemy cruiser.

Detmers was received home as a hero and was highly respected until his death in late 1976. With the help of his former crew who engaged in gradually less restrained hero worship, Detmers was a good naval officer who, with time and sentimentality, had become a great naval officer and a legendary figure. Those who served with Detmers in *Kormoran* continue to honour his memory and see his grave as a focal point for their memories and their collective commemoration. They have naturally been unwilling to accept even the faintest possibility that their former commanding officer could have done anything other than act in a perfectly lawful and honourable manner. But they have lost any ability to analyse the events of 19 November 1941 with open minds and critical spirits.

It is very likely that almost all of them have revealed all they know about what occurred off Carnarvon and believe implicitly and with complete sincerity all that Detmers and other officers told them of the action with *Sydney*. I am not convinced that Joachim von Gosseln even revealed all that he knew about the engagement. Although von Gosseln was never likely to add anything substantial to his wartime account, he was the last *Kormoran* survivor with the potential to alter the existing accounts with firsthand evidence. He was curiously close to Detmers and seems to have been especially trusted by his captain. In being a party to any post-action deception, von Gosseln would have acted from his personal devotion to National Socialism. However he might regard the Nazi Party in old age, von Gosseln as a young man displayed an overt enthusiasm for Nazism and revealed a capacity for deception. He remained silent.

Was, then, Detmers guilty of committing any war crime and how serious was the offence he may have committed? If Detmers did signal to *Sydney* that he intended to surrender or was, at least, not intending to fight, he was *prima facie* guilty of a breach of international law which made such a ruse illegal. However, there is nothing in the 1907 Hague Conventions which required Detmers to fly the German ensign although international tribunals have generally ruled that aggressors must reveal their true identity before hostilities begin. As *Kormoran* was approached while wearing the Dutch flag, rather than the Australian flag, that being his opponent's flag, Detmers could have argued that he was not obliged to hoist the German ensign before firing.

Detmers could have defended such a charge in various ways given that the only evidence would have come from his own men. The most attractive course would have been to plead guilty with mitigating circumstances. In the first instance he could have disputed the evidence that he had surrendered or had intended to surrender. He could have argued that he misunderstood international law; that the signal was sent without his knowledge; that he surrendered then changed his mind; and that *Sydney* seemed to have ignored his surrender and was going to fire on *Kormoran* at close range and inflict unnecessary casualties on his crew.

To assess the gravity of such an offence is to make another subjective judgment. It would depend on the success of Detmers' defence and how one regards international law. While it is unlikely that Detmers could defend successfully such a charge, it is likely that he could have persuaded a tribunal to accept a degree of uncertainty about his role in a German surrender and find that he had a diminished level of personal culpability. Such an outcome would have reduced the seriousness of the charge and his prison sentence. Additionally, if one agrees with John Hampden, the English statesman who defended the rights of the House of Commons against King Charles I, that 'Moderation in war is imbecility', and believes that to expect restraint in life-threatening situations is humanly unrealistic, the moral blameworthiness of Detmers' actions is further reduced. My personal opinion of international law is somewhat less than that of those who have demanded the trial of the *Kormoran* survivors for war crimes. For instance, Montgomery states that

> to make false distress calls and signal false requests for assistance were both, of course, offences against international law, which if proved would have relegated the *Kormoran*'s survivors from the status of prisoners of war to that of common pirates liable to summary execution.

Although Montgomery is wrong about the legal status of such ruses, his view of the seriousness of the crimes he imputes to *all* the *Kormoran* survivors led him to pursue their guilt with vigour.

I regard the declaration of war as the greatest evil and the all-encompassing crime because rarely does it conform to the criteria of the classic *jus ad bello* theory. All behaviour within war reflects the totality of its immorality and is barely made just by adherence to what are, in effect, rules of convenience for belligerents. Rules relating to the tactical and operational conduct of warfare have, in my opinion, no origin in natural moral and ethical law, and are illegitimate. However, international laws relating to the treatment of non-combatants and prisoners in warfare possess a different standing because they do emanate from natural law.

Whether or not Detmers violated international law during *Kormoran*'s engagement with *Sydney* will never be proved conclusively. But even if it were, the morality of such action has no bearing on my preparedness to arrive at such a conclusion. I would emphasise that I do not regard it as possessing the gravity that some would wish to attribute to it. I doubt that Detmers

would have even been imprisoned by a war crimes tribunal had
it been reasonably proved that he violated international law.
Those who were prosecuted and punished for war crimes after
the war were those men who were guilty of conspiring to make
war, such as Goering, Himmler and Ribbentrop, and those who
committed offences against prisoners and non-combatants. In
any event, Burnett was imprudent in assuming that international
law would be observed by *Kormoran*, if indeed that was his
assumption.

In this chapter I have offered a reconstruction of the
Sydney–Kormoran action. It is not the only reconstruction that
the evidence allows but I have attempted to show why it should
be favoured over generally accepted accounts of the action. It
makes better use of all the available evidence and embodies a
more sceptical approach to the German evidence. I have tried to
avoid bias in what I have accepted and rejected as evidence.

In the case of Detmers, there is an echo of truth in his account
but he remains an advocate of his own cause. Were his account
not embellished to give the impression of complete stupidity on
the part of the Australian ship, his contentions might be more
palatable. The inconsistencies in his statements over time and his
obvious efforts to portray events to suit his own ends, make him
the least reliable source of evidence among the *Kormoran*'s crew.
His efforts to manufacture an account from which he emerges in
the most favourable light draw attention to his actions and create a feeling that he has something to hide. Beneath the facade
that Theodor Anton Detmers has constructed, the truth is somewhere to be found.

17

The Unknown and the Unknowable

In 1946, John Ross concluded his book *Stormy Petrel* by acknowledging that 'the true story will not be known for some time yet—if ever—and *Sydney*'s end may go down in history as yet another unsolved mystery of the sea'.[1] Others have compared the loss of *Sydney* with the mystery surrounding *Marie Celeste*; the brigantine found abandoned with sails set between the Azores and Portugal in 1872. The ship's boat, sextant, chronometer, register and crew were missing and no trace was ever found of them. But whereas the stricken *Marie Celeste* stayed afloat, practically nothing remained from *Sydney*.

Explaining why the ship sank without trace and where the wreck of *Sydney* might lie were complicated questions. I have not covered these subjects in any detail for three reasons. There was very little information on which to base any judgment on why the ship practically vanished. There was also great variation in the German accounts of where *Sydney* headed after the action and when, in their opinion, the ship possibly exploded. Whenever this occurred, it is almost certain that the ship sank in water between 3000 and 1000 metres in depth.

This great depth of water made any search for the wreck a very difficult, although not impossible, task. RMS *Titanic* was located in 4000 metres of water; *Bismarck* was lying below 4800 metres of water. However, in both these instances, the search teams had reasonably accurate last known positions in latitude and longitude on which to focus their efforts. In the case of *Bismarck*, it took the search team three weeks to locate the wreck although the position of the ship was thought to be reliably recorded by the navigator of the battleship HMS *King George V*, who was 5000 yards distant from the sinking *Bismarck*. The leader of the *Titanic* and *Bismarck* search teams, Dr Robert Ballard from Woods Hole Oceanographic Institute in Massachusetts, remarked that finding the wreck of *Sydney* could not be described as looking for a needle in a haystack because the haystack had not yet been found!

In the 1980s, the RAN survey ship HMAS *Moresby* made several searches for the wreck of *Sydney* in addition to a number of hydrographic surveys of the area in which the action is reasonably believed to have taken place.[2] Although none of these searches was successful, the equipment deployed in *Moresby* was not ideally suited to locating sunken wrecks in deep water off the continental shelf.

Before the 1991 *Sydney* Forum held at the Western Australian Maritime Museum in Perth, a panel of experts was asked to give their opinion on whether the *Sydney–Kormoran* action could have taken place at the position stated in the German accounts—26 degrees 34 minutes S, 111 degrees E. In arriving at an answer, they were supplied with information on the sighting of flotsam and jetsam during the week following the action; details of the *Kormoran* lifeboats and when and where they were sighted; extracts from the diary of Lieutenant von Malapert describing the weather; and the stated German position for the action.

The experts agreed that both ships could have been lost in the position stated by the Germans. However, the panel, consisting of Associate Professor Kim Kirsner (University of Western Australia), Sam Hughes (Australian Maritime Safety Authority), Alan Pearce (CSIRO), John Penrose, Madeleine Gauntlett and Kim Klaka (Curtin University of Technology), and Mark McCormack and Ray Steedman (Steedman Engineering), produced 'a range of possible locations which cover up to one degree of latitude and as much as two degrees of longitude'.[3] In other words, the action could have taken place somewhere within several hundred square miles. After further analysis, consultation and discussion was co-ordinated by Kirsner, a revised position of 26 degrees 1 minute (+/– 5 minutes) S, 111 degrees 16 minutes (+/– 3 minutes) E was obtained. This position took into account the methodologies and calculations used by each member of the panel. In the area enclosed by the variation, 80 per cent consists of water more than 1000 metres in depth. At the time of writing, no progress had been made in finding the two wrecks.

In any case, the wrecks of either *Sydney* or *Kormoran* might not have added very much to what was then known about the action. Positively establishing their positions adjacent to the coast and relative to each other would certainly be useful information. If the wrecks were found near Dirk Hartog Island or 300 yards apart, this would dictate a substantial re-writing of the history. Neither result was rated as likely. It was also possible that the wreck of *Sydney* would confirm that she was hit by one torpedo on the port side, indicate other battle damage, and perhaps disclose why none of her crew survived.

Most experts were agreed that the *Sydney* wreck was likely to be in one or two large pieces, rather than a number of small pieces strewn across the ocean floor. As Kirsner argued from his brief survey of the loss of ships comparable to *Sydney* in similar circumstances—USS *Astoria*, USS *Atlanta*, USS *Juneau*, *Bartolomeo Colleoni*, HMAS *Perth*—it was most likely that the ship was broken in two by the major explosion that is assumed to have killed all on board:

> By and large, twentieth century ships which suffered major damage including magazine explosions typically broke in two, and the trend away from complete structural failure probably increased after World War I as greater attention was paid to safety and compartmentation in turret design, the shelf-life, stability and location of stored propellants, controlling the rate at which powder burned.

Finding the *Sydney* wreck would be a major undertaking requiring the involvement of the Commonwealth and State governments. The RAN, with its knowledge of the sea floor in the area where *Sydney* was lost, was ideally placed to assist. Allegations that the Navy was hindering efforts to resolve the *Sydney* mystery and locate the wreck did not stand up to scrutiny, as one case study demonstrated.

A retired commercial diver from rural New South Wales, Colin Sampey, wrote to Fleet Headquarters in Sydney in July 1987 stating that he had dived on *Sydney* in 1969 during the production of a documentary on dugongs for a Japanese television network. Sampey claimed that he was diving 120 miles south-west of Carnarvon at a depth of 110 feet when he came across a warship which was later allegedly identified as *Sydney*. He stated that there were three torpedo holes on the port side and that her loss must have been rapid as external watertight doors were open. Sampey then relayed finding numerous skeletal remains scattered throughout the ship. Although he did not report this startling find in 1969, he had come forward in 1987 because he heard a reference to *Sydney* on a television quiz program and this brought back memories.

It transpired in a subsequent personal interview with an officer from Fleet Headquarters that the dive conducted by Sampey was in 1979, not 1969, and that his sketch of *Sydney*'s bridge was altered to show a wheel where one did not exist. The Navy was unable to trace the Australian with whom Sampey claimed to have dived while the Japanese television company for whom the dugong documentary was made had no knowledge of the Japanese producer named by Sampey. While the alleged discovery of *Sydney* seemed most unlikely, one of Sampey's statements was pursued by the Navy.

Sampey claimed that a hermit on Dirk Hartog Island saw *Sydney* sink and rowed his boat out towards the wreck in search of survivors. One sailor, Able Seaman Radio Operator Williamson, from Melbourne, was allegedly recovered. However, according to Sampey, he died two days later from burns and was buried on Dirk Hartog Island by the hermit who apparently spoke with Sampey in 1979. On closer investigation by the Navy, neither the police or the local residents on the island knew anything about a hermit or a grave while neither of the two sailors on board *Sydney* with the name Williamson was a radio operator or from Melbourne.

To avoid the charge that it was not interested in *Sydney*, the Navy arranged for the despatch of an RAAF P-3C Orion maritime patrol aircraft to conduct a magnetic anomaly survey of the waters around Dirk Hartog Island. The survey sweep was to cover 50 square miles with a 95 per cent chance of detection. Meanwhile, an RAN patrol boat was tasked with landing a shore party adjacent to the site of the grave. Although the RAAF Orion search found nothing, the shore party located a small area of cleared ground set back from the cliff edge surrounded by rock which had evidently been brought from the beach. Regrettably, little conclusive evidence could be drawn from the find as many rough graves of men and women who were shipwrecked in these waters line the West Australian coast.

When the Navy confronted Sampey and stated that it was unable to find any corroboration for his claims, he provided further information. He stated that he had travelled to Japan and learned that *Sydney* had been sunk by a Japanese I-Class submarine named *Tiger Lily*, commanded by a Captain Fujita. According to Sampey's latest revelations, the submarine was to rendezvous with *Kormoran* to take on some British prisoners from a sunken tanker. The submarine allegedly machine-gunned some of the survivors in the water but took others back to Japan where they were imprisoned in a camp near Kobe. It appeared as though Sampey had been reading some rather sensational newspaper reports. After several months of work in assessing Sampey's claims, there was nothing to corroborate his statement and nothing to show for the effort. However, the Navy could say that initially it had taken the claims seriously and was interested in finding the wreck.

For the Navy to have played a useful role in finding the wreck as part of a consortium of interested groups, an additional allocation of funds and strong political support was required. The cost of finding the *Sydney* wreck was estimated in the early 1990s to be in the order of several million dollars. Without this magnitude of commitment from public and private institutions, the *Sydney* story would continue to be incomplete and the last and most substantial piece of forensic evidence would remain unexamined.

As I was completing the first edition of this book in late 1992 in the hope that it might diminish further speculation about the loss of *Sydney*, I received a highly emphatic letter[4] from a long-retired merchant mariner setting out yet another alternative theory. Captain Edgar Whish claimed that a trap, possibly devised by Admiral Doenitz, was set for *Sydney* by three German raiders in Shark Bay who sank the Australian ship, possibly with the help of a U-boat, at dawn on 20 November and later killed all the survivors. His statement was flawed as the raiders which he claimed were available for the flotilla operation were, in fact, either on their way back home or already in Germany. This information was readily available in published works. Whish should have also been aware that *Kormoran* was practically the only fully operational raider still operating in November 1941. He also seemed not to know that Doenitz's responsibilities were limited to U-boat operations until Raeder was sacked by Hitler in early 1943.

With a deficient knowledge of the available source materials but with a complete faith in his surprisingly crystal-clear recollections from 1940–41, Whish stated that the photographs of *Kormoran* published in Gill's account were inconsistent with his recalled 'impressions' of the raider's appearance.[5] He remarked that Barbara Winter was 'incapable of rational debate' and stated that the German raider captains of World War II 'were no better than the brown-shirts whose behaviour disgusted me during my last visit to Germany in 1936'.[6]

He asserted that the evidence given to the master of *Koolinda* by a *Kormoran* survivor, which was discussed earlier, revealed that *Kormoran* had been waiting for *Sydney* to pass before springing the trap. As has been shown, it revealed no such thing. Whish also claimed that he had been in contact with a former German naval officer who had assisted him in obtaining important information from the German side. He hoped I would accept his demonstrably false 'Australian alternative to enemy propaganda'[7] and enclosed copies of letters setting out his claims which he had earlier sent to the *Australian*, the *Sydney Morning Herald* and the Brisbane *Sunday Mail*. None of the letters was published. When I asked for the name of the former German naval officer and any documentary proof for his claims, Whish declined to disclose any names and 'at the same time refuse your request for documents'.[8]

The continuation of an historical debate of such importance by such ill-informed individuals was regrettable. Although Whish was fully entitled to write letters to newspapers and public officials expressing his views, it was a pity that his enthusiasm was not matched by a sense of responsibility.

Whish and others of similar sentiment failed to understand that there is much similarity between the discipline of history and the practice of law. Both the historian and the lawyer are searching for the truth. They rely on material evidence, which must be independently tested, and statements from witnesses which need to be corroborated separately. When the evidence and the facts have been marshalled into some logical order, a case for or against a proposition or a charge can be made. Nothing is proved until the evidence is presented and argument is heard. The burden of proof remains with those making allegations or proposing conclusions. It is invalid to base either a legal or an historical case on the premise that an allegation or a conclusion stands until it is refuted. In history as in the law, it is vital to have academic reticence, intellectual fairness and an abiding respect for the limitations of the available evidence. These virtues have not been applied uniformly to writing on the loss of *Sydney*.

Gill's account can be described most easily as a display of poor analytical writing. Montgomery suffered from inaccuracy, exaggeration and a form of bias and prejudice that he could easily have detected or corrected. Montgomery doubted the German accounts and selected only those accounts which tended to upset the prevailing view of how *Sydney* was lost. Whereas Montgomery was sloppy in his use of primary sources, Winter's research was impeccable. However, her interpretations of some of her evidence are suspect and open to challenge. Winter worked from a premise opposite to Montgomery's. She tended to accept those German accounts which worked to confirm the conventional view. In the absence of evidence that challenged the German view, such evidence being practically non-existent with the total loss of *Sydney* and her ship's company, Winter argued that the accounts of Detmers, in particular, ought to be accepted. However, she was too ready to overlook the inconsistencies and inaccuracies in the German accounts and the possibility that some of these accounts may have been meant to deceive. Winter should have asked: why should the German accounts be believed when they portray an entirely inexplicable and most unlikely interpretation of an event to which they are the only witnesses?

I have argued that the German accounts are individually unreliable, particularly that offered by Detmers in December 1941 and January 1942. However, when all of the German evidence which is gathered from late November 1941 until the release of Detmers' published account in 1959 and considered as a whole, a reasonably persuasive account of the action can be fashioned. The account of the action put forward in this book (and it has not changed since the first edition appeared in 1993) is intended to be no more than a possible reconstruction. There was so much about the action that required any account to be hesitant if not tentative.

In concluding her book *The Guns of August* dealing with the opening stages of World War I, one of the most well-documented periods in modern history and also one of the most contentious, Barbara Tuchman offers sound advice to her fellow historians. In the midst of the special pleading that usually accompanies historical controversy

the historian gropes his way, trying to recapture the truth of past events and find out 'what really happened'. He discovers that truth is subjective and separate, made up of little bits seen, experienced and recorded by different people. It is like a design seen through a kaleidoscope; when the cylinder is shaken the countless coloured fragments form a new picture. Yet they are the same fragments as made a different picture a moment earlier. This is the problem inherent in the records left by the actors in past events. That famous goal, 'wie es wirklich war' is never wholly within our grasp.

In the case of *Sydney*, there were reasonable doubts that we would ever know how it *really* was. There were, however, Australians who refused to accept any suggestion that the fate of *Sydney* was either unknown or unknowable. They were obsessed with finding the ship and resolving the mystery. Ending the controversy would prove much more difficult.

18

The Controversy Continues

The initial release of this book in November 1993 was accompanied by the screening of a one-hour television documentary entitled *No Survivors* on the Nine Network. The film-makers Julia Redwood and Ed Punchard of Prospero Productions used my book as a resource and I appeared throughout the film in the role of general commentator. By this time I believed the *Sydney* story had been exhausted. It had been told from almost every conceivable angle and few fresh insights had emerged. Without new source material becoming available, I concluded that the circumstances surrounding the sinking of the Australian light cruiser were probably beyond the reach of historians. They were largely unknown and likely to remain unknowable. In reflecting on this emotionally unsatisfactory outcome, I counselled those who mourned the loss of *Sydney*'s 645 officers and sailors to be prepared for permanent uncertainty. They would probably never know how or why this celebrated warship sank without survivors so near the Australian coastline.

While reviewers of the first edition were complimentary, there were also a number of complaints. Retired Commodore Sam Bateman, writing in the *Sydney Morning Herald*,[1] thought my criticisms of other writers were unfair and that I was too ready to dismiss accusations of a wartime cover-up aimed at concealing the Navy's failings in searching for *Sydney* after her final action. He was uneasy about my ambivalent attitude towards the morality of wartime rules of engagement and suggested I was a little too sympathetic to the conduct of Theodor Detmers. Vic Jeffrey chastised me for 'not visiting Western Australia in my research for the book'. He also said I should 'have interviewed people from the wartime era'. Jeffrey was disappointed, too, that I chose to 'criticise other researchers in the same way that Barbara Winter attacks anyone who has an alternative viewpoint'.[2]

I was taken to task by several reviewers, including Bill Guy writing in the *Weekend Advertiser*, for failing to contact some of the key surviving *Kormoran* personnel. Guy was a little disappointed that the best I could achieve was a 'reconstruction—only a possibility. In other words, just a theory to add to all the other theories. So the grand mystery remains'.[3] Barry Ralph was a little harsher in his assessment of the book's overall tenor.

> The essence of this new work is the assimilation and analysis of previous writing on the subject . . . the result is that his work concentrates far too much on the shortcomings of the previous major works and offers very little revelation. Frame's book is impressive for the obvious academic commitment and the desire to refute the many erroneous and quite often mischievous theories regarding the incident. However, a conspicuous aspect of the work is the author's pragmatism. His conclusions are few and reserved.[4]

Ralph thought 'no-one would take Frame to task for putting forward a theory'. Noting that I was born twenty years after *Sydney* was lost, he also thought I failed 'to convey the emotive aspects of the tragedy and the subsequent impact throughout wartime Australia'. Ralph concluded: 'the book has merit but it is an analytical product'.

Readers of this edition will make their own judgments about the fairness of these comments and criticisms. To respond briefly and selectively, I continue to stand by my decision not to interview the *Kormoran* survivors or to rely on what I considered rather stale wartime recollections. Personal memories of the engagement and its aftermath could not be relied upon to establish any contentious claim or to prove any serious point. Throughout the 1990s the Germans continued to assert that the entire ship's company of *Sydney* were taken by surprise on 19 November 1941, embellishing their accounts of Australian stupidity as the years passed with inconsistent claims about what *Sydney* did and did not do in the minutes before guns were fired. In a personal letter to me dated 1 January 1994, Otto Jurgensen, a former petty officer in *Kormoran*, claimed that Burnett 'had not the slightest knowledge of the war at sea!' This is plainly untrue and highly defamatory of Burnett personally and the Royal Australian Navy collectively.

There remains the possibility, of course, of a 'death-bed confession' among the German survivors. There is a body of received wisdom which holds that human beings cannot endure guilt forever and will inevitably succumb to the need for absolution gained through confession. According to this belief, there is a chance that one of the *Kormoran* survivors will 'break ranks' and make a confession of the 'true' circumstances of *Sydney*'s sinking in order to assuage his guilt before death. This is a remote and, I believe, a most unlikely possibility. Most of the *Kormoran* survivors, including Theodor Detmers, have already died and none have yet felt the need to make a confession of any undisclosed crime. I have argued consistently that precise knowledge of the crucial sequence of events which led to the sinking of *Sydney* was restricted to a handful of people. The 'confession' of someone who remained in the engine room throughout the entire action is as good as hearsay. If one of the *Kormoran* survivors were to 'break ranks' by disclosing startling new 'facts' about the engagement with *Sydney*, it would have happened by now. The Germans have given their version of events and nothing new of substance could be gained from them in the 1990s. Even less of value would be extracted from them now.

As for Australian recollections of matters touching on the loss of *Sydney*, there is a need for each and every claim to be solidly corroborated by a number of independent claimants. They are, after all, more than six decades old. If one person's recollections are tested and found to be inconsistent with what is generally accepted, that person's recollections ought to be marginalised if not rejected outright. The fact that a person is prepared to offer a recollection in the form of a statutory declaration misses the point being made about evidence. A statutory declaration merely denotes that an individual sincerely believes what they are saying is true. Unless a claim based on recollection is supported by strong corroborative evidence, it is unusable in the context of the *Sydney* debate. Stronger evidence, not yet more vague anecdotes, is needed.

Concerning my criticisms of the methodology employed by other writers, I defend the severity of my remarks on the grounds that poor research, shoddy analysis, fanciful assertion and scurrilous accusation have complicated the *Sydney* debate and distracted historians from key questions about the ship's final action and sinking. Bad writing and poor reasoning deserve to be denounced when they display a wanton lack of regard for evidence or a complete lack of respect for the reputations of those who cannot defend themselves. Given the controversial nature of the subject matter, published accounts of the *Sydney–Kormoran* action demand the exercise of absolute respect for primary source materials. Historians who depart from the available evidence, however seductive or momentary the departure might be, are in danger of sacrificing the sharp analytical focus this subject demands. As for the absence of 'revelations' in my work, they cannot be offered when they do not exist in the body of evidence with which historians must work. Are any 'revelations' likely?

History is considered a discipline because it demands an orderly gathering and patient sifting of thoroughly corroborated evidence. Documents are usually the primary sources from which historians produce a narrative. I have explained many times that every document with a bearing on the loss of *Sydney* was made available to the public some time ago. While I readily concede that some documents might have been lost, mislaid or destroyed, I do not think their absence amounts to, or is consistent with, an orchestrated attempt to withhold the truth or frustrate inquirers. Much of what is presently in the public domain has been so for some time. Although this material can be systematically re-examined in the hope of devising stronger or more compelling theories, I believe that nothing new can be gleaned from this body of evidence. As historians sometimes say, the subject area has been virtually 'trampled flat' by eager researchers.

When a revised edition of *HMAS Sydney: Loss and Controversy* appeared in 1998 there did not seem to be any reason to either modify or abandon my main conclusions. Of the book's minor conclusions, I made some significant concessions on the matter of the Christmas Island carley float. The exhaustive work of Rosslyn Page and John Bye demonstrated to my satisfaction that, on the balance of probabilities, the most likely source of the float washed up on Christmas Island was indeed HMAS *Sydney*.[5] But I contended that still more work needed to be done in establishing a direct material connection between that particular float and *Sydney*. I was also opposed to any government-funded attempt to locate the grave of the unknown sailor or to disturb any human remains on Christmas Island until much of the uncertainty surrounding the grave site was resolved.

By this time, criticism that I had not scoured the archives as thoroughly as I might in search of previously overlooked or unknown documents was muted by the publication in early 1997 of *The Sinking of HMAS Sydney: A Guide to Commonwealth Government Records* by Richard Summerrell, a professional archivist employed by the National Archives of Australia. Summerrell's guide ran to nearly 200 pages and 'described all Commonwealth government archival records that are known to exist on the loss of HMAS *Sydney*.' He included records 'still held by the Department of Defence and records held by the Australian War Memorial in privately donated collections'. He noted that 'apart from one manuscript in the National Library of Australia, details of which are also given, no other Commonwealth government agency or institution is known to hold relevant archival material'. Summerrell's guide built 'upon an earlier "source analysis" published by the archives in 1991' and was based on 'unlimited access to all the records described'. A second edition of the guide was published in late 1997 with a third edition appearing in 1999. (A fourth edition to which I contributed a short introduction has recently been published.) The entire guide is available on the National Archives of Australia website and can be downloaded free of charge. Summerrell's guide demonstrated that I had not overlooked any significant documents or collections of papers.

Between the publication of the first and third editions, Summerrell was able to identify several new items of minor relevance to the loss of *Sydney* but nothing that substantially affected what was known of the engagement. They included a file on 'Raiders in the Pacific' and the papers of Major Roland Seymour (both held at the Australian War Memorial), a series of dossiers containing reports on internees and POWs held in Australian camps between 1939–45, and intelligence reports from RAAF Headquarters Station at Pearce, 1941–42. He also dealt with a document that I cited in this book—a report on the loss of *Sydney* produced by Commander Emile Dechaineux RAN—which subsequently eluded detection. Regrettably, I quoted from the report but did not provide a citation. When Summerrell contacted me in late 1996 to inquire about the location of this document, I was unable to recall exactly where I had seen it although I believed it was at the National Archives of Australia reading room in Mitchell, ACT. In my defence, I explained that it was one document among several hundred that I consulted in various archival holdings while researching this book. I continue to regret this oversight and hope the document will eventually be located.

I was certain that no-one would grant me the final word on *Sydney* when this book was first released in 1993 or when the revised edition appeared in 1998. In a way, I tried to offer a sort of 'final word' when I claimed that researchers had proceeded to the extent of the available evidence and that nothing more could be reasonably concluded from primary source material about why *Sydney* was lost with all hands. This did not prevent a new group calling itself 'End the Secrecy over *Sydney*' being formed with the express intention of remaining vigilant in what its members considered their noble pursuit of the 'truth'. This group excited controversy when its members took a rather belligerent attitude to the second HMAS *Sydney* forum which was

held in Fremantle in February 1997. As most of the participants
sensed some advantage in an official investigation into the loss
of *Sydney*, an unexpected consensus emerged around a resolution calling on the Commonwealth government to sponsor such
an inquiry. The participants apparently thought the same government they believed had consistently misled them in the past
could be trusted to find 'the truth' more than 50 years after the
event. One delegate, Judith Bennett, was reported by the Perth
Sunday Times as saying: 'We want to see an inquiry because we
are entitled to know the whole truth, not just where the ship
is'.[6] However, precisely what a government inquiry might find
was not made clear. The forum's resolution was conveyed to the
Federal Parliament by several members and senators.

The Hawke and Keating Labor governments were opposed
to a public inquiry into the loss of *Sydney*. The attitude of the
Howard Coalition government was no different. The Department
of Defence believed there were insufficient grounds for conducting an inquiry and considered that little of practical value could
come from its deliberations. In what amounted to a back-flip,
the Federal Labor caucus supported demands for an inquiry in
1997. This was surprising because the Opposition Leader, Kim
Beazley, had been personally against holding an inquiry when he
was Minister for Defence (1984–1990). On several occasions he
stated in writing that an inquiry would serve no useful purpose.
The loss of *Sydney* was a matter for historians. Beazley's successor in the Defence portfolio, Senator Robert Ray, was even
more adamant that an official inquiry could not be justified and
would not be supported. However, when the necessary Parliamentary 'numbers' were mobilised, most of the major questions
relating to the loss of *Sydney* were summarised in quite comprehensive terms of reference that were subsequently conveyed to
the Defence Sub-Committee of the Joint Standing Committee
for Foreign Affairs, Defence and Trade (JSCFADT) by the then
Minister for Defence, Ian McLachlan, on 26 August 1997.

The inquiry's terms of reference were extremely broad. The
Joint Standing Committee was to investigate and report upon
'the circumstances of the sinking of HMAS *Sydney* off the West

Australian coast on 19 November 1941, with particular reference to'

the extent to which all available archival material has been fully investigated and whether any relevant material has been misplaced or destroyed;

all relevant archival material available from allied and former enemy forces;

the desirability and practicality of conducting a search for the HMAS *Sydney* and the extent to which the Commonwealth Government should participate in such a search should one be deemed desirable and practicable;

the practicability of accurately locating the grave of an alleged body from HMAS *Sydney* which was allegedly buried on Christmas Island;

the identification of any scientific procedures now available which could verify the identity of human remains alleged to be those of a crewman of HMAS *Sydney* buried if and when such remains were located;

measures which should be taken to protect and honour the final resting places, if and when located, of HMAS *Sydney* and KSN [sic] *Kormoran*.

The government's inability to prevent the inquiry from being held was widely reported by the media while notices calling for submissions were placed in newspapers and magazines. When the Committee began its public hearings in March 1998, nine volumes of written submissions had been received. The range of contributions was striking in both quantity and quality. From handwritten personal testimonials to comprehensive typeset essays, and from thoroughly researched scientific dissertations to witnessed statutory declarations, contributors were motivated by a host of concerns and interests. A number of submissions were from former members of *Sydney*'s ship's company who wanted to share their knowledge of the ship's strengths and weaknesses in combat. *Sydney*'s next-of-kin told the Committee that the wives of many men lost in the ship were never satisfied with what they had learned of the light-cruiser's final engagement, either during or after the war. One submission remarked that 'we next-of-kin sincerely hope that this sub-committee can reverse Tom Frame's closing paragraph . . . "that we will never know how it really was".'[7] Several archaeological and oceanographic groups commented on the possibility of finding the wreck of *Sydney* and canvassing the clues it might give to the circumstances of the ship's final engagement.

I declined involvement on three grounds. First, I had assumed responsibility for a large rural parish in the Anglican Diocese of Canberra and Goulburn and had said publicly everything I wanted to say about the loss of *Sydney*. Second, since publishing the first edition of this book I had avoided every opportunity for being drawn back into the fray, despite invitations to do so from organisations as diverse as the *Australian* newspaper and ABC Television's *Lateline* program. I had my chance to contribute to the debate and believed it was right to leave room for others. My third reason for keeping away from the inquiry was abhorrence at the level of personal abuse which seemed to accompany every attempt to identify and discuss the key issues in any type of public forum. Maintaining a silence embodied my feeling that nothing useful could be gained from pursuing the matter further. Other than whatever insights the sunken wreck of *Sydney* might yield if found, I was convinced that the evidence had been exhausted of all its possibilities.

I did, however, give the Committee members an informal briefing on 13 February 1998 on the condition that my co-operation, which was in response to a personal request from Senator David McGibbon (the Committee's chairman), was neither reported publicly nor referred to in subsequent hearings. In my two-hour meeting with the Committee, it was plain to me that they recognised the difficulty of their task and the virtual impossibility of meeting the public expectations of what they would find. I was assured that each of the parliamentarians maintained an open mind and hoped their deliberations and report might bring some comfort to those who still mourned and grieved loved ones lost in *Sydney*.

After months of public hearings and the acceptance of a torrent of public submissions, the Joint Standing Committee released its recommendations in March 1999. The report, which is a balanced and impartial document displaying signs of the careful scholarship usually associated with the work of Professor Peter Dennis (the Committee's historical consultant), did not come to any firm conclusions about how *Sydney* was sunk or why it was lost with all hands. This was a sensible decision as 'history by committee' is, in my view, contrary to the spirit of the discipline. The Committee did take the view that there has never been sufficient evidence to provide the answers to every question. Indeed, the report quoted my conclusion that 'there are some things that will remain unknown and unknowable'.

The Committee recommendations included: another thorough examination of archives in Australia and Britain, principally the Public Record Office in London, to ensure no relevant material was located in files that had not been assessed for public release or which remained veiled by the persistence of wartime secrecy provisions; that further research be conducted into the likely location of the grave of the unknown sailor on Christmas Island; that the appropriate Federal minister be asked to issue an exhumation order if the grave was located with the remains, if positively identified as a member of *Sydney*'s crew, to be reinterred in the nearest Commonwealth War Grave; that the Navy sponsor a seminar to consider the most likely search area for the wrecks with an initial search for *Kormoran* being conducted at or near 26 degrees, 32–34 minutes S, 111 degrees E; that the Commonwealth fund a full-scale search for the wrecks once a high probability search area had been ascertained; and, that a suitable memorial service for those lost in *Sydney* be held in conjunction with commemorative services. The Committee could find no credible evidence of Japanese involvement in the sinking of *Sydney* or anything to confirm the allegation that Australian survivors were machine-gunned while in the water. Nor was there anything presented to the Committee which showed that the Navy had ever conspired to withhold information from the public about the circumstances of *Sydney*'s disappearance. In a sombre note, the Committee explained that:

The search for *Sydney* and *Kormoran* is not guaranteed of success. If it does succeed, it may provide those interested in the fate of the ships some further insights into the events of 19 November 1941. If the search is unsuccessful, it does not mean that people will no longer wonder about the final resting place of the ship. However, an attempt to find the *Sydney* will be a sign that Australia cares about the 645 men who gave their lives in defence of their country, as well as family and friends.[8]

The Committee also offered some constructive advice to those involved in 'the *Sydney* debate'. It suggested that all parties needed 'to move beyond animosity and antagonism and find common ground. No one group "owns" *Sydney*, or has a monopoly on truth. The Committee hopes that in future researchers will rise above the personal acrimony and suspicion that has marred so much of the debate thus far. The "dialogue of the deaf" that characterises so much of this debate is counter-productive. An exchange of differing views is a positive process, and can only lead to a better understanding of the events of November 1941. HMAS *Sydney* deserves no less'.[9]

The Minister for Defence, Peter Reith, tabled the government's response to the report on 29 June 2000. The government noted that 'of the 21.6 shelf metres held by the National Archives [of Australia] . . . the Archives has released for public access all the records directly relevant to the HMAS *Sydney*'. The government agreed to assist and support any further surveys of archival holdings, including in Britain, which might yield relevant information. Concerning the unknown sailor buried at Christmas Island, the government commented that the remains, 'should they be proven to come from HMAS *Sydney*', would be buried in the closest war cemetery to Christmas Island—which happened to be Geraldton—because there was 'no way of knowing the place of death'. The government also canvassed the possibility that 'the family may wish the remains to stay where they have lain on Christmas Island for the past 57 years. If this were the case, Office of the Commonwealth War Graves would . . . mark the grave, record its location and maintain it in perpetuity.' But if the remains 'are not identified as an Australian serviceman, they should be reinterred on Christmas Island.' The government indicated that while it was willing to fund a search for the grave of the unknown sailor, it was not prepared to provide 'up to a total of $2 million' to fund a search but was 'prepared to provide assistance as indicated in its responses to the other recommendations in the report'.

The Committee and the government shared my belief that the only pieces of unexamined evidence that could have affected our understanding of the *Sydney–Kormoran* action were the undiscovered wrecks. Submissions to the parliamentary inquiry from marine archaeologists and salvage experts conceded that the task of finding the ships was not straightforward. For the previous two decades, both vessels had resisted every attempt at detection in very deep water. There was, however, good reason to believe that the wrecks could be located if enough money were provided to support a prolonged search. But was such an expensive undertaking worth the expense, given the possibility that little might be gained from an examination of the vessels? Those wanting to locate the ship recognised there was a window of opportunity they needed to exploit because interest in the loss of *Sydney* was expected to wane when those who served in the ship from 1935 to 1941 and those who lost close relatives in its final engagement had died.

Despite the lack of any additional primary source material, a number of new books dealing with HMAS *Sydney* appeared between 1997 and 2007. The quality of these works varied considerably. The most recent but least useful was *HMAS Sydney 1941: The Analysis* by Greg Bathgate, a former draftsman and civil designer for the Water Corporation in Perth, published in 2007.[10] Bathgate implied that previous studies had been based on 'pre-conceived ideas' which, if eliminated, would make it 'possible to assess all aspects analytically and on a logical basis in order to arrive at justifiable conclusions'.[11] His principal aim appeared to be identifying the most likely location of the *Sydney* wreck. Bathgate did not engage with the work of other authors or provide an adequate critique of their conclusions (the book does not contain any endnotes and is without a bibliography). He made false claims about the Navy's recent attitude to the loss of *Sydney*, revived old controversies such as the alleged involvement of a Japanese submarine in *Sydney*'s final engagement (without mentioning its chief proponent, Michael Montgomery), speculated without precision on *Sydney*'s course and speed after the battle, and failed to separate possibilities and likelihood from facts and conclusions.

Bathgate claimed, without making reference to the extensive work of Kim Kirsner, Cathy Norman and John Dunn, that the most likely location of *Sydney* was 25 degrees 46 minutes S 111 degrees 40 minutes E and *Kormoran* 25 degrees 33 minutes S 111 degrees 30 minutes E. He said that *Sydney* 'should lie within 8 to 23 nm south-east of *Kormoran* on a bearing of 145 degrees . . . *Kormoran* can be expected to be discovered in depths ranging from 1100 to 1300 metres and Sydney in about 950 metres'.[12] Every element of Bathgate's analysis would prove to be wrong—from the actual positions of the ships to the distance separating the two wrecks and the depth of water in which they were lying. *HMAS Sydney 1941: The Analysis* was a poorly written and badly constructed work. There were typesetting problems, unfinished sentences and deficient editing, such as whole paragraphs repeated verbatim without explanation. This book added nothing new to what was known about the loss of *Sydney* nor did it help efforts to locate the wreck.

Equally unproductive was *Somewhere Below: The Sydney Scandal Exposed* by John Samuels which appeared in 2005.[13] The biographical note on the back cover explains that Samuels is 'a journalist and an intelligence analyst'. There was no other disclosure of his competence to comment on the *Sydney* story. This book was superficial and shrill, unreliable and unbalanced.

The text was marred by many spelling mistakes, sentences with missing words and small factual errors. The reasoning was poor and the development of argument was weak. There was no mention of other researchers or their conclusions and there was an absence of any discussion of the limits of evidence and the other historiographical difficulties associated with writing about HMAS *Sydney*. Lacking in modesty, the publisher claimed that *Somewhere Below* 'rewrites the war history of Britain, Germany and the Australian Navy, in the lead up to Pearl Harbor'.

Samuels did not accept the conventional accounts of *Sydney*'s demise because the Germans were 'the enemy, with a truth to conceal'.[14] Although noting that a 'multitude of theories has been advanced' to explain the loss of *Sydney* and insisting they 'derive from little or no evidence and foster continuing baseless speculation',[15] Samuels revived the Japanese submarine conspiracy theory (he actually named the *I-58* as the boat involved) with the additional claim that hundreds of bullet-ridden bodies washed ashore and were buried on Dirk Hartog Island and along the West Australian coast. The burial of these men was apparently kept secret from the Australian people to conceal the fact of Japanese involvement. Samuels called for the bodies to be exhumed and examined to determine whether they died from wounds caused by Japanese bullets. The reason he cited for the Commonwealth's initial refusal to disclose the existence of the bodies was to avoid alerting the Japanese to Allied success in penetrating the secret Ultra and Purple communication codes used by the Axis Powers, and to ensure that Japan proceeded with her plans to attack Pearl Harbor leading to a war that London, Washington and Canberra were eager to fight.

Samuels based his claims on a re-assessment of existing evidence, a painting seen after the war in a Japanese naval academy, an interview with a member of *I-58*'s crew and 'evidence' from the family members of those who formed military burial parties in Western Australia. Although there had been several detailed critiques of possible Japanese involvement, Samuels wrote as though none of this analysis had ever cast any doubt over these claims. There was no evidence that *I-58* was anywhere near the coast of Western Australia in November 1941 nor was Samuels able to provide series, file or folio numbers for the facts on which he bases his description of *Sydney*'s fate. The book contained a great deal of fanciful interpretation, uncritical surmise and a general willingness to grab at any hint or inference that would sustain a line of argument that Samuels appeared to have embraced before he had written one word. He also misrepresented the attitude of the Joint Standing Committee to the Navy's contributions to the 1998 inquiry, implying that the Navy was accused of conspiring to continue a long-running cover up. The Committee's report (which appeared in 1999 and not in 2000 as reported by Samuels) made clear its belief that no cover-up had ever occurred nor had the Navy any reason to conduct a cover-up—in 1941 or subsequently.

Like several commentators before him, Samuels refused to interrogate his own interpretations and ignored obvious objections to his theories. When a reasonable alternative appeared to exist, Samuels claimed those who failed to support his allegations or who offered a discordant view were constrained by confidentiality provisions in Commonwealth law or were party to the continuing *Sydney* conspiracy being perpetrated by government. His faith in the readiness of large numbers of otherwise decent Australians to lie and deceive the public knew no bounds leading me to wonder whether he had ever worked closely with parliamentarians, political staffers or historians. If so, he would have known that the prospect of furthering one's career and enhancing one's professional standing by uncovering a conspiracy or exposing a scandal militates against their collusion or complicity in a cover-up. Speaking personally, if I could find just one document that merely hinted that the Navy had details about *Sydney*'s fate that it conspired to withhold from the public in 1942 or thereafter, I would be rushing into print with a full disclosure of what I knew. That I served in the Royal Australian Navy would not prevent me (and never has) from discharging my public responsibilities as a historian.

Samuels appeared intent on defiantly maintaining his theories until they were proved to be false. This is not, of course, the way the discipline of history operates. Given the anxieties and uncertainties faced by the families of those who lost relatives in HMAS *Sydney*, unsubstantiated claims and flimsy arguments about mass graves on Australian soil harmed rather than helped their interests. *Somewhere Below* was a very poor book that inflamed old animosities and required the consumption of energy on largely unnecessary refutations.

By way of contrast, Captain Peter Hore's edited work *HMAS Sydney II: The Cruiser and the Controversy in the Archives of the United Kingdom* was a careful and reasoned analysis that did much to advance the conversation.[16] It was published in 2001 by the Royal Australian Navy Sea Power Centre in Canberra. Hore, a retired British naval officer, explained that his aim was 'to find records in British archives about the disappearance of HMAS *Sydney* in November 1941, and to investigate opinion of that period which might be relevant to knowledge of the disappearance of the cruiser'.[17] After providing a summary of the action and the outstanding issues to be resolved, Hore provides extracts from a range of documents, including the text of signals and official reports, that disclose the extent of the British government's knowledge of the engagement and the Admiralty's view of what might be learned from the action in terms of intelligence, tactics and communications. He explains that 'no first hand accounts of the loss of HMAS *Sydney* or any type of inquiry into her loss have ever been found in British archives'.[18]

After searching likely and even unlikely collections of records for material relating to *Sydney* (a very useful schedule of documents in British archives is provided as an annex), Hore doubted 'whether there was ever a conspiracy, either by the Germans or the Australians, to hide the truth about the fight between the two ships. The interval between the various reports, particularly in the early days as the dreadful news broke, allows no opportunity for this, and there is no sign . . . of altered documents'.[19] Hore concluded: 'the author is only sorry that he has not been able to draw any line under the enduring mystery which surrounds the disappearance of HMAS *Sydney* in November 1941 and the deaths of so many brave men'.[20] His book was an important source of primary source material that helped to tie up several possible loose ends and to close off several possible avenues of inquiry. But it was still not the final word.

Glenys McDonald published *Seeking the Sydney: A Quest for Truth* in 2005.[21] Her interest in the *Sydney* story was aroused after she settled in the small coastal fishing town on Port Gregory on the coast of Western Australia in January 1988. She was intrigued by the claims of elderly local people that they had witnessed a great naval battle 'some time early in the war' which might have been the *Sydney–Kormoran* action. McDonald then interviewed local families and found that several individuals had similar memories of an evening during which there appeared to be more noise and light than usually accompanied a thunderstorm.

McDonald wrote to me on 12 February 1994 asking for my assessment of the claims of '10 local families in the [Port Gregory] area about a night where they saw flashes out to sea west of Port Gregory between midnight and 2am. Some actually describe what they saw as a "naval battle" with different sounding guns . . . several of these people link what they saw with events associated with HMAS *Sydney*'. She asked me whether there was 'any good reason why the *Sydney* could not have limped towards Geraldton? She would have come in the Geelvinck Channel and been off Port Gregory, where she may have blown up. Some feel she could have been involved in a second battle. I have no evidence for this second version except eye witnesses who are sure what they watched was a "battle".' I replied that the veracity of these recollections was questionable and that their historical value was virtually nil. In my view they were undated, poorly corroborated memories offered by individuals without knowledge of naval warfare.

Those who spoke with McDonald were not alone in believing, however, that the action occurred not far from the coast. I received a letter from Mr B.J. Bradshaw from Bentley in Western Australia on 18 November 1993 claiming that *Sydney* was '20 to 30 miles' off the coast and that 'my father has seen the wrecks of both boats off the coast in 1954 and in

1958. I have also seen them. This is no hoax'. Around the same time I received a letter from Rob Cleeve of Seaford in Victoria relating information from the owner of Quobba Station, a Mr Bastian, who claimed that *Sydney*'s final action was just off the coast south of Carnarvon which was where the wreck would be found.

Throughout the 1990s McDonald persisted with her research, exploring the possibility that the action took place much closer to the coast than any other previous researcher had postulated. She was ably assisted by her son David, a specialist navigator serving in the Royal Australian Navy, who concluded that 'a position north west of Port Gregory 27 degrees 51 minutes S 112 degrees 01 minutes E fitted all the environmental and sighting considerations as the likely battle area' which served to 'validate the possibility that the coastal sightings were of the *Sydney–Kormoran* encounter'.[22] McDonald was 'willing to accept the *Kormoran* survivors' testimony of the battle' but could not 'accept the official version of the aftermath and search for *Sydney*. I also believe that the debris field from the sinking of *Sydney* was located and never made public'. She felt it was 'now time for those who know the whole truth, or even portions of the truth, to come forward'.

While I believe McDonald is entirely mistaken about a Navy cover-up and am convinced that anyone with any useful information to contribute has already come forward with their insights, McDonald offered a helpful window into the determination of those who wanted to keep the loss of *Sydney* in the public gaze and the tactics of those who thought a parliamentary inquiry would advance the cause of historical scholarship. Her claims about the location of the action would eventually be disproved but her energetic campaigning for a search to locate the wreck made her a significant player in the unfolding HMAS *Sydney* story.

Another Sydney 'convert' was Wes Olson, an employee of the National Rail Corporation and Army Reserve member, who put aside his long-term interest in military matters for naval history in 1992. His very substantial and detailed book *Bitter*

Victory: The Death of HMAS Sydney appeared in 2000.[23] Its impact would have been greater had Olson been prepared to engage with existing works. It is not clear from the text where he went beyond the work of Gill, Montgomery, Winter or Frame, and whether and why he felt their interpretations were inferior to his own. His introduction did not outline his approach, his sources or the historiographical issues involved in writing about *Sydney* after nearly 20 years of intense debate. This was a disappointing element of the book because Olson did uncover new material that had the potential to better explain some of the tactical aspects of the engagement and the effect of the damage sustained by *Sydney* during the opening phase of the battle on her ability to return fire. *Bitter Victory* also provided a wealth of detailed material on the weaknesses and vulnerabilities of Modified *Leander* Class Light Cruisers, and measures taken by the Admiralty and the Australian Commonwealth Naval Board to deal with them.

But the enormous amount of technical data was not matched by equal attention to either the developing of interpretations or the drawing of nuanced inferences. In fact, Olson stated his conclusions in two short sentences and they were not too dissimilar from those found in this book. In contrast to other works, Olson's tone was measured and careful. He refused to engage in unwarranted speculation, showed a keen appreciation of the limits of evidence and was clearly conscious that his words would affect the family and friends of *Sydney* men. His main achievement was gathering and assessing evidence, publishing previously unknown material (including photographs and technical drawings) and providing a detailed list of primary references. It was an impressive achievement and Olson deserved the positive response his book generated among reviewers.

With the publication of *Bitter Victory* it was clear that dialogue among researchers could only become more inward looking. Every piece of information with the potential to make a material difference to what was known of the action had been brought to public attention. But after the mid-1990s this information served to expand the footnotes more than it enhanced the narrative. The loss of HMAS *Sydney* was easily the most researched, examined, discussed and debated episode in the nation's naval history. No other action had ever prompted anywhere near the sustained interest. The *Sydney* story had drawn in professional and amateur historians and attracted people with no previous connection to ships or the sea. Coming to terms with the loss of HMAS *Sydney* was virtually a national obsession. It was perhaps not surprising then that an increasingly unpopular Coalition government in Canberra which was keen to improving its standing with the electorate, especially in Western Australia, changed its mind about the importance of finding *Sydney* and the identity of the man who might have been its only survivor.

19

The Sea Retains her Secrets

The recommendations of the Joint Standing Committee inquiry into the loss of HMAS *Sydney* and the Commonwealth government's response were focussed on two main practical outcomes. The first was determining whether the unknown sailor buried in Christmas Island was from the ill-fated Australian light cruiser. The second was finding the submerged wrecks and perhaps coming to some firmer conclusions about why none of *Sydney*'s ship's company survived the engagement with *Kormoran*. These two activities represented the last chance for anybody to say anything new about Australia's greatest naval loss.

Backed by the parliamentary inquiry and prompted by growing public interest, the Navy attempted to locate the grave of the unknown sailor in 2001. But an extensive excavation of numerous possible locations during an expedition led by Lieutenant Commander Richard Chartier RAN proved to be unsuccessful. No remains were located despite a determined effort that involved systematic digging in what were considered the most likely places. Despite continuing community agitation, the Navy was adamant there would not be another search until new evidence could be produced. Owing to the efforts of Ted McGowan, who believed the unknown sailor might have been his brother, and Glenys McDonald, fresh assessments of existing evidence convinced the Navy Sea Power Centre in Canberra that a second expedition was justified. This search would benefit from the assistance of Mr Say Kit Foo, who was born on the island in

1936 and played as a child in the cemetery. A photograph taken in 1950 by Brian O'Shannassy, a former Navy wartime signal-man who worked as an accountant-bookkeeper on Christmas Island from 1950–52, also improved the chances of locating the grave. The second expedition would focus on an area more than 20 metres away from the ground excavated by Richard Chartier. The new search team consisted of a senior naval officer (Captain Jim Parsons), an archaeologist, a forensic anthropologist and two forensic orthodontists.

After careful but fruitless excavation along a row of existing graves, the search team found the unmarked grave in a two-metre gap situated between two marked graves in October 2006. It was set at right angles to the other graves and was facing the harbour. The coffin was 1.4 metres long and 0.8 metres wide, and appears to have been specially constructed to accommo-date the badly decomposed remains. The remains, consisting of a largely intact and complete skeleton, were repatriated back to the mainland for analysis by the Shellshear Museum of Physical Anthropology and Comparative Anatomy at the University of Sydney's Department of Anatomy and Histology.

The first stage of the identification process—examination of dental records—did not produce a positive identification although the survivor had numerous gold fillings and was miss-ing some teeth despite previous reports that the man had perfect teeth. But as half of those serving in the light cruiser at the time of the *Kormoran* action had their dental records ashore (rather than in the ship) more than 300 men of the ship's company could be eliminated. The second process concerned anthropo-logical examination of the skeletal remains to assess the man's height and age. As he was relatively tall, this narrowed the list of possibilities to around 100 men. When forensic analysis of the fabric found within the press-studs located in the vicinity of the grave revealed that the body was wearing white overalls, denoting an officer or warrant officer, rather than blue ones sug-gesting the occupant was a sailor, the list of names was reduced again. There was further confirmation that the man was not a sailor when research into the distinctive features of wartime naval clothing revealed that overalls made with press-studs were usually worn by officers. The overalls issued to sailors had buttons. The weave of the fabric found in the press-stud was also inconsistent with the cloth from which the overalls issued to sailors were made.

The forensic evidence pointed to a junior engineering officer or warrant officer assuming that the individual was wearing his own overalls at the time of the action. This led to the possibility that the survivor was Lieutenant Allan Wallace Wilson (aged 31), Sub-Lieutenant Allen James King (aged 26) or Sub-Lieutenant Frederick Harold Schoch (aged 22). The Navy contacted the relatives of the three men. With a small pool of possibilities, DNA testing held out the greatest likelihood of making a positive identification. Despite the technical difficulties of extracting viable DNA from the remains, genetic evidence actually excluded Wilson, King and Schoch. Further investigation suggested that officers and warrant officers of the Ordinance Branch were also issued with 12 yards of white drill material which they could have made into overalls. At the time of writing, no positive identification of the remains has been made. DNA analysis continues.

Examination of the Christmas Island remains disclosed evidence of injuries that were probably consistent with those sustained by most of the men who perished with *Sydney*. It appears that the man suffered from numerous broken ribs and two head wounds. It was these wounds rather than exposure to the elements that caused his death. Initial visual examinations of the skull and X-ray analysis suggested the man had been shot in the back of the head with a small calibre bullet which had been disfigured on impact. This news rekindled speculation that the survivors from *Sydney* were machine-gunned after their ship sank. Metallurgical analysis of the fragment showed that it was a piece of shrapnel containing silicon and manganese that was consistent with German metal hardening technology used for large-calibre armour piercing projectiles. The Minister Assisting the Minister for Defence, Bruce Bilson, explained in a public statement: 'As the fragment does not contain either nickel or copper the War Memorial has assessed that the fragment is unlikely to come from a Japanese-manufactured projectile'.

It now appears that the first injury was caused by shrapnel that struck the front of the man's skull and lodged in the left forehead. It also appeared that the man had fallen and injured his head, possibly after receiving the initial wound. But how and when did the man receive the injury that probably caused his death? Did he manage to get into the carley float that eventually conveyed him to Christmas Island alone or was he assisted by others? There were no answers to these questions in any Australian files. Captain Peter Hore's examination of files maintained by the Admiralty, the War Office and the Colonial Office did not uncover any 'reference to a coroner's inquest on a body washed ashore on Christmas Island in early 1942'. In sum, 'no evidence or any other relevant record has been found'.[1]

The Commonwealth has accepted on the balance of probability that the man indeed originated from HMAS *Sydney* and, in accordance with government regulations at the time of writing, has proposed that the remains be reinterred in the nearest Commonwealth War Cemetery to the site of the *Sydney–Kormoran* action (Geraldton). There are also plans to place a suitable memorial on Christmas Island marking the original burial site. Notwithstanding extensive forensic investigation and DNA analysis, it is quite possible that the man's name might never by known. For as long as his identity remains unknown, he could have been anyone on board the Australian ship. And if he could have been anyone, he represents everyone who was lost at sea on 19 November 1941. With the Christmas Island 'survivor' laid to rest, the task of locating his shipmates gathered even greater momentum.

Finding the wreck of *Sydney* depended on defining a high probability search area. As with all things associated with the *Sydney* story there was a great deal of speculation about where the action occurred, whether the stated German position could be relied upon, the direction in which the Australian ship headed after the engagement, how long she remained afloat, and the prevailing weather conditions on the afternoon and evening

of 19 November 1941. Although two main theories developed
as to where a search should best begin, known simply as the
'northern' and 'southern' theories, researchers took very different approaches to nominating their preferred position for the
engagement and the most sensible place to search. Those who
favoured the northern theory were inclined to accept the position nominated by Detmers, which was 26 degrees 34 minutes S,
111 degrees E although noting that his navigator (Meyer) mentioned 27 degrees S 111 degrees E. The parliamentary inquiry
recommended a search at or near 26 degrees 32–34 minutes S,
111 degrees E, a position which is approximately 180 nautical
miles south-west of Carnarvon. Those embracing the southern
theory held that the position given by the Germans was deliberately false and that *Sydney* was more likely to be located around
200 nautical miles to the south at a position near to the Abrolhos Islands, south-west of Geraldton.

In a newspaper article published in July 2006, private
researcher Warren Whittaker was critical of the Commonwealth
government's decision to fund a search for *Sydney* based on the
northern theory because 'a search that clings unquestionably to
the German location is doomed to failure'.[2] Whittaker placed
great weight on the accounts provided to Glenys McDonald that
the action was much nearer to the coast and argued these witness statements were more reliable than German evidence that
had been tainted by wartime considerations. He also pointed to
'the hotly disputed direction and distance travelled by lifeboats
from the *Kormoran* and flotsam recovered from both ships.'
Based on meteorological data from November 1941 and the
movement of drift cards, Whittaker insisted that the action must
have occurred off the Abrolhos Islands.

Whittaker also hinted at the existence of dark motives behind
the northern theory and its 'official' endorsement. He claimed
that in spite of strong arguments against the northern theory
and positive proof for the southern theory, 'the navy remains
super-glued to the German location, apparently content to con-
demn the proposed search to failure before it even puts to sea'.
Ean McDonald was equally critical. He said: 'They are basing

their theories on the German story alone, which I and many others believe is nonsense. Unless they also do a fully umpired search of the area off the Abrolhos, then the expenditure on the northern area is an utter waste of money'.[3] A lot of energy had been devoted to testing both theories.

Among those favouring the northern theory, Kirsner and Dunn had used cognitive psychology in applying a 'systems approach' to the analysis of personal memories of the engagement. They contended that the position 26 degrees 04 minutes S, 111 degrees 02 minutes E was to be preferred.[4] Neil Brown, Frank Leahy and Joseph Leach from the Department of Geomatics at Melbourne University and Timothy O'Leary from Pricewaterhouse Coopers Consulting used survey network theory to assess the reliability of the evidence upon which other researchers had based their likely search area.[5] They explain that 'survey network theory uses a least squares algorithm to provide a rigorous technique for combining all measurements and their assigned precisions to estimate the position of the unknown points'. After examining signal data and the location of debris, they concluded that 'there are no sources of evidence that can reasonably be called reliable. Even if the positions given by the Germans are correct they are still only quite rough'.

Defining a high probability search area, which was a challenge in itself, was just the start. A successful search consisted of three other vital ingredients: funding, expertise and technology. The Commonwealth government decided to support 'The Finding *Sydney* Foundation' because it was a not-for-profit group established to raise money that would be used solely to locate the *Sydney* wreck, and because it had managed to secure the services of the notable American search director David Mearns (the business office of his Blue Water Recoveries is located in England) who had found the British battle-cruiser *Hood* and relocated the German battleship *Bismarck* (after it was initially discovered by the American Robert Ballard). Mearns had been studying the loss of *Sydney* for a number of years, assisted by Captain Peter Hore, and believed the ship could be found. The Foundation also had access to high-powered, high-resolution sonar equipment. The Commonwealth government promised Federal funding of $4.2 million ($1.3 million approved in August 2005 and another $2.9 million in August 2007) with the West Australian and New South Wales state governments contributing $500,000 and $250,000 respectively.

The Finding Sydney Foundation was upbeat about the chances of finding the wrecks while Mearns helped to reinforce the significance of the search. Mearns remarked in November 2006 that he had 'worked on some very high-profile, high-stake projects, but with regard to from-the-heart passion involved in why this ship sank and why it needs to be discovered, nothing comes close'.[6] Mearns thought the Sydney story 'actually exceeds the significance of Titanic and the Hood and that's why she means so much to Australia'. As for the probability of success, Mearns noted that the longer a search vessel could remain at sea the greater the chance of Sydney being found. In any event, he said, 'I have absolutely no doubt it will be found. If not by us, then somewhere in the next generation somebody will find it'.

Mearns initially identified two possible positions for the wreck site: 25 degrees 57 minutes S, 110 degrees 48 minutes E and 26 degrees 30 minutes S, 110 degrees 52 minutes E. He refined his preferred position after managing to track down a German dictionary that Detmers had kept throughout his imprisonment in Australia in which he had produced a secret account of Kormoran's loss by placing faint dots under the letters in the dictionary which was later given to Detmer's nephew in Hamburg. The information Detmers had encoded in the diary provided sufficient collaborative evidence to lead Mearns and others to believe that the extant accounts of the action were reliable. Mearns was confident in the 'quality and veracity of the German accounts about where the action took place, even though there were many other researchers who strongly took an opposing view'.

But it appeared for several days in August 2007 that Mearns was badly mistaken. A group of amateur salvage divers claimed to have found the wreck of HMAS Sydney off Dirk Hartog Island in very shallow water (150 metres). The 'find' was reported in several major newspapers. If this wreck was Sydney, much of what researchers thought they knew about the action would need to be revised. I confessed to the *Age* newspaper that I simply could not believe it was *Sydney*, a judgment the Navy soon confirmed. The search for *Sydney* would continue accompanied by just a little more scepticism after one more false alarm.

When Mearns had completed his analysis the Finding *Sydney* Foundation announced that its search area would encompass 1800 square nautical miles of ocean—an area 2.5 times the size of the Australian Capital Territory—approximately 120 nautical miles off continental Australia's most westerly point, Steep Point. The depth of the water ranged from 2000–4000 metres. The Foundation explained that

> the search for *Sydney* can only be conducted after the wreck of *Kormoran* is found. The simple reason for this is that the navigational coordinates recorded by *Kormoran*'s captain, Theodor Detmers, and other physical clues such as the location of floating debris recovered by Australian ships days after the sinking, are all referenced to the position of *Kormoran* and not *Sydney*. While there is reasonable information about where *Sydney* may have sunk and thus where to begin the search for her wreck, this information is relative to the final position of *Kormoran* and thus dictates that the wreck of *Kormoran* is found first. Once *Kormoran* is found the search for *Sydney* can begin in earnest.

The search ship SV *Geosounder* sailed from Geraldton with side-scanning sonar technology embarked in early March 2008. The search team were expecting to be at sea for at least five weeks. The Foundation explained that the search was to be carried out in two phases.

> The first phase involves using deep tow side scan sonar imaging equipment to sweep the seabed for any wreck site indicators such as debris fields, other seabed anomalies or the wreck itself. Should any of these indicators be found a more detailed sonar imaging process will be implemented that will more accurately identify the anomalies or wreckage fields discovered. Subject to budget, phase two may commence.

This involves deployment of a remotely operated vehicle to investigate and confirm the sites and to record video and photographic records of the wreckage fields.

The first week of the search was unproductive owing to technical problems and bad weather. In a surprising turn of events, everything changed with the weather. The discovery of a badly damaged hull confirmed the search had focussed on the right area.

The news that the wreck of *Kormoran* had been found was announced by the Foundation on 16 March although the ship was actually detected on 12 March. The wreck was located at 26 degrees 05 degrees 49.4 seconds S, 111 degrees, 04 minutes 27.5 seconds E, some 112 nautical miles off Steep Point in 2560 metres of water, four miles south of the main battle site. This was astounding news that attracted enormous media interest. I was asked by several news outlets when I thought *Sydney* would be located. There seemed to be no reason why the light cruiser would not be found within a few weeks. I suggested that the Australian ship would be lying 16–20 nautical miles to the south-west of *Kormoran*.

Just as news of *Kormoran*'s discovery was announced, another minor controversy gathered momentum. It started when Ludwig Ernst, the President of the *Kormoran* Survivors' Association, told the *West Australian* newspaper that Captain Burnett was so grossly 'incompetent' and even 'criminal' that the Germans effectively owed him their lives. Ernst stated: 'I observed *Sydney*'s incompetent command structure from the moment *Sydney* appeared over the horizon and turned to pursue us'. Ernst claimed that 'eventually Australians will have to comprehend that the guilty party for *Sydney*'s sinking is Captain Burnett'. The German allegations were rather predictably supported by Alastair Templeton whose criticisms of Burnett's performance as *Sydney*'s commanding officer were canvassed in an earlier chapter. The 86-year-old Templeton continued to claim that Burnett was reckless and foolhardy. He told the media that *Sydney* was not ready for action, that her gunners were in the ship's cafes having dinner rather than being in their designated places of duty, and that *Sydney* was not 'in a state to deal with *Kormoran*.' Templeton asserted that Captain Burnett had a flippant attitude that was typical of British naval officers (Burnett was, of course, Australian) and that he was overly confident in *Sydney*'s superior main armament. Although he had made these comments 15 years earlier, Templeton was now alleging that Burnett was not even qualified to command *Sydney*: 'He had 29 years in the Navy, had never commanded a ship of any kind and was simply not attuned to the job in hand and paid the price'.[7]

I was unwilling to comment on Templeton's allegations, which I concluded were simplistic and spurious. But I firmly believed that the German claims needed some response because they received more attention than they deserved and wilfully and unfairly damaged Captain Burnett's reputation. In an interview with the *Sydney Morning Herald* I contended that:

Mr Ernst is not, and was never, in a position to comment on the manner in which HMAS *Sydney* was commanded. I have consistently argued that *Sydney*'s movements can only be explained by Captain Burnett believing that the raider had surrendered. Burnett was a prudent, even cautious man who was reasonably entitled to believe the suspect ship might have been carrying Allied POWs from earlier successful operations. Firing on the unidentified ship from a safe distance might have led to hundreds of sailors being lost—as had happened earlier in the war. In my view, Burnett approached *Kormoran* from the safest bearing for a boarding and the Australian ship would certainly have been at action stations. The German claim that the Australians took a cavalier attitude to the encounter has been long abandoned. We now know that these claims emerged when questions were first raised about how an armed merchant raider might have sunk a light cruiser. While there are good reasons for Australians wanting to defend Captain Burnett who has been terribly defamed by Mr Ernst, we should not withhold credit from Theodor Detmers who was one of the finest raider captains of the twentieth century. Although I am not convinced finding the wreck of either ship will answer every question we might pose of this devastating engagement, it does not serve any useful purpose for speculation to surge beyond the bounds of evidence.[8]

The heat produced by this exchange would soon dissipate. It was, in any event, blown away by some startling news.

At 11.03 a.m. (West Australian time) on Sunday 16 March, just hours after Prime Minister Kevin Rudd announced that the wreck of *Kormoran* had been found, those on board SV *Geosounder* noted that 'a small dark shape was detected coming into view on the starboard side of the SM30 side scan sonar in an otherwise featureless seabed. David Mearns soon classified this contact as being man-made, displaying all the characteristics of a major shipwreck. Within minutes a debris field came into view confirming this belief.' Further examination of the site and the debris occurred throughout the day. Early on the morning of Monday 17 March 2008, the Australian people learned that the most enduring mystery in Australian naval history had ended. After nearly 67 years on the seabed, HMAS *Sydney* had finally been found. The identity of the wreck had been confirmed the previous evening although *Sydney* had taken longer to positively identify than *Kormoran*. A media frenzy began. Finding *Sydney* made national and international headlines.

A press conference was hastily convened. The news that *Sydney* had been located was confirmed by Prime Minister Kevin Rudd, Defence Science and Personnel Minister Warren Snowdon, Ted Graham, the chairman of the Finding *Sydney* Foundation, Chief of Defence Force, Air Chief Marshal Angus Houston and the Chief of Navy, Vice Admiral Russ Shalders. Prime Minister Rudd described the announcement as 'a historic day for all Australians, and a sad day for all Australians.' He hoped the discovery would bring 'some closure to the families of the 645 defence force personnel who lost their lives bravely in this naval action in World War II'. Minister Snowdon congratulated the Foundation and the Navy 'on this memorable discovery which will bring some peace to the relatives of the brave crew who gave their lives while serving our nation'. Vice Admiral Shalders explained that 'this nation has wondered where the *Sydney* was and what occurred to her. We've uncovered the first part of that mystery . . . the next part of the mystery is, of course, what happened'. Ted Graham stated that underwater imaging equipment attached to a remote operated vehicle would be deployed when the weather conditions were favourable. Visual images could then be transmitted ashore.

After all the heated debate about where the search should concentrate and criticisms of the Foundation's methodology, Mearns was right and his critics and detractors were proved wrong. *Sydney* was located at 26 degrees 14 minutes 37 seconds S, 111 degrees 13 minutes 3 second E, 12.2 nautical miles from *Kormoran* and 10.5 nautical miles south-east of the site, of the engagement. She was lying under 2468 metres of water. The Minister for the Environment, Water, Heritage and the Arts, Peter Garrett, was consulted about legal protection for the site, which was immediately listed under the *Historic Shipwrecks Act*. A relative of Stoker Lindsay Rowe who lost his life in *Sydney*, Wayne Fisher, told the *Sydney Morning Herald* he had 'mixed feelings' about the discovery of the wreck. He remarked: 'I feel a bit teary to tell the truth—closure is always a difficult thing. I'm pleased it's been found, it's a very important chapter in our history. My grandmother always lamented that her brother never came back, she lamented until her dying days that he never received a Christian burial. She passed away talking and crying about it.'[9]

After encountering big seas and some technical problems, the *Geosounder* returned to Geraldton to prepare the remotely operated undersea vehicle to film the wreckage. The pictures sent back to the mainland the following week were stunning for their detail and drama. The clarity of the images was arresting and surprised even seasoned analysts. The cameras revealed every damaged fitting and the badly torn superstructure. *Sydney* was, in every sense, a wreck with mangled metal strewn across the upper deck and on the surrounding seabed. But as John Perryman remarked, although *Sydney* was 'in a badly damaged state, this great warship retains a powerful aura in her final resting place'. Images of the battered warship disclosed the destructive force of *Kormoran*'s weapons. Mearns explained that 'because the [remote vehicle] landed nearer to the stern we began moving slowly in that direction to see if we could locate *Sydney*'s bell on the quarterdeck. Sadly, it was nowhere to be found'.

Contrary to my belief that the wreck would probably be in two large pieces because only a catastrophic midship explosion would have led to the ship being lost with all hands, the hull was largely intact. *Sydney* was, in fact, standing upright on the seabed although inclined slightly to starboard. Some of the upper deck was still in place although the Borneo whitewood planking had clearly suffered the effects of being submerged in deep water for more than 60 years. The light cruiser appears to have hit the seabed stern first and then slid 50 metres to her final resting place. The propellers were sheered off and the stern was buckled by the impact. Mearns reported that 'both funnels and masts were gone and all the lifeboats were missing from their cradle stands, but all four turrets were retained in place'. The bridge and gunnery director control tower had been battered and confirmed the widely-held belief that *Sydney*'s command team were killed in the first seconds of the engagement.

Pictures of the wreck also confirmed that the ship was hit by a torpedo on the port side. It would appear that the bow, which was severely damaged and weakened by the torpedo strike just forward of A turret, detached from the ship before her descent to the bottom. The upturned bow was situated 450 metres from the rest of the hull. The two forward turrets were facing to port with the barrels set at 90 degrees to the centreline of the ship. B turret had been blown apart with evidence of a direct shell hit. The roof had also been torn away. Noting that the German survivors credited the crew of *Sydney*'s X turret with inflicting the damage that led to *Kormoran*'s demise, Mearns observed that 'our pictures of X turret not only show it pointing forward frozen in its final shooting position, but they also reveal the turret's two forward hatches swung wide open, possibly to allow better aiming and firing by the gunners inside'.[10] Y turret was covered in debris with the barrels in skewed positions. The starboard side of the ship appeared to be much more heavily damaged than the port side. Five of the ship's boats were detected in the debris field with clear evidence of battle damage and the effects of an upper deck fire. There was no sign of four other ships' boats, which were probably obliterated in the engagement or possibly consumed by the flames that were observed by *Kormoran*'s crew during the hours after the engagement. The debris area contained several shoes and a gasmask. As expected, there were no human remains. They had long ago been dissolved by the seawater.

The location of the two wrecks off the West Australian coast, their positions relative to each other and to the site of the initial engagement, and the visible battle damage sustained by both ships was entirely consistent with German accounts of the engagement in all major respects with the exception of the claim that *Sydney* was unprepared for a gun battle. To have been able to fire on *Kormoran* within a very short space of time, the Australian ship needed to have been at action stations. The aspect of the main armament on the wreck shows clearly that *Sydney* was ready for a fight with gun crews closed up and ready to execute orders to fire. German claims about *Sydney*'s casual attitude to the encounter and their reiteration by Alastair Templeton, which amounted to a serious slur on Captain Burnett and his officers, were simply wrong.

The battle damage confirms that after being hit by *Kormoran*'s weapons on the port side, the Australian ship turned sharply to port. After crossing *Kormoran*'s wake, she presented her starboard side to the German raider which responded with sustained heavy calibre gunfire at short range. The wreck confirms that *Sydney*'s main armament was rendered immobile by *Kormoran*'s initial barrage. The state of the battered hulk suggests that a substantial number of the ship's company were almost certainly killed in the initial exchange while the few remaining survivors were effectively denied the use of life-saving equipment that had been damaged by *Kormoran*'s guns or destroyed by fire. The lateral separation of the two wrecks confirms that *Sydney* remained afloat for approximately six hours before the inflow of seawater saw her quickly sink below the water line and plunge to the seabed more than two kilometres below. It is impossible to ascertain from an examination of the wreck when the man exhumed from Christmas Island entered the carley float, whether there were others with him in the float or if they abandoned *Sydney* before she sank. The number of men killed during the actual battle, the number who subsequently died of their wounds, and the number who perished when the ship sank cannot be reliably established from images of the submerged vessel.

In one sense, precise detail of this kind matters little. Every member of the ship's company died in the action. No Australian would ever be able to say what had happened on board *Sydney* in the six chaotic hours after the engagement. The widow of Leading Stoker Alfred Cooper, the 90-year-old Dorothy Cooper was nonetheless relieved to see the pictures. She said: 'I feel great peace and relief knowing the ship is mostly intact and that he and his comrades are probably all together still on board. I always feared what was left of the ship would simply be fragments, but to know that it is intact, is a sacred site and will be observed as a war grave makes me emotional but happy'. Mrs Cooper was married the day before she farewelled her husband and never saw him again.

As the nation absorbed the significance of these developments, the Deputy Prime Minister, Julia Gillard, announced on 31 March that Terence Cole QC, a former Judge of the New South Wales Supreme Court, would head a commission of inquiry into the loss of *Sydney*. She said that Commissioner Cole, who had already headed public inquiries into the building industry and the Australian Wheat Board, was selected because, she said, he was an expert in maritime law. She did not say why expertise in maritime law would be relevant when no legal issues were involved in the loss of *Sydney*. Commissioner Cole would report his findings directly to the Chief of the Defence Force. Ms Gillard stated that it would be a complicated inquiry and 'will take some time, but it's a task worth doing because we do want an answer to this long standing mystery.' She also said that there were documents spread 'across 23 kilometres of shelf space that must be worked through in the course of this inquiry because they all pertain to *Sydney*, and so may include information that is relevant to the inquiry'.

Air Chief Marshal Houston explained that 'at the moment there is just one term of reference and that is to inquire into the circumstances that led to the loss of HMAS *Sydney* and all of her crew'. He suggested that the inquiry would take some time because 23 kilometres of documents had to be examined and that 'a lot of this material has not been looked into before'. He went on to say that 'we must leave absolutely no doubt as to what happened. We have to establish the facts . . . because, strange as it may seem, no board of inquiry was conducted during World War II. So this is very much unfinished business and we think that this is the best way to go'. Vice Admiral Shalders stressed that the key questions were why *Kormoran* managed to mortally damage *Sydney* and why the Australian ship sank without trace.

The decision to hold an inquiry made little sense to me. In fact, I thought it was pointless. There had not been any public agitation for such an inquiry and, if the absence of clearly defined terms of reference were an indication, the government did not have a considered idea of what it wanted the inquiry to achieve. Writing in the *Weekend Australian Financial Review*, journalist Brian Toohey was scathing of the government's decision.[11] He asked why Cabinet had endorsed a decision before any cost estimates were provided and 'why, as Education Minister, did Gillard let a lawyers' plaything, called an official commission of inquiry, anywhere near the writing of history'. Toohey believed 'the loss of the ship has been exhaustively examined by skilled historians and by a parliamentary committee that released a high quality report in 1999 after accessing the same material that Cole will re-examine'. He said 'there is no great remaining mystery—certainly nothing to warrant the expense of a cumbersome commission to cover a topic best left to naval historians and other experts'. Toohey noted that the government had paid Justice Cole $1.05 million to conduct an inquiry into the building industry in addition to expenses of $250,000 and another $850,000 to head the Wheat Board inquiry. 'There is', Toohey complained, 'nothing of any importance for Cole to do. The parliamentary committee debunked all the usual conspiracy theories.' Toohey's criticisms were, in my view, entirely justified.

As I told ABC Radio's *PM* program several hours after the inquiry was announced, the statements that 23 kilometres of documents needed to be examined, that these documents related to *Sydney* and perhaps to the final engagement, and that most had not been seen before were all completely untrue. In fact, the converse was the case. There was no event in Australian naval history more thoroughly examined than the loss of *Sydney* and no 'new' documentary material had been uncovered in years. I received several letters and emails from individuals highlighting Ms Gillard's 'admission' that the Commonwealth was sitting on a mountain of documents relating to *Sydney* previously denied to the public. Worse still, these correspondents stressed, naval authorities had never examined them. The origin of statements about the existence of 23 kilometres of unexamined documents is unknown. It would certainly not have come from anyone with more than a passing knowledge of the *Sydney* story.

In my view, no useful purpose will be served by the inquiry trawling for documents in obscure places that might, just might, have some bearing on the *Sydney–Kormoran* action and its aftermath. To make the point again: there are no unexamined files in the records held by the National Archives of Australia; every known item has been identified and brought before the public. If documents cannot be found, they have either been misplaced or destroyed. While this might sound suspicious, every government department and major private company encounters problems with its filing systems. Documents are placed in the wrong files by junior staff or papers mistakenly deemed to be unimportant by someone without subject matter expertise are discarded. Governments and businesses routinely destroy vast quantities of printed material. This is part of modern information management.

In the course of several radio interviews I expressed my opinion that the decision to conduct an inquiry was a mistake. I explained that history is written by historians not judges and that inquiries of the kind established by the Rudd government were not well placed to write or to rewrite history. It was also fanciful to suggest, as Ms Gillard did, that Commissioner Cole would be any more likely to arrive at 'an answer' when his 'findings' would be little more than yet another opinion that would be added to the vast array that had already been offered. Cole's 'findings' were entitled to no more respect than those of other researchers. There was also what I suggested was the inevitability of Justice Cole's 'findings' being deemed part of the Navy's continuing cover-up because, I am sure the conspiracy theorists will say, Commissioner Cole served in the RAN Reserve and his was a government commissioned inquiry.

Although the judicial impartiality and personal integrity of Commissioner Cole are beyond question—his conduct of previous high level inquiries more than justifying such a view—the acrimony associated with the *Sydney* story and the persistence of passionate beliefs that sometimes stand in defiance of material evidence, is bound to have an influence on both the conduct of his inquiry and its 'findings'. Indeed, shortly after the wreck of *Sydney* was found rumours began to circulate that the Navy had known the whereabouts of the ship all along and used the opportunity afforded by the search to 'come clean'. As the SV *Geosounder* entered the search area it has been suggested that the Navy's observer, John Perryman of the Navy Sea Power Centre, laid a piece of paper on the chart table and suggested the position shown on it was worth investigating. This apparently explains why the wreck was found so quickly. This did not happen. John Perryman is a man of unquestioned honesty and high moral principle. Like every other person on board SV *Geosounder*, he was stunned when the side-sonar detected the submerged object that proved to be *Sydney*.

There was nothing either new or startling in Commissioner Cole's statement at the opening of his inquiry on 30 May 2008. The inquiry would essentially cover the same ground as the Joint Standing Committee a decade earlier. I told Counsel Assisting the Inquiry, Commander J.T. Rush RANR, that I would not be making any submissions. In my view, the only useful purpose the inquiry could serve would be to arrange for experts to examine images of the two wrecks and then to draw some conclusions about the conduct of the engagement. The inquiry might assess the battle damage sustained by both ships and suggest some possible reasons for *Sydney* sinking with virtually all hands. Analysis of this kind could, however, have been conducted without the expense and the inconvenience of a government inquiry. An assessment of the wrecks could have been managed through the auspices of a leading Australian cultural institution or university. That such a course of action was not taken was a mistake and something the government might regret.

With the wreck found there remained only the need for commemoration. Much good work had already been done in preserving the memory of those who died. Most evocative is the HMAS *Sydney* Memorial at Geraldton, which is located on a hill overlooking the Indian Ocean. Its central theme is 'symbolic of eternity and the circle of life' and features sculptures, a stele and a dome. At Carnarvon, the HMAS *Sydney* Memorial Drive is lined with 645 palm trees with the name of each man lost in the ship inscribed on a plaque located at the base of each plant. One of those men was Able Seaman Bill Pitt.

He did not know that a letter written to his mother on 8 October 1941 would be the last she would ever receive from him. His words, written after a short visit to Melbourne, were brimming with life and hope.

> When we left [Sydney], we had a very rough trip, and the ship did everything but capsize. The first week out was not a very pleasant one for me . . . I am now going to go for a gunnery rate, and then I would, or hope, to have a better chance of going overseas. I would like to get a draft off this ship more than ever now but I don't want you to start worrying about me.

He managed to see a girl called Betty during his brief stay in Melbourne but spent most of the evening in the company of her parents drinking cups of tea and eating sandwiches and cakes. At about 1 a.m., he took his leave and Betty walked to the tram with me and I think that was about the only time that I spoke with her all the evening. She is a very nice girl, and I am sending a snapshot of her that she sent me, so you can write and tell me what you think of her. I think I must be in love . . . I hope Betty keeps on writing to me, for she writes very nice letters.

He finished the letter by telling his mother that on his mess deck 'they are all on draft but me, but still, I hope to be going soon. I have done my best to write an interesting letter this time, and must say cheerio for now, hoping it finds you as well as I am feeling at present.' It was signed 'I remain your loving sailor son' and carried a PS: 'I do not think I will be home for my birthday, but can I still have a party when I do come home . . . I'm beginning to feel old, 21'. Six weeks later, Bill Pitt and every other man on board HMAS *Sydney* was dead. He would never again embrace his mother or enjoy another birthday party.

Those who hoped beyond hope for news of their loved one's fate will, of course, continue to ask questions about the loss of HMAS *Sydney*. Despite the sentimental talk of 'closure', they will continue to ponder life's possibilities had *Sydney* not encountered *Kormoran* all those years ago. For them, the awful 'ifs' accumulate. Their lives would have been different had the dreams and aspirations of the young men to whom they were bound not disappeared with their ship. Of course, no-one else could take their place. They were unique and irreplaceable. The dull pain of their absence might have been dissipated by the years but their enduring grief will not be dissolved. This is the essence of war's tragedy. It is destructive and wasteful. It knows no restraint and stares callously into the face of its victims—the living and the dead. Perhaps worst of all, it leaves so many painful questions that can never be adequately answered—not even now.

APPENDIX I

Alleged HMAS Sydney *Letter of Proceedings— 19 November 1941*

NARRATIVE OF PROCEEDINGS INVOLVING H.M.A.S. SYDNEY IN ACTION WITH A GERMAN ARMED MERCHANT CRUISER ON THE EVENING OF 19th. NOVEMBER, 1941, SOUTH-WEST OF SHARK'S [SIC] BAY, ON THE COAST OF WESTERN AUSTRALIA.

All the times and positions given in this narrative of proceedings are approximate only.

1400 G.T. (–7) MST 14hrs. 24min. Proceeding on course 155 deg. direct towards Fremantle at 23 knots. Weather medium to rough in patches. Wind S.S.E.—Force 4; Swell from S.W.—4; Visibility B.V.—9: Extreme. Estimated position 25deg. 42min. S: 110deg. 56min. E. Fourth degree of readiness with the hands at cruising stations, cleaning ship and make and mend.

1442: Small electrical fires with short circuits involving the generators, motor alternators and rotary converters put our W/T and R/T equipment out of action but we were soon able to restore reception and extinguish the fires although the main defects could not be made good due to lack of some important spares.

1457: Action Stations were sounded and all gun crews closed up. Masthead and the S2. lookouts reported bearing Green 17 deg. distance three miles a submarine proceeding on the surface. 26deg. 01 min. S: 110deg. 00min. E.

1459: Bridge confirmed the sighting as an 'I' Class Japanese ocean-going submarine headed S.S.W. and diving.

1503: The submarine submerged.

1505: We resumed our course towards Fremantle at 20 knots. The U.D.C. was stood down. Still unable to transmit submarine sighting report.

1507: Reverted to fourth degree. A.B.C. watertight doors and openings checked and all found to be closed and fully secured.

1556: A suspicious merchant vessel sighted by the masthead lookout at a distance of 12 miles bearing 192deg. T. and heading S.E. dead slow towards coastal waters and making a large volume of smoke.

1558: Action stations sounded, and our course altered to intercept at 22 knots and revolutions increasing to A.F.P.

1600: Our estimated Position is 26deg. 19min. S.: 111deg. 06min. E.

1620: Merchant vessel showing the Norwegian flag at her ensign staff and on her hull sideboard.

1622: Our speed is now 27 knots and our course corrected to intercept at 10 miles by graphic plot.

1650: The merchant vessel is now showing no national flag at all. Captain Burnett now believed that she might be Raider 'G'.

1652: Made V/S Lamp (out): WHAT ARE YOUR SIGNAL LETTERS. NOT ACKNOWLEDGED.

1700: Still makin [sic] V/S Lamp (out): WHAT ARE YOUR SIGNAL LETTERS. NOT ACKNOWLEDGED. 14200 yards and closing. The suspect vessel then made a four letter hoist with individual flags obscured but read as L.H.G.J. She then commenced transmission of a W/T 'Q' signal.

1704: Made V/S Lamp (out): CANNOT READ YOUR SIGNAL. SHOW YOUR FLAGS CLEAR.

1708: The suspect cleared her hoist which was then read as P.K.Q.I. She ran up the Dutch national flag and began transmitting another 'Q' signal. She was then assumed to be Raider 'G' rendezvousing with the Japanese submarine we had sighted earlier. All guns were loaded and tubes readied. Made V/S Lamp (out): HOIST YOUR SIGNAL LETTERS CLEAR. V/S Flag (in): P.K.Q.I. Not on V.A.I.

1710: Alphabetical Index—P.K.Q.I. is Straat Malakka which had similar initial letters to Raider 'G', the Steiermark. Made V/S Lamp & Flag (out): WHERE BOUND. V/S Flag (in): BATAVIA TO LOURENCO MARQUES. Made V/S Lamp (out): WHAT CARGO. V/S Flag (in): GENERAL.

1712: Made V/S Lamp (out): MAKE YOUR SECRET CALL-SIGN. NOT ACKNOWLEDGED. Courses now parallel with all guns and tubes bearing at 5500 yards. Made V/S Lamp (out): SHOW YOUR SECRET CALLSIGN. V/S Flag (in): SIGNAL NOT UNDERSTOOD BUT FLAGS DISTINGUISHED.

1715: Opening and turning to starboard. Made V/S Lamp (out): STOP INSTANTLY OR I WILL FIRE. Flag (out): STOP INSTANTLY. V/S Lamp (out): DO NOT ATTEMPT TO SINK SHIP. V/S Flag (in): ACKNOWLEDGED.

1718: Turned into the wind S.S.E. at 15 knots opening range and then slowing to launch aircraft. The Walrus crew which stood by with Lieutenant Bacon was all killed by the sixth enemy salvo. Weather was too heavy to launch and recover the aircraft but the motor was kept running slowly. The raider broke out a large white flag about the size of a table cloth from her triadic stay halyards and hove to on our port beam. We swung back in an arc to deal with her.

1748: We closed bows on to 3000 yards and hove to with our screws just turning over. Made V/S Lamp (out): CLOSE UP TO HALF A MILE AND HEAVE TO FOR RECEIVING ORDERS AND A BOAT. V/S Flag (in): ACKNOWLEDGED.

1749 to 1755: The prize made smoke as if she was on fire and trying to scuttle. We stopped both engines at a range of 1650 yards. The seaboat was ordered awaay [sic] with boarders and the anti-scuttling party but before it could be slipped we were struck heavily underwater aft of 'A' Turret by a torpedo from a concealed tube of the raider. Another torpedo passed ahead of us. Three enemy ranging rounds probably from her secondary armament fell short and two rounds passed well over. The bridge attempted to go full ahead both and the motion caused by this and our torpedo hit affected the accuracy of our fire so that our whole first salvo pitched over the enemy ship. A full enemy salvo from her main and secondary weapons along with heavy and light automatic fire hit the bridge structure killing or fatally wounding everybody on it. Captain Burnett although mortally wounded continued to fight the ship until 1807, when he fell dead from wounds and loss of blood. The enemy poured in deadly four inch explosive shells which caused dreadful burns with splinter wounds. The bridge, charthouse, rangefinder, gunnery control, fore-mast, navigating bridge and the fore-funnel were wrecked. Our upper deck was raked by her secondary armament, H.M.G. and automatic fire. The raider ran up the Nazi Battle Ensign at 1751, to her fore-top and then struck the Dutch flag and White Flag in that exact order. Nobody can respect their piratical behaviour and arrant cowardice in opening fire wearing false colours after they had already surrendered. They acted like Dagoes and not like regular German navalmen. Two torpedoes passed astern of us while the enemy weapons were firing S.A.P. and H.E. nose-fuse projectiles which caused terrible wounds. The range then opened to 1850 yards and we gathered way and moved steadily ahead.

1750: 'A' Turret which had been trained manually to port was found to be jammed solid on its roller path and could not be budged. After the first enemy salvo all turrets moved to independent fire. Both 'B' and 'Y' Turrets were damaged by enemy fire early in the action from the third and fourth salvo. We commenced firing at 1700 yards and our first salvo pitched over from the motion that was imparted by our torpedo hit forward and our screws starting up suddenly. Our second salvo hit the raider heavily in her waterline. Our third salvo caused even heavier damage as well as starting a high flaring petrol or oil fire on her upper deck just abaft the funnel.

1756: Our speed had by now reduced to 9 knots and we turned south to pass the enemy with both our rear turrets bearing but the tenth enemy salvo destroyed 'B' Turret and the great concussion combined with the effect of having too much rudder on as well as being down by the head and the bows rising when the turret was hit we swung back closer than was comfortable to within 2000 yards under the stern of the enemy without 'X' or 'Y' turrets being capable of bringing effective fire to bear on the enemy. It was observed that some of our rounds failed to detonate even after a direct hit upon the enemy vessel.

1802: There were large fires burning above decks forward and also in our shambles amidships. Slowed to 5 knots and fired four torpedoes at 5000 yards. Three of these ran wide but the fourth hit the raider somewhere under her engineroom sending up a great gout of flames and sparks shooting vertically upward from her funnel.

1808: I assumed command of H.M.A.S. Sydney upon the death of our gallant Commanding Officer, Captain Joseph Burnett, R.A.N.

1808: The enemy lost way rapidly and then she altered her course so that our 'X' and 'Y' Turrets could not bear. The raider was burning fiercely as the range opened to 7500 yards and so making our Vickers' fire ineffective. We were still taking hits at that time from the guns of the enemy although their vessel was in a bad way.

1825: Most of our superstructure between the bridge and the after funnel was either on fire or burnt out by now. We were making thick brown smoke from the burning charges on the deck and around the remains of 'B' Turret. We commenced clearing away all the damage we could and plugging of the holes where it was at all possible. The raider altered course at that time by swinging very slowly to port.

1845: Sporadic but ineffective fire was received from the raider whose side was glowing from the fires raging inside her hull. Our own plating in places is also really hot.

1926: It was at this time we fired our last round from 'Y' Turret.

The range had now opened to 1600 yards. We fired two torpedoes well within M.E.R. but without results. We then ceased fire. The raider then fired a single round which was observed to drop short. The enemy also finally ceased fire.

2005: We turned towards the Western Australian coast which should lie about 220 miles due E. of our present position. I posted the lookouts to watch for shorelights. Our speed is now reduced to 7 knots, but we are hoping to raise it to 12 knots in the next hour or so. We have started to lay out the dead and the wounded. We have collected all identity discs of the wounded we could but a few are not wearing them or were wearing metal discs instead of the standard issue. We placed the dead in the waist of the ship and the wounded it was possible to move in the highest part of the ship aft. The ship is still making water but the inflow is being checked and emergency lighting has been rigged. The steam loss from our holed and fractured pipes is being contained and reduced. We cannot raise our engine revolutions much further quickly because of our extensive damage near the bows. We found almost all useful equipment and gear burnt or destroyed. There is neither food nor medical supplies. I have very severe burns and minor wounds to my hands and arms which makes this slow dictation necessary. The plight of our dying and wounded is dreadful in the extreme. The list of 7 degrees to port at the bows is not increasing but the duplicate set of magazine keys which was placed forward are now inaccessible. All the most important keys for the ship are lost. The Watch and Quarter Bills, Station and Fire Bills have been lost along with the compasses and chronometers in their war positions. I am heading towards Geraldton and I will attempt to beach in Champion Bay area as close to the port as is possible with the least damage to the hull below the waterline so that we may become an effective fighting unit again in the shortest time possible.

ALL WERE BRAVE THIS BLOODY NIGHT.

2015: The burning raider we have destroyed is still visible as a glare with flaring flames which should attract aircraft attention and bring to us the assistance we so sorely need.

2100: All the fires have now been brought completely under control but two which although they are small are still causing us some concern especially as the decks and the superstructure are still dull red hot in spots.

2200: All the hands have been mustered for roll call from the temporary nominal list. All the fires have now been extinguished except for a small fire below deck up in the bow section. The ship is at present under a fair degree of control and is still headed in the general direction of Geraldton inner harbour. We will all be very pleased to see the roof of the Shamrock Brewery on the skyline.

0000: All hands appear to have been accounted for but several ratings have been reported to have abandoned ship without permission whatever. It is not possible to make an estimate of the ammunition expended in the action but 'Y' Turret expended a total of 53 rounds.

20th November, 1941

0030: High flames seen to shoot up in the N.E.

0033: Blast wave and explosion presumed to be the enemy vessel destroyed by a sudden explosion.

0100: The sea is now becoming rougher and the rolling period is affected by the period of encounter but the sea on the bows causes heavy pitching while lifting of the stern makes the screws race when the sea is kept more or less on the beam.

0230: Estimated PROBABLE POSITION is 27deg. 23min. S.: 110deg. 52min. E.

0300: This Narrative of Proceedings, Casualty List and Captain Burnett's Cap Badge prepared for casting adrift in a small wooden box in case of the ship foundering.

Signed

Sub-Lieutenant B.A. Elder, R.A.N.

B A Elder

His Mark—20th. November, 1941.

APPENDIX 2

Officers and Men Lost at Sea in HMAS Sydney

Captain Joseph Burnett RAN

Commander Edmund Wybergh Thrushton DSC RN
Commander (E) Lionel Sydney Dalton DSO RAN
Commander (S) Thomas Francis Maynard RAN
Surgeon Commander John Reid Hasker RAN

Chaplain the Rev. George Stubbs RAN

Schoolmaster Percy Francis Skewes RAN

Lieutenant Commander Clive Alexandra Craig Montgomery RN
Lieutenant Commander Michael Morgan Singer DSC RN
Lieutenant Commander Alexander Mackay Wilkinson RAN
Lieutenant Commander (O) Jack Cawston Bacon RN
Lieutenant Commander (E) Richard Daniel Handcock RAN
Surgeon Lieutenant Commander Francis Harrison Genge RAN

Lieutenant Thomas Garton Brown RAN
Lieutenant John Alan Cole RANR(S)
Lieutenant Thomas Edgar Davis RAN
Lieutenant Andrew Ian Keith RANR(S)
Lieutenant Eric Elton Mayo RAN
Lieutenant Ian Thomas Roy Treloar RAN
Lieutenant (E) William Thomson Anderson RANR(S)
Lieutenant (E) Allan Wallace Wilson RANR(S)
Lieutenant (S) Robert Ernest Ridout RANR
Surgeon Lieutenant (D) Mervyn Clive Townsend RAN

Sub-Lieutenant Albert Edwin Byrne RANR
Sub-Lieutenant Alexander Vinrace Eagar RANR
Sub-Lieutenant Edwin Ross Eddy RAN
Sub-Lieutenant Bruce Alfred Elder RANR
Flying Officer Raymond Barker Barrey
Sub-Lieutenant (E) Allen James King RANVR
Sub-Lieutenant (E) Frederick Harold Schoch RANVR
Sub-Lieutenant (S) James Irvine Clifton RANR
Sub-Lieutenant (S) Charles McGregor Mitchell RANR
Acting Sub-Lieutenant (S) Donald Wolsey McCabe RAN

Gunner Frank Leslie Macdonald RN
Gunner (T) James Edward Peterson RAN

Acting Gunner John Kerr Houston RAN

Warrant (E) William George Batchelor RAN
Warrant (E) Alexander Baillie Biggs RAN
Warrant (E) Frederick William Reville RAN
Warrant (H) John Albert Ernest Fuller RAN
Warrant (L) Robert Wesley Nicholson RAN
Warrant (S) William Albert Owen RAN

Abernethy, Roderic Bell – Petty Officer Telegraphist
Absolem, John Francis – Acting Leading Seaman Stoker
Addison, Roy Hilton – Acting Leading Seaman
Agar, Lavington Henry – Chief Mechanician
Allison, John Albert Curtis – Able Seaman
Anderson, Cecil John – Ordinary Seaman
Anderson, Ronald Harry – Able Seaman
Andrews, Arthur John – Able Seaman
Archbell, Allen Walter – Acting Leading Seaman
Armstrong, Harold James – Ordinary Seaman
Aumann, Cyril – Acting Leading Stoker
Avery, George William – Able Seaman
Aylott, William Lewis – Acting Petty Officer
Ayton, Leslie George – Ordnance Artificer

Bain, William John – Able Seaman
Baker, Victor Leslie – Ordinary Seaman
Baker, William Alfred – Stoker
Balding, Harold Ross – Able Seaman

Barclay, Victor Nathaniel – Supply Assistant
Barham, Eric Ralph – Sick Berth Petty Officer
Barker, Benjamin Joseph Herbert – Able Seaman
Bartlett, Maxwell Edwin – Able Seaman
Bath, Walter James – Ordinary Seaman
Batten, Keith Carrington – Stoker
Baverstock, Ernest George – Able Seaman
Beattie, Alexander – Leading Stoker
Beattie, Eric Peter – Stoker
Beckett, Richard James – Stoker
Belcher, Edgar Raymond – Wireman
Bennie, Graham Russell – Able Seaman
Berwick, George Ross – Wireman
Bettany, John Henry – Able Seaman
Betterman, Donald Richard – Able Seaman
Bettinson, Walter Edward – Leading Seaman
Bevan, Hanbury Victor – Able Seaman
Beverton, John Troy – Stoker
Bibby, Ivo Ignatius – Engine Room Artificer First Class
Biram, Bernard Frank – Petty Officer Cook (O)
Birch, James William – Acting Leading Stoker
Blackwood, James – Stoker
Blake, John Shaldis – Acting Leading Stoker
Blom, Leslie Michael – Stoker
Bodman, Anthony Arthur – Able Seaman
Bone, Gordon Frederick – Able Seaman
Bonham, Henry George – Engine Room Artificer Fourth Class
Bonner, Reginald – Mechanician First Class
Bool, James – Ordinary Seaman
Booth, Ernest Albert – Able Seaman
Bowden, Laurence – Stoker Second Class
Bowes, Keith Andrew Joseph – Stoker
Box, Robert Aubrey – Stoker Second Class
Boyd, David William – Acting Leading Sick Berth Attendant
Bradley, Ross – Ordinary Seaman
Brennan, Ernest Norman – Able Seaman
Brind, Max – Able Seaman
Brodie, Raymond Roy – Acting Leading Seaman
Brooks, Donald Leslie – Ordinary Seaman
Buchanan, Allen Ridley Morton – Stoker Petty Officer
Buck, Clifton Charles – Able Seaman
Buckingham, Clarence Frederick Parett – Able Seaman

Buckley, Daniel Stanley – Ordinary Seaman
Budden, Keith Eric – Acting Yeoman of Signals
Bundy, Frederick Philip Keith – Petty Officer
Bunting, James – Able Seaman
Burgess, William Robert – Signalman
Burgoyne, Maxwell Aubrey – Leading Steward
Burke, Kenneth Thomas – Telegraphist
Burke, Leslie – Leading Cook (S)
Burke, William – Chief Engine Room Artificer
Burns, John Roardon – Acting Stoker Petty Officer
Burnsyde, William Edmund – Stoker
Burrowes, Douglas James – Able Seaman
Burt, Alwyn Stewart – Wireman
Butler, Kenneth Norman Hilton – Supply Assistant
Butler, Stanley Wilfred – Able Seaman

Cabban, Victor Roy – Stoker Second Class
Cannon, Lionel James – Telegraphist
Carey, Henry Robert Joseph – Able Seaman
Carey, Thomas Leslie – Chief Petty Officer Cook
Carr, John William Aaron – Able Seaman
Carthy, George Thomas – Able Seaman
Cartwright, Alexander Mitchell – Able Seaman
Catley, Raymond Rex – Able Seaman
Caudle, Douglas William – Ordinary Seaman
Challenger, Charles William – Chief Stoker
Chapman, Neville Owen – Ordinary Seaman
Chapman, William Roy – Stoker
Charlton, Claude Leyshon – Cook
Christie, Albert Thomas Norton – Stoker
Christison, John Maxwell – Ordinary Seaman
Clark, Daniel Murchie – Acting Leading Stoker
Clark, Thomas Welsby – Able Seaman
Clarke, Arthur – Leading Aircraftman
Clarke, Harry – Acting Leading Stoker
Clayton, Alfred Stockdale – Stoker
Clement, William – Ordinary Seaman
Clive, Alfred Walter – Stoker
Colbey, Robert Sabey – Ordinary Seaman
Cole, John Vincent – Ordinary Seaman
Cole, Sydney Arthur William – Able Seaman
Coleman, George Edward – Wireman

Colhoun, Robert Alan – Stoker Second Class
Collie, Cyril Brian – Stoker Second Class
Collier, Richard Thomas – Acting Leading Seaman
Collins, Charles Ernest – Able Seaman
Collins, William Henry – Able Seaman
Conquit, William Clarence – Able Seaman
Cookesley, Clifford William – Stoker
Coonan, Bevis Royal – Acting Leading Seaman
Cooper, Alfred Langley – Leading Stoker
Cooper, Arthur Donald Wilfred – Stoker Second Class
Cooper, Bertie – Able Seaman
Cooper, Reginald – Stoker
Cooper, Rex Albert – Able Seaman
Coppin, George William – Assistant Steward
Cork, William James Morris – Ordinary Seaman
Cormick, Thomas George – Engine Room Artificer Fourth Class
Courtis, Roy John – Stoker
Cox, Harold William – Acting Leading Stoker
Cox, John Lionel – Signalman
Cragg, George Louis – Stoker
Craike, Brian Wesley – Able Seaman
Cranwell, Henry Alfred Geoffrey – Stoker
Craske, Benjamin Jack – Ordinary Seaman
Crawford, Thomas Alfred – Acting Able Seaman
Crocker, Leslie Joseph – Petty Officer Cook
Crowle, Jack Alfred Francis – Stoker Second Class
Cummings, James – Able Seaman
Cunnington, Alan Leonard Fyffe – Ordnance Artificer Fourth Class
Curtis, Clifford Leslie James – Wireman
Curtis, Richard – Petty Officer
Curwood, Walter Leslie – Wireman

Daniel, Kevin Henry – Ordnance Artificer Fourth Class
Darby, Stanley Maurice – Able Seaman
Daunt, Arthur Robert – Stoker
Davey, John Stanley – Petty Officer Cook
Davies, Sidney John – Electrical Artificer
Davis, Stanley Roy – Leading Seaman
Deacon, William Frank – Able Seaman
Deane, Wallace Bertram – Ordinary Seaman
Dee, Thomas – Leading Steward
DeForest, McAdam Carruthers – Stoker

DeGracie, John Philip – Ordinary Seaman
Dempster, Herbert James – Stoker
Devereux, Eric Gordon – Able Seaman
Dhu, Lionel Edward – Able Seaman
Diews, Bernard Albert – Able Seaman
Dimmock, Donald Charles – Able Seaman
Dix, Gordon Kenneth – Acting Leading Stoker
Dixon, Thomas Charles – Leading Stoker
Dobson, Herbert Hartfield – Able Seaman
Dodds, Richard – Leading Aircraftman
Doxey, Alexander Harold – Able Seaman
Doyle, Edward Francis – Able Seaman
Drake, Albert Reginald – Able Seaman
Drake, John Richardson – Stoker
Duncan, Emanuel Robert Thomas – Supply Assistant
Dundon, Stephen – Able Seaman
Dunin, Thomas – Steward

Edenborough, Alan Grosvenor – Ordinary Seaman
Edgoose, John Franklin – Ordinary Seaman
Edwards, Ernest John – Able Seaman
Edwards, Frederick – Acting Stoker Petty Officer
Evans, Francis Richard – Petty Officer
Ewens, Robert Underdown – Able Seaman

Fahey, William Richard – Able Seaman
Farrand, Leonard Charles – Ordinary Seaman
Faulkner, Arthur John – Able Seaman
Ferguson, David Wallace – Able Seaman
Ferguson, Kenneth Charles – Ordinary Seaman
Fibbens, William Sidney – Telegraphist
Findlay, Gordon Lindsay – Acting Ordnance Artificer Fourth Class
Finlayson, Harry – Mechanician First Class
Fisher, John William – Leading Cook (S)
Fitzgerald, Augustine Francis – Blacksmith Fourth Class
Fitzgerald, Lloyd Gerald – Acting Supply Petty Officer
Fleming, Wilfred Stafford – Able Seaman
Foote, Reginald Eric – Cook (S)
Forbes, Robert Gordon Staunton – Ordinary Seaman
Forsyth, Glenbervie Edwin – Electrical Artificer Fourth Class
Forth, Herbert – Able Seaman
Foster, Norman Douglas – Engine Room Artificer Fourth Class

Foster, Roy – Leading Aircraftman
Foulkes, Robert Eugene – Telegraphist
Franklin, Edward William – Leading Seaman
Fraser, Noel James – Ordinary Seaman
Freer, Walter Edward Albert – Able Seaman
Friar, Jack Allan – Engine Room Artificer Third Class
Frisch, Ernest Dudley – Able Seaman
Frith, William Railton Oliver – Petty Officer, RN
Fry, Robert Aubrey – Stoker
Fryer, Kenneth James – Ordinary Telegraphist

Gamble, Frank Harold – Petty Officer Telegraphist
Gamble, Ronald Frederick – Acting Petty Officer Telegraphist
Gardiner, Heathcote Diggery – Ordinary Seaman
Garnett, William Henry – Acting Leading Stoker
Garrett, Basil Farmer – Able Seaman
Gale, Raymond – Leading Supply Assistant
Gentles, Harry Spencer – Chief Stoker
Gilsenan, Dudley John – Steward
Glackin, Thomas Nevin – Stoker
Glasby, Harold – Able Seaman
Goodwin, Neil Francis – Able Seaman
Goodwin, Wilfred James – Able Seaman
Gothard, Edwin – Acting Petty Officer Telegraphist
Graco, Henry Mathias – Able Seaman
Graham, George Albert – Ordinary Seaman
Greaves, Sidney – Able Seaman
Green, Arthur Eric – Acting Stoker Petty Officer
Green, John Rex – Ordinary Seaman
Green, Theo Lawrence – Cook (O)
Greenwood, James Herbert – Ordinary Seaman
Gregson, Michael Oswald – Ordinary Seaman
Grinter, Norman Francis – Acting Leading Stoker
Gronberg, Ernest Edward – Stoker
Gwynne, David Andrew – Able Seaman

Haag, Francis Vincent – Stoker
Hagan, Allan – Steward
Hammond, Lawson – Able Seaman
Hare, Richard William – Able Seaman
Harricks, Sydney William – Able Seaman
Hass, Mervan Loui Wallace – Able Seaman

Harrington, Albert Frederick – Acting Leading Seaman
Harris, Ronald Charles – Able Seaman
Harrison, Leslie Alexander – Petty Officer Steward
Hartmann, Frederick Holland Reg – Petty Officer
Haslam, Aubrey Cecil – Acting Leading Seaman
Hattersley, Jack Osberg – Able Seaman
Hawker, George Clarence – Steward
Hawkes, Sydney William – Able Seaman
Haynes, Frank James – Stoker
Haywood, George James – Ordinary Seaman Second Class
Heaton, Edmund – Acting Electrical Artificer Fourth Class
Henderson, William Laurence Douglas – Stoker
Henrickson, John Olaf – Stoker
Herington, Henry Foster – Stoker Second Class
Heritage, Roy George – Able Seaman
Herrod, Herbert Frederick – Acting Leading Stoker
Hewett, Edmund Herbert – Able Seaman
Hickey, Robert Arthur – Able Seaman
Hill, Douglas Hugh – Stoker
Hill, Peter – Able Seaman
Hill, Robert Henry – Engine Room Artificer Fourth Class
Hobbs, George James – Able Seaman
Hogan, Michael Henry – Ordinary Telegraphist
Holder, Edward Harrison – Telegraphist
Holm, Clarence Kenneth Asby – Able Seaman
Homer, Arthur Wilfred – Chief Stoker
Honor, Charles Leslie – Telegraphist
Hooper, Edgar Norman – Ordinary Seaman
Hopcraft, Robert Beauchamp – Shipwright Third Class
Hore, Keith Beresford – Able Seaman
Horrigan, Cornelius – Able Seaman
Howard, Keith – Aircraftman First Class
Howard, Leonard John – Able Seaman
Hudson, James Lloyd – Signalman
Hutchinson, Richard – Able Seaman
Hutchinson, Roy Harold – Able Seaman
Hutchison, James Robertson – Stoker Second Class

Ingham, John Wakelin – Acting Leading Stoker

James, Martin Curtis – Able Seaman
Jarvis, William John – Stoker Second Class

Jeffs, Francis William – Ordinary Seaman
Jennings, David Mathias – Able Seaman
Jesnoewski, Leslie Albert – Ordinary Seaman
Johnson, Percy Albert – Stoker Second Class
Johnston, Donald Erskine – Able Seaman
Johnston, George – Writer
Johnston, Edgar William – Able Seaman
Johnstone, Trevor James Armistice – Able Seaman
Jones, David James – Acting Stoker Petty Officer
Jones, Donald Edgar – Able Seaman
Jones, Ivan David – Acting Engine Room Artificer Fourth Class
Jones, John Banks – Engine Room Artificer Fourth Class
Jones, Philip Trevor – Chief Petty Officer
Jones, Wilfred George – Chief Shipwright
Jordan, Ernest John – Able Seaman
Jordan, Horace David – Able Seaman
Joyce, William Robert John – Able Seaman

Keane, Walter John DSM – Chief Ordnance Artificer
Kearnon, Rex Allan – Ordinary Seaman
Keenan, Francis Bernard – Stoker
Kelly, James Vincent – Able Seaman
Kelly, Neville Andrew – Stoker Second Class
Kennedy, Robert John – Stoker Second Class
Kenney, Arthur Henry Lawrence – Chief Petty Officer
Kent, Lloyd Shackleton – Signalman
Kettle, Edward James – Able Seaman
Kettyle, James Thomas – Leading Stoker
Keys, Rodger Francis – Able Seaman
Kirkham, Eric James – Able Seaman
Kitchin, Clayton Peter – Stoker
Kleinig, Arthur Albert – Telegraphist
Knapman, Wesley Bowden – Engine Room Artificer Fourth Class
Knapp, Douglas John – Stoker Second Class
Knight, Neil Kenneth – Steward
Kreig, Archibald Douglas – Assistant Steward

Laffer, Peter Morton – Ordinary Seaman
Lang, John – Able Seaman
Lang, William Hugh – Stoker Second Class
Lawler, Neil Charles – Ordinary Seaman
Lawson, James Neil – Supply Assistant

Laxton, Stewart Thomas – Sick Berth Attendant Second Class
Laycock, Royce Stanley – Stoker
Lewis, Ambrose Henry – Stoker Petty Officer
Lewis, Desmond Henry – Bandsman
Lewis, Leslie Raymond – Acting Leading Seaman
Lillywhite, Harry Edgar – Shipwright First Class
Lockard, Terence Godfrey – Acting Signalman
Love, Snowden Edward – Stoker
Lowenstein, William – Stoker
Lowry, Frederick William – Able Seaman
Lynch, Stephen Maxwell – Able Seaman
Lyne, Raymond Vivian – Ordinary Seaman

Mackinnon, Murdo – Petty Officer
Males, Trevor – Shipwright Fourth Class
Mann, Keith Arthur – Ordinary Seaman
Manning, Maurice – Leading Cook (S)
Marley, Sidney – Sergeant
Marson, Albert Richard – Mechanician Second Class
Martin, Alan Douglas – Ordinary Seaman
Martin, James Hearle – Able Seaman
Martin, Leslie Frank – Steward
Martin, Leslie James Frederick – Ordinary Seaman
Matheson, Edward Austin John – Ordinary Seaman
Mathews, John William – Able Seaman
Maxwell, Ian Maxwell – Ordinary Seaman
Medlen, Lindsay James – Sick Berth Attendant
Melandri, Percy Ernest Vincent – Bandsman
Menzies, William – Able Seaman
Miller, George James – Cook (S)
Miller, James Douglas Haig – Able Seaman
Miller, Kenneth Roscoe – Ordinary Seaman
Miller, Martin Patrick – Steward
Miller, Robert Alfred – Stoker
Milverton, Peter Frederick – Able Seaman
Minns, Leslie Charles – Sick Berth Attendant
Mitchell, Francis Joseph – Supply Assistant
Mogler, Richard Charles – Stoker
Mordaunt, Francis Xavier – Petty Officer Writer
Morisey, Ronald – Able Seaman
Morphett, Merton James – Cook (S)
Morris, Edgar Percy – Petty Officer

Morris, Raymond Keith – Able Seaman
Moule, Albert – Stoker
Mudford, Leslie Francis – Able Seaman
Mulhall, John Dillon – Bandsman
Murdoch, Raymond Charles – Able Seaman
Murray, Malcolm – Able Seaman
Mutch, Hector MacDonald – Able Seaman
Myers, Henry William – Stoker
McAulay, Angus Campbell – Bandsman
McAuslan, Arthur Robert – Chief Engine Room Artificer
McBain, Joseph Henry – Chief Engine Room Artificer
McCabe, Ernest Victor – Able Seaman
McCallem, Duncan – Canteen Assistant
McClaren, Alfred Allan – Petty Officer
McConnell, Robert Nicol – Stoker
McCulloch, Sydney – Able Seaman
McCullough, Samuel James – Wireman
McDonald, John Denis – Able Seaman
McDougall, Wallace – Able Seaman
McGregor, Donald Alexander – Cook (S)
McGowan, Thomas Henry – Able Seaman
McHaffie, Edward Hunter – Painter First Class
McKay, Allan Murdoch – Leading Supply Assistant
McKechnie, Glen Morton – Ordinary Seaman
McKenzie, Donald James – Able Seaman
McKeown, Malachi James – Able Seaman
McLean, William Ernest – Stoker Petty Officer
McLeod, Herbert Charles – Acting Leading Stoker
McLeod-Smith, Albert Fraser – Petty Officer

Nesbitt, Jackson – Able Seaman
Newman, Charles Albert – Able Seaman
Nicholls, Malcolm Godfrey – Able Seaman
Nichols, Francis Roy – Ordinary Seaman Second Class
Nichol, Thomas Enright – Wireman
Noble, Charles Taylor Reg – Petty Officer
Noell, Alfred John – Stoker
Norbery, Stephen William – Able Seaman
Norman, Charles George James – Able Seaman
Norman, Frederick William – Leading Seaman
Norton, John Thomas Henry – Leading Stoker
Norton, Montague Alfred Huxley – Engine Room Artificer Fourth Class

Norton, William Frederick Cecil – Able Seaman
Nugent, Cyril James – Stoker
Nyal, Leslie John – Stoker Second Class

Oakford, Phillip James – Ordinary Seaman
O'Brien, Edward Bedford – Shipwright First Class
Ogilvie, Laurence – Able Seaman
Oliver, Alan Henry – Ordinary Seaman
Opas, Maurice – Canteen Manager
Owens, Edward Harold – Able Seaman

Paling, Dennis Ross – Able Seaman
Parkes, Douglas Leon – Able Seaman
Parr, George Frederick – Chief Electrical Artificer
Partington, Leslie Warburton – Bandsman
Pascoe, Percival Holman – Stoker
Pastoors, William Cecil – Stoker Second Class
Patrick, Charles William – Ordinary Seaman Second Class
Paul, Stanley Robert – Stoker
Payne, John Robert – Sick Berth Attendant
Peak, John McGhie – Stoker
Pearce, Eric Victor – Acting Engine Room Artificer Fourth Class
Pelham, Frederick Charles – Bandsman
Perger, Frederick James – Able Seaman
Perryman, Richard Severn – Able Seaman
Peters, Maxwell Wesley – Telegraphist
Peterson, Peter William – Stoker
Phillips, Frederick Ernest – Able Seaman
Pike, John William – Able Seaman
Pitt, William Harold – Able Seaman
Platt, Robert – Stoker Second Class
Pople, Alfred – Band Corporal
Potter, Alfred William – Ordinary Seaman
Potter, Clyde Ashby – Acting Supply Petty Officer
Powell, Lyal Llewellyn – Able Seaman
Prike, Joseph John – Able Seaman
Primmer, John Foster Roy – Able Seaman
Pritchard, Herbert Lloyd – Ordnance Artificer Fourth Class
Psaila, Samuel – Canteen Assistant
Pulham, Edward George Montague – Acting Leading Stoker
Purdon, Eric Thomas – Leading Seaman
Purkiss, Cecil Edward – Wireman

Putman, Albert Edward – Ordinary Seaman

Quilty, John Edward – Acting Leading Seaman
Quinn, George Frederick – Petty Officer Cook (S)

Ramsay, Ernest Wilson – Able Seaman
Ranford, John Irvine – Ordinary Telegraphist
Ray, Harold George – Able Seaman
Redfearne, Charles Hugh – Stoker
Redmond, Eric Neville – Ordinary Signalman
Reed, George Percival – Writer
Rees, Robert John – Ordinary Seaman
Reeves, Ellis Leslie – Able Seaman
Reeves, Raymond Henry – Ordinary Seaman
Reid, Graham Roy – Signalman
Reilly, James Brian – Acting Engine Room Artificer Fourth Class
Remfry, Ernest John – Able Seaman
Ricardo, John Layton – Chief Petty Officer Butcher
Rice, Desmond Maxwell – Stoker Third Class
Richards, Harold Nelson – Acting Engine Room Artificer Fourth Class
Richter, Arthur John – Acting Supply Petty Officer
Riley, Edwin Martin – Ordinary Seaman
Rippen, Adolph Heinrich Gerhard – Telegraphist
Riters, Edward – Able Seaman
Roberts, Lyndon Irvine – Stoker
Roberts, Ronald Charles – Assistant Cook (O)
Robertson, Michael John – Leading Seaman
Robertson, Thomas Noel – Acting Stoker Petty Officer
Robertson, William James – Leading Cook
Rogers, Charles Allan – Able Seaman
Rogers, Ralph Carey – Signalman
Rolfe, Edmund Sturgeon – Able Seaman
Rolley, Ernest David – Steward
Rosevear, Geoffrey – Able Seaman
Rosevear, Lance – Able Seaman
Ross, Donald – Petty Officer Steward
Ross, James Thompson – Supply Petty Officer
Rothbaum, Lionel – Assistant Steward
Rowe, Allan Lawrence – Able Seaman
Rowe, James Ronald – Telegraphist
Rowe, Lindsay Thomas – Stoker Second Class
Rowlands, Harold Edward – Supply Chief Petty Officer

Rudwall, Peter Sutherland – Ordinary Seaman

Salmon, John – Able Seaman
Sampson, Louis Nicholas – Supply Chief Petty Officer
Sands, William Archibald Martin – Chief Petty Officer
Savage, Leonard Roydon – Stoker
Sawbridge, George William – Bandsman
Schache, Walter Herbert – Chief Petty Officer Cook
Schmidt, Alan Hartley – Ordinary Seaman
Schulz, Raymond Arthur – Stoker
Scott, George Gillick – Acting Petty Officer
Shadlow, Eric Henry – Stoker Second Class
Shepherd, Alfred Horwood – Acting Engine Room Artificer Fourth Class
Shepherd, David John – Chief Petty Officer Telegraphist
Shiers, Arthur Ernest – Able Seaman
Shipstone, Henry Buccleuch – Petty Officer
Short, Harry Kenneth – Able Seaman
Sievey, Richard Thomas – Ordinary Seaman
Silk, Stanley George – Chief Petty Officer
Simpson, Benjamin – Petty Officer Telegraphist
Simpson, Charles Henry – Able Seaman
Simpson, Reginald Austin – Ordinary Telegraphist
Slater, Alec George Hamilton – Assistant Cook
Smith, Allen Leslie – Chief Electrical Artificer
Smith, Alfred James – Stoker Second Class
Smith, Cornelius Francis – Able Seaman
Smith, Douglas William Charles – Engine Room Artificer Fourth Class
Smith, Ernest Edward Frederick – Able Seaman
Smith, George William – Stoker Second Class
Smith, Ronald George Singleton – Engine Room Artificer Fourth Class
Smith, Roy Clarence – Supply Assistant
Smith, Roy Somerville – Stoker
Smith, William Frederick Albert – Able Seaman
Smith, William Harrison Randall – Engine Room Artificer Third Class
Smith, William Reginald Devine – Acting Petty Officer
Soutar, William Nicoll – Supply Assistant
Spiller, Harold James – Able Seaman
Staff, Robert Frank – Steward
Stammers, Robert – Cook
Standish, George Frederick – Able Seaman
Stear, Ernest Victor Lloyd – Bandmaster
Steed, Philip William – Ordinary Seaman

Steele, Roy McLellan Morgan – Able Seaman
Stenton, Stanley Peter William – Stoker
Stephens, George – Acting Yeoman of Signals
Stephenson, Walter Thomas William – Stoker
Sterling, Leslie – Able Seaman
Stevens, Horace John – Bandsman
Stevenson, Robert – Stoker Third Class
Stride, Cecil Meadus – Stoker Second Class
Striethorst, Raymond Conrad – Able Seaman
Stripe, Alexander Edward – Able Seaman
Strugnell, John William – Petty Officer
Stuart, James Richard Keith – Stoker
Stuart, William Fancourt – Writer
Stubbs, Kimberley – Stoker Second Class
Sturla, James Robert – Chief Stoker
Sutton, Denis O'Reilly – Able Seaman
Sutton, Kingsley – Acting Stoker Petty Officer

Tabor, Frederick Arthur – Acting Leading Seaman
Tassel, Harry Woodrow – Petty Officer
Tatters, George Nelson – Able Seaman
Taylor, John – Telegraphist
Taylor, John Ernest – Able Seaman
Taylor, John McLean – Able Seaman
Taylor, Keith – Ordinary Seaman
Taylor, Kenneth George – Able Seaman
Taylor, Rupert Allenby – Leading Stoker
Tennant, Ronald George – Engine Room Artificer Third Class
Thompson, Harry Edward – Wireman
Thompson, William Raymond – Stoker
Thomson, Archibald James – Stoker
Trenbath, Jack Stephen – Stoker Third Class
Trenwith, Harry George – Stoker Petty Officer
Triggs, Robert – Master-at-Arms
Tuffin, Edwin Daniel – Able Seaman
Turk, Herbert – Able Seaman
Turner, George Alfred – Ordinary Seaman Second Class
Turner, Harold – Signalman
Turner, Kenneth James – Ordinary Seaman
Turner, William Ross – Able Seaman
Tyldsley, James – Chief Yeoman of Signals
Tyler, Charles Desmond – Bandsman

Unwin, John Edward – Able Seaman
Uren, Thomas William James – Leading Steward

Vassett, Alexander William – Electrical Artificer First Class
Vogt, Ronald Matthew – Able Seaman

Wait, Howard Thomas Charles – Acting Supply Petty Officer
Waldron, Thomas Arthur – Stoker Second Class
Walker, Arthur Joseph – Cook
Walker, Edward John – Yeoman of Signals
Walker, Kenneth James – Able Seaman
Walker, William Albert Gordon – Leading Signalman
Wallace, William Raymond – Stoker
Walsh, Gordon Stuart – Supply Assistant
Walsh, Michael Henry Joseph – Able Seaman
Ward, Frederick Ernest Charles – Able Seaman
Ward, James Joseph Richard – Leading Stoker
Ware, Leonard Frank – Joiner Third Class
Warren, Vincent – Bandsman
Waye, Leonard William – Acting Leading Stoker
Webb, Arthur Charles – Able Seaman
Webb, Oliver Ernest Raymond – Acting Petty Officer
Weller, Royce Henry – Acting Shipwright Fourth Class
White, Hans James Leo – Signalman
White, Robert George – Able Seaman
Whitfield, Leonard William – Chief Petty Officer Writer
Whithear, Alan George – Stoker
Williams, Alfred David – Able Seaman
Williams, David Leslie – Acting Petty Officer
Williams, John Bruce – Stoker Second Class
Williams, John Harris – Stoker Second Class
Williamson, Maurice Douglas – Leading Stoker
Williamson, Sydney Thomas Lawrence – Acting Petty Officer
Willis, George Boyd – Able Seaman
Willis, Percy John Christian – Plumber First Class
Willis, Lloyd Martin – Cook (O)
Willis, Ronald Verdun – Steward
Wilson, Clifford – Telegraphist
Wilson, Jack Stanley – Able Seaman
Wilson, Roderick Richard – Sick Berth Attendant
Wilson, Roy Weddon Dawes – Ordinary Seaman
Windham, Russell Bertram – Ordinary Telegraphist

Witton, Bertram Linsay – Acting Leading Telegraphist
Wixted, Ronald James – Stoker Second Class
Wood, Arthur Thomas – Able Seaman
Woodcroft, William George – Leading Steward
Woodhams, Reginald Bernard Craig – Stoker Second Class
Woods, William Raymond – Acting Engine Room Artificer Fourth Class
Woodsford, Alfred Charles – Acting Leading Seaman
Woolmore, Laurence Thomas – Ordnance Artificer Second Class
Worsley, William Cornelius – Acting Electrical Artificer Fourth Class
Wright, Charles Alan – Able Seaman
Wright, Charles Patrick – Signalman
Wright, Harold Douglas – Assistant Steward
Wyatt, Eric William – Telegraphist

Yeoman, Walter Clifford – Stoker
York, Leonard Denis – Able Seaman
Young, John Robinson – Able Seaman

Zammitt, Salvatore – Canteen Manager

APPENDIX 3

Officers and Men Lost at Sea in HSK Kormoran

Heinz Aron
Alex Barthel
Josef Bednareck
Werner Berges
Alfred Bez
August Bilges
Willi Bolt
Paul Brachvogel
August Breer
Franz Breitenstein
Erich Bruchig
Ludwig Bussjager
Reinhard Czech
Hein Dein
Bruno Demandt
Willi Dobileit
Johann Duismann
Eduard Eberhard
Hermann Ebert
Heinz Feldmann
Willi Fischer
Gerhard Gause
Egbert von Gaza
Ernst Georg
Theo Glander
Fritz Grabow
Gerhard Haarnagel
Erich Haase
Hans Haase

Johann Hahn
Willi Havekost
Franz Heinze
Helmut Heinzemann
Fritz Hemmerich
Otto Herstel
Eugen Heumann
Albert Hille
Wilhelm Hinkel
Fritz Hoffmann
Fritz Holzel
Karl Hudasch
Kurt Hufer
Josef Hurter
Heinrich Knupper
Willi Kreutzer
Robert Kummel
Hermann Lange
Erich Langenbach
Franz Leger
Otto Lenz
Dietrich Lohmann
Rudolf Losche
Fritz Martin
Paul Meyer
Heinz Muller
Freidrich Nagel
Oskar Pakosch
Franz Pastuschka

Hubert Pregler
Herbert Prystuppa
Kurt Quednau
Alfred Rennig
Herbert Rickert
Alfons Ross
Hans Salinsky
Georg Salzgeber
Ernst Schonberg
Horst Schuster
Karl Siller
Hermann Stehr
Alfons Storney
Fritz Tiemann
Leonhard Trentler
Josef Tschznter

Bernhard von der Tweer
Rudolf Ulbricht
Kurt Wachter
Robert Wulf
Karl Zeitler

Died during *Kormoran*'s cruise
Erich Dembnicki
Kurt Hofmann

Died as prisoner of war
Erich Meyer

Notes and References

Introduction
1. Michael Montgomery, *Who Sank the Sydney?* (Cassell, Melbourne, 1981).
2. Barbara Winter, *HMAS Sydney: Fact, Fantasy and Fraud* (Boolarong, Brisbane, 1984).
3. Source Analysis [from ANGAM II] for HMAS *Sydney* and HSK *Kormoran*, 20 December 1991, p. 2.
4. ibid., p. 17.
5. Barbara Tuchman, *Practising History* (Macmillan, London, 1981) p. 60.

Chapter 1
1. There are four different international time zones relevant to this narrative. International Time Zone Zulu (Z), also known as Greenwich Mean Time (GMT), was the time at the observatory at Greenwich in England. East and west of Greenwich, time is referred to as being Zulu Time +/– a number of hours depending on longitude. The time zones are designated alphabetically to the East. *Kormoran* kept Golf Time: GMT + seven hours. HMAS *Sydney* and the District Naval Office in Fremantle kept Hotel Time: GMT + eight hours. In other words, they kept the next time zone to the east of that used by *Kormoran*. The Naval Board in Melbourne and the Naval Headquarters in *Sydney* kept Kilo Time: GMT + ten hours.
2. *Aquitania* was a passenger ship with the Cunard Line when she was requisitioned for war service in 1939. Launched in April 1913 at Clydebank in Scotland, *Aquitania* displaced 45,000 tons and was capable of 24 knots. She was requisitioned for service in the 1914–18 war as a troop transport for the Dardanelles campaign, and as a hospital ship in the Mediterranean. *Aquitania* was broken up in 1950.
3. Distances at sea are always given in nautical miles. One nautical mile equals 2000 yards; one land mile measures 1760 yards. The other relevant distance used at sea is the cable, a distance of 200 yards.
4. Details of the search for *Sydney* are included in Navy file, 'Search for HMAS *Sydney*', MP 1049/5 2026/3/457, AA ACT.
5. CNS (Royle) to Minister for the Navy (Makin), 24 November 1941, Papers of Sir Frederick Shedden, Permanent Secretary of the Department of Defence (hereafter 'Shedden Papers'), 'HMAS *Sydney* – Sinking of by German Raider *Kormoran*, 1941', A 5954 Box 2400/21, AA ACT.
6. *Trocas* was built in Rotterdam by Rotterdam Drooyd Matts and launched in 1927. She displaced 7406 tons and was operated by Shell Oil until being sold in 1960.

7. The Hudson aircraft were used by the RAAF for utility reconnaissance, transport and bombing during World War II.

8. Prime Minister from Private Secretary, 25 November 1941, Shedden Papers, A 5954 Box 2400/21, AA ACT.

9. *Koolinda* carried passengers and cargo on the coastal ports service to Darwin. Built in Belfast in 1926, *Koolinda* displaced 4227 tons and was operated by the State Shipping Service. After being used to evacuate civilians from Singapore, she reverted to coastal service until 1958.

10. *Centaur*, a 3066-ton cargo ship, was lent to the Australian government for war service in 1939. Owned by the Ocean Steamship Company, she was built in Scotland in 1924. After conversion to a hospital ship in early 1943, *Centaur* was sunk by a Japanese submarine off the Queensland coast in May 1943. Controversy has surrounded the sinking of the ship and the submarine captain has been criticised for his decision to attack the ship. The best account and analysis of the *Centaur* controversy is chapter sixteen of David Jenkins' excellent book, *Battle Surface! Japan's Submarine War Against Australia, 1942–44* (Random Century, Sydney, 1992).

10a. The Advisory War Council was established on 28 October 1940 by Prime Minister Menzies. It consisted of four Cabinet members and four Labor parliamentarians. Menzies' aim was to achieve political stability with respect to the conduct of the war. In return, the Labor members of the Council had access to information on planning and operations with a capacity to make recommendations.

11. Sec, Naval Board to Prime Minister, Cable M 2797, 27 November 1941, Shedden Papers, A 5954 Box 2400/21, AA ACT.

12. Sec, Naval Board to CNS, Cable M 2755, 26 November 1941, Shedden Papers, A 5954 Box 2400/21, AA ACT.

13. AWM OW 89/5, 'HMAS *Sydney*—casualty list—missing presumed dead—19 November 1941'.

14. Sec, Naval Board to Prime Minister, Cable M 2799 dated 27 November 1941, Shedden Papers, A 5954 Box 2400/21, AA ACT.

15. HMAS *Yandra*, a 990-ton coastal cargo vessel, was requisitioned for war service from Coast Steamships of Adelaide in June 1940. As part of her war service as an anti-submarine and harbour patrol vessel, *Yandra* operated out of Fremantle from October 1940 to April 1941, and from June to December 1941. She saw active service around New Guinea in the latter part of the war and paid off from RAN service in 1946.

16. Details of the sighting are contained in AWM, PR 88/119 'Flying logbook and navigators log sheets maintained for the search for *Sydney* and later discovery of the German raider *Kormoran* life boat with survivors', Flight Lieutenant Rooke, 26–29 November 1941.

17. The signal from Fremantle was sent to the Naval Board in Cable M 2801, 28 November 1941, Shedden Papers, A 5954 Box 2400/21, AA ACT.

18. R.T. Crooke to Western Australian Maritime Museum, 1991.

19. See 'Complaint re: official release of the names of personnel of HMAS *Sydney*', SP 109/3 342/14, AA ACT.

20. In spite of a prohibition on any press or broadcast mention of *Sydney*, several Melbourne radio stations failed to comply with the censorship order and were suspended from broadcasting. See 'Suspension of radio stations for breaches of instructions regarding the sinking of HMAS *Sydney*', SP 109/3 357/06, AA ACT.

21. Teleprinter Message D.3265, dated 30 November 1941, 'HMAS *Sydney* and HMAS *Parramatta*—Expressions of Sympathy', AA A 1608, S/51/1/6.

22. Prime Ministerial Statement No. 78, 20 November 1941, Shedden Papers, A 5954 2400/21, AA ACT.

23. Department of Prime Minister and Cabinet file, 'HMAS *Sydney*', A 816 40/301/290, AA ACT.

24. *West Australian*, 1 December 1941.
25. ibid.
26. Sec, Department of the Navy to the Prime Minister's Private Secretary, CS 2674, 1 December 1941, Shedden Papers, A 5954 Box 2400/21, AA ACT.
27. Prime Minister's Private Secretary to Assistant Secretary, Department of Defence Coordination, CS 2666, Shedden Papers, A 5954 Box 2400/21, AA ACT.
28. War Cabinet Minute No. 1528, dated 4 December 1941, A 2673, Vol. 9, AA ACT.
29. 'HMAS *Sydney* and HMAS *Parramatta*—Expressions of Sympathy', A 1608 S51/1/6, AA ACT.
30. *Bulletin*, 10 December 1941.

Chapter 2

1. A small British survey brig launched in 1825 was named HMS *Sydney*. She subsequently saw a decade of uneventful service and was paid off.
2. Adolf Hoehling, *Lonely Command* (Cassell, London, 1957) p. 111.
3. Navy file A 2911 1834/14, 'European War 1914. *Emden*, destruction of by HMAS *Sydney*', AA ACT.
4. Erich von Manty (ed.) *Der Krieg Zur See, 1914–18* (Mittler, Berlin, 1920–37) vol. 3.
5. Fred McClement, *Guns in Paradise: The Saga of the Cruiser* Emden (McClelland and Stewart, Toronto, 1968).
6. See the index and history cards relating to drawings, plans and specifications for HMAS *Sydney* (II) contained in MP 547/1 Boxes 12 and 13, AA Melbourne.
7. H.T. Lenton, *British Cruisers* (Macdonald, London, 1973) p. 86.
8. *Commonwealth Parliamentary Debates* [hereafter *CPD*] (Representatives [hereafter Reps]) 31 July 1934, p. 915.
9. A. Raven and J. Roberts, *British Cruisers of World War II* (Arms and Armour Press, London, 1980) p. 161.
10. Navy file, 'New cruiser to replace HMAS *Brisbane*—name to be HMAS *Sydney*', MP 124/6 603/263/2, AA Melbourne.
11. The following narrative of Sydney's operational service is drawn from several sources including her log books for the period 1935–41, SP 5551/1 bundles 526, 527 and 528, AA ACT.
12. W.H. Ross, *Stormy Petrel: The Life Story of HMAS* Sydney (Pattersons Printing Press, Perth, undated but actually 1943).
13. Navy file, 'HMAS *Sydney*—attachment to the Royal Navy, 1935', MP 124/6 603/263/147, AA Melbourne.
14. No relation to Commander H.M.L. Waller RAN.
15. Navy file, 'HMAS *Sydney* protection of fire control systems and alternative controls', MP 1049/5 2026/3/294, AA Melbourne.
16. ibid.
17. ibid.
18. Dominions Office cablegram No. 191, 8 September 1939, attached with minute from Shedden to Boucher (Second Naval Member), 19 September 1939, 'HMAS *Sydney*—Sinking of Italian Cruiser—Congratulatory Cables, 19–24 July 1940', A 5954, Box 582/1, AA ACT.
19. Macandie (Secretary to the Naval Board) to Shedden, 26 September 1939, AA A 5954, Box 582.
20. Vice Admiral Sir John Collins, *HMAS* Sydney (NHSA Monograph, Sydney, 1971) p. 8.
21. When joined by *Sydney*, the Squadron consisted of the 6-inch cruisers *Orion* (flagship), *Neptune*, *Sydney*, *Gloucester* and *Liverpool*, See S.W.C. Pack, *Cunningham: The Commander* (Batsford, London, 1974) p. 93.

22. ADM 234/323, 'Bombardment of Bardia, 21 June 1940, 17 August 1940 and 3 January 1941', *Battle Summary No. 6*.
23. Collins, op. cit., p. 14.
24. For a detailed account of naval operations around Crete see ADM 234/319, 'Naval operations of Battle of Crete', *Battle Summary No. 4*.
25. Navy file, 'HMAS *Sydney*—reports of action, 9 July 1940', MP 1049/5 2026/3/350, AA Melbourne.
26. ADM 234/323, 'Mediterranean operations: operation MA 5, 7–15 July 1940; action off Calabria, 9 July 1940', *Battle Summary No. 8*.
27. P.C. Smith and J.R. Dominy, *Cruisers in Action 1939–45* (Kimber, London, 1981) pp. 87–92.
28. 'Engagement of HMAS *Sydney* with *Bartolomeo Colleoni*', SP 112/1 352/7/13, AA ACT.
29. The *Bande Nere* was sunk on the night of 22–23 March 1942 by the submarine *Urge*.
30. The fullest account of the engagement is contained in ADM 234/317, 'Mediterranean operations and action off Cape Spada (Crete) 19 July 1940', *Battle Summary No. 2*.
31. Pack, op. cit., p. 98.
32. A list of signals sent to and from *Sydney* during and after the Cape Spada action, and the associated plain text, is held by the author.
33. 'HMAS *Sydney*—sinking of Italian cruiser—congratulatory cables, 19–24 July 1940', A 5954 518/1, AA ACT.
34. Navy file, '*Return of Sydney, 9 February 1941*', MP 1049/5 2026/3/410, AA Melbourne.
35. Ross, op. cit., p. 269.
36. Navy file, 'Passages of HMAS *Sydney* and Admiral Colvin to Singapore', AWM 124 4/151.
37. In addition to *Sydney*, the only ships from the *Leander* and the Modified *Leander* Classes to have been lost during the war were HMS *Neptune*, which was sunk off North Africa by mines in December, and HMAS *Perth* which was lost during a fierce surface action with a vastly superior Japanese force in the Sunda Strait on the night of 28 February–1 March 1942. There is no suggestion that the loss of either ship was hastened by defects or shortcomings in the design of the fire control system. See W.D.G. Blundell, *Royal Navy Warships, 1939–45* (Almark, London, 1971) p. 43.
38. Navy file, 'Report of suspicious sighting by HMAS *Yandra*', MP 1049/5 2021/5/596, AA.
39. ibid.
40. ibid.

Chapter 3

1. CID Memorandum dated 1910, quoted by Hyde to Minister for Defence, in 1931, CRS A 5954, Item 1001/1, AA ACT.
2. *Sydney Morning Herald*, 18 July 1914.
3. Two histories of the RAN College have been written: Frank Eldridge, *A History of the RAN College* (Georgian House, Melbourne, 1949); and, Ian Cunningham, *Work Hard Play Hard* (AGPS, Canberra, 1988).
4. 'Chephren', 'The RAN College—Its History and development', *Journal of the Royal United Services Institute*, Vol. 38, No. 3, January–March 1930.
5. The original proposed site for a naval college was in Sydney. Admiral Sir Reginald Henderson in his report to the Commonwealth government of March 1911 (generally known as 'Recommendations') stated that the college should be located at Middle Head in Sydney near the present site of HMAS *Penguin*. Papers Relating

to the Henderson Report, mimeographed minute, AWM 124 'RAN Historical'.

6. Eldridge, op. cit., p. 76.

7. See Tom Frame, 'Fitted by training and character: the Report of the RAN College for 1916', *Journal of the Australian Naval Institute*, November 1986, pp. 61–67.

8. Quoted in the *Times*, 23 December 1918.

9. 'Naval Defence Report of Admiral of the Fleet Viscount Jellicoe, 1919', A 5954, Item 1004/4, AA ACT, p. 7.

10. CNS to Minister for Defence, 'Officering the RAN', 19 November 1931, A 5954, Item 1001/1, AA ACT, p. 1.

11. Quoted in G. Hermon Gill, *The Royal Australian Navy 1939–42*, Vol. I, *Official History of Australia in the War of 1939–45* (AWM, Canberra, 1957) p. 269.

12. Commander Patrick Burnett, 'Captain Joseph Burnett RAN', *Naval Historical Review*, December 1973, p. 7.

13. ibid.

14. Much of the information about Farncomb's career has been obtained from A.W. Grazebrook, 'First to a Flag: The Life of Admiral H.B. Farncomb' in T.R. Frame, J.V.P. Goldrick and P.D. Jones (eds), *Reflections on the RAN* (Kangaroo Press, Kenthurst, 1991) pp. 189–205.

15. Promotion to the rank of lieutenant commander was, in the normal course of events, automatic after eight years in the rank of lieutenant.

16. Most of Collins's career details have been obtained from his autobiography, *As Luck Would Have It: The Reminiscences of an Australian Sailor* (Angus & Robertson, Sydney, 1965).

17. *Hermann Schoemann* was later sunk during a surface action with HMS *Edinburgh* in the Arctic on 2 May 1942.

18. Captain Theodor Anton Detmers, *The Raider Kormoran* (William Kimber, London, 1959) p. 9.

19. Detmers, op. cit., p. 12.

20. Winter, op. cit., p. 12.

21. ibid.

Chapter 4

1. Robert Stern, *Kriegsmarine* (Arms and Armour Press, London, 1979) p. 5.

2. 'Reflections of the Commander-in-Chief, Navy on the Outbreak of War, 3 September 1939'. A copy of this document and a collection of others relating to high-level German naval planning were captured by British and American Naval Intelligence officers at Tambach during the war. They were reproduced and published by the Admiralty in October 1947 as 'Fuehrer Conferences on Naval Affairs' [hereafter referred to as *Fuehrer Conferences*], with Volume I covering the period 1939–41 and Volume II, 1942–45. A copy is held by the Australian Defence Force Academy library.

3. Report of Commander-in-Chief, Navy (Raeder) to Hitler, 6 September 1940. *Fuehrer Conferences 1940*.

4. Conference of the Commander-in-Chief, Navy with the Fuehrer, 14 November 1940. *Fuehrer Conferences*.

5. Detmers, op. cit., p. 17.

6. ibid, p. 19.

7. ibid, pp. 20–21.

8. ibid, p. 22.

9. ibid, p. 21.

10. ibid, p. 22.

11. ibid, p. 27.

12. ibid, p. 30.

13. ibid, p. 31.
14. ibid, p. 33.

Chapter 5
1. A.K. Muggenthaler, *German Raiders of World War II* (Hale, London, 1978) p. 13.
2. Detmers, op. cit., p. 46.
3. ibid, p. 54.
4. ibid, p. 56.
5. HSK *Kormoran* 'War Diary', translated copy held by author.
6. Detmers, op. cit., p. 71.
7. ibid, p. 83.
8. ibid, p. 90.
9. Raeder to Hitler, 20 April 1941. *Fuehrer Conferences 1941*, p. 43.
10. Detmers, op. cit., pp. 102–3.

Chapter 6
1. An almost complete set of 1941 *Weekly Intelligence Summaries* (including the 'Raider Supplements') are contained in MP 1580/1, AA Melbourne.
2. Detmers, op. cit., p. 115.
3. Detmers, op. cit., p. 119.
4. Russell Pattee, 'The Raider *Kormoran—Sydney*'s Nemesis', *United States Naval Institute Proceedings*, December 1950.
5. There is inconsistency between *Kormoran*'s war diary and Detmers' later published account regarding the disguise *Kormoran* adopted when she entered the Indian Ocean. In my view these inconsistencies contain no sinister import. There is little doubt, however, that *Kormoran* was disguised as the Dutch freighter *Straat Malakka* after she entered the northern Indian Ocean.
6. Raeder to Hitler, 25 July 1941, *Fuehrer Conferences 1941*, p. 94.
7. Raeder to Hitler, 17 September 1941, *Fuehrer Conferences 1941*.
8. Detmers, op. cit., p. 136.
9. Raeder to Hitler, 13 November 1941, *Fuehrer Conferences 1941*.

Chapter 7
1. See also the War Diary of 6 Battalion, Citizens Military Forces, AWM 52.
2. 'Recovery of Enemy Survivors by HMT *Aquitania*', MP 1185/8 2026/3/453, AA Melbourne.
3. MP 1587/1 /164M, AA Melbourne.
4. The records of individual *Kormoran* POWs are included in A 7919, AA ACT.
5. Detmers' action report was probably produced in January 1942. When he was captured after a failed escape attempt in January 1945, the document was found in his possession. It was given the title 'Detmars [sic] Diary' by Australian naval intelligence staff. Originally written in a cipher code, the document was translated into English. A folder of papers containing encrypted, German plain text and translated English versions of the action report is held by the Melbourne office of Australian Archives, CA 6966 B 5823/1.
6. War Cabinet Minute No. 1528, dated 4 December 1941, AA ACT, 2673, Vol. 9.
7. ibid.
8. A 5954, 'Shedden Papers', Box 2400/21, AA ACT.
9. Heinrich Ahl, the pilot *of Kormoran*'s aircraft, stated in 1979 that the sailing ship 'was at first thought to be the ex-German square rigged ship *Pamir*, which had been in Australia at the beginning of the war and was supposed to be under the Australian flag'. 'Report on the Engagement Between HMAS *Sydney* and

the German Auxiliary Cruiser *Kormoran*', *Naval Historical Review*, December 1979, p. 33.
10. The forward turrets were designated Alpha and Bravo; the after turrets were X-ray and Yankee.
11. MP 1587/1/164M, AA Melbourne. To avoid an excessive number of references, information cited or quoted from the interrogation reports contained in MP 1587/1/164, parts L, M and N, and MP 1587/1/165K, will not be individually referenced.
12. 'Notes for Commander Dechaineux, Re: Survivors ex *Trocas*', MP 1587/1/164M, AA Melbourne.
13. The contents of these reports is quoted by Barbara Winter, 'The German Ultra', *Naval Historical Review*, 1990.
14. A report which systematically reviewed the evidence of the *Kormoran* survivors was also prepared by Frank Burgess Eldridge, a master at the RAN College, in early 1942. See 'Compilation of Report on Loss of *Sydney*', MP 1185/8 2026/19/6, AA Melbourne.

Chapter 8
1. 'Dr Habben's Diary', MP 385/7 53/101/78, AA Melbourne.
2. Quoted in Jonathan Robotham, Eagle in the Crow's Nest (unpublished manuscript) pp. 49–50.
3. Cable M 2825, Navy file PC 419/2/115, AWM 124 2/224.
4. *Age*, 3 December 1941.
5. HMAS *Canberra* letter dated 30 November 1941, Enclosure 1 to Australian Fleet (AF) letter 1503/8 dated 8 December 1941, Navy file PC 419/2/115, AWM 124 4/224.
6. Barbara Winter, 'The Writing of HMAS *Sydney*' in T.R. Frame et al (eds), op. cit., p. 154.
7. Laffer to Lightfoot, date obscured but probably 1986. Copy held by author.
8. Public Record Office (London) ADM 199/736.
9. ADM 234/324, *Actions with enemy disguised raiders 1940–41*, Battle Summary No. 13, pp. 11–12.
10. HMAS *Canberra* letter dated 29 November 1941, Enclosure 1 to Australian Fleet (AF) letter 1503/8 of 8 December 1941, Navy file PC 419/2/115, AWM 124 4/224. The records of interrogation for the *Kormoran* survivors recovered by *Aquitania* are also included in AA 1979/318, AA Melbourne.
11. ibid.
12. Blau to author, 17 November 1991.
13. ibid.
14. ibid.
15. HMAS *Canberra* letter, ibid.
16. HMAS *Canberra* letter dated 1 December 1941, Enclosure 2 to AF letter 1503/8 of 8 December 1941, Navy file PC 419/2/115, AWM 124 4/224.
17. H.B. Farncomb, 'The Loss of HMAS *Sydney*', *White Ensign*, December 1946.
18. Quoted in Robotham (undated), op. cit., p. 52.
19. Assistant Director of Naval Intelligence (Melbourne) to Director of Naval Intelligence (Admiralty), 28 January 1947, '*Kormoran*—Interrogation of Survivors', MP 1587/1/165K, AA Melbourne.
20. Bruce Stock to author, 9 September 1991.
21. Director of Naval Intelligence (Melbourne) to Director of Intelligence RAAF, minute dated 29 August 1947, MP 1587/1/165K, AA Melbourne.
22. ibid.
23. Director of Naval Intelligence (Melbourne) to Director of Naval Intelligence (Admiralty), letter dated 20 November 1947, MP 1587/1/165K, AA Melbourne.

Chapter 9

1. The raider problem is covered in 'Enemy raiders, Pacific (1940)', MP 1049/5 1835/2/734, AA Melbourne.
2. The laying of mines by *Orion* is covered in chapter 5, 'Mines in Hauraki Gulf', of *The Black Raider* (Elek, London, 1953) by Captain Kurt Weyher.
3. Colvin to Hughes, memorandum, dated 10 December 1940, A 5954, Box 531, AA ACT.
4. 'Intelligence report—sinking *of Coburg*', MP 1185 2026/3/418, AA Melbourne.
5. Gill, op. cit., p. 369.
6. Colvin to Hughes (Minister for the Navy), undated staff paper but probably 2 December 1940, A 2680, 10/1940, AA ACT. This paper was in response to Advisory War Council Minute No. 34, 'Review of Naval Dispositions—November 1940, General Review', dated 25 November 1940.
7. ibid.
8. S.W. Roskill, *The Strategy of Sea Power* (Collins, London, 1962) p. 160.
9. *Leander* was manned by the New Zealand Division of the Royal Navy. The Royal New Zealand Navy (RNZN) was not established until 1 October 1941.
10. 'Ramb' stood for Royal Associated Monopoly of Bananas. *Ramb 1* had entered the Indian Ocean disguised as a raider but met no merchantmen to the time of her sinking.
11. Jack Harker, *Well Done Leander* (Collins, Auckland, 1971) pp. 107–109.
12. S.W Roskill, *The War at Sea, 1939–45*, Vol. 1 (HMSO, London, 1954) p. 549.

Chapter 10

1. BR 1738, 'Preliminary Narrative, *The War at Sea*, Volume II, January–December 1941', Admiralty Historical Section, 1944.
2. W.A. Jones, *Prisoner of the* Kormoran (Australasian Publishing Company, Sydney, 1943).
3. ibid., p. 29.
4. ibid., p. 48.
5. Jack Bottomley, *Naval Historical Review*, Vol. 12, No. 3, September 1991.
6. Jones, op. cit., pp. 127–8.
7. Ross, op. cit., 'Acknowledgments'.
8. The probability that newspaper reports were indeed the origin of the information that *Kormoran* was flying the Norwegian flag is enhanced by the repetition of this information in E. Keble Chatterton's *Commerce Raiders* (Hurst and Blackett, New York, 1943) p. 72, which was based entirely on published accounts. Writing during the war, Chatterton stated, 'We are still lacking some pieces of knowledge, although it is practically certain we shall never obtain a British version'.
8a. Letter to author, 24 February 1993.
9. This book also appeared as Theodor Detmers and Jochen Brennecke, *Hilfskreuzer* Kormoran (Koehlers, Herford, 1959).
10. Geoffrey Scott, *HMAS* Sydney (Horwitz, Sydney, 1962).
11. ibid., p. 6.
12. ibid., p. 103.
13. ibid., p. 128.
14. ibid.
15. Collins (1971), op. cit.
16. Burnett, op. cit., p. 7.
17. Ahl, op. cit., p. 33.
18. ibid.
19. ibid., p. 35.
20. Montgomery, op. cit., unnumbered preface.
21. ibid.

22. ibid., p. 199.
23. ibid., p. 202.
24. ibid., p. 108.
25. ibid., p. 113.
26. ibid., p. 214.
27. Navy file, '*Kormoran* (Raider No. 41) "G"—German AMC', MP 1587/1/164L.
28. Navy file 429/201/363, letter dated December 1941, MP 1049, AA, Melbourne.
29. Montgomery, op. cit., pp. 215–16.
30. F.A.H. King, *Journal of the Australian Naval Institute*, Vol. 7, No. 4, November 1981, p. 50.
31. Captain Sam Bateman, *Journal of the Australian Naval Institute*, Vol. 8, No. 1, February 1982, p. 3.
32. Winter, op. cit.
32a. See my chapter on Lord Fraser in Malcolm Murfett (ed.), *The First Sea Lords and British Naval Policy: From Fisher to Mountbatten* (Praeger, New York, forthcoming).
33. Winter, in Frame et al, op. cit., p. 154.
34. Templeton to author, 4 March 1992.
35. Templeton to author, 23 March 1992.
35a. Letter to author, 24 February 1993.
36. Montgomery, op. cit., pp. 56–7.
37. AWM PR 89/122, Albert Edward Putman, letters to his aunt while in HMAS *Sydney*.
38. Ean McDonald, unpublished paper delivered to the HMAS *Sydney* Forum held at the Western Australian Maritime Museum in Fremantle, 21–23 November 1991. The papers and proceedings of this forum were compiled and edited by Michael McCarthy and Kim Kirsner. The author delivered two papers at this forum. Subsequent citations and quotations from papers delivered at this forum will be shown as 'HMAS *Sydney* Forum'.
39. McDonald, HMAS *Sydney* Forum, op. cit.
40. Quoted in Montgomery, op. cit., p. 57.
41. Winter (1984), op. cit., p. vi.
42. John Robertson, 'Introduction to the 1985 Reprint' of G.H. Gill, *Official History of Australia in the War of 1939–45, The Royal Australian Navy, 1939–42* (Collins, Sydney, 1985) pp. xx–xxi.

Chapter 11

1. Montgomery, op. cit., second page of unnumbered preface.
2. In his single-volume companion to the official history series, Gavin Long, the general editor of the entire series, makes only brief mention of the loss of *Sydney*. He states that the action took place 150 miles south-west of Carnarvon and that *Kormoran* tried to pass herself off as a Dutch ship. At 1730 when *Sydney* was less than 2000 yards from the raider, the signal 'Show your secret sign' was made. *Kormoran*'s captain, incorrectly referred to as Captain Anton Detmers, then opened fire. At 1745 according to Long, both ships were crippled and burning. Forty minutes later, he states that Detmers ordered *Kormoran* abandoned and that at 2200, the last was seen of *Sydney*. Long concludes by stating that 'Why Burnett did not keep his distance from an unidentified ship remains a mystery'. See Gavin Long, *The Six Years War: Australia in the 1939–45 War* (AWM & AGPS, Canberra, 1973) p. 119.
3. Gill, op. cit., p. 453.
4. ibid.
5. ibid., p. 454.
6. ibid.

7. ibid.
8. ibid., p. 457.
9. ibid., p. 459.
10. Bean to Secretary for Defence, 9 October 1919, MP 472/1, file 2/21/15183, AA Melbourne.
11. Department of the Navy, file 19/11298, part II, p. 3, copy of minute by Military Board, AA Melbourne.
12. Peter Edwards, 'Official history: does it merit suspicion?', *Canberra Historical Journal*, No. 17, March 1986, p. 17.
13. ibid.
14. A.W Jose, *Official History of Australia in the War of 1914–18*, Vol. IX, *The Royal Australian Navy* (AWM, Canberra, 1928).
15. The dispute between Jose and the Naval Board is examined in great detail by Ross Lamont in his introduction to the Queensland University Press edition of Jose's volume (Queensland University Press, St Lucia, 1987) pp. xxiii–xxxix, and Stephen Ellis 'The censorship of the official naval history of Australia in the Great War', *Historical Studies*, Melbourne, Vol. 20, 1983, pp. 367–82.
16. Sir Julian Corbett, *History of the Great War, Naval Operations*, Vol. 1 (Longmans, London, 1921). See also discussions of censorship and freedom of expression relating to writing on the Great War in *The Jellicoe Papers, Vol. II 1916–1935* (Navy Records Society, London, 1968) and Commander P.G. Hore, 'Free Expression—A Commentary', *Naval Review*, 75th anniversary issue, 1988, pp. 77–81.
17. Gill, op. cit., p. xiv.
18. Sir Keith Hancock, lecture entitled 'The History of Our Times', reprinted in W.K. Hancock, *Perspective in History* (Canberra, 1982) and quoted in Peter Edwards, op. cit.
19. Winter, op. cit., p. 225.
20. ibid.

Chapter 12

1. Montgomery, op. cit., p. 182.
2. ibid, pp. 182–6.
3. ibid, p. 186.
4. ibid, p. 188.
5. *Northern Times*, 6 December 1941; quoted in Montgomery, op. cit., p. 189.
6. Montgomery, op. cit., p. 189.
7. ibid., p. 190.
8. ibid.
9. ibid.
10. ibid.
11. ibid., p. 191.
12. ibid., p. 192.
13. ibid., pp. 192–3.
14. ibid., p. 193.
15. ibid., p. 191.
16. Detmers, op. cit., p. 194.
17. ibid., p. 194.
18. Interrogation reports, MP 1587/1/165K, AA Melbourne.
19. L.H. Pyke, *Journal of the Australian Naval Institute*, Vol. 8, No. 1, February 1982, p. 54.
20. Montgomery, op. cit., p. 195.
21. Public Record Office (London), ADM 1/19211.
22. Montgomery, op. cit., p. 195.

23. Laffer to Lightfoot, date obscured but probably 1986. Copy held by author.
24. Montgomery, op. cit., p. 196.
25. Michael Montgomery, *Imperialist Japan: The Yen to Dominate* (Christopher Helm, London, 1987) pp. 493–4.
26. Montgomery (1981), op. cit., p. 210.
27. See my review of Chris Coulthard-Clark's book, *Action Stations Coral Sea: The Australian Commander's Story* (Allen & Unwin, Sydney, 1991) in the *Journal of the Australian War Memorial* No. 19, November 1991, pp. 64–5, for an alternative assessment of Crace's administrative performance as RACAS in the period before the Pacific War began.
28. Tom Frame (1992), *Pacific Partners*, op. cit., chapters four and fourteen.
28a.*Canberra Historical Journal* No. 28, September 1991, pp. 50–51.
29. Michael Montgomery, 'The *Sydney–Kormoran* action: contradictions between the evidence and the official accounts', HMAS *Sydney* Forum.
30. Montgomery (1981), op. cit., p. 195.
31. Jenkins (1992), op. cit.
32. *Sydney Morning Herald*, 17 September 1992.
33. ibid.
34. ibid.
35. 'Sinking of submarine I-124', MP 1932/3/51, AA Melbourne.
36. Jim Davies, 'Another version of historic encounter', *No Survivors*, 50th Anniversary Commemorative Booklet produced by West Australian Newspapers Limited, 19 November 1991.
37. Kawano to Stevens, 7 February 1991. Copy held by author.
38. John Costello, *The Pacific War* (Pan, London, 1981).
39. In *Pearl Harbor: The Verdict of History* (McGraw Hill, New York, 1986), Gordon Strange makes a pertinent observation on Costello's *The Pacific War* and other Pearl Harbor conspiracy theorists. 'In support of their theories concerning Roosevelt's villainy, revisionists have presented a number of incidents, enough to fill a book. A careful scrutiny of these reveals one characteristic in common, namely, a complete lack of proof of Roosevelt's evil intentions or, in many cases, that he was involved at all. The evidence against the President lies in the judgement of the writers submitting them, not in the incidents themselves', p. 45.
40. Montgomery (1987), op. cit., pp. 492–3.
41. ibid., p. 494.
42. James Rusbridger, 'The Winds of Warning', *Weekend Australian Magazine*, 11–12 January 1986.
43. James Rusbridger and Eric Nave, *Betrayal at Pearl Harbour* (Summit, London, 1991).
44. AWM 124, 'ATIS translation of documents captured from Nachi', 2/273, p. 4 of translation.
45. John Chapman (ed. & trans.), *The Price of Admiralty: The War Diary of the German Naval Attache in Japan, 1939–1943*, Volume IV, 10 September 1941–31 January 1942 (Saltire Press, Sussex, 1989).
46. Arthur Marder, *Old Friends, New Enemies, The Royal Navy and the Imperial Japanese Navy, Strategic Illusions, 1936–41* (Clarendon Press, Oxford, 1981) pp. 126–27.
47. Chapman, op. cit., p. xxxvi.
48. Winter, in Frame et al, op. cit., p. 155.
49. Beesley to Montgomery, 26 September 1979, MLBE 2/35, Churchill College Archives, Cambridge, quoted by Winter in her paper at the 1991 HMAS *Sydney* Forum.

Chapter 13

1. Benson's relationship with the Navy is covered in detail in my book *Where Fate Calls: The HMAS* Voyager *Tragedy* (Hodder & Stoughton, Sydney, 1992) pp. 122–24, 183–84.
1a. W.P. Evans, *Deeds not Words* (Hawthorn Press, Melbourne, 1971).
1b. 'The *Sydney* Letter of Proceedings—a case for the defence', Stephen Allen, 9 September 1988, unpublished paper presented to a group of historians at the Australian War Memorial.
2. HMAS *Cerberus* letter 1/28/5, 13 November 1981, Navy file 89/24512/1.
3. Commodore I.H. Richards, 'Loss of HMAS *Sydney*—The Evans Papers', unpublished naval staff paper.
4. Minute from Mackenzie to the Secretary to CNS, 23 November 1981.
5. CNS 557/81 to NOC VIC, Navy file 89/24512/1.
6. 'The Second HMAS *Sydney* (1935–41); a 6830 ton cruiser', DASETT file 81/3574.
7. 'Inquiries, Consultancy and Research on Material Allegedly from HMAS *Sydney* II', AWM file 422/1/16.
8. 'Examination of the Evans Relics, Allegedly from HMAS *Sydney*', 27 October 1989, AWM file 88/0269, p. 1.
9. 'Fluorescence of the Bag', ibid., folio 44.
10. Winter, in Frame et al, op. cit., pp. 156–57.
11. Bryan Clark, HMAS *Sydney* Forum.
12. The copy was kindly provided by Ean McDonald of the *Sydney* Research Group.

Chapter 14

1. 'Australia's shame—*Sydney* secret was hidden for 50 years', *Sunday Times*, 27 October 1991.
2. *Sunday Times*, 27 October 1991.
3. Paper delivered at the HMAS *Sydney* Forum.
4. *Sunday Times*, 27 October 1991.
5. *Sunday Times*, 8 March 1992.
6. Paper delivered at the HMAS *Sydney* Forum.
7. ibid.
8. SWACH log held in Australian Archives, East Victoria Park, Perth, K 809/1. A microfiche of the portions of this log relevant to the loss of *Sydney* is contained in AWM CA 6978, ORMF 0037.
9. ibid.
10. McArthur, op. cit.
11. ibid.
12. Montgomery (1981), op. cit., p. 206.
13. HMAS *Sydney* Forum.
14. HMAS *Sydney* Forum.
15. D.J. Killen to Senator J.A. Mulvihill (undated but probably January 1982), Navy file 89/24512/P1.
16. Both these incidents are dealt with in detail in my book, *Pacific Partners*, op. cit.

Chapter 15

1. The two Navy files which deal principally with this subject are 'Relic ex HMAS *Sydney*—carley float', MP 150/1 635/201/1507, AA Melbourne; and 'Relic ex HMAS *Sydney*—carley float: transfer to Australian War Memorial, 1942–43', MP 150/1 635/201/1607, AA Melbourne.
2. Montgomery (1981), op. cit., p. 155.
3. John Ashton and Cathy Challenor, 'The scientific investigation of a carley float by the Conservation Section of the Australian War Memorial', unpublished AWM report dated October 1992, p. 17.

4. ibid., p. 21.
5. ibid., p. 18.
6. ibid.
7. ibid., abstract.
8. ibid., p. 20.
9. Quoted in Bryan Clark, 'Australia's Forgotten Son', *Naval Historical Review*, 1991, p. 15.

Chapter 16

1. See *Sydney*'s reports of proceedings for the period May–November 1941, AWM 78 329/3.
2. MP 1049/5 1984/2/350, AA Melbourne.
3. Although both ships were fitted with masts that permitted observation at much longer ranges—in the case of *Kormoran* 20 miles and of *Sydney* 16 miles—the evidence suggests that *Kormoran* did not alter course towards the west until 1630 when a positive identification of *Sydney* had been made. Given that the reported heat haze may have obscured visibility slightly, the range would have been between seven and nine miles when *Kormoran* altered course.
4. Detmers, op. cit., p. 140.
5. ibid.
6. ibid., p. 141.
7. Gill, op. cit., p. 454.
8. Montgomery (1981), op. cit., p. 212.
9. *Daily Telegraph* (Adelaide), 9 June 1960.
10. The Allies wanted to try several German naval officers for war crimes after the 1914–18 war. However, they were not very successful in having the crimes dealt with appropriately by the Supreme Court of the Reich at Leipzig. By way of example, Lieutenants Ludwig Dithmar and John Boldt from the submarine *U-86* were accused of illegally torpedoing the troopship *Llandovery Castle*. Although 230 men were killed, the two Germans received gaol sentences of four years. Shortly after incarceration, they escaped.
11. Muggenthaler, op. cit., p. 284.
12. Vice Admiral Friedrich von Ruge, *Sea Warfare, 1939–45* (Cassell, London, 1957) pp. 140–41.
13. Montgomery says that the First Officer from *Eurylochus* told him that Detmers had punched him in the face when he inadvertently observed one of *Kormoran*'s torpedo crews practising a drill. Montgomery (1981), op. cit., p. 74.
14. Detmers, op. cit., p. 153.

Chapter 17

1. Ross, op. cit., p. 276.
2. 'Search for wreck of HMAS *Sydney*—hydrographic aspects', Navy file 339/16/71, part I, and the paper delivered by Commander Lindsay Gee RAN at the HMAS *Sydney* Forum.
3. Working paper produced by Associate Professor Kim Kirsner, 'The Search for HMAS *Sydney* and HSK *Kormoran*: A Proverbial Needle', unpublished, 30 April 1992.
4. Whish to author, 15 June 1992.
5. Whish to author, 16 December 1992.
6. ibid.
7. ibid.
8. ibid.

Chapter 18

1 Sam Bateman, 'Was *Sydney* a sitting duck?', *Sydney Morning Herald*, 20 November 1993.
2 Vic Jeffrey, 'Book Review', *Westcoast Bulletin*, December 1993.
3 Bill Guy, 'Author torpedoes sinking theories', *Weekend Advertiser*, 13 November 1993.
4 Barry Ralph, 'Sinking bad theories', *Courier Mail*, 11 December 1993.
5 John A.T. Bye, Flinders Institute for Atmospheric and Marine Sciences, Flinders University, SA, 'Results from drift card releases at the site of the sinking of HMAS *Sydney*', 1997; and R.A. Page, 'The grave-site of the unknown sailor on Christmas Island, Part I: HMAS *Sydney* drift-card study', 1997.
6 Frazer Guild, 'Push for Sydney Probe', *Sunday Times*, February 1997.
7 JSCFADT Submission No. 81, W.P. Aylott, 31 December 1997.
8 JSCFADT, *Report on the Loss of HMAS Sydney*, March 1999, p. 162.
9 Ibid., pp. 171–72.
10 Greg Bathgate, *HMAS Sydney 1941: The Analysis*, Boolarong Press, Brisbane, 2007.
11 Ibid., p. 12.
12 Ibid., p. 136.
13 John Samuels, *Somewhere Below: The Sydney Scandal Exposed*, Halstead Press, Sydney, 2005.
14 Ibid., p. 7.
15 Ibid.
16 Captain Peter Hore RN, *HMAS Sydney II: The Cruiser and the Controversy in the Archives of the United Kingdom*, Papers in Australian Maritime Affairs No. 9, RAN Sea Power Centre, Canberra, 2001.
17 Ibid., p. 13.
18 Ibid., p. 167.
19 Ibid., pp. xviii–xix.
20 Ibid., p. xix.
21 Glenys McDonald, *Seeking the Sydney: A Quest for Truth*, University of Western Australia Press, Nedlands, 2005.
22 Ibid., p. 184.
23 Wesley Olson, *Bitter Victory: The Death of HMAS Sydney*, University of Western Australia Press, Nedlands, 2000.

Chapter 19

1 Hore, op. cit., p. 263.
2 Warren Whittaker, 'Wrong turn in the hunt for an old wreck', *Weekend Australian*, 22 July 2006.
3 Victoria Laurie, 'In Search of HMAS *Sydney*', *Weekend Australian Magazine*, 17–18 September 2005.
4 Kim Kirsner and John Dunn, 'The Search for HSK *Kormoran* and HMAS *Sydney* II: A Cognitive Perspective', unpublished paper dated 1 December 2004, copy held by author.
5 Neil Brown, Tim O'Leary, Frank Leahy and Joseph Leach, 'Modelling Uncertainty in the Search for HMAS *Sydney*', FIG XXII International Congress, Washington DC, April 2002, copy held by author.
6 Braden Quartermaine, '*Sydney* riddle may be solved', *Sunday Herald Sun*, 12 November 2006.
7 Steve Gee, 'HMAS *Sydney*'s 645 lost shipmates', *Daily Telegraph*, 15 March 2008.
8 The text of the interview appeared in the *Sydney Morning Herald* on the morning of 17 March 2008, just as the announcement was made that the wreck of *Sydney* had been found.

9   Arjun Ramachandran, 'HMAS *Sydney* found: PM', *Sydney Morning Herald*, 17 March 2008.
10 Elizabeth Gosch, 'Pictures show *Sydney* fought on after bridge destroyed', *Australian*, 7 April 2008.
11 Brian Toohey, 'Hard to understand a million-dollar joke', *Weekend Australian Financial Review*, 12–13 April 2008.

Bibliography

PRIMARY SOURCES (Published)

Naval Staff Histories (Battle Summaries)
ADM 234/317 No. 2 *Mediterranean operations and action off Cape Spada (Crete) 19 July 1940*
ADM 234/319 No. 4 *Naval operations of Battle of Crete*
ADM 234/323 No. 6 *Bombardment of Bardia, 21 June 1940, 17 August 1940 and 3 January 1941*
ADM 234/323 No. 8 *Mediterranean operations: operation MA5, 7–15 July 1940; action off Calabria, 9 July 1940*
ADM 234/324 No. 13 *Actions with enemy disguised raiders 1940–41*
BR 1738 Vol. 2 Preliminary Narrative, *The War At Sea, Vol. II, January–December 1941* (Historical Section, Admiralty, 1944)
International Code of Signals (HMSO, London, various years)
Joint Standing Committee on Foreign Affairs, Defence and Trade, *Report on the Loss of HMAS Sydney*, Commonwealth Parliament, Canberra, March 1998

PRIMARY SOURCES (Archival)

Australian Archives
Records relating to HMAS *Sydney* and HSK *Kormoran* are located in Australian Archives Regional Offices in the ACT, New South Wales, Victoria and Western Australia. The major collection is in Victoria where Navy Office was located until 1959 when moved to Canberra. See 'Source Analysis [from ANGAM II] for HMAS *Sydney* and HSK *Kormoran*', produced by Australian Archives, 20 December 1991. And the first edition of Richard Summerrell's *The Sinking of HMAS Sydney: A Guide to Commonwealth Government Records*, National Archives of Australia, Canberra, 1977.

Australian Archives (ACT)
A 816 40/301/290 HMAS *Sydney*
A 1608 A51/1/12 War—1939—Messages of Congratulation—HMAS *Sydney*
A 1608 S51/1/6 HMAS *Sydney* and HMAS *Parramatta*—Expressions of Sympathy

A 2911 1834/14 European War 1914. *Emden*, destruction of by HMAS *Sydney*

A 5954, Item 1004/4 Naval Defence Report of Admiral of the Fleet Viscount Jellicoe, 1919

A 5954 518/1 HMAS *Sydney*—Sinking of Italian Cruiser—Congratulatory cables, 19–24 July 1940

A 5954 Box 2400/21 HMAS *Sydney*—Sinking of by German Raider *Kormoran*, 1941 [Shedden papers]

A 7919 Individual POW records

CRS A 2670 War Cabinet Secretariat agenda 262/1940, 91/1941 and 401/1941

CRS A 2682 Advisory War Council Minutes

MP 547/1 Box 12, 13 HMAS *Sydney* [index and history cards relating to drawings, plans and specifications]

SP 109/3 342/14 Complaint re: official release of the names of personnel of HMAS *Sydney*

SP 109/3 357/106 Suspension of radio stations for breaches of instructions regarding the sinking of HMAS *Sydney*

SP 112/1 352/7/13 Engagement of HMAS *Sydney* with *Bartolomeo Colleoni*

SP 5551/1 Bundles 526, 527 and 528, Log Books, HMAS *Sydney* (II) (1935–41)

Australian Archives (Melbourne)

MP 124/6 603/263/2 New cruiser to replace HMAS *Brisbane*—name to be HMAS *Sydney*

MP 124/6 603/263/147 HMAS *Sydney*—attachment to the Royal Navy, 1935

MP 150/1 635/201/1507 Relic ex HMAS *Sydney*—Carley float

MP 150/1 635/201/1607 Relic ex HMAS *Sydney*—Carley float: Transfer to Australian War Memorial, 1942–43

MP 151/1 429/201/374 Inquiry from Chinaman who was a P/W on the *Kormoran*

MP 151/1 443/201/946 *Sydney* re: loss. Copies of circular correspondence sent to next of kin and dependants by Navy Office, 1944

MP 385/7 53/101/78 Dr Habben's diary

MP 742/1 175/1/103 German Raider *Kormoran*, 1941–44

MP 1049/5 1835/2/734 Enemy raiders, Pacific (1940)

MP 1049/5 2021/5/596 Report of suspicious sighting by HMAS *Yandra*

MP 1049/5 2026/3/108 Modernisation of cruiser—Conference at Navy Office

MP 1049/5 2026/3/196 HMAS *Sydney*—transfer to the Royal Australian Navy

MP 1049/5 2026/3/294 HMAS *Sydney* protection of fire control system and alternative controls

MP 1049/5 2026/3/350 *Sydney*—reports of action 9 July 1940

MP 1049/5 2026/3/410 Return of *Sydney*, 9 February 1941

MP 1049/5 2026/3/454 HMAS *Sydney*—raider publicity

MP 1049/5 2026/3/457 Search for HMAS *Sydney*

MP 1049/5 2026/19/6 Interrogation of German Survivors ex Raider 41—*Kormoran*

MP 1103/1 Box 26 Four volumes: No. 1—Service and Casualty Forms (AAF A112), *Kormoran*—Germans; No. 2 Merchant Seamen—transferred from Internee Section
MP 1185/8 2026/3/418 Intelligence report—sinking of *Coburg*
MP 1185/8 2026/3/453 Recovery of Enemy Survivors by HMT *Aquitania*
MP 1185/8 2026/19/6 Compilation of Report on Loss of *Sydney*
MP 1580/1 *Weekly Intelligence Reports*, 1941 [and 'Raider Supplements']
MP 1587/1 Navy Historical Records Files
MP 1587/1/164L *Kormoran* (Raider No. 41) 'G'—German AMC
MP 1587/1/164M *Kormoran* (Raider No. 41) 'G'—German AMC—Interrogation of Survivors
MP 1587/1/164N *Kormoran* (Raider No. 41) 'G'—German AMC—Translation of Log, Voyage Dec. 1940–Nov. 1941
MP 1587/1/165K *Kormoran*—Interrogation of Survivors
MP 1587/1/165P *Sydney–Kormoran* Action, Signals etc.
MP 1932/3/51 Sinking of Submarine I-124
Navy Office Confidential and Secret Correspondence Files Registers
B1125
B1127
B4081

Australian Archives (Western Australia)
K 809/1 South Western Area Combined Headquarters log book, 2 July 1941–2 May 1942 [microfiche of relevant portions of this log are also held at the Australian War Memorial, CA 6978, ORMF 0037]

Australian War Memorial
AWM 52 War Diary of 6 Battalion, Citizens Military Forces
AWM 78 329/1, 2 & 3 Report[s] of proceedings—*Sydney*, 1939–41
AWM 124 Papers Relating to the Henderson Report, mimeographed minute, 'RAN Historical'
AWM 124 4/151 Passages of HMAS *Sydney* and Admiral Colvin to Singapore
AWM 124 4/183 *Sydney* class cruisers—alterations and additions, Vol. 2
AWM 124 4/224 Loss of *Sydney* [two files concerning censorship of loss and interrogation *Kormoran* survivors]
OW 89/5 HMAS *Sydney*—casualty list—missing presumed dead—19 November 1941
PR 83/109 Seaman Karl Ropers, confiscated diary
PR 88/026 Philip Jay—Notes regarding the sinking of HMAS *Sydney* by the *Kormoran* in 1941
PR 88/119 Flying logbook and navigators log sheets maintained for the search for *Sydney* and later discovery of the German raider *Kormoran* and life boat with survivors, Flight Lieutenant Rooke, 26–29 November 1941
PR 89/122 Albert Edward Putman, letters to his aunt while on board HMAS *Sydney*

Australian Defence Force Academy (Library)
'Fuehrer Conferences on Naval Affairs', 1947 Admiralty mimeographed

duplicates of translated original documents, Volume I (1939–41) and Volume II (1942–45)

Department of Arts, Sport, the Environment, Tourism and Territories (file)
81/3574 'The Second HMAS *Sydney* (1935–1941) a 6830 ton cruiser'

Department of Defence (files)
94/1/913/1 'Defence Force Assistance—Search for Wreck of HMAS *Sydney*'
339/16/71/1 'Search for Wreck of HMAS *Sydney*—Hydrographic Aspects'

Australian War Memorial (files)
422/1/16 'Inquiries, Consultancy and Research on Material Allegedly from
    HMAS *Sydney* II'
748/2/34 'Relics Official—Navy Relics HMAS *Sydney* WWII'

Monographs
Collins, J.A. *As Luck Would Have It* (Angus & Robertson, Sydney, 1965)
Collins, J.A. *HMAS* Sydney (NHSA monograph, Sydney, 1971)
Cunningham, A.B. *A Sailor's Odyssey*, Vol I (Arrow Books, London, 1961)
Detmers, T.A. *The Raider Kormoran* (William Kimber, London, 1959)
Doenitz, K. *Ten Years and Twenty Days* (Weidenfeld & Nicolson, London, 1959)
Jones, W.A. *Prisoner of the Kormoran* (Australian Publishing Company, Sydney, 1944)
Raeder, E. *Struggle for the Sea* (William Kimber, 1959)
Rogge, B. *Under Ten Flags* (Weidenfeld & Nicolson, 1957)
Weyher, K. *The Black Raider* (Elek, London, 1955)

PRIMARY SOURCES (Unpublished)

Ashton, J. and 'The scientific investigation of a carley float by the Challenor,
    C. Conservation Section of the Australian War Memorial', AWM report
    dated October 1992
Evans, WP. HMAS *Sydney* Relics—Errata and Additional Information
    (undated)
Richards, I.H. 'Loss of HMAS *Sydney*—The Evans Papers', report produced
    for the Chief of Naval Staff, 22 February 1982
Winter, B. 'Assessment of alleged "Letter of Proceedings" regarding loss of
    HMAS *Sydney*', report produced for the Department of Home Affairs, 10
    September 1982

Newspapers and Periodicals

Australian
Age
Bulletin
Courier-Mail
Naval Historical Review
Sun-Herald
Sunday Times (Perth)
Sunday Mail (Brisbane)
Sydney Morning Herald
Times (London)
United States Naval Institute Proceedings
West Australian
White Ensign

SECONDARY SOURCES (Published)

Monographs
Anon. *No Survivors*, 50th Anniversary Commemorative Booklet produced by West Australian Newspapers Limited, 19 November 1991
Bathgate, G. *HMAS Sydney: The Analysis* (Boolarong, Brisbane, 2007)
Beesley, P. *Very Special Intelligence* (Hamilton, London, 1977)
Bergamimi, D. *Japan's Imperial Conspiracy* (Heinemann, London, 1971)
Brennecke, H.J. *Ghost Cruiser HK 33* (William Kimber, London, 1954)
Blundell, W.D.G. *Royal Navy Warships, 1939–45* (Almark, London, 1971)
Burdick, C.B. *The Frustrated Raider: The Story of the German Cruiser Cormoran in World War I* (Southern Illinois University Press, Carbondale, 1979)
Carpenter, D. and Polmar, N. *Submarine of the Imperial Japanese Navy* (Conway, Polmar, N. New York, 1986)
Carter, B.J. *Naval War Games: World War I and World War II* (David & Charles, Newton Abbott, 1975)
Chapman, J. (ed. and trans.) *The Price of Admiralty: The War Diary of the German Naval Attache in Japan, 1939–1943*, Volume IV, 10 September 1941–31 January 1942 (Saltire Press, Sussex, 1989)
Chatterton, E.K. *Commerce Raiders* (Hurst & Blackett, London, 1943)
Coulthard-Clark, C.D. *Action Stations Coral Sea: The Australian Commander's Story* (Allen & Unwin, Sydney, 1991)
Corbett, J. *History of the Great War, Naval Operations*, Vol. 1 (Longmans, London, 1921)
Costello, J. *The Pacific War* (Pan, London, 1985)
Cunningham, I.J. *Work Hard Play Hard* (AGPS, Canberra, 1988)
Eldridge, F.B. *A History of the Royal Australian Naval College* (Georgian House, Melbourne, 1949)
Evans, W.P. *Deeds Not Words* (Hawthorn Press, Melbourne, 1971)
Forstmeier, F. *SMS* Emden, Warship Profile Series No. 25, London, 1972
Frame, T.R. and Swinden, G.J. *First In, Last Out! The Navy at Gallipoli* (Kangaroo Press, Kenthurst, 1990)
Frame, T.R. *The Garden Island* (Kangaroo Press, Kenthurst, 1990)

Frame, T.R., Goldrick, J.V.P. and Jones, P.D. (eds) *Reflections on the RAN* (Kangaroo Press, Kenthurst, 1991)

Frame, T.R. *Where Fate Calls: The HMAS* Voyager *Tragedy* (Hodder & Stoughton, Sydney, 1992)

Frame, T.R. *Pacific Partners: A History of Australian–American Naval Relations* (Hodder & Stoughton, Sydney, 1992)

Gill, G.H. *The Royal Australian Navy 1939–42*, Vol. I, Official History of Australia in the War of 1939–45 (AWM, Canberra, 1957)

Gill, G.H. *The Royal Australian Navy 1942–45*, Vol. II, Official History of Australia in the War of 1939–45 (AWM, Canberra, 1968)

Harker, J. *Well Done* Leander (Collins, Auckland, 1971)

Hoehling, A.A. *Lonely Command* (Cassell, London, 1957)

Hore, P. *HMAS Sydney: The Cruiser and The Controversy in the Archives of the United Kingdom*, Papers in Maritime Affairs No 9, RAN Seapower Centre, Canberra, 2001.

Hoyt, E.P. *The Last Cruise of the* Emden (Andre Deutsch, London, 1967)

Johnston, G.H. *Grey Gladiator: HMAS* Sydney *with the Mediterranean Fleet* (Angus & Robertson, Sydney, 1941)

Jose, A.W. Official History of Australia in the War of 1914–18, Vol. IX, *The Royal Australian Navy* (Angus & Robertson, Sydney, 1928)

Jenkins, D. *Battle Surface! Japan's Submarine War Against Australia, 1942–44* (Random Century, Sydney, 1992)

Langmaid, K. *The Sea Raiders* (Jarrolds, London, 1963)

Lenton, H.T. *British Cruisers* (Macdonald, London, 1973)

Marder, A.J. *Old Friends, New Enemies: The Royal Navy and the Imperial Japanese Navy, Strategic Illusions, 1936–41* (Clarendon Press, Oxford, 1981)

Marder, A.J., Jacobsen, M. and Horsfield, J. *Old Friends, New Enemies: The Royal Navy and the Imperial Japanese Navy, The Pacific War, 1942–45* (Clarendon Press, Oxford, 1990)

McDonald, G. *Seeking the Sydney: A Quest for Truth* (University of Western Australia Press, Nedlands, 2005)

Mohr, U. and Sellwood, A.V. *Atlantis* (Werner Laurie, London, 1955)

Montgomery, M. *Who Sank the* Sydney? (Cassell, Melbourne, 1981)

Muggenthaler, A.K. *German Raiders of World War Two* (Hale, London, 1978)

Olson, W. *Bitter Victory: The Death of the HMAS Sydney* (University of Western Australia Press, Nedlands, 2000)

Pack, S.W.C. *Cunningham: The Commander* (Batsford, London, 1974)

Powell, A. *The Shadow's Edge: Australia's Northern War* (Melbourne University Press, Melbourne, 1985)

Raven, A. and Roberts, J. *British Cruisers of World War II* (Arms and Armour Press, London, 1980)

Roskill, S.W. *The War at Sea, 1939–45*, Vol. 1 (HMSO, London, 1954)

Roskill, S.W. *The Strategy of Sea Power* (Collins, London, 1962)

Ross, W.H. *Stormy Petrel* (Pattersons Printing Press, Western Australia, 1946)

Ruge, von F. *Sea Warfare 1939–45* (Cassell, London, 1957)

Rusbridger, J. and Nave, E. *Betrayal at Pearl Harbour* (Summit, London, 1991)

Samuels, J. *Somewhere Below: The Sydney Scandal Exposed* (Halstead Press, Sydney, 2005)

Schmalenbach, P. *German Raiders: A History of Auxiliary Cruisers of the German Navy 1895–1945* (Patrick Stephens, Cambridge, 1979)

Scott, G. *HMAS* Sydney (Horwitz, Sydney, 1962)

Smith, P.C. and Dominy, J.R. *Cruisers in Action 1939–45* (Kimber, London, 1981)

Stern, R. *Kriegsmarine* (Arms and Armour Press, London, 1981)

Strange, G. *Pearl Harbor: The Verdict of History* (McGraw Hill, New York, 1986)

Thomas, L. *The Sea Devil: The Story of Count Felix von Luckner the German War Raider* (Heinemann, London, 1928)

Tracey, N. *Attack on Maritime Trade* (Macmillan, London, 1991)

Tuchman, B. *Practising History* (Macmillan, London, 1981)

Watts, A.J. and Gordon, B.G. *The Imperial Japanese Navy* (Macdonald, London, 1971)

Woodward, D. *The Secret Raiders* (William Kimber, London, 1955)

Articles

Ahl, H. 'Report on the Engagement Between HMAS *Sydney* and the German Auxiliary Cruiser *Kormoran*', *Naval Historical Review*, December 1979

Bateman, W.S.G. '*Who Sank the* Sydney?', review article, *Journal of the Australian Naval Institute*, Vol. 8, No. 1, February 1982

Bottomley, J. Untitled article dealing with the loss of *Mareeba*, *Naval Historical Review*, Vol. 12, No. 3, September 1991

Burnett, P.R. 'Captain Joseph Burnett RAN', *Naval Historical Review*, December 1973

'Chephren' 'The RAN College—Its history and development', *Journal of the Royal United Services Institute*, Vol. 38, No. 3, January–March 1930

Edwards, P. 'Official history: does it merit suspicion?', *Canberra Historical Journal*, No. 17, March 1986

Farncomb, H.B. 'The Loss of HMAS *Sydney*', *White Ensign*, December 1946

Frame, T.R.'Fitted by training and character: the Report of the RAN College for 1916', *Journal of the Australian Naval Institute*, November 1986, pp. 61–67

Gill, G.H. 'The Australian Navy: Origins, Growth and Development', *RAHS Journal and Proceedings*, Vol. 45, No. 3, 1959

Hore, P.G. 'Free Expression—A Commentary', *Naval Review*, 75th anniversary issue, 1988

King, F.A.H. '*Who Sank the* Sydney?', review article, *Journal of the Australian Naval Institute*, Vol. 7, No. 4, November 1981

Kirsner, K. 'The Search for HSK *Kormoran* and HMAS *Sydney*: A Preliminary Analysis Based on Modified Search and Rescue Procedures', *Great Circle*, Vol. 14, No. 2, 1992, pp. 88–102

Pattee, R.S. 'The Raider *Kormoran*, *Sydney*'s Nemesis', *United States Naval Institute Proceedings*, December 1950, pp. 1299–1306

Pyke, L.H. '*Who Sank the* Sydney?', review article, *Journal of the Australian Naval Institute*, Vol. 8, No. 1, February 1982 von Gosseln, J. 'The Sinking of the *Sydney*', *United States Naval Institute Proceedings*, March, 1953, pp. 251–55

Winter, B. 'The German Ultra', *Naval Historical Review*, 1990

SECONDARY SOURCES (Unpublished)

Robotham, J. Eagle in the Crow's Nest (manuscript copy held by author)

Index